PORTUGAL AND THE PORTUGUESE WORLD

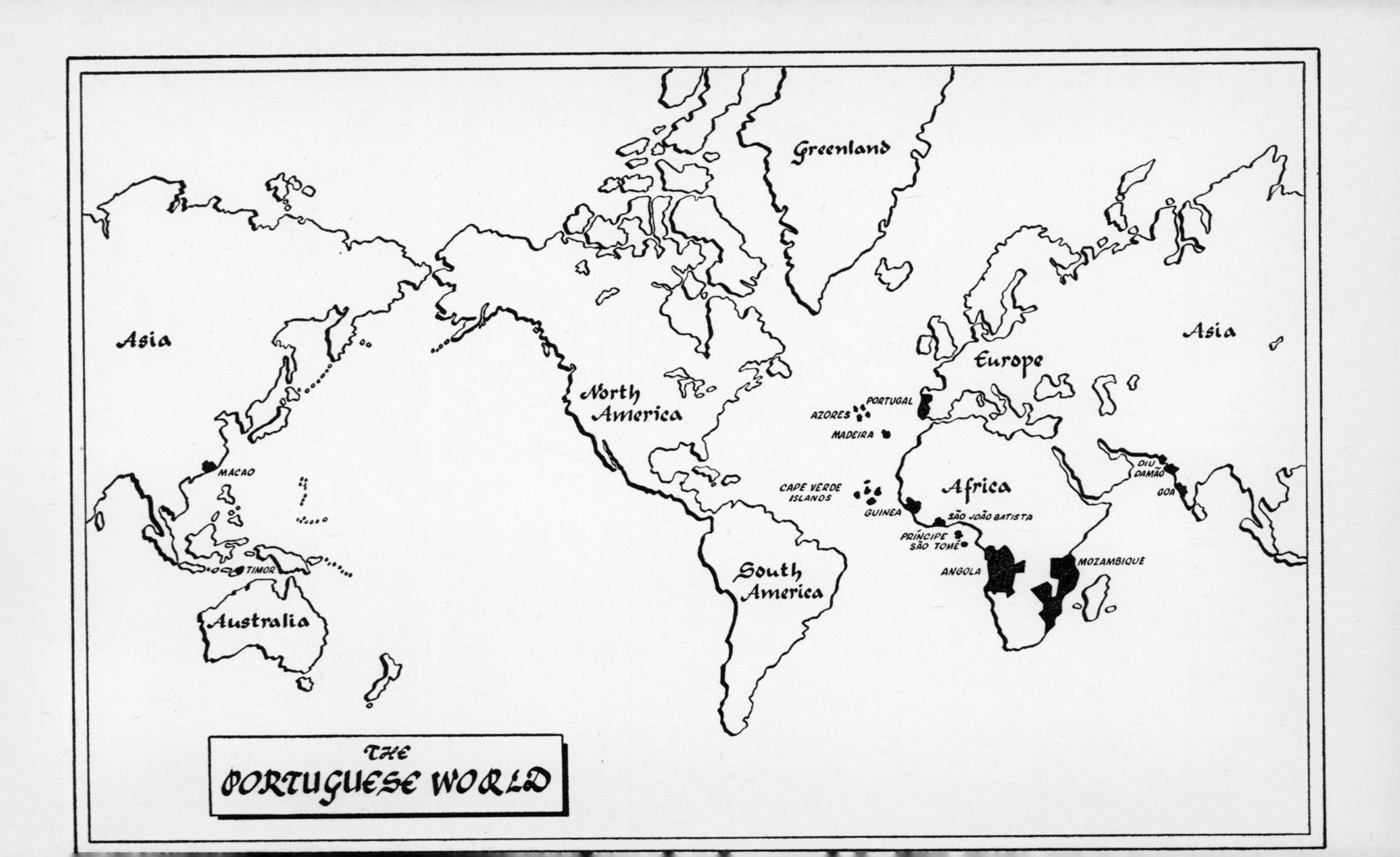
THE PORTUGUESE WORLD
Greenland
Asia
North America
Europe
Asia
Africa
South America
Australia
PORTUGAL
AZORES
MADEIRA
CAPE VERDE ISLANDS
GUINEA
SÃO JOÃO BATISTA
PRÍNCIPE
SÃO TOMÉ
ANGOLA
MOZAMBIQUE
DIU
DAMÃO
GOA
MACAO
TIMOR

PORTUGAL and the Portuguese World

BY RICHARD PATTEE

THE BRUCE PUBLISHING COMPANY
MILWAUKEE

Library of Congress Catalog Card Number: 57–12347

MADE IN THE UNITED STATES OF AMERICA

INTRODUCTION

The present work is intended primarily as a portrait of contemporary Portugal, the Portuguese people, and the world beyond the frontiers of Europe that were occupied by this enterprising nation and which still form a part of the empire. Since the volume is a synthesis of both the past and the present, there has been no effort to open up heretofore untapped documentary sources or perform what is commonly known as an original research job. I have limited my effort to calling attention to some of the principal printed sources of information, and especially those that exist in the Portuguese language.

In the midst of the convulsions that agitate the world in this mid-twentieth century, Portugal appears as a relatively peaceful oasis, dedicated to the internal task of social and economic reconstruction and eager to put its own house in order as the essential preliminary to an effective role in international affairs. To what extent this purpose has been achieved may be judged by the survey contained in these pages. Portugal cannot be separated from the vast territories beyond the seas and I have undertaken therefore to place in the proper context the development of the Portuguese province in Africa, Asia, and Australasia. The lessons of Portuguese history, as well as its contemporary accomplishments, are of profound significance at a time when racial tensions, ethnic antipathies, and "colonialism" are among the liveliest issues of the day. The Portuguese solution — if it can be called such — to these and related matters, is not without interest as an example of conduct by a European people toward those of other races with whom historical destiny has placed it in direct contact.

To acknowledge individually all those who have been of assistance in the preparation of this study of the Lusitanian world would be impossible. My interest in the subject has been unflagging over a period of thirty years since the time, long ago, when I first matriculated at the University of Coimbra. To the numerous professors under whose guidance this interest was kindled and enlivened: João Providencia Sousa Costa, presently Dean of the Faculty of Letters at Coimbra, Mendes dos Remedios, Farrand d'Almeida, Lopes de Almeida, and a host of others, a word of appreciation. I am grateful to the Instituto de Alta Cultura in Lisbon for innumerable publications and for the opportunity to return to Coimbra in 1956 to lecture. The Overseas Ministry has been most helpful in providing material regarding the territories in Africa and Asia.

My hope is that this volume may serve as a modest contribution to the knowledge of a gallant and courageous people whose survival has not always been easy and whose historical mission frequently most difficult of accomplishment. Through all Portuguese history, in spite of vicissitudes and moments of despair, there runs the thread of a fidelity to its high vocation and a conviction that although small in area in Europe and blessed with few natural resources, destiny has so placed the nation that its achievements have far surpassed the meager means with which it was endowed.

RICHARD PATTEE

Coimbra, Portugal
August 15, 1956

CONTENTS

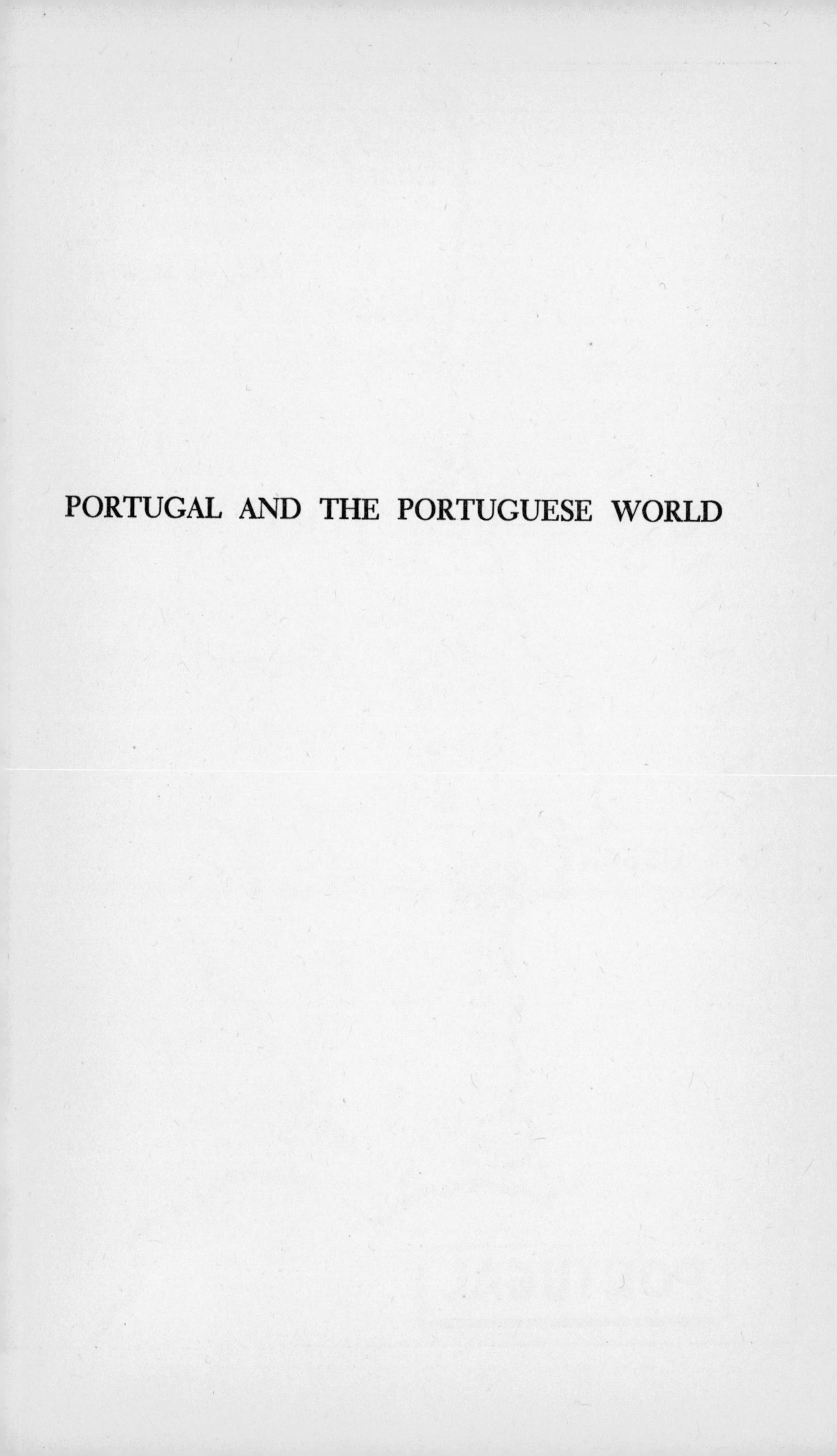

PORTUGAL AND THE PORTUGUESE WORLD

ATLANTIC OCEAN
SPAIN
ENTRE MINHO E DOURO
TRAZ OS MONTES
BEIRA
ESTREMADURA
ALEMTEJO
ALGARVE
Minho R.
Tamega R.
Douro R.
Mondego R.
Tejo R.
Xarrama R.
Guadiana R.
Bragança
Braga
Vila Real
Porto
Aveiro
Viseu
Guarda
Coimbra
Covilha
Sa. da Estrella
Leiria
Castelo Branco
Santarem
Portalegre
Sa. d'Ossa
LISBON
Setúbal
Évora
Sa. de Monchique
Faro
PORTUGAL

Chapter I

LUSITANIA: THE LAND

De Europa toda, o Reino Lusitano,
onde a terra se acaba e o mar começa.

Luis de Camões, Os Lusiadas, *Canto III,* xx.

PORTUGAL, says Eugenio d'Ors, the Spanish essayist, is a "balcony on the infinite," and that infinite is the vastness of the Atlantic Ocean along which the country stretches for some 340 miles. From this proximity to the ocean Portugal derives not only its moderate climate but many of the characteristics of its spirit which has made it one of the more unique civilizations in Europe. Separated from the rest of the continent by the Spanish land mass and the formidable political influence that has always emanated from Madrid, Portugal gives the superficial impression of an artificial entity which the vagaries of the Middle Ages threw up as an autonomous state and of a people whose distinction from their fellow Iberians is merely one of degree and not of kind.

It is no exaggeration to state that any profile of the Portuguese people must begin by a definition of their illusive personality and the general affirmation that, whatever they may be, they are not Spaniards, in spite of the oft-repeated contention of the distinguished Salvador de Madariaga, who sees in them a variant of the common peninsular stock that happen to be so placed that for centuries they have looked outward across the seas rather than inward in the kind of introspection to which the Castilians have been addicted.[1]

[1] "The Portuguese is a Spaniard with his back to Castile and his eyes on the Atlantic Sea . . . ," Madariaga, Salvador de, *Spain*, London, 1946, p. 185.

The dictates of geography have made Spain a nation keenly aware of its role in the Mediterranean. This awareness has operated simultaneously with its decided vocation for overseas expansion. Portugal, on the other hand, is Mediterranean only in a limited sense and shares with Norway, both physically and historically, a vocation for transoceanic movement. "Portugal is Mediterranean by nature and Atlantic by position," in the sense that there is definitely an air about the land that partakes of the Mediterranean while, on the other hand, geographical position has provided Portugal with very slight opportunity for collective action within the great enclosed sea around whose shores so much that is significant in human history has developed.[2]

Every observant traveler to Portugal, unless he arrives via the cosmopolitan air routes, is alert to the details which proclaim that he has set foot in another land. From across the Spanish frontier this may not always be evident. Unless one is acquainted with the misty, damp, and somewhat melancholic Galicia, he may scarcely recognize that frontier has been crossed because Galicians and Portuguese, although of different nationalities, share to a very high degree a similar past and, above all, a similar culture. "Our country abroad" is the expression for Galicia, employed by the Portuguese writer Antero de Figueiredo, in a vivid chapter of his *Espanha* in which he evokes the centuries of spiritual comradeship between the two peoples whose language, folklore, customs, and even superstitions partake of a common source.[3] M. Gonzague de Reynold, the well-know Swiss historian, his remarked that the eye accustomed to the spectacle of Spain and the spirit long attuned to the peculiarities of the Spanish temperament may not, on first glance, perceive any radical difference when one crosses into Portugal either from Castile via Salamanca or in the south from Andalusia.[4] The villages look much alike, the people seem quite the same, the land and its cultivation vary but little and, were it not for the customs and other entrance formalities, the superficial impression would be that here was at the most only a minor variant in the general symphony of Iberia.

But underneath this surface there is a world of subtlety that

[2] Pequito Rebelo, José, *A terra portuguesa*, Lisbon, 1929, p. 55.
[3] Figueiredo, Antero de, *Espanha*, Lisbon, 1944, p. 39 *seq.*
[4] Reynold, Gonzague de, *Portugal*, Paris, 1936, p. 63.

rewards the more penetrating observer. Houses are decorated with the colorful Portuguese *azulejos*, or glazed tiles, which, in their multiple coloration, lend an air of gaiety and charm to the drab environment. The hissing sibilants of the Portuguese tongue assail the ear and gradually, as one moves westward toward the coast, the oceanic qualities of Portugal become increasingly apparent. There is quite tangibly another atmosphere, another climate, and even the light seems different — no longer the glare and the intensity of Castile but a softness mitigated by the humidity. Portugal is an oasis in the Iberian land mass with a nature whose rough and rugged contours have been smoothed by the tempering influence of the sea. The sea moves inland in Portugal to make the whole country maritime; whereas in Spain the land and the ocean are divided by a sharp and impenetrable frontier, a sort of defiant arrangement in which the two elements are maintained in rigid separation, one from the other. The soft and often melancholy light of Portugal reflects in the natural order the temper of its inhabitants, and of this we shall have occasion to say a word later. It is sufficient to indicate here that the Portuguese live in a land which has molded their character to its image. The Portuguese landscape is indisputably more human than the Spanish, and even the mountains, as they incline toward the sea, lose something of their abruptness and their rigor. The abundance of vegetation, save perhaps in certain areas in the south, and the far greater density of population make of Portugal a garden, and, what is more significant, a garden in which the hand of man is ever present. Compare, for example, the impression of infinite vastness which one experiences on the Castilian plain — where there is often no sign of human dwelling and no sound to denote the presence of man — with the normal Portuguese landscape. It is man himself who has created his own environment in Portugal.

In this narrow strip of territory that ranges from 75 to 135 miles in width, live over seven million people who have vanquished their isolation and remoteness from the main currents of international life by a systematic exploitation of the resources and possibilities of the sea. Portugal may more properly be considered as an anchor holding in place the Lusitanian world and it is a commonplace, but one to which we shall return constantly in these pages, to say that Portugal is merely one element — the most important to be sure — in the elaborate structure that forms the Portuguese speaking and governed world. This world extends to the Atlantic islands of the Azores and Madeira, the African islands of Cape Verde, the territories on the continent of Africa and the possessions in India, China, and the Indonesian Archipelago. All of this is authentically Portugal, and the relative insignificance of the tiny land that achieved this expansion is modified in the light of the place it has made for itself in the community of nations.

European Portugal may be divided for the sake of general description into two broad areas: the North and the South. The North is mountainous, misty, damp, with abundant rainfall on the coast, while in the dryer highlands the predominant note is that of pine forests; groves of chestnuts, oaks, and poplars abound, and bracken and heather grow. "Except . . . for the ox-carts creaking along the narrow roads, one might fancy oneself in Scotland."[5] This is the territory of Tras-os-Montes, "beyond the mountains," the name itself evoking the impression of impregnability and isolation, and the province of Minho. The Portuguese nationality was born here and except for the Roman conquest, whose profundity or superficiality is open to debate, no other invading force ever subjugated it. It constitutes in the annals of Portugal what Asturias does in those of Spain: the bulwark of the national consciousness, the irreducible *Festung* of the defense of national integrity. From these northern provinces have come most of Portugal's leaders and the talent which forged such a considerable place for the country in history. North of the Mondego River, which roughly divides the two Portugals, the Arabs left only the faintest traces or, in most parts, none at all.

The population of Minho is dense and the land split up into infinitely minute parcels, cultivated with rare assiduity. Fruit trees mark the dividing line between the properties of the small land owners, and in this damp climate the grape vine thrives, constituting the chief characteristic of the area. The division of the land explains the absence of village life and the dispersion of the population, each on its small farm. The region has its outlet to the sea and its ports are part of the vitally important Portuguese fishing industry: Viana-do-Castelo, from which the sailing vessels

[5] Bridge, Ann, and Lowndes, Susan, *The Selective Traveller in Portugal*, London, 1949, p. 19.

depart regularly for Newfoundland and Greenland; Povoa-do-Varzim, one of the most characteristic of the fishing communities and quite different in its way of life from the rural hinterland; and Matozinhas, a suburb of Porto, where the coastal sardine fishing enterprises are centered. In spite of its cities, the commercial Porto and the traditional Guimarães, the Minho area is primarily rural and with its 1,700,000 inhabitants, now concentrated in the three districts of Entre Douro e Minho, it represents 23 per cent of the entire population of the country in an area of approximately 8 per cent.

Agriculture has reached the point where only through a technical revolution will the region be able to maintain this dynamically growing population. But the Minho has always been a primary export center of people as well as wine and grain. "Ever since the sixteenth century, with admirable vitality, these fertile valleys, overflowing with people, have sent forth waves of settlers to that tropical world which their ancestors helped to found."[6]

Outside of Porto, the second Portuguese city which is a kind of synthesis of the whole area, most of the urban centers are of modest proportions: Viana-do-Castelo (13,000 inhabitants); Braga (30,000 inhabitants), the seat of an ancient religious tradition; and Guimarães (11,000 inhabitants), the court in the Middle Ages of the Counts of Portugal and in the shadow of whose castle the nation itself was born.

As one penetrates inland toward the mountainous country that separates Minho from Tras-os-Montes, the economy as well as the climate undergoes a startling transformation. Villages appear more frequently, with an agriculture that is often carried out by the community in common. Barley predominates over other grains. Tras-os-Montes is a poor land and has felt for centuries the constant pressure of a population incapable of living off its sterile resources. There is no city with more than 10,000 inhabitants in the whole area. Its remoteness, proximity to Spain, and general inaccessibility have given this province an air of "splendid savagery about its climate and landscape."[7]

[6] *Portugal Breviário da Pátria para os portugueses ausentes*, Lisbon, 1946; "Territory and Population," by Orlando Ribeiro, p. 12. "The human fecundity of the Minho explains how this civilization permeated the whole country. It is the basis of the colonial expansion that produced the present empire and of the fact that the Portuguese language is spoken in the largest nation of South America." Birot, Pierre, *Le Portugal. Etude de géographie régionale*, Paris, 1950, p. 63.

[7] Bridge and Lowndes, *op. cit.*, p. 207.

If this district is physically impressive and architecturally intriguing with the incomparable city of Bragança, it is full of all sorts of odd references in the history and folklore of Portugal. Its churches defy enumeration in their number and charm. Whole towns such as Lamego are built in the baroque style. Remote villages near Bragança still contain the descendants of Jews who fled to these fastnesses during the period of the Inquisition and have retained many of their rites. The city of Miranda do Douro is not only attractive to the tourist but one of the most fascinating of problems to the philologist, since it is one of the rare towns in the world having its own dialect.

Within the limited expanse of these two provinces, the accident of geography has produced marked differences in temperament and way of life. The inhabitants of Tras-os-Montes are described as lively, active, robust, and quite distinct from the somewhat obtuse *minhoto*, whose outstanding traits are their perseverance, patience, and capacity for hard work. In Tras-os-Montes, the atmosphere is dry and bracing with severe winters, freezing temperatures, and peaks covered with snow. In Minho, on the other hand, the abundant rainfall is the source of constant mistiness; small streams spring up everywhere . . . a fertile, damp, climate that makes for a much easier life than in the rugged highlands. "The Minho is Flanders, not Attica," says the distinguished historian Oliveira Martins.[8]

From the Douro River that flows out to the sea at Porto to the Tagus at Lisbon, is a part of Portugal that is far harder to define and resists the generalizations that come so easily to mind in describing both the northern and the southern provinces. This is the region of the Beira Alta and the Beira Baixa and along the coast on the southern tier, Estremadura. The area lacks natural unity and is, in fact, largely a transition zone between north and south. From the human point of view, a good portion of the most significant in Portuguese life is to be found here: the great monuments of Tomar, Alcobaça, and Batalha, the hallowed ground of Fatima, Coimbra, the Mondego valley, and, of course, Lisbon itself. It is here, perhaps, that the most authentic national life is to be found.

The south central region of Alentejo borders on Spain, and, in

[8] Article, "A terra e o homem," in Nemésio, Vitorino, *Portugal, a terra e o homem*, Lisbon, n.d., p. 15.

the rolling plains, the fields of grain, and the bronzed humanity, there is no perceptible difference from the Spanish Estremadura across the frontier. The intensity of the sun produces a sort of sun-baked monotony under the canopy of blue sky. "It is a queer province which combines my untravelled ideas of what the climate of the Sahara and that of the South American pampas must be like."[9] The descriptions of the Alentejo invariably emphasize the velvety skies of a night, the clarity of the atmosphere, the marked contrast of the scorching heat of the day and the chilling cool of the evening, and, above all, the dust and heat miasma that hangs over these underpopulated plains in the daytime.

The southern tip of Portugal is the Algarve, designated in the classic writings as "The Kingdom of the Algarve," and in every respect a segment of Morocco that by some curious trick has remained on the European side. Although the evidences of Arabic material influence are perhaps not very numerous, this is the region of Portugal in which their blood and customs have left the deepest imprint. At every step across the Algarve it is necessary to reflect consciously that this is not Africa after all but the tip of Europe. "There is a brilliantly white house with its narrow chimney; a Moorish balcony; an inside patio in the center of which is a well; a palm tree clearly silhouetted against the sky. The appearance of the people, darker and less vigorous than elsewhere, attest to centuries during which Moorish blood was transmitted to their veins."[10]

The Atlantic island groups of Madeira and the Azores are, to be sure, integral parts of Portugal and can in no way be considered as appendages and much less "colonies." Madeira, prior to its discovery in 1419, was uninhabited and therefore has been Portuguese from the time it was first settled. It is, in fact, a sort of northern prolongation of the Canaries, volcanic in origin and structure, with a rich soil that has long made it one of the principal producers of wine and sugar. From the days of Henry the Navigator, Madeira became, on a minor scale, a preview of the sugar economy that was to be instituted in Brazil and in many parts of Africa. Oddly enough, much of the responsibility for the economic development of the island is due to English initiative. Madeira wine has a noble

---

[9] Goldring, Douglas, *To Portugal*, London, 1934, p. 131.

[10] *Guia de Portugal. Extremadura, Alentejo, Algarve*, Lisbon, 1927, Vol. II, p. 187.

past and renowned history, since it was popular in Elizabethan England and has maintained its reputation down through the centuries.

To the north and west of Madeira, almost straight out from the southern tip of continental Portugal, lies the archipelago of the Azores, a group of nine islands a thousand miles from Europe and the only important land between Europe and the Western Hemisphere. The Azores have been populated by enterprising and energetic Portuguese ever since the fifteenth century, and the hardy, adventurous Azoreans retain a great deal of the curiosity and wanderlust of their fellows of five centuries ago. It is from the Azores that a very large proportion of the Portuguese immigrants to the United States have come since, like the Minho, these tiny islands have been unable to support their population of a quarter of a million people. It may be remarked that the largest of the islands of the archipelago, São Miguel, is only 41 miles long by 9 miles wide.

Far down the West African coast are the Cape Verde Islands, fourteen in number, with an area of a little over 1500 square miles and less than 200,000 inhabitants. The people are the "Black Portuguese," descendants of the slaves imported from the continent of Africa and, among other things, they have developed a form of Portuguese which is quite unique, known as the *lingua crioula*, as different in its phonetics and structure as the modified Portuguese of the Far East. Unhealthy at certain times of the year and with indifferent inter-Island communication, the Cape Verde Islands have been distinguished also by the great number of their people who have sought to better themselves in America and, especially, in Brazil.

One of the most revealing and at the same time most intriguing of sources for the examination of influences on the Portuguese people is the language. The Islamic conquest left profound traces in vocabulary, place names, and usages all over the land, except in the north above the Douro River, where the Moors never penetrated. It is therefore not surprising that the same object, measure, or operation should frequently bear a designation of Arabic origin in the south, whereas, in the north it is Latin or Germanic.[11] Eco-

[11] Ribeiro, Orlando, *Portugal, o Mediterrâneo e o Atlântico. Estudo geográfico*, Coimbra, 1945, p. 89.

nomically, the two regions show the same marked differentiation. In the north, the land system has always been one of small property holdings with the individual farmer the owner of his own piece of land; in the south, the Roman tradition of *latifundium* developed and to this day the Algarve and Alentejo are characterized by the concentration of agricultural holdings in relatively few hands.[12]

Even the production reflects this fundamental difference: in the north corn predominates, while in the south, where agriculture is far less of an individual enterprise, it is wheat. The north, as has been suggested, is more densely populated. As one moves southward, there is less rain, the vegetation becomes more scarce, the cultivation of the soil less intensive, and rural property less divided. South of Lisbon the land merges into an open plain, easy of access and traversed with facility. It is not astonishing, perhaps, that the Islamic conquerors clung so tenaciously to this region rather than make futile attempts to dislodge the Christian strongholds in the mountainous north. This part of Portugal is so like Africa as to be indistinguishable: the same sun beats down on the Alentejo and Algarve as in Morocco; the same baked, parched qualities strike the eye. It was through this territory that every Mediterranean cultural influence, Greek, Roman, Phoenician, and Moslem, moved unrestrictedly marching northward to meet a dogged resistance. The south of Portugal accepted every influence that was brought to bear on it; the north, with equal fervor, resisted these influences.

In spite of these variations which, in a larger land, would have resulted inevitably in mutual isolation and deep regionalism, Portugal is small enough to have avoided the more pronounced consequences of separatism. Lacking a high central plateau comparable to that of Spain, Portugal is essentially a coastal country, in that 41 per cent of the whole land area can be classified as littoral or coastal. The degree to which the nation is oriented oceanward is demonstrated most eloquently perhaps by the fact that, in contemporary times, 96 per cent of the foreign trade passes through its seaports and only 4 per cent overland. Physically speaking, Spain and Portugal are like the two sides of a watershed — the precipitation flowing normally away from each in spite of the intimate proximity.

[12] Amorim Girão, Aristides de, *Atlas de Portugal*, Coimbra, 1941, Section XV, "Rural property holdings." In this excellent study of the geography of Portugal, the author notes that there are sometimes five farms per square kilometer in the south and as many as 700 in the north.

Portugal is low lying, demonstrated in the fact that 71.4 per cent of its land is less than 1200 feet above sea level and only 11.6 per cent is higher than 2100 feet. Even the Portuguese rivers show an essentially different character, once they cross the frontier, than in Spain. The Douro rises in Spanish territory and moves toward Portugal, sluggish, shallow, and unnavigable. Once it enters the latter country, it widens, deepens, and becomes a useful and important means of communication between the coast and the hinterland. Easy communication has long facilitated the uniformity of Portugal in contrast with Spain. Aside from the one barrier of the Serra de Estrela, most Portuguese mountains are crisscrossed by valleys and routes that offer no serious obstacle to human traffic. Spanish geography is rigidly compartmentalized; Portuguese is relatively uniform, which does not exclude, to be sure, a very considerable variety.

This oceanic quality, to which we return again and again, is further evidenced by the location of Portuguese cities. Only one of any importance is located on the plains, and the coast, or the area that may be considered as the coastal zone, accounts for nearly five and a half million of the population.[13]

It cannot be too much emphasized that in a study of contemporary Portugal, it would be improper to limit our consideration to the continental European territory. The Portuguese empire of history has become, thanks to the evolution of its institutions and the decision of the present regime to incorporate the possessions beyond the seas as provinces in a world-wide Portugal that is more than a colonial empire, a loose commonwealth or even an association of regions. Portugal is European, Asiatic, and African. The inhabitant of the farthest reaches of its domains, in Macao off the coast of China or Timor in Indonesia, is a Portuguese citizen, subject to the same laws and the same authority as the citizen of Lisbon or of Braga. He may be a tribesman from Angola or an Indo-Portuguese from Damão, but, regardless of his racial origins or the particular geographical habitat he may occupy, his juridical position is identical and as such he is not to be classified as a "colonial," whereas the people of European Portugal are the rulers and dispensers of favors.

---

[13] Ribeiro, *op. cit.*, p. 146: "In Portugal there are scarcely any plains cities; with an exception of Aveiro on a sandy plain linked by canals, all other centers of major population are on the coast or on rivers."

This is the political and spiritual Portugal of today, remnants (and very considerable ones at that) of the far vaster empire that the Portuguese had conquered from the beginning of their expansion. Visible evidence of this past grandeur remains everywhere on three continents. Morocco is covered with the ruins of Portuguese fortresses and strong points which attest the time when this corner of North Africa was part of the dominions of the monarchy. Innumerable geographical names along the African coast evoke vividly the epic of the Portuguese explorations and the achievements of their navigators. In America, Brazil, Portuguese speaking and closely attached culturally to the former motherland, is the greatest and most permanent monument to the genius of the Portuguese as colonizers. Far to the north, Newfoundland, the Terra Nova of the early explorers, and Labrador, perpetuating the name of João Fernandes Lavrador, bear the names that were given them by the Portuguese, and the fishing banks are still a rendezvous for the intrepid and daring fisher folk. Asia still bears the imprint of the Portuguese who set up permanent trade routes across its waters and whose merchants and missionaries trod its soil in every direction. The island of Formosa was baptized with this Portuguese word and in almost every portion of the great continent, from India through Burma, Siam, the Malaya peninsula, Indonesia, Indo-China and up the China coast to Japan, the mark of Portugal is indelibly engraved. The frequent occurrence of Portuguese family names in Ceylon and India, such as the Fonsekas and the Sousas, reveals the predominant trait of Portuguese colonization, which was racial intermixture and religious conversion. The Portuguese language, although long since ousted as official in most parts of Asia, lingers on in dialectal form in India, Ceylon, and elsewhere. Portuguese is used in Java, with Malayan admixture; in Malacca, which was conquered by Albuquerque in 1511; and a patois known as the *dialecto malaqueiro* persists in Singapore and in Timor.

In many places the use of Portuguese outlasted the empire and continued as the *lingua franca* under the French and the British rulers. In Bombay, Salsette, Bassein, south of Bombay, and on the Malabar coast among the Christians of Mangalor, Cananor, Cochin, Mahé, Pondicherry, Kairkal, Cuddalore, and Tranquebar, Portuguese has persisted through the centuries in various modified forms. Dutch and British efforts in Ceylon never managed to eliminate Portuguese completely, especially among those who professed the Catholic faith from the time of the first Portuguese conquerors.[14]

Many of the Portuguese trading posts that dotted the coasts of Africa have disappeared, absorbed in the forward movement of other empires or more aggressive European communities. In some cases, like fragments after a cataclysm, pieces of territory continue to float on the Portuguese sea such as Guinea, wedged in between British Gambia and French Guinea; the islands of São Tomé and Príncipe in the Gulf of Guinea that are scarcely distinguishable on a map; Cabinda near the mouth of the Congo and separated from Angola by Belgian territory; São João Batista de Ajudá, in Dahomey where French control prevails and is so tiny that John Gunther says of it that it "must be the smallest political entity in the world."[15] We are familiar enough, in view of the events of the past few years since the independence of India, with Goa. As a matter of fact, Goa is only one — the largest to be sure — of the enclaves under Portuguese sovereignty on the coast of India. In addition there is Diu and Damão, farther up the coast and quite separated from Goa physically. Inland from Damão, to make things more complicated, is a prolongation called Pragana de Nagar Avely. Thirty-five miles from Hongkong and hanging precariously on the periphery of China, is the five-square-mile province of Macao, the continuous occupation of which dates from 1557 and is the oldest European outpost for trade with China. Far off in the lush Indonesian archipelago, the Portuguese occupy the northwestern end of the island of Timor and an enclave called Ocussi-Ambeno, surrounded entirely by the Indonesians who rule the rest of the island. The Portuguese had been in this remote outpost for a hundred years before the Dutch arrived in 1713, and through war and isolation, occupation and attempts at eviction, they have clung to their half of this island which enjoys today the status of a full-fledged province within the empire.

The giants among the Portuguese possessions are Angola and

[14] For a short résumé of Portuguese overseas see Entwistle, William James, *The Spanish Language*, London, 1936, Chapter IX, "The Portuguese Language Overseas." Pimpão, Alvaro da Costa, "La langue portugaise dans le monde," *La Revue de l'Université Laval*, Québec, P. Q., Vol. X, No. 10, June, 1956, p. 888 *seq.*

[15] Gunther, John, *Inside Africa*, New York, 1955, p. 599.

Mozambique. The former, on the west side of Africa, is fourteen times as large as the homeland but with scarcely more than half the population of Portugal itself. Of this population, less than 100,-000 are Europeans. Angola is old Portuguese territory, antedating the discovery of America, and remains today as one of the major potential outlets overseas for the pressure of population at home. Across the continent lies Mozambique, nearly 300,000 square miles in area with something short of six million people, a choice bit of territory if there ever was one, with the Belgian Congo, South Africa, and Tanganyika as neighbors. East Africa has figured largely in the historical and literary annals of Portugal, and the Lusiads devote numerous stanzas to the observations of Vasco da Gama along the coast, a goodly portion of which is Portuguese today.

Portugal is, therefore, one of the smaller of the European nations, continentally speaking, and one of the major powers globally that exists today, with territories that rank third, after Great Britain and France, among the empires of the world. It is of this Euro-Afro-Asiatic combination that we shall speak in these pages, for, under the present political dispensation in Lisbon, Portugal is the seat of administration for these overseas provinces, and national citizenship has nothing to do with place of origin or color of the skin. The dark-hued Goan from India, the *assimilado* or Europeanized Angolan or the native of the Cape Verde Islands is equally Portuguese and suffers from no perceptible color bar to his advancement or movement. The integration of this empire demands, quite obviously, considerable effort in the way of transportation and communication, both of which have been insufficient up to the present time. The temporary occupation of Timor during the last war by the Japanese armed forces could not be prevented by the strength Portugal could muster. Although Macao has not been directly threatened and has figured only occasionally in Communist Chinese pronouncements on expansion, it is clear that Portugal could not hope, from the great distance of the home base, to put up an effective defense of this miniscule province so utterly exposed to China.

Although the solidarity of the Portuguese empire was seriously breached in the early nineteenth century by the independence of Brazil, it would not be entirely improper, perhaps, to include mention at least of the very strong attachments that exist between the former mother country and its gigantic offspring. Brazilian independence left no aftermath of malice or ill will; rather the contrary, to such an extent that during the remainder of the nineteenth and the twentieth centuries the relations have grown more and more cordial. Large Portuguese immigration to Brazil has made more secure the bonds between the two Portuguese-speaking peoples of the world, who tend to cling together, partly at least because of the cultural isolation in which they live, in a world in which Spanish-speaking people, particularly, greatly outnumber them.

The story of Portugal is, then, that of a relatively small people on a strip of land in southwestern Europe whose resources and natural wealth have placed strict limitations on the possibility of their economic evolution. From the beginning of their history, they have been forced to look outward toward the sea and the lands that lie beyond it, and from the peculiar combination that has always distinguished the Lusitanian strain of imagination and a sense of adventure, came the remarkable impact that the Portuguese race has made on the history of mankind. Rarely has a small people, so little privileged from the material point of view, achieved so solid a place in the annals of mankind as have the Portuguese.[16]

---

[16] The "visionary" quality of the Lusitanian spirit is evoked by Mario de Vasconcelos, "Condições geográficas," in the monumental work, *História de Portugal*, under the direction of Damião Peres, Barcelos, 1928, Vol. I, p. 18.

Chapter II

HOW PORTUGAL CAME TO BE

Esta foi Lusitânia, derivada
de Luso ou Lisa, que de Baco antigo

Camões, Os Lusiadas, *Canto III*, xxi.

The Origins

The Portuguese have always been keenly aware of the complexities of their own national origin and the apparently insoluble historical problems that it poses; in fact, this problem may be said to constitute one of the obsessions of the nationality and is a source of constant speculation and surmise.

During the period of the Renaissance, men of letters evoked as a historical truth the idea that modern Portugal was the lineal descendant of ancient Lusitania and that the contemporary Portuguese were the heirs of the prowess and glory of Viriatus and his men, who have gone down in annals and in legend for their obdurate and tenacious defense of their land and customs against the pressure of the Roman Legions. André de Resende, in his *De Antiquitatibus Lusitaniae*, published in 1593, gave permanent form to this thesis and from that date until the appearance of the fundamental *História de Portugal* of Alexandre Herculano in 1842, no one challenged this pleasant notion of a modern nation that had persisted, unaltered, since the days when Rome established its sovereignty over all Iberia. The great nineteenth-century historian asserted categorically that Portugal, prior to its emergence as an independent state, had been merely one of the welter of peoples during Celtic, Punic, and Roman times in the peninsula, and that this shadowy past was no solid basis for erecting the superstructure of a formal interpretation of the national institutions.[1]

To Herculano, Portugal was a miracle of creation in the absence of almost all of the factors commonly associated with nationhood. No connection can be established between medieval Portugal as it enters the light of history and the primitive tribes that inhabited Lusitania; no clear territorial frontiers existed that could be ascribed to the Portuguese at any time in their long evolution; no undisputed racial traits welded them together as a people and assured their survival; no common language, uninterrupted in its transmission, attests to the existence of a Portuguese community. Portugal was born in the northwest corner of Spain in the twelfth century through political circumstances and maintained its precarious independence long enough to gain strength and fortitude to subsist, expanding southward against the Moors until a territory had been rounded out that corresponds essentially to the nation today. In a word, Herculano argues that Portugal was merely one fragment of Iberia which, through fortuitous circumstance, managed to become autonomous, and this autonomy, in turn, thanks to the perseverance and tenacity of the medieval rulers, laid the ground work for the creation of a nation. The Portuguese state, in a certain sense, existed before the nation, and provided the separate framework within which it evolved and became personalized.

Thirty years later, the French geographer Reclus sought to establish the physical basis for Portugal, developing a theory whereby natural factors have conspired to set this country apart from its Iberian neighbors.

Oliveira Martins, whose *História de Portugal* and his well-known *História de civilisação ibérica* are landmarks in nineteenth-century Portuguese historiography, suggested a theory not entirely contradictory with that of Herculano, which may be summarized in his phrase that "the audacious, avaricious and turbulent barons of the time were quite ignorant of theories and systems — they could see no further than the points of their blades." This thesis would have Portugal the work of a band of noblemen animated by one simple ambition: the extension of their domain by the sword. Carving out

[1] Herculano, Alexandre, *Historia de Portugal*, Lisbon, n.d., Vol. I, p. 29. "Portugal . . . detached from the Leonese trunk, had no visible and exclusive relation with anything prior to the conquest of the Goths. . . ."

a small piece of Galicia, a bit of Leon, and a goodly segment of Islamic Spain, they patched together a territory that somehow managed to survive, thanks to the general turbulence which characterized life in the Iberian peninsula in the twelfth century.

The romantic epoch in Portugal, as elsewhere in Europe, was intrigued and bemused by these theories of origins lost in the nebulous and misty past. Whether they were anthropologically or historically sound was a secondary matter: they ought to be true because they were far more exciting than the more probable and prosaic reality. By the end of the past century, Portugal was the scene of a vast amount of useful and competent scholarship, ranging from prehistory to philology and ethnography. Men of the stature of Martins Sarmento, Leite de Vasconcelos, Alberto Sampaio, and many others brought to light abundant new materials for a more balanced and a more penetrating assessment of Portugal's past. The accidental or spontaneous creation so dear to the thinking of previous generations gave way to a resurgence of the conviction that Portugal was in fact something different from the rest of the peninsula.

In more recent times, Portuguese of great scholarly distinction, such as the anthropologist Mendes Corrêa, have gone over the ground once more and modified, revised, or refashioned the older theses to fit the demands of modern science. Jaime Cortesão, historian of Portuguese expansion overseas, laid stress on the fact that neither Herculano nor Oliveira Martins were correct in denying all connection with the ancient Lusitanians or in denying the effect of geographical and social community prior to the formation of the nation. Dr. Amorim Girão, professor of geography at the University of Coimbra, has asserted that Portugal has no definite geographical demarcation differentiating it from Spain and that precisely this absence is conclusive evidence of the *élan vital* of the Portuguese people toward their constitution as a nation, since they have demonstrated that in spite of the lack of a physical configuration they have established and maintained a national personality which has resisted the conspiracy of history for eight centuries.[2]

This same authority, in a later publication, argues that "The

[2] Amorim Girão, *Geografia física de Portugal, Coimbra,* 1915, pp. 12–13.

dismemberment of the Kingdom of Leon from which the Portuguese nation was created, consisting of the territories south of the Minho, is an event better explained by historical chance and the personal ambition of a prince than the character of its geography. . . . more than a nationality, what existed at that time in this corner of the Iberian peninsula, was a confusion of nationalities which, at a later date, were joined by well defined political ties."[3]

When the dictates of geography and history seemed to fail, other Portuguese have fallen back on the argument of national character. Nothing, obviously, is more difficult to define than the national temperament of a people and nothing perhaps is quite as seductive as the effort to do so. Antonio Sardinha developed the thesis that the Portuguese lyricism and innate melancholy were features that set the nation sharply apart from Castile. Others have seen even in the development of the primitive institutions of the two parts of the peninsula, and particularly in the forms of municipal government, external evidence that from the beginning the two peoples have been led instinctively to seek different paths in their history.

The soundest approach would seem to be that of Damião Peres in his *Como nasceu Portugal* when he says that "Portugal is a national fact . . . as the result of a process that began obscurely in the ninth century with the liberation of the territories south of the Minho which had been devastated by the Reconquest. Later, vague political sentiments became evident which culminated in the twelfth century in the establishment of autonomous Portugal."[4]

The brilliant Spanish scholar, Américo Castro, has devoted some attention to the problem in his recent publications, the purpose of which is to establish the fundamental character of the peoples of the peninsula. This writer developed the thesis that Portugal originated from *outside* forces, that is, the activity of Count Henry, the Burgundian, ably seconded by the Cluny reform. "Portugal was born and developed as a result of her will not to be Castile to which she owed much of her greatness and not a little of her tragedy."[5] Burgundy attempted to accomplish in Castile what

[3] Amorim Girão, *Condições geograficas e históricas da autonomia de Portugal*, Coimbra, 1935, p. 19. Mendes Corrêa, A., *Raizes de Portugal*, Lisbon, 1944, Chapter I, "Portugal ex-nihilo."

[4] Peres, Damião, *Como nasceu Portugal*, Barcelos, 1938, p. 30.

[5] Castro, Américo, *La realidad histórica de España*, Mexico, 1954, p. 176. Appendix II, p. 647 seq., entitled "The Independence of Portugal."

the Norman knights achieved in Britain; that is, the implantation of a foreign dynasty and the reduction of the territory to its service. Portugal did not arise out of the internal consent of its own people, as did Castile under Fernán González, but from outside influences, the consequence of foreign ambitions. The proof of this is that the Portuguese Galician was continued unbroken and that at no time during the birth pangs of the Portuguese nationality did epic poetry develop, one of the natural manifestations of a people whose local heroes and protagonists were the forgers of its own existence.

But enough of reference to this classic polemic that has agitated the Portuguese mind for centuries. Suppose we now attempt to trace as rapidly as possible how Portugal came into being and the visible forces that contributed to what is an undeniable fact of history; that Portugal became a nation and that its people achieved that sense of community and of oneness without which a national life is impossible.

Portugal is not lacking in evidences of primitive population which antedate all historical reckoning. Fable and picturesque legend envelop this obscure and impenetrable period before a people known as the Lusitanians appear in the brighter light of recorded history. One is tempted to give credit to the amiable account that would have Tubal, grandson of Noah, reach the western shores of Europe a century and a half after the deluge and whose son, Iberus, was given the direction of a number of families who had fled the tyranny of Nemrod of Babylonia. Seven hundred years later, according to another legend, Bacchus disembarked on the peninsula and persuaded its undoubtedly astonished inhabitants to accept his compatriot, Lysias, as king. Later, Ulysses of Ithaca, who pulled up stakes after the destruction of Troy, gave the name of Ulissipo or Olissipo to a city already in existence at the mouth of the Tagus — from which our modern Lisbon stems. A great drought set in after this which forced the inhabitants to seek refuge beyond the Pyrenees and it was only when the rains returned and the land became fertile once more that they found their way homeward, bringing with them numerous companions among those with whom they had sojourned in France: Celts and Gaulish tribesmen.

As we approach the chronicles of the historians of antiquity, we are in a certain sense on firmer ground, although nothing is as unsatisfactory as the determination of contemporary place names in the light of ancient nomenclature. Strabo tells us of how, long before Homer, the enterprising Phoenicians had set up trading stations in the Iberian peninsula, and centers such as Gades (Cádiz), Malaca (Málaga), Hispanil (Seville), and others were flourishing emporiums of commerce centuries before Christ. Of the primitive Iberians we have scant knowledge. The Celtic invasions from the north pertain more properly to known history for one of the most valuable sources is the recurrence of place names such as Conimbriga (Coimbra) which bear witness to their passage. The racial amalgamation that occurred before the epoch-making conflict of Rome and Carthage drew the peninsula into the orbit of civilized Europe is a matter of conjecture. The Lusitanians appear as a specific element during this time, and it is probable that the name was extended to numerous peoples in the region between the Tagus and the Douro.

Who were the Lusitanians whose name has been perpetuated to designate poetically the modern Portuguese? They may have been the descendants of a vague people known as the Ligurians, or they may have been one more of the numerous nuclei of Celtiberi who populated the peninsula. Strabo writes of the Lusitanians as the "most powerful of the Iberian nations and which managed for a longer period of time than any other to resist Roman advances." These Lusitani clung with remarkable tenacity to the mountain fastnesses of the Serra da Estrela, among whose inhospitable rocks and crags they developed a warlike culture that despised the softer ways of the inhabitants of the plains and the valleys.

As the great struggle between Rome and Carthage moved toward its dramatic climax, the Lusitanians were scarcely affected, remote as they were from the normal currents of contact between the two giants. Carthaginian attention was focused on Iberia after the defeats of the First Punic War and, in the process of extending this work of pacification and penetration, Hamilcar came into contact with the tribes of the west, a number of which he defeated decisively in battle. After the Battle of Zama (201 B.C.) Carthaginian aspirations were dashed forever, and the presence of Rome became more and more evident to these restless, rough peoples who disdained the works of civilization as represented by the occupants. Instead of waiting for the Roman assault and ultimate incorporation, the Lusitanians set out in a series of *razzias* against the settlements of the Algarve in southern Portugal and Andalusia. Defeated by Cornelius Scipio, they returned to the attack two years later and killed the Roman commander Aemilius Paulus and six thousand of his troops.

For fifteen years after this, the Lusitanians waged ceaseless guerrilla warfare against the legions of Rome, in an interminable series of incursions and even full-fledged invasions such as the passage of the Straits of Gibraltar and the attack on Roman settlements in North Africa. Rome mounted a counterattack that carried its armies clear to the Tagus with devastation and destruction in its wake. The Lusitanians, momentarily thrown back, were led to lay down their arms and accept terms with the result that thousands of them were sacrificed by Servius Sulpicius Galba in a frenzy of vengeance.

The Lusitanians were not cowed by the disaster and among them rose up a remarkable leader, whose personality may be said to be the first of the Portuguese chieftains in genius and ability. Viriatus, a humble shepherd, seemed providentially to have harkened to the call of duty at a critical moment in the history of his sorely tried people. In Viriatus, we have a primitive combination of Joan of Arc and the Cid Campeador, who bursts into history in 147 B.C. when his plea to the beleaguered Lusitanians to carry on the struggle against Rome was heeded. In the ravines of the Serra de Ronda, Viriatus and his followers destroyed four thousand Romans and their leader, Vetilius. A year later a vast Roman force estimated at more than ten thousand infantry set out to reduce this indomitable warrior. Through stratagem and a reliance on the arts of guerrilla warfare, the Lusitanians escaped, following the destruction of a considerable portion of the enemy force.

With the death of the shepherd-warrior, Lusitanian resistance was broken and the lands in the west of Iberia were now open to conquest and occupation by the Romans. Decimus Junius Brutus was the first. Between 138 B.C. and 136 B.C., he pushed northward above the Douro into the territory that had served as the center of the Lusitanians. He is reputed to have founded a settlement at Cale, the future Oporto, and from which the name of modern Portugal is derived — "Portus-cale."

Under Viriatus, tough tribesmen had fought to prevent the imposition of Roman rule and customs. Under Quintus Sertorius, sent in 83 B.C. as praetor to Hispania Citerior, the Lusitanians found a second leader, who led them in opposition to the existent powers in far-off Rome and who, for a period of years, defeated the best forces that Rome could send to the peninsula. But the work of Viriatus and Sertorius was profoundly different; the former was a native leader bent on preventing Roman penetration; the second was a Roman, ambitious for himself and bent on autonomy, who was guided by the desire to Romanize the tribesmen whose leader he had become.

The century before Christ, under Caesar and Augustus, witnessed the end of such resistance and the effective Romanization of Lusitania. In brief, suffice it to say that Romanism penetrated deep into this Lusitanian soil and, sometimes by force and sometimes by sheer superiority, won the adherence of the indigenous population. The Portuguese ceased to be an assortment of rustic tribes and were molded into a compact and stable community somewhat on the fringes, to be sure, of the great currents of Roman life, but nevertheless impregnated with the ideas and the conceptions that made Roman civilization what it was.

Christianity came early to this corner of Europe, and tradition has it that St. James himself preached the Word in Iberia and the splendid shrine at Compostela attests the enduring quality of this belief. The truth of this visit and that the tomb venerated in the Galician capital is indeed that of the Apostle merited the recognition of St. Jerome, St. Isidore, St. Julian of Toledo, and the Venerable Bede; and in the consciousness of the Hispanic peoples it has been accepted as a reality. During the years 64 and 65, when Nero was emperor, it is known that seven zealous propagandists of Christianity found their way to Iberia and churches were founded here and there in what is today Spain.

Let it be remembered that we are dealing with a period in which the names *Spain* and *Portugal* are quite arbitrary, for neither of these nations existed as such, in fact. Both were there in embryo, in gestation, so to speak, and the leaven of Roman culture had already begun to do its work in terms of language and spirit. To the amorphous mass that was the Iberian peninsula, the introduction of Christianity was to bring an incalculably important element, the most important in all the centuries of their history, for if ever two closely related nations displayed a positive vocation for Christianity and its expansion, those were Spain and Portugal. It is difficult to overemphasize not only the ennobling influence of the doctrine of Christ on people long habituated to semibarbarism and idolatry, but the sense of national cohesion that a common religion provided. Of this we shall have occasion to refer later in discussing the religious element in the impulse that led the Portuguese to pioneer in the discovery and exploration of the world that lay beyond the narrow limits of antiquity.

Until 313, when Christianity was formally recognized, Portugal shared with the rest of the empire the glory of its Christian martyrs. Gradually historical records speak with growing clarity of bishops and councils, of Christian feasts and practices over the peninsula. A Bishop of Evora appears at a council held near Granada in 300 and the periodic persecutions produced their crop of virgins and martyrs. Curiously enough, the Portuguese city of Braga achieved some renown in this early period as one of the principal seats of the Priscillian heresy. Between 380 and 400, Priscillianism established itself firmly in the Iberian peninsula.

Fifty years before the formal collapse of Roman power in 476, the Pyrenees had been crossed by venturesome Germans and that extraordinary period called the "Barbarian invasions" had begun. For three centuries of the Dark Ages they were to penetrate peninsular life, set up kingdoms, adapt themselves to the Roman models found everywhere, and become Christians. Vandals, Goths, Swabians, and Alans divided up the territories and, once the centralized machinery of Roman administration had broken down, gave vent to a marked propensity for internecine strife and the fragmentation of the unity of the peninsula. Some Barbarians settled down to carve out kingdoms; others, such as the Vandals, Goths, and Alans, were attracted by the rich lands of Mauretania and crossed into Africa. In Lusitania, the Swabians had entrenched themselves in what was, for all purposes, a Galician-Portuguese kingdom extending from the Tagus to the northwestern tip of Spain. Thus by the end of the fifth century, there existed a Swabian state in what is now Portugal and beside it a Visigothic one covering the major part of contemporary Spain. Obviously it would be incorrect to conclude that here we have the origins of the two nations. It is significant, nevertheless, that even in times as tumultuous and anarchical as these, the peninsula was not held under a single sway and that the division took place along lines that resemble somewhat Portugal and Spain today.

Racially it is inevitable that the Germanic invaders should leave more than a casual trace of their presence. They very quickly became a part, religiously and culturally, with the rest of the population, and it is not uncommon now to note what seem to be very definite "Germanic" traits in many Portuguese in the north of the country. It is, in fact, a source of amusing speculation to attempt a guess at racial origins in the features of the peasantry one sees from Braga far south to Faro or Lagos in the Algarve. Many times in the towns, villages, and on the highways of Portugal, I have noticed those magnificently built peasant women, blonde, blue eyed, stalwart, swinging along majestically with all sorts of burdens on their heads — perfect specimens of the legendary Germanic breed of womanhood. It is not difficult to imagine that these folk, who might easily merge into the background of a Norwegian or Swedish community, are descendants of the barbarians who, for a very short time between the decay of Rome and the impact of Islam, held precarious sway over Portugal.

Any more detailed description of what the presence of the barbarians meant to Portugal would take us far afield. Obviously they left an imprint ethnically and, to a very considerable extent, juridically and administratively. Although they came as seekers of booty and as pillagers, they remained to create a stable and orderly society and, until their conversion, sought to impose a rigid class system in which the interlopers were the privileged. As usual, Christianity served as the leaven which reduced Goths and Iberians to the same level. The Visigoths encouraged the development of the Church which attained a position of considerable eminence during the period. Culture was not as low or as insignificant as might be thought, although Portugal was still looked upon, by those who partook of Latin culture, as a remote and probably semi-barbarous province in the West.

From what has already been said, it is clear that Portugal was a nationality *in potentia* among the welter of ethnic groups that formed the mosaic of Visigothic and later Islamic Iberia. The definite emergence is intimately linked to that epic struggle, with its moments of heroism and its plateaus of depression, which we call the *Reconquista.* The common Christian tradition that had sunk deep roots in the Iberian soil became the rallying point for resistance to the prolonged presence of the Arab as he settled most of the peninsula after the eighth century. From the tiny beginnings in the fastnesses of Asturias and the north of Portugal, Christians dreamed of liberation and of the expulsion of the infidel and with an absorption that was exclusive of almost all other preoccupations, desperate men banded together through generations to push back step by step the lands occupied by the invader and reassert the supremacy of Christ.

This glorious achievement, which must rank as one of the most moving crusading enterprises of all times, was not unmarked by dark and ominous episodes. There were numerous cases of defection, acts of treason, gross betrayals, and what we would call, in the parlance of our day, "appeasement." Long periods of quiet succeeded outbursts of energetic reprisal, and internal dynastic controversy was far from absent among the Christian states, each bent on consolidating its own hegemony at the same time as the rolling back of the Moslem.

There was a note of the providential in the grim struggle which now took place. The dissension, rivalries, and petty quarreling of the Visigoths that had opened the gates of the peninsula to the African hordes gave way to a new birth of fervor and consciousness of mission. In a quite literal sense, the Iberian peoples found their souls and under the pressure of adversity manifested, as they so frequently have in their history, that outstanding capacity to rise to sublime heights when their existence was menaced.

Pelayo, in the Asturian mountains, infused an ardor in his rustic warriors that recalls Viriatus and his resistance to Rome or, to transpose the analogy to a modern period, to the obdurate and uncompromising Carlists who, for generations, carried on guerrilla combat in the name of their dynasty. The common Hispanic quality of endless fighting for a cause that seems lost even before it is begun, distinguished the *Reconquista.* None could have foreseen that when the Moslem sweep was stopped by Charles Martel and the flood ebbed back across the Pyrenees, the little islands that had not yet been submerged in the peninsula would become the nuclei of the future Hispanic kingdoms. Out on this remote frontier of Christendom — remote from the great centers of Europe — lonely men fought against the opulence and the might of a power which had the stretches of Africa and the riches of Asia behind it and theirs was to be the final victory. Pelayo was responsible for the foundation of the Asturian state sometime between 722 and 725 and its first expansion was westward to Galicia.

The first monarch who emerges from the mists of this period is Alfonso I, who promoted a number of raids and *razzias* in Moslem territory, carrying Christian arms as far as Braga, Porto, and Viseu in Portugal, and to Leon, Zamora, Salamanca, and Ávila in Spain. He harassed the Arabs as far as the Douro and created for himself a solid tradition as a first-class guerrilla fighter.

The violence of these encounters, in fact the whole character of this clash of two civilizations, was enormously mitigated and softened by the plastic quality of large segments of the population, notably the Mozarabs and the Mudejars,[6] whose long experience of living under alien rule and in the presence of a hostile religion had provided them with a flexible and adaptable character that proved most useful during the Reconquest. Indeed it would be no exaggeration to conclude that the necessity of working out some kind of compromise, if life was to be tolerable at all, was the origin of that extraordinary elasticity which is a predominant Portuguese characteristic.

In the sense that the struggle to oust the Arabs provided a long and arduous experience in dealing with non-Christians and non-Europeans, it was an exceedingly useful training ground for those who were to become the foremost among all Europeans in the understanding of the mind and heart of peoples of fundamentally different cultures outside Europe.

The Mozarabs and Mudejars formed the population that during these times of stress carried on the ordinary operations of social and economic life. They continued to till the soil, harvest the crops, and provide the food during periods when warfare raged across the land. Their passivity was often reflected in the way in which they welcomed the Christian conquerors and, once the territory thus occupied had to be again given up to the Moslems, these same people readjusted themselves to the former way of life with

[6] The expression "Mozarab" has already been used to designate the Christian population under Moslem rule. "Mudejar" refers to the reverse process, Moslems under Christian rule.

a minimum of difficulty. The period was essentially fluid and these critical years can be considered rightfully as the truly formative period of the Portuguese and Spanish character.

The Heritage of Islam

The penetration and influence of Islam in Portugal must be treated necessarily within the framework of peninsular unity. There was no Arab occupation of one country as distinct from the other, for both were part of the great impulse that led the original religious zealots of the desert to extend their sway across the straits into continental Europe. No period of history is perhaps more obscure than the generations which immediately preceded the eruption of the Islamized hordes into Europe. We lack sound historical evidence as to the state of mind, the administration, and the attitude of the Visigothic sovereigns on the eve of the arrival of the Arabs, which was destined to produce one of the greatest transformations ever wrought in Spain and Portugal in their long history of contacts with alien peoples.

The distinguished Spanish Arabist, Emilio García Gómez, has written brilliantly of the *lacunae* and pitfalls in the examination of this turbulent and dark period when Iberia was obviously disintegrating and overready for the formidable incursion of the African and Asiatic horsemen. What did the Visigoths think as Islam moved like a tidal wave across North Africa, took over Morocco and its Berbers, Islamized these nomadic peoples and lapped dangerously at the coasts of the peninsula? The chronicles are painfully silent on this score. It was obvious that Spain and Portugal were torn by dissension and weakened by internecine strife and no match for the energy and evangelizing spirit of the intruders.

The Arabs themselves have written their history *ex post facto*, and have perhaps understandably adorned the tale of their conquest with the embroidery of retrospection. Later Arabic sources are abundant, although in their pages it is the invader and not the invaded who bear witness to the tremendous experience. As we look at the event across the centuries, the wonderment never ceases that a handful of impetuous and enterprising Arabs from the fringes of the Mediterranean world, accompanied by recently converted Berbers — stock hands and mountaineers — should have managed to enter, subdue, organize, and rule the lands that later were to constitute Spain and Portugal. Stranger still was the prospect that clashing tribesmen far removed from the central authority of the Caliphate should achieve a political stability that was to produce such extraordinary fruits in the realm of culture and the social order.[7]

The Iberian peninsula had already suffered numerous invasions from Africa, and indeed it may be said that it had become the natural terminal point in the movements of population from the neighboring continent. It is possible that the prehistoric Iberians, coming from the Caucasus, may have followed the classical route along the Mediterranean shores, over the straits, and into the south-western European land mass. Under Carthage the peninsula was entered from Africa and in the year 150 B.C., as a result of revolts in North Africa, numerous denizens of the area found their way into Spain. At the time of Marcus Aurelius, groups of Berbers crossed the narrow straits to contribute one more population contingent to the motley assortment of races being slowly amalgamated into the modern Portuguese and Spanish.[8] In the reverse sense, the Germanic invaders in turn entered Africa and set up garrisons in such places as Ceuta and Tangier. The Moslem invasion of 710–712 was, therefore, no novelty in a certain sense, although it would be impossible to overestimate the shock that it produced not only on the peoples immediately subjected to the new rulers but to civilized Europe as a whole.

It would be foolhardy, obviously, to conceive of the invasion as comparable to modern, Western forms of political penetration and control. The Arabs moved westward across Africa along natural communication routes, carrying with them the peoples they encountered on the way, and the Berbers were simply incorporated among the conquerors, and their natural propensity for pillage amply satisfied. There was no political cohesion, no administrative structure as we conceive it in the West, in the movement. Iberia was precisely the type of society that had proved most attractive to the Arabs — civilized, economically developed, socially stable,

---

[7] See García Gómez, Emilio, Introduction to the *Historia de España*, "España musulmana hasta la caída del califato de Córdoba," under the direction of Ramón Menéndez Pidal, Madrid, 1950, Vol. IV, p. xiii.

[8] Brémond, Général, *Berberes et arabes*, Paris, 1950, pp. 222–223.

and with abundant opportunities for the enjoyment of the luxuries of life without the necessity of creating them.

One of the most remarkable facts of this wholly remarkable episode in history is that the Arabs set out on a career of conquest quite unparalleled in the annals of mankind without the preliminary organization of their own land of origin. Islam established itself predominantly in centers already highly developed: in Syria, Mesopotamia, Egypt, and later the Iberian peninsula. On the foundation of what was already existent, Islamic influence was brought to bear to modify, perfect, and refine into a curious hybrid culture which is no less extraordinary because of its origins.[9]

The Islamic campaign into Spain and Portugal was the last of the great waves of expansion through which the religion of the Prophet was carried far and wide across the world.[10] It marked the high point in the spread of the teachings of the Koran to Africa and Europe. One is struck, in reviewing this event, by the rapidity with which it was carried out and the feeble opposition which seemed to have been offered to the conquerors. In the summer of 710, Musā ibn-Nusayr, the governor of North Africa under the Umayyads, dispatched one Tariq to reconnoiter the approaches to Europe. In 711, Phillip Hitti, the historian of the Arabs, suggests, "actuated more by the desire for booty than for conquest, Musā dispatched his Berber freedmen, Tariq ibn Ziyad, into Spain with 7,000 men, most of whom were Berbers."[11]

Tariq landed near the rock that ever since that memorable date bears his name, Jabal Tariq (Gibraltar). The precise circumstances in which Tariq crossed the straits and began the great assault on Christian Europe have been so embellished with legend and fiction as to make impossible an accurate judgment. One version — and the most popular — has it that Count Julian of Ceuta had suffered the humiliation of the violation of his daughter Florinda by Rodrigo,

[9] Gautier, E. F., *Le passé de l'Afrique du Nord*, Paris, 1952, p. 282.

[10] Simultaneously with the conquest of Iberia, the Arabs were operating in the East: "While the armies of Syria under expert leaders such as Maslama e Abbas carried the war to the Byzantine provinces — other captains of no less courage. Qutaybah ibn-Muslim, Muhammad ibn-al-Qasim, Musā ibn-Nusayr, Tariq Ziyad extended the empire in the east and west" (Pareja, F. M., *Islamologia*, Rome, 1951, p. 82).

[11] Hitti, Philip K., *History of the Arabs*, London, 1931, p. 493.

who had seized the Visigothic throne from Akhila, son of Witiza. The Visigothic court was a confusion of dynastic claims and intrigue, and once the Arabs reached the Atlantic in North Africa, like all conquering forces far from their home base, they were faced with the problem of alternatives. South lay the stretches of the Sahara and Black Africa; with the topography of which they were familiar and an area which they could, in all probability, have successfully occupied. To the north, separated by the narrows between the Moroccan tip and the extremity of Spain, lay not only a lush and fertile country with its cities and wealth, but the gateway to Europe itself. The preference for the expedition northward is easy to understand.

The Arabic chronicles are replete with accounts of how Count Julian sought out Musā in his court to expound the ease with which Spain could be invaded. After the preliminary soundings to which reference has been made, Tariq crossed, in the summer of 711, with several thousand Berbers and began the march toward the north. Rodrigo was disastrously defeated in the first encounter and the Islamic forces moved on Cordova. The ease with which Andalusia was overrun led the Arabs to push on at once to Toledo, capital of the Visigothic kingdom, and there they found an abandoned city from which everyone had fled.[12]

Musā, jealous perhaps of the lightning success of his lieutenant, crossed into the peninsula in June of 712 and laid siege to Seville, the center of intellectual life and former capital under Roman rule. By 713 the fortified cities that Tariq had avoided had been largely reduced, and some, such as Mérida, had offered a tenacious and prolonged resistance.

The peninsula now assumed its Arabic name of al-Andalous, and after seven years of fitful campaigning and meager resistance one of the great provinces of medieval Europe had fallen to the Arabs, not as a temporary occupation but as a permanent annexation to the newly created world of Islam. The quarrels of Tariq and Musa, which led to the humiliation of the former, foreshadowed in a certain sense one of the great sources of the weakness of the Islamic empire in Spain and Portugal, that is, the internal dissensions and personal rivalries which ultimately, seven centuries later, would provide the opening wedge for their expulsion from Europe. Musā

[12] Menéndez Pidal, *Historia de España*, *op. cit.*, IV, p. 15.

returned to Damascus laden with the booty of the conquest and with hundreds of Gothic captives, a display which has long fascinated the Arab chroniclers who have outdone themselves in vivid descriptions of the triumphal march across Africa back to the Middle East and the seat of Moslem power.

In 717 or 718, the third successor of Musā crossed the Pyrenees, encouraged by the vision of vast spoils to be found in the Frankish cities and the lure of conquest in the heartland of Christianity itself. Much later, in the spring of 732, the Moslems undertook seriously to invade France, stormed Bordeaux and Poitiers, and reached Tours, an especially sacred spot to the Christians as the resting place of St. Martin, apostle of the Gauls. There, after days of skirmishes, Charles Martel stopped Islam from further inroads into Europe, although in all probability the battle was far less decisive than it has been depicted in the European chronicles. Moslem power had already reached a breaking point and it is dubious that the Arabs, even had victory been theirs, could have pushed on indefinitely, standing as they were a thousand miles from Gibraltar and an infinitely longer distance from the centers of Islamic authority in the East. Here and there in the Iberian peninsula, little nuclei of resistance continued, especially in the less accessible areas in the north and the west. In Asturias, Covadonga was to become celebrated in history and in verse as the symbol of the Christian resistance and the point of departure of that splendid epic of the Reconquest.

Up to 755 Iberia depended on governors who were in turn dependent on the caliphs of Damascus. These were troubled and restless times: Arabs quarreled and clashed with Berbers; Syrians were hostile to their coreligionists from elsewhere in the far-flung empire; and the spirit of the clan or tribe tended to overcome the more or less imposed cohesion of rulers in a land that was not yet effectively subjugated. In reality the Moslems in the peninsula were too removed from Damascus to maintain effective contact. In addition they were faced by the twin difficulties of unrest within the area and dissatisfaction on the part of the Berbers in North Africa behind them. In 755, Abd-al-Rahman, an Umayyad, proclaimed himself king of Cordova and roused the population against the last of the governors. The peninsula became a separate Moslem state. During the period of his rule, until 787, this remarkable ruler fought the forces of Charlemagne who had been invited in by his enemies, suppressed rebellions of the Berbers instigated by Damascus, and built up a permanent army for the maintenance of order in his territory.

Under Abd-al-Rahman II, Cordova was expanded and attention paid to the development of letters and the arts. The outlines of the rich cultural expression that was to distinguish Islamic Iberia began to take form, although political difficulties continued unabated. Further complications during this reign were caused by the first incursions of the Northmen, valorous and predatory seamen who infested the coasts, pushed up the navigable rivers and, in one instance, rode the Guadalquivir to Seville, sacking and looting the city. The pressure of the Christians in the north became more intense, and something like a permanent "cold war," which frequently blew hot, existed for years between the two portions of the peninsula. The Islamic policy of broad toleration of the non-Moslem minority gave way to active persecution and religion became in a very real sense the standard by which loyalty was judged.

It would be an error nevertheless to assume that the seven odd centuries of Islamic-Christian coexistence in Portugal and Spain were ones of unmitigated warfare or even high tension. In many cases the Christian population continued under Moslem rule to practice their religion and preserve the essentials of their way of life, each element reacting upon the other in a constant process of what the anthropologists call "acculturation." There were Hispanic Christians who became Islamized and adopted Arabic as their instrument of expression; there were Arabs who employed the romance of the day, the Latin, that was already becoming transformed through the alchemy of philological change in the parent of modern Portuguese and Spanish; there were Jews who accepted Arabic and wrote in the language of the conquerors.

In the heart of Andalusia — southern Spain and Portugal south of the Tagus — large nuclei of Christians remained faithful to the traditional religion after the invasion of Tariq. These were the Mozarabs, that is to say, natives of Hispania as it may be called who retained their religion and their Visigothic laws and continued to live under the authority of their bishops and nobility, while paying a special tribute to the Islamic rulers and living, for the most part, in separated or restricted areas; a sort of Christian ghetto as tolerated by Islamic practice.

Here and there were individual Christian noblemen who had resisted the invasion and preserved a precarious independence even when surrounded by the flood of the new culture. It was not unusual to find these scattered Christian landowners respected in their autonomy by treaties with the Moslem rulers. Record exists of one of these islands of Christianity in the sea of Islam in the person of the Aragonese, García Aznar, who fell prisoner to the famous Cid Campeador in 1083 and who had proclaimed in 1057 that he and his ancestors had never been bound by any ruler and had systematically refused to pay tribute to the Caliphs of Cordova or Almanzor "quia libertas nostra antiqua est."[13]

For the sake of clarity in this brief summary of Islamic Hispania, the long period of Arab domination may be classified as follows:

I. The conquest of the peninsula, A.D. 711–756
II. Independent al-Andalous, A.D. 756–912
III. The Caliphate of Cordova, A.D. 912–1030
IV. From the fall of the Caliphate and the advance of the Reconquest, A.D. 1031–1284
V. Decline and extinction of the Moslem kingdoms in the peninsula

The Reconquest, which lasted eight centuries with its humble beginnings in a cave in Asturias, was a very special kind of war, whose military operations tended to be sporadic and limited to certain periods of the year. In the intervals of peace which were sometimes inordinately prolonged, Christians and Moslems engaged in trade and other activities including mutual assistance and aid in a number of fields. After the collapse of the Caliphate and the creation of numerous small Moslem kingdoms, rivalry with the Christians was not infrequently superseded by an equally intense rivalry among the Moslems themselves. These kings often called on their Christian colleagues for assistance while the latter were not reluctant to accept Moslem aid both in international and internal wars. Hardpressed monarchs such as Sancho I of Leon and Alfonso VI of Castile were not averse to seeking refuge in Moslem cities.[14]

[13] Quoted in Menéndez Pidal, Ramón, *La España del Cid*, Buenos Aires—Mexico, 1939, p. 53.

[14] Altamira y Crevea, Rafael, *Manual de historia de España*, Madrid, 1934, p. 169.

It may be well to outline rapidly the process of the Reconquest since in this confusion Portugal was to emerge as an independent kingdom. The fall of the Caliphate was an event of outstanding importance. The brilliance and prestige of united Moslem Hispania had given way by the opening of the eleventh century to discord, feud, and unabashed pillage on the part of the Caliphate authorities. Internal tension exploded in 1031 with the overthrow of the regime and the split of Moslem controlled territory into numerous fragments which came to be known as *taifas*. Seville became a republic and landed aristocrats carved out domains for themselves in the midst of the anarchy. Badajoz became the center of a principality while in other parts of Portugal, south of the Tagus, three states came into being, each insignificant in its dimensions and definitely limited in its power. Obviously this situation of progressive Balkanization played directly into the hands of the Christian princes ready and willing to advance at the expense of the historic adversary, so weakened now as to offer little more than token resistance.

From the end of the Caliphate to the middle of the thirteenth century, three events dominated the historical scene: the progress of the Reconquest which, from the Douro, reached in the tenth century, gained the Guadalquivir on the south and the Mediterranean coast on the east; the concentration of the disparate political entities such as the kingdoms of Astures-Leon, Navarra, Castile, Aragon, Catalonia, and the Basque provinces in two major units, the kingdom of Leon and Castile with two of the Basque provinces attached, and the kingdom of Aragon and Catalonia with Navarre dependent; and finally the marked development of the various Romanic languages — Castilian, Galician, Catalan, and others which were to constitute the natural regions into which the Iberian peninsula was to be divided permanently.

If this trend toward greater unity was pronounced in the Spanish part of the peninsula, a decisive factor in the contrary sense was the separation of the west, from the Minho southward, that is, the creation of Portugal, the outstanding event of the twelfth century. For the first time since Roman rule, Hispania was divided politically into two national units. The Hispanic kingdoms up to that time, although numerous and often clashing, never lost sight of the fact that they were all part of the same broad stream of culture and history. The birth of Portugal was to establish a line of cleavage that has lasted to this day and which has had profound repercussions on the evolution of the Hispanic spirit. The story of how the Spanish kings pushed the Moslem back into Andalusia and ultimately into Africa belongs properly to the history of Spain and not to that of Portugal.

It may be useful, however, in the presentation of the main lines of Islamic rule to deal for a moment with the character of the Arab influence, not in external political terms but in the more intimate effects on the Hispanic peoples. It was true that Islam in Spain and Portugal revealed itself singularly tolerant in many respects, the result perhaps of the minority position of the Moslems themselves and the fact that they were divided and any manifestation of Christian unity was bound to have the most uncomfortable repercussions. The Mozarabs found it possible in many cases to rise to high position under the Moslems. Many served in the armed forces; others attained positions of significance in the civil service or in the cultural life of the Caliphate.[15]

The Moslem courts were centers of refinement and learning in marked contrast to the rustic and somewhat primitive Christian. By the eleventh century, the Islamic kingdoms were characterized by a curious contradiction; side by side with great wealth, luxury and material splendor, with great cultural advancement in the case of the Hispanic-Andalusians but not the descendants of the Berbers in Granada, was a weakening of Islam itself and an almost total lack of political and military intuition and organization. An effeteness set in that was in marked contrast with the austerity of the first conquerors and with the spirit of Islam itself. There is the impression that the essence of Islamic *raison d'être* had been sapped and that the brilliance achieved in the realm of the mind was at the sacrifice of vigor in the realm of the body.

The Iberian peninsula was for three centuries almost entirely within the orbit of Islam and received its cultural contacts from the East. The absence of close relations with the rest of Europe

---

[15] Aguado Bleye, Pedro, *Manual de Historia de España*, Madrid, 1947, Vol. I, p. 415. Islamic writers have insisted that this was the inevitable consequence of the teachings of the Koran. Ali Zaki, *Islam in the World*, Lahore (Pakistan), 1947, p. 110 *seq.* "The Quran declares: There is no compulsion in religion. Everywhere the subject races were allowed freedom of worship; non-Muslims obtained under the tolerant rule of the conquerors, security for their religious beliefs, their lives, their honour and their property."

reduced the Christian states to a lower and lower cultural level while at the same time increasing the power of attraction of Arabic thought and ways on those who were eager for such experience. The Christians of the peninsula were unable, because of their religion, to partake fully of Islamic thought; and, because of their isolation, were deprived of normal, constant contact with the West. It is not astonishing that a certain sterility or shriveling should set in until such a time as a reintegration with the currents of occidental culture could be re-established.

During four centuries, the Arabic speakers dominated world culture, and its finest fruits were produced on what may be called the fringes of Islam, that is, Central Asia and the Iberian peninsula with Morocco. It would be hazardous indeed to seek to assess, with precision, the specifically Arabic or even Islamic contribution to the rich harvest of literary, philosophical, and scientific thought that flourished under the Moslem rulers. Indeed it would be difficult to judge to what degree these rulers could properly be called orthodox Moslems. There is little doubt that the Islamic courts of the peninsula were a very far cry from the austere and self-denying existence of the desert. The fine flowering of speculation and disputation in the Iberian centers seems remote from the inflexible simplicity of the Koran which taught that man was to obey the law of God and not to discuss his nature.

Islamic Iberia, during the years of peace before constant warfare debilitated the population, knew a very considerable prosperity which in turn was favorable to the pursuits of culture and the production of articles of luxury. Toledo was famous for the making of arms, a reputation it has still retained; Málaga was outstanding in ceramics; and Almería in glasswork. Cordova as the administrative center and Seville as the commercial served as vast emporia for the growing trade of the western Islamic state. This material well-being contributed to the advancement of culture. Libraries were created and the annals recount from time to time the rich collections, both private and royal, that were the wonder of Islamic Spain.

The existence of schools and centers of higher learning in which not only the Koran and related subjects were studied but also philosophy and the natural sciences proved a point of attraction for the rest of Europe. Gerbert of Aquitaine, later to become Pope

Silvester II (999–1003), found his way to Cordova and there occupied himself in his insatiable curiosity for knowledge with the study of geometry, astronomy, and other sciences. To him is attributed the introduction of the Arabic numerals into France on his return from Spain. The peninsula was fundamentally, from the cultural point of view, the meeting place, the *trait d'union* between Europe and the East and no single center was more significant in this regard than Catalonia and Toledo. The former was noteworthy in the tenth century whereas Toledo gained great prestige in the twelfth as a center of translators. In Toledo the school of translators gained lasting fame in the diffusion of classical and Arabic texts. The *Organon* of Aristotle was translated and science owes an everlasting debt to Domingo González, Juan Hispalense, and others who made available an infinite number of sources to the scholarly and humanistic world of Europe. The place of Averroës in the constellation of Arabic commentators scarcely requires elucidation, so well established has his prestige become through the dependence of many Christian writers on his writings.

The literary apogee of the Arabs in the West coincides with the reign of Abd-al-Rahman III (912–961) and the dictatorship of Almanzor who led the Moslems to the peak of their achievement. Even during the years of the decline, from the capture of Toledo by the Christians in 1086 to the later shift in dynasty, this cultural life persisted and in the case of Granada was still lively right down to the final fall of the curtain in 1492. The origins of Hispanic Moslem letters is obscure although it would seem to have commenced in earnest as an outburst of verse in the popular vein. In the beginning it was subservient to Syrian and Iraqui models and, by the eleventh century, this special form of Spanish literature in the Arabic language may be said to have attained its autonomy. Women, love, flowers: these are the themes that predominate and in turn were forerunners of the troubadour poetry of Christian Europe. Abject and submissive love appears as the natural attitude of the lover, and a good bit of the verse revolves around the idea of the anguish and torment which the lady quite reasonably inflicts on her swain.

Ibn Abdi Rabbihi (860–940) is one of the notable savants and men of letters of the Arabic age, known principally for his anthology *al-Iqd,* in which he inserts a number of his own erotic, historical, and ascetic compositions.[16] It was not until the tenth and eleventh centuries that the more original verse makers appeared. The courts all had their officially designated poets such as Ramadi (died in 1013 or 1022) who performed this function for the Caliph Hakam II and his son Hicham II. But this milieu was also known for the production of a totally new genre in poetic literature known as the *muwassahas* or *zegels* and brought about a literal revolution in the style and meter of Arabic verse which heretofore had been extremely long. The *zegel* seems to have been a popular form and the *muwassaha* the more refined or literary development from it. The *zegels* were destined for popular consumption, to be sung in the market places and in the road houses and spread far and wide over the Arabic-speaking empire.[17] Love, wine, and the enjoyment of life constitute the theme of this verse which obviously is not in line with the strict interpretation of the teachings of the Koran but which reflects, perhaps as perfectly as anything, the element which the Moslems introduced into the Iberian peninsula.

But this brief indication of the wealth of Arabic letters should not conclude without mention of the importance of the Jews in the Spain and Portugal of the time. In fact, no single influence is probably more striking than this persistent recurrence of the Hebraic at almost every moment in the history of the two Iberian peoples. The Jews prospered in general under Islam and in many cases they expressed themselves in Arabic and were indistinguishable from their fellow literary craftsmen in that language. In other cases they composed religious verse in Hebrew, the purpose of which was for use in the synagogue. In the *taifa* states of the eleventh century, various modifications and renovations in Hebrew verse brought forth a veritable renaissance in the capacity of the ancient tongue to express the emotion and sentiment of the age. Figures as famous as Solomon ibn Gabirol and Yehuda Halevi shed luster on the Hebrew letters of the peninsula in this period.[18]

---

[16] Brennan, *op. cit.*, pp. 28–29. This is an excellent summary of this relatively little known period of Hispanic literature. Nicholson, R. A. A., *Literary History of the Arabs*, Cambridge, 1953, p. 420.

[17] Pellat, Charles, *Langue et littérature arabes*, Paris, 1952, p. 121.

[18] See *Historia general de las literaturas hispánicas*, under the direction of Guillermo Díaz Plaja, Barcelona, 1949, Vol. I. The study entitled, "Hebraic-Spanish Literature," by Prof. Millás Vallicrosa, p. 145 *seq.* Pires de Lima, J. A., *Mouros judeus e negros na Historia de Portugal*, Porto, 1940.

It would be unfair to conclude that there was nothing but unmitigated eroticism abroad during the many generations of Moslem rule. There was a lively and fascinating development of the ascetic life among the Christian populations and the Moslems themselves were not immune to its influence for among them, as a reaction perhaps against the laxity of the courts, arose innumerable groups, confraternities, and individuals who sought to apply to their personal or collective lives the more rigorous tenets that had been so largely abandoned.[19]

The Moslem domination in Portugal lasted for five centuries as against eight in Spain and, even with their departure, the influence was felt and is perhaps felt to this day. The justification for the space occupied by these considerations of the Moslem conquest is the permanent effect on the Hispanic peoples of this intimate association which, in a religious sense, vanished after the Reconquest but which, in a more subtle if less tangible way, has endured in the temperament, manner of thought, customs, speech, and habits of the descendants of those who lived for so long in close contact with a vigorous and novel civilization, many aspects of which contrasted markedly with the Hispano-Gothic background of the local inhabitants.

Moslem institutions and forms of organizations left a deep imprint on the conquered territory and no source reveals this more eloquently than the vocabulary of the modern peninsular languages, from which Arabic words have been taken precisely to designate those objects of operations which were superimposed on the life of the people during these critical centuries. The Portuguese language is rich in words and expressions of Arabic origin, many of them relating directly to forms of activity for which the Moslems were primarily responsible. The Mozarabic population quite naturally took over convenient words from the Arabic, many of which have become so much a part of the Portuguese vocabulary as to be scarcely recognizable.[20]

---

[19] A suggestive study is contained in González Palencia, Angel, *Moros y cristianos en España medieval*, Madrid, 1945.

[20] *Aldeia* (village) may very probably derive from the Arabic *adday'at* and some of the most ordinary terms in everyday Portuguese are straight from the Arabic: *alface* (lettuce), *Alfaiate* (tailor), *Alfandega* (customs house). Oddly enough no verbs seemed to have been taken over, although certain current expressions such as the indefinite *fulano* (someone) and the interjection *oxalá* (Ar. 'in sa 'a l-lah)

What did the Arabs really leave as their heritage in the Iberian peninsula? A goodly amount of their blood, beyond reasonable doubt and certainly many of their practices and preferences: the inside patio; the heavy grilles on the windows of the house; and perhaps the traditional seclusion of women, are all Moslem in origin. One may speculate that the complicated social customs that up to very recently made it almost impossible for young men and women to meet may have been the offshoot of the Moslem practice of seclusion.

Individual characteristics of the Iberian peoples coincide in many cases with the Moslems: the keen sense of personal dignity, self-reliance, the fervent devotion to personal independence, the capacity for enduring pain and privation, and the zeal with which, on the basis of the most mediocre material resources, great historical enterprises have been carried forward to brilliant success. The Portuguese explorations and conquests can only be compared in their proportions and breath-taking dimensions with the spread of Islam across Africa to the outposts of Europe. This militancy, this sense of crusade and of national destiny, so inextricably bound up with each other, may conceivably flow in some small measure from the heritage of Islam. The softness and tender melancholy of the Portuguese may, too, derive from the sensibility which the Islamic conquerors developed to so remarkable a degree while in the peninsula.

At any rate, even though it may be impossible to fix, with the fine precision one would wish, the frontiers or delimitations of character to which each of the component ethnic elements in Iberia have contributed, there can be little doubt that the Moslem impact was fundamental and transcendental; that it revolutionized the thought and the spirit of the Spanish and the Portuguese; opened up to them a new world and by the same logic obstructed the classic one. It is no exaggeration to say that Portugal was thrust into this world of Africa and Asia in part, at least, by the presence of Islam, for five centuries, on her soil. The Moslem conquest was Asia's revenge on Europe after Rome; the Portuguese expansion beyond the seas was, in a very real sense, the retrieving by Europe

---

which may be translated broadly as "Would be to God" are in use. See Bourciez, Edouard, *Eléments de Linguistique romane*, Paris, 1956, 4 ed., pp. 421–422. Groult, Pierre, *La formation des langues romanes*, Tournai-Paris, 1947, p. 151.

of the challenge and the exerting once more of the initiative in a new Reconquest.

The Emergence of the Independent State

The founders of what we know as Portugal were not Portuguese at all but a Leonese monarch, a Burgundian prince, the Benedictine monks of Cluny, and the nobles, camp followers, and divers adventurers who found their way to this western corner of Iberia to engage in the wars of liberation against the infidel. They remained to enjoy the fief that was carved out for Henry of Burgundy and which bore the name of *Portucale.*

The eleventh century was one of the decisive, exciting, dramatic periods in the history of mankind when, by rare coincidence, a host of colorful personalities dominate the scene and great issues are debated and resolved. The magnificent Gregory VII was performing a yeoman task in asserting and securing the primacy of the seat of Peter; Henry of Germany had been laid low and had come groveling to Canossa; and it was the time when St. Robert of Champagne took himself off to Citeaux to live under the rule of strict observance of religion that became known as the Cistercian. It witnessed the plenitude of the Cluniac reform under the able abbots whose impulse meant so much in the spread of this beneficent influence, while in Spain it was an era dominated by the figure of Alfonso VI of Leon, a romantic, dashing, compassionate and impetuous monarch, whose deeds — and misdeeds — fill the latter part of the century and a portion of the succeeding. The king who styled himself emperor and laid claim to all parts of the Iberian peninsula was a disconcerting example of every medieval virtue and vice: bold and tender; pious and outrageous; chivalrous and conspiratorial — the vicissitudes of his reign account in very large measure for the birth of Portugal. He was a character straight out of a *chanson de geste* and it was the logic of fate that he should be called upon to deal with no less a figure than Ruy Díaz de Vivar, the Cid Campeador whose exploits are a high point in the constant struggle of Islam against Christianity in medieval Iberia.

Alfonso's own life was a maze of contradictions. In the *cantar de gesta* of the poets, he was celebrated as worthy of the greatest honors — in a category with Charlemagne. The *jongleurs* and *troubadours* sang of his struggle with the nobility and his passion for aiding the oppressed. He fled from imprisonment by his brother and fell into the hands of Almamum of Toledo, one of those Moorish heroes whose gentility and courtliness belie all description. He was the synthesis and epitome of that remarkable age when chivalrous friendship for the hated Moslem infidel went hand in hand with intrigue and treason. Shrouded as is the career of Alfonso VI in legend and poetical invention, it is clear that he was a fighter for the unity of Spain and for its Christian consolidation; that he understood perfectly the issues that had been joined in his time and was determined to see them through to a happy conclusion.

It would be hazardous, perhaps, to attribute to this brilliant and glowing century too much in the way of retrospect or read into its annals sentiments and emotions that belong to our own age. It was true, however, that Spain was in the throes of an inchoate, nebulous nationalism that was simply a primitive stage in the long struggle of the peninsula for the defense of its own particularism against European universalism.

The regions south of the Pyrenees have always lived both within Europe and outside it; torn in conscience as well as in spirit between belonging to the stream of continental culture or forming a current apart. In Alfonso's case, one senses dimly this inner conflict. To be sure it would not be proper to speak of a Leonese imperialism bent on molding the rest of Spain to the image and likeness of this particular pattern nor is it legitimate to assert that out of the clash of ideas and ideals around Alfonso and stimulated by his action, the shape of the Iberian peninsula emerged clearly in a way that was to endure for centuries. Alfonso called himself, in his more felicitous moments, "*Adefonsus imperator totius Hispaniae*" and, a little later, in a variant on the same theme, "*Constitutus imperator super omnes Hispaniae nationes.*"[21]

It is noteworthy that even at this stage reference was made to the "Hispanic nations" in the plural, implying that the peninsula was not one, but a sort of loose federation of several peoples and political entities. Whatever may have been the "nationalist" aspiration of Alfonso of Leon, the power and prestige of Gregory VII were sufficient to impose the kind of universality toward which the Papacy aspired.

[21] Menéndez Pidal, Ramón, *La España del Cid*, *op. cit.*, p. 161.

French influence penetrated Spain on a scale comparable to that which was to take place centuries later when the Bourbons mounted the throne. Only in the eleventh century it was Christian in character and was brought by the Cistercians and with them Bernard, a Frenchman, first Archbishop of Toledo. The king took, in a second marriage, Constance of Burgundy, and somewhat later his two daughters, one legitimate and the other a bastard, married Burgundians. The Latin rite of the Holy Mass was propagated and the Mozarabic gradually eliminated or curtailed.

This crisis of nationalism, if it may be called such, reached its culmination in the proclamation by the Holy See that Spain was a fief to the Papacy and the presence of an increasing number of monks of Cluny aided what might be called, in the broad sense, the process of denationalization.[22] The chain of Cluniac monasteries across the land assured the presence of a clergy loyal to the Supreme Pontiff and free from local entanglements so that the Spain that was being rapidly liberated from the Islamic yoke was vigorously and effectively reincorporated into the common Christian fold. The work of Gregory assured the rule of orthodoxy and offset that almost uncontrollable tendency in Hispanic affairs toward localism and anarchy.

In 1087, a new crusade was preached against the Moslem intruder and from France came a host of warriors and gentry to break lances on behalf of Christendom, among them the Duke of Burgundy, his brother Henry and cousin Raymond, with noblemen from Languedoc and Provence, Limousin, Poitou, and Normandy. Many of the Frenchmen displayed a considerable reluctance to press on to the rough frontier and undergo the hazards of border fighting, preferring to remain in the Ebro valley and near the frontier where there were few Moors. Raymond of Burgundy reached Leon, ostensibly to visit his aunt, Constance, wife of Alfonso VI, and it was here in the same year, 1087, that he was wed to a child of seven, Urraca, daughter of the Leonese king. Eight years later, Henry of Burgundy married the illegitimate daughter of Alfonso, Teresa, and it is that marriage that determined the emergence of Portugal as a state because *Portucale*, as the narrow territory north of the Mondego was called, was a part of the dowry of the princess.

---

[22] "The monks of Cluny were charged with disrupting Spanish nationalism," says Menéndez Pidal, *op. cit.*, p. 169.

There is no point in tracing in more than the broadest outline, the complicated history of this period, with its confused genealogy and welter of passions and ambitions, sometimes sordid and frequently heroic. Suffice it to note that with the death of Alfonso VI in 1109, the land that had gone to Teresa reverted to Urraca as the legitimate heiress. Henry of Burgundy was in no mind to give up what he and his wife had come to enjoy as theirs and his defiance of Leonese authority was the first faint expression of Portuguese national conscience. But it was not Henry who was to carry through the operation of severing *Portucale* permanently from the common Iberian trunk, but his widow and infant son, Afonso Henriques.

Portuguese historians have long been perplexed at the precise nature of this turbulent, shadowy period of their history when the nation itself was in a state of gestation. Did *Portucale* separate from Leon in a legal, normal procedure or did it come into being by revolution and an act of defiance? In other words, did the grant of territory to Henry constitute a purely personal arrangement that was conceived only as compensation for his aid during his own lifetime? Portuguese separatism would seem to have been a rebellion in which a keenly felt localism refused to come to terms with the still very strong Leonese imperialism.[23]

The Portuguese church was not alien to this process and it is curious to note that even at this stage there was resistance and opposition to the preponderance of Spain, an eloquent example of which is the effort of Portuguese Braga to assert its own primacy against Toledo. *Portucale*, as we may properly call this ill-defined little land, was showing that obdurate tenacity and will to survive which was to characterize it for the next eight hundred years. Rome was forced to come to terms with the remote warriors and bishops on the rim of the Atlantic and to accept, as a *fait accompli*, the separation from the common Iberian unity. The Church was basically concerned with the maintenance of unity of the Christian world against Islam, and internal upheavals, such as the Leonese-Portuguese, were not conducive to the effective pursuit of the

[23] "Portuguese separatism was, then, an illegal act, a long insurrection, we might say, an evolutionary insurrection, if the terms are compatible." Ramos, Manoel, "O condado Portucalense," in Peres, Damião, *Historia de Portugal*, *op. cit.*, Vol. I, p. 487.

reconquista. It was precisely because of this situation and the desire of the Holy See to mollify the bishops and leaders of Portugal that the latter managed to win its point and to become ecclesiastically, as well as politically, independent of Spanish domination.[24]

Portugal's definitive independence was the direct outcome of the struggle between two very energetic women who were half sisters: Teresa and Urraca. It is difficult, across the centuries of time and in view of the opaqueness that enshrouds this period, to visualize the life of these courts in the northwest corner of Spain. Urraca fought with the weapons of legitimacy and a sense of national unity; Teresa responded with the zeal of a widow who had no intention of seeing her son done out of his rights. Alfonso VII, of Leon, waged war against Teresa; laid siege to her castle at Guimarães and was probably a happy spectator of the struggle which broke out between Teresa and Afonso Henriques, her son — for there were many of the Portuguese who wanted no part of Teresa in view of her stormy love affair with the Leonese Count Fernando Peres.

The civil war that ensued divided mother and son, and it was around the young and attractive figure of Afonso Henriques that the Portuguese rallied. On June 24, 1128, on the field of São Mamede near Guimarães, Teresa and Peres were defeated in battle and expelled from *Portucale*. This engagement has been brilliantly depicted in one of the great patriotic canvases of the Portuguese painter, Acacio Lino, as "the first Portuguese afternoon." For the first time there was a Portuguese nation willing to take up arms to defend its territory against encroachment and aggression. São Mamede was decisive in that it placed the affairs of the little country definitely in the hands of its own leaders and created the conditions for the first national dynasty under a prince who was born and bred on Portuguese soil. The relation of vassal or liege to Leon was broken forever. It was not, however, until eleven years after that Afonso Henriques assumed the formal title of king: "*Alfonsus portucalensium rex*," which left no serious doubt that a nation had been born.[25]

Iberian unity was definitely broken and all pretense of a future

[24] Erdmann, Carl, *O papado e Portugal no primeiro século da história portuguesa*, Coimbra, 1935, pp. 7–13.

[25] Peres, Damião, *Como nasceu Portugal, op. cit.*, p. 86.

consolidated monarchy for the entire peninsula was cast aside. Portugal's outlook in the mid-twelfth century was not particularly brilliant. The Saracens were still in possession of a goodly portion of the territory to the south and, instead of an ally to the east and north, the Portuguese were now faced with a hostile and embittered Leon, all too eager to contribute in every possible way to the undoing of the work of Afonso Henriques. The Portuguese were squeezed into a tight little corner with no outlet but the sea — a dilemma which might be compared with that of Israel after 1948 in which the surrounding world was uniformly inimical to its very existence. That Portugal survived at all was a miracle of tenacity, persistence, and ingenuity as well as downright determination to preserve what had been achieved by force of arms.

The events of 1128–1139 did, nevertheless, lay down the pattern for Portuguese development for centuries to come, for once Leon and, with the Leonese, Spain itself was repudiated, Portugal was left to its own devices. For twelve years, Afonso Henriques waged almost constant war against Christians and infidels until the Peace of Zamora in which all semblance of allegiance to any Spanish sovereign was terminated. The Portuguese entered, as of that moment, on that long and singularly lonely road which they have trod down to the present; relatively uncomprehended by anyone else and unaided by those who share the same land mass with them. To the Leonese and by extension to the rest of Spain, Portugal, after 1128, was a center of insurrection and disloyalty and a source of danger to the Christian community as a whole in the struggle against the Moslems which culminated in the successful liberation of Lisbon in 1147. Even the sea which washed their coast was no protection for the Portuguese, since these waters were infested with pirates and corsairs, so that Afonso's range of action was, therefore, extraordinarily limited and it is not surprising that his whole reign should have been devoted to fighting.

Free momentarily through a truce from the danger of conflict with Leon, the founder turned his full attention to the Saracens and in the Battle of Ourique in 1139 inflicted on them a crushing defeat. It was during this engagement that the Crucified Christ appeared before his startled eyes and he heard words of encouragement from the Saviour.

The progress of the king-founder is like a map of Portugal

itself. Ourique was followed some years later by the siege of Santarem and the surrender of this fortress. Lisbon was the objective of the Christian forces, filled with enthusiasm by the repeated defeats of Islam and the promixity of the greatest of strong places in Moslem-held Portugal. The national frontiers were still ill defined and it was supremely necessary for the precariously held north of the country that Lisbon, and what lay beyond, be brought under Afonso's control as a counterpart to Leon and as a basis for operations in the event that Castilian and Leonese patience be exhausted. The conquest of Lisbon had long haunted the king and as early as 1140 he had probed its defenses and enlisted the aid of a certain number of crusaders from France, who had landed at Lisbon on their way to the East — ex *partibus Galliarum*, as the old chronicles have it.

It was after the collapse of Santarem that the siege of Lisbon could be seriously envisaged. When, in June, 1147, a flotilla of over two hundred sails entered the Douro estuary bringing hundreds of crusaders from every part of northern Europe: Germans, Flemings, English and Bretons, Aquitains and Lorrainers mixed joyously in this motley company which was happy to interrupt the long voyage to Palestine for the purpose of laying siege to the Saracen in one of his proudest cities.

This was not the first time, nor would it be the last, that Portuguese history has been determined by foreign aid nor would it be the last in which the integrity of the Portuguese nation was assured by close collaboration with the north. The preparations for the siege of Lisbon and the international bridges that composed the advancing armies, seemed like a forerunner to the English alliance two centuries later which gave Portugal what she so badly needed in the time of her birth — the steadying influence of a strong arm from abroad.

Lisbon fell after an interminable series of battles and attacks in which valor, stratagem, ingenuity, and ruse all played their part. With the loss of the city, a dozen secondary fortresses around it were delivered over to the Christians, including Sintra, Almada, and Palmela. Afonso Henriques, after the consolidation of these appreciable gains, pushed on southward over the Tagus; in 1159, Evora, then Beja, and the wave of conquest turned eastward toward peninsular Spain itself. Out of the remnants of the Arab kingdoms, the Portuguese took Cáceres, Trujillo, and innumerable other strongholds, thereby completing a process that not only assured Portugal of survival — which was vital — but of adequate territory for the essential mobility of its forces and people. Until the land south of the Mondego was cleared of the infidels, the Portuguese nation could exist only on sufferance of its more powerful neighbors. The prestige of Afonso Henriques increased by leaps and bounds and the Holy See, in gracious recognition of the fact that Portugal was now a reality, accepted the primacy of Braga with its suffragans, Coimbra, Viseu, and Lamego, thus assuring the spiritual and ecclesiastical independence of Portugal.

The work of Afonso was facilitated by the common Spanish practice of splitting up large kingdoms among the various heirs. This operation was performed by Alfonso VII, who left Leon to his son Fernando and Castile to his son Sancho. Spanish unity was broken at precisely the moment when Portugal was becoming a substantial reality, a factor of appreciable importance in assuring the survival of the latter. Afonso's attention was by no means limited to the south, for with equal zeal he undertook to place Galicia under his sovereignty. While engaged in these multiple and far-flung operations, Badajoz was in grave danger and Afonso hastened to its aid. Both Leonese and Moslems were particularly sensitive to Badajoz and its capture by the Portuguese had been a source of lively distress. It was Fernando II of Leon, Afonso Henriques' son-in-law, who sought to restore it to his own sovereignty. The Portuguese king and a band of his followers, in order to avoid capture, managed to break through an opening in the city walls and, in so doing, the monarch suffered a broken leg from one of the iron bolts. The unconscious ruler was made prisoner and taken before his son-in-law, who released him on condition that he abandon all of Galicia that the Portuguese had occupied. From that moment on, the king's decline was rapid and with him the fortunes of the country he had carved out by the sword. Weak and exhausted, he could offer but feeble resistance to the Moors who poured back into the lands south of the Tagus. Pope Alexander III, in the Bull *Manifestis probatus*, in 1179, recognized Afonso Henriques as king of Portugal and a forerunner of that long line which was to perform such valiant services for Christ and his Church.

The rule of Afonso Henriques was one of the longest in history, especially in medieval history where longevity among monarchs was not the rule; for fifty-seven years he guided the destinies of a country that was scarcely conscious of its own personality and left it substantially, as far as its political frontiers are concerned, as it is today. After 1185 there can be no doubt that Portugal was on the European political scene; perhaps in many ways the oldest of all united countries on the continent, for none preceded it in the achievement of an integrated, coherent, and fully conscious national life.

The warrior-king had had scant time for anything but the eternal passages at arms in which he had indulged for two generations. Portugal was a poor and exhausted land, whose peasantry eked out a sordid existence in constant fear of the destruction and death that the shifting fortunes of war might bring. The Moslems came and went like the waves of the sea and there was no indication that the time had come when their return would not have to be feared. In the shadow of a few castles and under the protection of the Cistercians whose great monasteries were encouraged, a more sober and productive life began to evolve. There was ever an overshadowing uncertainty about the future during these early years when the first chieftains of the nation were carving out its territory and seeking by diplomatic means to assure its continuity.

Even at this early stage it was evident that a prefiguration of Portugal throughout its history was taking place, revealing one of the primary characteristics of the nation and peoples as a group — the capacity to achieve very great things on the basis of a most modest economic organization.

Many of the crusaders who had engaged in the liberation of territory coveted by the Portuguese remained to settle down on lands placed at their disposal by the monarchs and, not infrequently, whole communities such as those of Vila Verde dos Francos, Azambuja, Lourinha, and Sezimbra were colonized by foreigners from the north of Europe who merged, within a few generations, with the Portuguese mass.

When the nation was created, the way of life was unencumbered and simple. During the great era of exploration and expansion beyond the seas, the manner of living in the homeland did not change substantially for the mass of the population, and today, under the austere guidance of Dr. Antonio Salazar, the Portuguese people have never achieved wealth or affluence nor, indeed, have they ever aspired to it. Their preoccupation has always been, from the eleventh to the twentieth century, to attain a modest place in the community of peoples consonant with the limited resources of their land.

Afonso's son, Sancho, undertook to repair the damage the land had suffered from the depredations and destruction of these years. It is said he envisaged the possibility of engaging in the Third Crusade but was restrained by the fear that departure from Portugal, at so precarious a moment in its history, would leave the territory wide open to invasion by the Saracens on the south and the Leonese on the north. Portugal was still in a state of convalescence. It was during his reign that the royal title was broadened to include Portugal and the Algarve, the southernmost province of the country, destined to play so decisive a role in the later work of expansion beyond the seas.

It would be a dreary task to outline, even briefly, the constant ebb and flow, the oscillation of rising Portuguese-Christian fortunes and the periodical restoration of Islamic rule over parts of the country. Large areas became a sort of permanent battlefield in which the victor was never installed for more than a short period of time, to be ousted once more by the perennial enemy.

The eclipse of the sun in 1199 unnerved people everywhere and foreboded the calamities which descended on the land during the early thirteenth century for floods and earthquakes, famine and diseases stalked Portugal to a degree unheard of before. There was the very real danger under Sancho and Afonso II that the necessity of defense which had led to the granting of numerous concessions to clergy and nobility would so weaken the incipient monarchical institution as to produce a chaotic and anarchical feudalism which in the end would make the survival of Portugal quite impossible. The early monarchs were devoted fundamentally to the task of creating and defending, with scant time or energy for the task of endowing the nation with a suitable political and social structure. Portugal was fortunate in its early monarchs in that each responded to the particular challenge of his time. With the first Afonso, it was the extension, militarily and diplomatically, of the national territory; under Sancho it was a continuation of the march southward plus the assurance that Portugal would not succumb to the pressures from without and, under Afonso II, it was a concerted effort to construct the administrative and political underpinning without which the Portuguese state could not function organically.

Portugal experienced the throes of growing pains in the form of internecine wars, *coups d'état,* and, more than once, open conflict with the Holy See. Even in this early period, the Portuguese state revealed an uncommonly modern attitude in undertaking to seize Church properties when the national treasury was at a particularly low ebb. This medieval prefiguration of anticlericalism, which reached its plenitude in the nineteenth century, was the cause of an interdiction on the entire land with the most grievous results for the community. By 1263 the province of Algarve became definitely Portuguese and Lisbon the capital of the united kingdom, whose territories from this date remain permanently fixed.

The prince who became king in 1279, Dom Diniz, as he is known in the annals of Portugal, was, by every light, a most remarkable personality. Here was no improvised sovereign who, sword in hand, had hacked his way to fame and fortune; no *parvenu* to the scepter with no knowledge of the affairs of state save the use of force. Dom Diniz had been most carefully educated in the delicate art of reigning. From France, the distinguished priest, Aymeric d'Ebrard, later Bishop of Coimbra, had come to take charge of the instruction of the heir to the throne. From across the frontier in Castile, Dom Diniz was subject to the influence of that extraordinary figure, Alfonso the Wise. The education of the prince was not limited to the legal and ecclesiastical sciences of the day but embraced as well the natural sciences, philosophy, and letters. Dom Diniz is still recognized as one of Portugal's great kings and had he never reigned he would remain secure in the niche he occupies in the history of Portuguese letters.

Dom Diniz was one of those complex personalities that appear from time to time in the life of a nation, endowed with an abundance of energy, a driving will, and a keen sense of the varied necessities of the state. He encouraged the expansion of agriculture, put into effect a policy designed to distribute lands more equitably and thus develop a class of small property owners. He was responsible for the draining of swamps, the opening of new mines, and the expansion of the Portuguese fleet. Near the city of Leiria may still be seen the remnants of the pine forest which King Diniz had planted as part of a general reforestation project. His whole reign reads like that of a very modern and up-to-date, socially minded ruler, intent on pulling his nation up to a standard compatible with social justice.

It was Dom Diniz of whom the historian Ruy de Pina said that "never did he lie nor break his word." Here was the almost conventional portrait of the enlightened, medieval monarch. He depended a great deal on the Order of Templars whose power in Portugal was very great. He founded a university at Lisbon, later transferred to Coimbra, which in time was to become one of the greatest medieval centers of learning. The queen, St. Elizabeth, still revered by the Portuguese people for her Christian virtues, was canonized in 1625 and has been accorded a lively devotion in the country even down to the present time.

Diniz had fought a civil war with his father and, on his own accession, engaged in a vigorous struggle with his brother before his own legitimate claim was firmly established. This pattern of family warfare was quite common to medieval Portugal and was generally complicated by the dubious relations with Castile and Leon. The war against Sancho IV and Ferdinand IV of Castile and Leon ended in 1297 with an alliance under the terms of which Ferdinand married Constance, daughter of Diniz, while Afonso, the heir to the Portuguese throne, took to wife Beatrice, Ferdinand's sister.

It was during the days of King Diniz that Portugal's relations with England began to take on the shape and form that was to become the most enduring association in European history and which today still plays a significant role in international affairs. Both Porto and Lisbon were well on the way to attaining the commercial prestige they have enjoyed for centuries and trade was becoming increasingly active with the north of Europe: France, Flanders, and England. It is a curious fact of Portuguese history that propinquity to Castile has never contributed to commercial or cultural contacts in any real sense. At every stage in its development, Portugal has looked out across the sea, first to central and northern Europe and, later, to America, Africa, and the Far East. A decree dating from December 26, 1253, mentions the expanding trade of the Portuguese cities with Rouen, Arras, Lille, Bruges, and Ypres.

Portuguese merchants were organized, as is attested by a document, from the reign of Diniz, and from the fourteenth century on there existed in Porto an exchange which concerned itself with such matters as maritime insurance, indemnity, mutual aid, and assistance to shipwrecked seamen. Portugal was rapidly ceasing to be a purely agricultural nation in which barter was the basis of the economy. Diniz undertook to encourage fairs and commercial expositions and to channel the energies of his people toward these extremely lucrative occupations. At the end of the thirteenth century, the country was still most backward. Internal communication was bad and a network of domestic customs houses made Portugal literally a checkerboard in which every obstruction was present to hamper the free flow of trade. The national population was small, probably between 500,000 and 1,000,000, after the expulsion of the Moslems or their retreat into Africa and the constant bloodletting that had been the lot of the country since its inception under Prince Henry.

There is a tradition that Afonso Henriques was the founder of the Portuguese navy, and the name of his commander, Fuas Roupinho, has come down to us. It is probable that something in the way of a primitive fleet existed very early to combat the Berber pirates and assure some degree of safety along the coasts. Under the monarchs who succeeded the founder, Portuguese men-of-war very certainly plied the immediate territorial waters to collaborate in the work of the reconquest. Under Afonso II, Portuguese vessels engaged in the siege of Alcacer; under Sancho II, a large fleet was equipped to carry on the war in the Algarve; and, under Afonso III, a still larger naval unit was placed at the service of Alfonso X of Castile. A Genoese, Manuel Pesagno, was hired as admiral of the Portuguese fleet, and some twenty seamen out of Genoa entered the service of the king of Portugal — a curious forerunner of a later Genoese whose exploits were to be considerably more significant for both Portugal and the rest of Europe. One of the main purposes of King Diniz in encouraging reforestation was to provide wood for shipbuilding, not only for war purposes but for commerce and for protection against the almost uninterrupted incursions of the corsairs.

Piracy was so lively that Edward I of England complained in a letter to Diniz, dated June 15, 1293, that Portuguese corsairs had held up and looted ships carrying merchandise from Bayonne to England. This was the beginning of a correspondence that was to have the most fateful consequences for both nations. A number of commercial treaties were signed which provided for facilities and freedom of commerce between Britain and Portugal and a tribunal for the settlement of such grievances or disputes as might arise. These documents expressly excluded the Spanish, and it was stated specifically that should Portuguese goods be shipped in Castilian bottoms, the privileges provided for in the treaties would be annulled.[26]

Edward II expressed his gratitude to the Portuguese monarch for his expressions of esteem and affection for his late father, Edward I, and continued the guarantee of privileges that had been initiated by his predecessor. A further treaty was signed in 1308 and, as of 1325, it is clear that the sovereigns were giving serious thought to uniting their families by marriage.

In 1344 Edward III sent two ambassadors to conclude a treaty of alliance with Afonso IV, and a later mission was dispatched to Lisbon to ask for the hand of Leonora, the king's youngest daughter, on behalf of Edward, Prince of Wales, known in history as the Black Prince. Although the proposed union did not come to pass at the time owing to complications elsewhere, the friendship of Portugal and Britain continued; and Portuguese wine flowed freely in England while English cloth covered many a Portuguese back.

The name of Afonso IV has gone down in history on two counts: first, for his courage at the battle of Salado against the Moslems; and, second, for his participation in the murder of Inez de Castro, the mistress of his son and heir, Dom Pedro. Murder in the Middle Ages was not particularly rare and diplomatic or official murder even less so. In the ordinary course of things, the liaison of Dom Pedro with the beautiful Castilian, Inez, would have constituted simply another amorous episode in the innumerable accounts that clutter up the annals of royal families and dynasties. But the case of Pedro and Inez is different from the normal run of these sordid extracurricular affairs and has long since become one of the most formidable and popular legends in Portuguese history. It happened in the following way:

[26] Marques Guedes, Armando, A *Aliança inglesa* (*notas de história diplomática, 1383–1943*), Lisbon, 1943, pp. 64–65.

Afonso IV had married his son Pedro to Constancia of Castile in the hope of cementing relations between Portugal and the Spanish kingdom. In the suite of Doña Constancia came one Inez de Castro, illegitimate daughter of the powerful nobleman, Pedro Fernandez de Castro, grandson of the Castilian king, Sancho IV. So beautiful and distinguished was Lady Inez that the contemporary chroniclers have spoken of her as "The Swan Neck."[27] Although Pedro was closely related to Inez through the fact that her father was his cousin, this did not detract from the fact that a violent passion was engendered once they met. Constancia, hopeful of putting a stop to what looked like a developing scandal, made Inez the godmother of her first child by Pedro, in the hope that the bond of spiritual kinship thus established would be an obstacle to the illicit relations of the two. Discretion was tossed aside and the whole court became aware of the situation.[28] Inez was exiled from the court, taking up temporary residence near the Spanish frontier from which vantage point she carried on an assiduous correspondence with Dom Pedro.

In 1345, the death of Constancia during childbirth left Pedro free to follow his whims and one of his first acts was to have Inez brought back to the court. Pedro had long been alienated from his father and he devoted himself exclusively to the interests of his mistress, her brothers, and his illegitimate offspring. The aged monarch was fearful that, since the circle was made up entirely of Castilians, the result would be a serious danger to the independence and integrity of Portugal. Needless to say, the courtesans and nobles of the Portuguese court were not amused at the increasing influence exerted over the future king by his Spanish mistress. When the king urged a second marriage upon his son and heir to assure the stability of the throne, Dom Pedro announced that the depth of his feeling for his late wife, Constancia, made any second marriage impossible. The king had been particularly affected by the prodigality with which Pedro and Inez were producing bastard offspring, whose claims and counterclaims would certainly form a source of

[27] The story of Pedro and Inez de Castro is contained in every manual of Portuguese history. I have used a splendid study of the history and the legend by Vasconcelos, António, *Inêz de Castro*, Porto, 1928. This highly illustrated volume examines every phase of the incident and the places and associations, both with the love affair and the murder.

[28] Lopes, Fernão, *Crónica de D. João I.*

great insecurity for the Portuguese crown. Inez' brothers awakened in the prince the most extraordinary ambitions, in the hope that in rebellion against his father he might ultimately come to rule over a combined Spain and Portugal. Afonso IV was equally convinced that the brothers of Inez would not hesitate to murder the legitimate son of Pedro, Dom Fernando, in order to remove the last obstacle to their plan for their sister's lover.

Dom Pedro set Inez up at Coimbra, in a residence that had been built by his grandmother, St. Elizabeth, not far from the convent of Santa Clara. The saintly queen had laid down as a rule that the residence was to be occupied by no one but the king and princes of the royal family and their legitimate wives. Within a few yards of the spot where St. Elizabeth had been laid to rest, Pedro settled Inez and their children in open defiance of the conventions and in cynical mockery, as it seemed to the court and to his father, of the memory and precise instructions of his grandmother. It was but a step, in the minds of those who surrounded Afonso, to urge that the welfare of the state demanded the elimination of Dona Inez, the obstacle that stood definitely in the way of the future of the reigning house and the stability of the nation: *Morra ela e viva Portugal.*[29] The sentence was carried out on January 7, 1355, when Inez was murdered in the palace at Coimbra.

Dom Pedro reacted violently; he sought to overturn his father by rebellion, failed, and then bided his time until the death of the monarch. Legend insists that one of his earliest acts was to vindicate the name of his murdered mistress by proclaiming his secret marriage to her and later in disinterring her body, clothing it in the garments of royalty, and having the crown placed on the head of the corpse, after which, in April, 1361, she was supposed to have been transported to Alcobaça and reburied with all solemnity.[30]

---

[29] "Let her die and let Portugal live."

[30] There is no basis in fact for this popular version which has been accepted almost universally. The older historian of Portugal, H. Morse Stephens, *Portugal* (London, 1891, p. 98), recounts how the "body was conveyed to the Convent of Alcobaça, where it was solemnly crowned and then buried." Virginia de Castro e Almeida in *Itinéraire historique du Portugal* (Lisbon, 1940, pp. 30–31) describes in considerable detail how the body of the late Inez was dressed, covered with jewels and seated next to the king, to receive the crown. Antonio de Vasconcelos (*op. cit.*, p. 175 *seq.*) dismisses the whole thing as an invention of the sixteenth century and after and as formed, most probably, not in

Pedro, as king, made a great reputation for himself as a dispenser of justice. His severity became proverbial and since the objects of his rigors were the nobles and persons of high rank, his actions were rarely displeasing to the common people. He traveled about the kingdom to mete out justice, personally and directly, in a sort of Haroun-al-Rashid tradition. This passion for justice, which could be compared only with the excesses of concupiscence of which he had been guilty before, became literally an obsession. He displayed this fierce spirit in the severity of the judgment against the assassins of Inez, whose tortured bodies were subjected to every inhumanity in the presence of the king himself. Today the tombs of Dom Pedro and Dona Inez are to be seen at Alcobaça, facing each other with the reclining statues foot to foot so that at the Resurrection, says tradition, on rising they may gaze on each other before seeing anything else.

Six centuries have so altered the story of Inez and Pedro that it is all but impossible today to disentangle fact from legend. Every great Portuguese poet who has treated the subject, and most of them have, from Garcia de Resende and Camões on down to the modern, have seen in the murder of Inez an act of vengeance; a monstrous crime in which Afonso IV personally was very probably the executor. History is sometimes more prosaic than this. Her death was the result of a formal sentence which, in the light of Portuguese law at the time, was perfectly valid and the execution, if we are to judge by the engravings that appear on the tomb at Alcobaça, was carried out by the proper functionaries charged with that grim task. The public, however, has embroidered the story down through the ages to relate that the innocent Inez was cruelly murdered by a hateful and vengeance-bent king. Camões has celebrated the event in one of the best known lines in the Lusiads and in the Quinta das Lágrimas in Coimbra the visitor is regaled with the version of how, in this delightful and bucolic spot, Inez was wont to meet with Pedro for long and tender passages at love.

Portugal, by this time, had reached a turning point in its history.

Portugal but in Spain. The comment of this noted historian is worth transcribing since it emphasizes the difference in mentality between the two Iberian peoples: "The Spanish imagination appreciates, far better than the Portuguese, these gruesome, terrible scenes, full of majestic and grandiose tragedy. The Castilian spirit is fundamentally epic, the Portuguese lyrical. It was in Spain that this strikingly original epilogue to the story of Inez had its origin."

The period of gestation had long passed and with the development of commerce and peaceful pursuits the nation settled down to a relatively placid and conventional existence. The nobility became less warlike and more indolent; the clergy and bishops were very far indeed from the stern moralists who had thundered their imprecations in the early days. A softness had crept into Portuguese life and even the Cortes or parliament, which had represented a popular voice in the management of public affairs, was silenced. The court, above all, was growing in dissoluteness and laxity. Under Ferdinand, Pedro's successor and the last of the Burgundian line, the general level of court morality remained about the same, for the new king displayed precisely the same tendencies which had brought so much tragedy to his father.

Once again, as before in the history of Portugal, high matters of state were decided in the boudoir rather than elsewhere. Ferdinand was particularly notable for entering upon liaisons that were even more complex than those of his predecessors, and this, it may be said in passing, was far from easy to achieve.

In 1369, Ferdinand had set forth claims to the throne of Castile and Leon on the death of Pedro the Cruel, but was forced to give up these pretensions under pressure from the nobility of Spain and the Pope, who was far from eager to have the Portuguese king occupy both thrones. Ferdinand agreed, among other things, to marry Leonor, daughter of Henry II, who had taken the throne of Leon in his stead.

Like Pedro before him, Ferdinand had a roving eye and during the ceromonies of the marriage of his half sister, Beatrice, the monarch saw and fell instantly in love with one Leonor Trelles de Menezes. The fact that the lady was already married was no insuperable obstacle to the realization of the royal hopes. The king repudiated his promise to marry the Castilian princess and thereby provoked the violent reaction of the Spanish, who were not accustomed to taking lightly this sort of affront. At the same time, he won the enmity of his own people who saw in his fickleness a sign of political danger for the nation. An obscure tailor headed a riot that came very close to liquidating the king once and for all, and which forced him to promise to fulfill his word and take the Spanish princess to wife. Ferdinand ordered the ringleaders beheaded, fled to Porto, and there entered into a bigamous marriage with Leonor, a sign of the low level to which affairs had fallen. In retaliation for the indignities that had been heaped on the head of the Infanta, Henry II invaded Portugal, laid siege to Lisbon, and lifted it only at the behest of the papal legate.

Ferdinand spent his life breaking treaties and oscillating between war and peace with his Castilian neighbors. Leonor, who had many of the less lovely traits of the Borgias, became the dominating influence in Portuguese life — a scheming, odious tyrant who attempted to poison her first husband and wreaked the most hideous vengeance on her sister who had opposed her marriage to Ferdinand. Adultery, forgery, murder, and treason were monotonously repeated as this tyranny reached heights which surpassed even the most brutalized and degraded reigns. The Portuguese people did not rebel, as might reasonably have been expected, which demonstrated the degree to which they were attached to the monarchical principle and how thoroughly the dynasty as founded by the first kings had become a deep-rooted national institution.

Leonor was a Lady Macbeth on the grand scale, for not only did she terrorize and subjugate her own people and court but dabbled in international politics and never quite gave up the idea of the dynastic union of Portugal and Castile. One of her lovers was dispatched as ambassador to Britain to secure aid against the Castilians and when English soldiers were sent, they found that, as usual, Ferdinand had betrayed them as well as his own countrymen to the Spanish.

In 1383, with the death of Ferdinand, Leonor became regent. The hatred that the queen's imperious and arbitrary conduct had aroused boiled up in collective indignation. Under the leadership of John, Master of the Order of Aviz, vengeance was taken on the queen's lover, the Count of Ourem, who was murdered in her presence. Leonor appealed to her son-in-law, John of Castile, to invade Portugal and save the throne. While the Portuguese had been willing, in the name of the monarchical principle, to tolerate this vicious woman for years and put up with the most unseemly affronts as long as she represented the dynasty, they were quite unwilling to accept subservience to a woman, legitimate or a usurper, who appealed to foreign aid to maintain her power and who was patently willing to deliver Portugal over to the Castilians. Immorality, cruelty, criminality even, might be borne until such a time as the queen should pass from the scene, but treason and the destruction of the nation was another thing entirely. At this time, as so frequently in the long and stormy history of Portugal, the keen and unflagging sense of nationalism was the mainstay of survival.

Portugal has been favored, at critical moments in its history when the outlook was grim and the chance of collapse imminent, with heroic personalities who have rescued her from calamity. In the fourteenth century, when there seemed that nothing could stop absorption by Castile, it was Nun' Álvares Pereira, a prototype of a medieval knight straight from the Round Table, who saw the salvation of the nation only in the overthrow of the queen and the placing on the throne of the bastard John, Master of Aviz, son of Pedro I and Teresa Lourenço.

Most of the nobility supported the queen, and preparations had gone so far forward in Toledo that the Castilian king had paraded his armed forces with standards bearing the coat of arms of Portugal, as though the Lusitanian kingdom were already a part of the greater Spain of which he dreamed. In an age when signs and portents were wondrous and full of meaning, it is recounted how, at the moment when the banner bearing the seal of the two countries combined passed by, the horseman fell and in the accident the pennant was ripped in two, separating the Castilian seal from that of Portugal.

Medieval history in Portugal as elsewhere is filled with incidents in which the popular will expresses itself clearly, eloquently, and invincibly. The notion that this was an age when kings and nobles played fast and loose with popular sentiment and that public opinion had no place in the affairs of state was never demonstrated to be more false than in the arrangements of John of Aviz to defend the national sovereignty against the threat of invasion and the intrigues of Leonor Trelles. If Nun' Álvares was the military leader of the cause headed by John of Aviz, João das Regras was its constitutionalist; for it was he, a deeply learned man and particularly competent in matters of jurisprudence, who advanced the arguments to justify the innovation of a new dynasty. The Cortes had to be convinced and, as in a modern parliament it was the eloquence, erudition, and forensic qualities of João das Regras that carried the day. John of Aviz was proclaimed monarch, to usher in an entirely new era in Portuguese affairs. But, like a much later France which debated matters of institutional reform when the enemy was smashing across the frontier, the Portugal of this time was faced with the infinitely difficult task of meeting the challenge from Spain.

The Battle of Aljubarrota must go down in history as one of the decisive actions of all time. The stage was relatively small, but the consequences were far reaching on the fortunes of the Iberian people involved. Nun' Álvares was a sort of medieval Portuguese counterpart of Joffre or Foch. Once the legal question of the succession had been settled by the proper procedure, the military took over. From the far north of Portugal to the south, Nun' Álvares labored with remarkable zeal and untiring energy to build up the defenses before the Castilian could attack. One of the gravest of obstacles was the reluctance of many of the Portuguese nobility to support John of Aviz, fearful as they were that if the fortunes of war favored the Spanish they would be irretrievably lost. The nationalistic fervor that swept the country was the sentiment of the masses — of the common people, far more than of the upper classes or the gentry.

On a blazingly hot day in mid-August of 1385, Nun' Álvares, now constable of Portugal, deployed his forces on the field of Aljubarrota not far from Leiria. The Castilians were superior in number with much of their strength depending on their mounted armor. The Portuguese were on foot, with a goodly number of crossbowmen and a small number of English archers. The Archbishop of Braga, bearing a standard with the image of the Virgin, rode among the ranks inciting the Portuguese to a maximum of effort. The Portuguese waited the onslaught on a hillock and so vast was the Castilian army which approached that the chronicler Fernão Lopes writes that "the Portuguese seemed like the tiny light of a mediocre star against the brilliant illumination of the moon." By nightfall the field had been cleared; the Castilian king was in flight to Santarem and John of Aviz and Nun' Álvares could relax in the warmth and glow of total victory. For the first time that day, the leaders and men of the Portuguese forces broke their fast for it was the day before the Assumption of the Blessed Virgin Mary and they had not as yet eaten.

Aljubarrota saved Portugal from extinction and at the same time infused new vitality into its institutions that had suffered so grievously from the decadence and incompetence of its last monarchs. Victory brought new hope and a fierce pride in the destinies of this little peninsular people whose salvation and mission seemed predestined by this obvious favor from God. Nationalism could scarcely be considered a characteristic of the fourteenth century (certainly not nationalism in the contemporary sense of the term), yet the sentiment that had turned to the Aviz branch of the royal family and had accepted the national arguments of João das Regras signalized a state of mind and an attitude that was far ahead of the times. Portugal may be called, without exaggeration, the first European state in which the popular sense of nationality, as against social or religious community, existed.

Nun' Álvares followed up the triumph at Aljubarrota with the invasion of Castile, where the remnants of the Spanish army had fled, and was wounded in one of the major engagements at a moment when Portuguese courage flagged. His presence was sorely missed until he was found alone, in a solitary cavern close by, in prayer, the holy relics that had been seized from John of Castile around his neck and the vow on his lips that if victory was Portugal's on this day he would erect a mighty temple to the Blessed Virgin in Lisbon.

John of Gaunt, Duke of Lancaster, had aided the Portuguese at Aljubarrota and it was now his purpose to follow up this victory by effectively exploiting the new alliance. Son-in-law of Pedro the Cruel, former king of Castile, the Englishman was not without hopes himself of securing the Spanish crown, and in this venture Portuguese assistance would be a most precious aid. On May 9, 1386, the Portuguese representatives and Richard II signed a treaty of alliance at Windsor. This document, which was sealed in Britain and ratified at the royal palace in Coimbra in August of that year, promised perpetual co-operation between the two peoples as is attested by the first article: "For the peace and well-being of the royal family and the vassals of the two kingdoms . . . friendship, and perpetual confederation is promised between the two states and each shall provide aid for the other if it is in danger of extinction."[31]

The Anglo-Portuguese alliance has been no dead letter, for it remains the oldest arrangement between states of this nature in existence today in spite of several lapses. Its validity as well as

[31] Marques Guedes, *Aliança inglesa*, *op. cit.*, p. 89.

its vitality was amply demonstrated during the twentieth century when Portugal joined Britain in World War I and made concessions in the Azores in World War II which were of fundamental importance to the success of British arms. An intriguing aspect of this treaty obligation arises in the present controversy between Portugal and India over the Portuguese province in India, commonly known as Goa. To what degree Portugal is justified in considering the defense of the integrity of Goa, Damão, and Diu as a part of the maintenance of its own national integrity is a moot point, with the interesting speculation of what Britain's precise obligations might be in the event of conflict.

In 1387 John of Aviz married Philippa, daughter of that Duke of Lancaster who had landed previously in La Coruna, preparatory to the invasion of Spain to lay claim to the crown. Although the expedition was a failure, in spite of the Anglo-Portuguese collaboration, the marriage was by no means lacking in consequence. It linked England and Portugal dynastically and opened up a very long period of time during which Englishmen found their way to Portugal in increasing numbers, and English interests became more and more vital to the economic and social welfare of that country.

With the vexing question of national independence settled and John firm on the throne, the Portuguese court opened one of the most promising periods in the nation's history — the prelude to the Golden Age which is to come, in all its splendor, in the fifteenth century.

John's task was fundamentally one of house cleaning, that is, a complete renovation of internal life, beginning with the somewhat discredited nobility and ending with his own household. It was true that the first dynasty, in spite of its inglorious and even ignominious end, had rendered signal services to Portugal. From Afonso I to Afonso II (1128–1267), the kingdom had been carved out of the peninsula in the midst of the constant struggle against the Saracens and their pressure; from 1267 to Aljubarrota, the second century of independent Portugal witnessed considerable progress in various spheres: in the political field by the encouragement of the *conselhos*, or local councils to be represented in the Cortes; in the development of letters and culture under Diniz; the administration of justice under Pedro; and the expansion of agriculture under Diniz and Ferdinand.

If, aside from the securing of independence, there was any lesson connected with Aljubarrota, it was that the Portuguese people had no longer any political mission in the Iberian peninsula itself outside the narrow confines of their own territory. The barrier that had existed, psychologically and linguistically, between Portugal and Spain was sealed off, so to speak, in a tangible and permanent fashion, and from 1385 onward the latent energies and restless temper of the Portuguese could be diverted in only two directions: westward toward the Atlantic and southward toward Africa. Aljubarrota made the Portuguese supremely conscious of their own identity as a people and of the precious heritage of a collective personality whose expansion from their cramped European quarters could only be realized toward the ocean and overseas.

The social revolution effected in the country under the House of Aviz began with the nobility, since a very large proportion of the privileged class had deserted during the recent hostilities to take the side of Leonor Trelles. This class was now replaced by those who had fought with John of Aviz, the "new generation" to which the historian Fernão Lopes refers as coming into prominence with this new era. Since the change of dynasty had been based both in military considerations and on law, it is not strange that, with the new dispensation, jurists should occupy a very special place in the hierarchy of things. *Legistas,* as they are styled in Portuguese, rose to distinction as the architects and defenders of the new order. They were responsible for the intellectual as well as legal basis of the system and contributed powerfully toward creating the new centralized monarchy which was rapidly emerging in the land. For two hundred years, Portugal had been ruled by the sword and was, in a literal sense, in a permanent state of siege and war psychosis. After Aljubarrota, as though an immense cloud had been suddenly lifted, the nation found itself free of the traditional tensions and liberated from the anxiety of conquest or reconquest that had haunted the preceding generations. In this new atmosphere, soldiers were less needed than administrators to provide the state with a solid constitutional structure.

If clergy and nobility — the new nobility, of course — were the source of fundamental support to the regime, it is impossible to overlook the role of the people in this renovated society. Medieval practice, and this is as true in Portugal as elsewhere, was very far from the "undemocratic" conception that it is taken to be today. Popular intervention in political matters was not only taken for granted but positively encouraged and considered as indispensable for the proper operation of a well-organized state. John of Aviz extended the privileges of the people through various channels that already existed to assure the expression of opinion.[32] One finds at this time an institutional life that bears a striking resemblance in certain of its details to the corporate state that Dr. Salazar has inspired in the twentieth century in which the "professional corporations" are the agency or vehicles for participation in national affairs. The corporations of *mesteres*, or craftsmen, had flourished before John's time and had supported enthusiastically the cause of Aviz. The organization of *gremios*, or guilds, existed in all the Portuguese cities and had long since assumed responsibility for the technical excellence of the product of the various crafts and as the exponent of the needs and interests of the craftsmen themselves. Each community had what was known as the *Casa dos Vinte e Quatro* (House of Twenty-Four), which represented twelve of the craft guilds, each with two representatives in this kind of municipal council which, in turn, spoke in the name of the entire body of workers who were thus represented. In Portugal, as in Spain, political genius in the Middle Ages, as well as in the modern period, manifested itself in local organization and especially in a highly developed form of popular representation at the municipal level. The absence frequently of a tendency toward the creation of national institutions for popular expression have often blinded observers to the fact that, through the craft organizations, guilds, and municipal councils of one variety or another, a very effective freedom of expression and influence existed.

The court of King John and Queen Philippa contrasted mightily with the crime, intrigue, and general dissoluteness of their predecessors. The English queen was austere, homely, and quite unconcerned about matters of high politics. The calm and well-balanced direction given by the royal household affected every phase of the national life, and it was refreshing to the Portuguese of the late fourteenth century to find their monarch once more a man of learned and refined tastes. According to the testimony of

[32] Prestage, Edgar, *The Royal Power and the Cortes in Portugal*, London, 1927, p. 2.

his son Dom Duarte, "my most excellent and virtuous father, the King, wrote a Book of Hours of the Blessed Virgin, a commentary on the Psalms and a treatise on riding and hunting."[33] Many of these texts have been lost and it is probable that the monarch, in the same way as Alfonso X of Castile, worked in collaboration with the learned men of his court to produce these writings and treatises. "There was never," says the historian of Portuguese literature, Alvaro Julio da Costa Pimpão, "a generation in Portuguese history, that occupied so high an ethical place in thought and culture, as that which grew up during the alliance of John and Philippa of Lancaster."[34]

The Renaissance was brought to Portugal by the Aviz dynasty. But before the Italian influence became strong and Portuguese men of letters more cosmopolitan, the events of the end of the fourteenth and commencement of the fifteenth centuries had given the country a pronounced taste for history and it is not particularly strange that this form of intellectual production should have overshadowed all else. Lyric poetry and history have always been Portugal's peculiar forte and with the attainment of national independence on a firm basis and the expulsion of the Moslems centuries before the Spanish managed to do it, the Portuguese were naturally led to take singular pleasure in the chronicles and annals of these stirring events. The full flowering of this spirit of historical recopilation and commentary belongs to the fifteenth century and is ushered in by the most famous of early Portuguese historians, Fernão Lopes.

The union of John and Philippa was fruitful in talented and brilliant sons. Dom Duarte, the eldest and heir to the throne, was of a chivalrous and literary bent and the author of a remarkable piece of writing called the *Leal Conselheiro*, which reveals the most extraordinary psychological penetration and understanding imaginable, especially when one takes into account the time and the circumstances of its composition. Sentiments, emotions, and states of mind are analyzed with an understanding that would do credit to a psychoanalyst. One of the intriguing and curious parts of the book is the attention devoted to that peculiarly Portuguese attitude known as *saudade:* the sweet melancholy that pervades the national

---

[33] Quoted in Mendes dos Remedios, *História da Literatura portuguesa*, Coimbra, 1921, p. 88.

[34] Pimpão, Alvaro Julio da Costa, *História da Literatura portuguesa*, Coimbra, 1947, p. 215.

atmosphere. Dom Duarte defines the word; breaks it down into a *saudade alegre* and *saudade triste* (happy and sad *saudade*) and notes that there is no adequate translation for the expression in any other language — a conception that has been labored *ad nauseam* from that date to the present time.[35] Dom Pedro, the second son, was energetic, enterprising, brilliant, and distinguished by an abundance of courage. The third, Dom Henrique, who has gone down in history as the Navigator, deserves, of course, a very large place in the history of Portugal and the world for his unflagging devotion to the cause of nautical science and exploration. Prince Fernando was the spiritually gifted one of the lot and destined to a very high place among those stalwarts who have gone far along the arduous and difficult way of mysticism. Warriors, writers, poets, mystics, and adventurers made up this exceptional family and, through the successors to John of Aviz, Portuguese history was to be shaped decisively for the next five centuries. No more effective team, if the expression may be used, could be found at this precise juncture of history to lead the nation along paths of greatness which up to then had scarcely been conceived. Portugal was now ripe and mature for the great adventure for which two hundred years of struggle and sacrifice had prepared her; it was the moment for expanding beyond the seas and the fulfillment of what, in the design of God, was clearly the peculiar national vocation.

The spirit of high adventure dominated the court in 1411 when a treaty of peace was signed with Castile. The burgeoning energies of princes, nobility, and people had no available outlets except in tournaments and feats of agility. It is said that on the occasion of the tournament held to celebrate the Castilian treaty, King John's sons expressed their dissatisfaction at engaging in make-believe combat when the proper thing would be to seek a real engagement that would bring honor and prestige to the nation and, at the same time, perform a useful service for Christendom. According to the *Chronica de D. João,* and repeated by historians down the ages, the king's adviser João Affonso de Azambuja whispered the word "Ceuta" in his ear and thereby stirred the imagination of the monarch most fatefully.[36] Ceuta was the key to North Africa and

[35] Pimpão, Alvaro da Costa, *op. cit.*, pp. 225–226.

[36] Oliveira Martins, J. P., *The Golden Age of Prince Henry the Navigator* (translated by J. Johnston Abraham and Wm. Edward Reynolds), London, 1914, pp. 19–20.

the gate through which the Moslems sought to maintain their hold on the Iberian peninsula. It was a rich and tantalizing prize that would, if besieged and captured, shed infinite glory on Christian arms. Portugal was blocked on the east in any enterprise of this sort for the Spanish would never have tolerated a Portuguese expedition against Granada, which was already well within what may be called, even though the expression is premature, Spain's "sphere of influence." If the Moroccan source of Moslem control were dried up, the service rendered both to Spain and to the Christian world at large would be incalculable and would redound quite naturally to the greater glory of Portugal itself.

John of Aviz was medieval; his sons were strictly modern — so modern in fact that it takes no great effort for us, in the twentieth century, to understand their minds or to grasp the motivations that were at work in them. The riddle of the universe was a matter that roused in them the greatest interest and we have, in Dom Duarte, numerous references to his disbelief in many of the superstitions of the Middle Ages that were still very much taken for granted.[37]

Their zeal was fired for the enterprise that seemed so much more productive of both glory and gain than bouts and tournaments, pageantry and pomp. Prince Henry was particularly keen on the Ceuta undertaking, for already in his adolescent mind was stirring that vision which was to endure with him for the rest of his life and which, accompanied by the tenacity of his will, was to open up for Portugal horizons which were not even suspected in the days of John of Aviz.

The serious proposal to conquer Ceuta was simply the concrete manifestation of ideas and hopes that were in the atmosphere of the time. Portugal was rife with legends and speculation regarding far-off lands. The Portuguese have always been conspicuously curious about peoples and customs that are alien to their own way of life, from the days of the pontificate of Calixtus II (1122) when a certain Oriental ecclesiastic appeared at Rome and told wondrous stories about the shrine of St. Thomas in India and a lost Christian people long since detached from the common stock of Christianity. Some years later, tales began to spread of Prester John, a combined warrior and priest, whose domains were understandably located in vague spots from Ethiopia to India. From the fourteenth

[37] Sanceau, Elaine, *Henry the Navigator*, London, n.d., p. 15.

century onward, Prester or Presbyter John was localized in Ethiopia. Later, when John II of Portugal was prosecuting inquiries regarding communication with the Indies, his first object was to establish contact with Prester John of the Indies, who was generally considered as an important and powerful Christian potentate in Africa. King John was not as easily persuaded as the *infantes* and, in view of his fifty-odd years, he took fire a little less easily than his impetuous sons. Nevertheless he interrogated his theologians and ascertained that a war against the infidels in Africa would be a holy war and a continuation of the glorious tradition that had begun at Ourique when God made manifest his will to his valiant Portuguese.

After elaborate preparations, carried out in the greatest secrecy, the fleet was ready to sail in the spring of 1415, at precisely the moment when the plague struck Portugal and laid low, among its victims, Queen Philippa. With her passing, there was the thought that the expedition against Ceuta simply could not sail nor could her sons, who had just lost their mother, be expected to depart for Africa. Nevertheless it was decided that the ships should sail — all two hundred and forty of them — and so it was that they set out, while the Moslems were ignorant of what was in store for them. Fifty thousand men were reputed to be on board, sailors, rowers, soldiers, and archers.

After various *contretemps*, the fleet reached Algeciras and, on August 12, prepared to cross directly to Ceuta. The infidels were lulled into false security by the storm and the indecision that beset the Portuguese before they finally decided to make the assault. The historian, Oliveira Martins, has pointed out that even at this date, long before the conquest of Constantinople, there was in the subconsciousness of Europe a feeling that unless the Moslem advance was halted and the presence of the enemies of the faith on the fringes of Europe eliminated, there was no safety for Christendom. The atmosphere was not unlike our own day in which the pressure from the communist-dominated world leads to the same sentiment of uncertainty and fear. Ceuta was taken without too vigorous a resistance and with it a vast amount of loot which whetted the appetites of the Christians and led them to the wildest hopes that beyond Ceuta was to be found infinite fields for new conquest and unlimited riches.

Oliveira Martins tells us that Ceuta was more filled with riches than Venice and that it gave the appearance of one vast bazaar.[38] This was the first time that the ordinary Portuguese peasant and countryman, fresh from the crags of Tras-os-Montes, or the thatched huts of his native Beira, had come in contact with the opulence and the refinement of the Orient; it was not to be the last, for this was literally the opening gun in the gigantic adventure that was not to conclude until India and Ceylon, Malacca and Japan had all come within the range of Portuguese interest and curiosity. But in 1415 it was all quite new and disconcerting and paneled ceilings and rich inlaid mosaic were very far from the artistic experience of the unlettered soldiery. The great mosque of Ceuta was converted into a Christian temple, a *Te Deum* sung, and the three sons of King John were solemnly anointed for their heroism in the capture of such a glorious prize. In Portugal, after the forty days of absence with so great consequences, men everywhere who had participated in the conquest were acclaimed and it was thought that the blow that had been struck the Saracen was the final event in the long and hazardous epic of the conflict between the two great spiritual forces. No one could foresee in 1415 that Ceuta was the toe hold, the initial step toward the conquest of Africa — and once the Portuguese had experienced the zest that came from accomplishment of this sort, there were no longer rational limits on the world nor were its frontiers circumscribed by what heretofore had been conceived of as reasonable and feasible.

Two objectives were clearly visualized at this moment: the first was the conquest of certain strong points in North Africa that were strategically necessary to contain Islam, and the second was the beginning of a gradual expansion of both knowledge and exploration of the dimly perceived African coasts, beyond which lay what no man could conceive and about which the wildest legends and accounts had been circulated.

This was one of those moments of supreme exultation which occur off and on in the Iberian world: of uncontrolled zeal for a vast and enticing enterprise; a fervor for the spread of the Christian faith; and, in the background, the ill-defined but very real presentiment that the successful conclusion of the effort will bring glory and riches to the land of Portugal. Unfortunately the capture of

[38] Oliveira Martins, *op. cit.*, p. 56.

Ceuta was a step in what was recognized before very long as a false direction. To be sure, it demonstrated to the Portuguese—and this was no mediocre achievement—that their destiny was not limited by continental Europe or even the sea that lapped their shores. On the other hand, it did not take the perspicacious Portuguese long to acknowledge that their force and vitality were inadequate to the task of conquering and occupying effectively a land mass such as North Africa, inhabited by a fanatical and warrior people. The ultimate consequence was the disaster that befell Dom Sebastian, and with it the end of Portugal's hope of carving out a domain among the Saracens. North Africa, then as now, became the graveyard of European hopes and led to that frustration and bloodletting that was to characterize European activity in that part of the world from the fifteenth century down to the twentieth in which the Spanish struggles to defeat Abd el Krim and the later French crisis in Morocco, Algeria, and Tunis are the final culmination.

The conquest of Ceuta completed, the princes turned their energies and talents to other fields. Dom Duarte became a sober and intelligent administrator and codifier of Portuguese law; Dom Pedro traveled widely, frequented the courts of Europe and, for lack of anything more profitable, participated in the struggle of the Teutonic knights against the Lithuanians on the far eastern marches of Europe, a prefiguration in a sense of the Portuguese propensity to seek adventure far afield and engage in undertakings that seem unconnected with the national life. Prince Henry, showered with honors and titles, settled down at Sagres on the tip of Portugal looking out over the Atlantic and toward Africa.

Crusading zeal as against scientific exploration was responsible for the ill-starred expedition against Tangier in 1437, a natural concomitant to the occupation of Ceuta but which was destined to have a tragic end. It was due in large part to the solicitations of Dom Fernando, whose burning ardor for the expansion of the faith had led him to refuse all ecclesiastical dignities and devote his energies to the destruction of the infidel. The eight thousand Portuguese troops, with more enthusiasm than caution, allowed themselves to be separated from their fleet before the African city and suffered the humiliation of having Dom Fernando himself imprisoned as a hostage. He died a heroic martyr's death in 1443, to pass into history under the title of the "Constant Prince," in homage of his preference for death rather than agree to the surrender of Ceuta.[39]

The course of glory for Portugal was not destined to be straight or undeflected. Although Prince Henry continued his ceaseless efforts to push the frontier of geographical knowledge further and further out until his death in 1460, the successors of John, and particularly Afonso V, his grandson, called "The African," became involved in two of the most unpromising activities in which Portugal could engage: the expansion of her claims in Moorish territory and the union of the crowns of Spain and Portugal.

Three expeditions were led by Afonso into the hinterland of Morocco, between 1458 and 1471, expensive and essentially fruitless ventures that exhausted his treasury and sapped the strength of his people. John of Portugal had understood very clearly that Spain and Portugal were fated to develop along separate and independent lines and that the accident of geographical juxtaposition was no basis for efforts to rectify what history had already made permanent. The Portuguese people had instinctively known this and, unless it were in defense of their legitimate interests and national integrity, there was no stomach for dynastic maneuvering or intrigue, the purpose of which was to unite the crowns and, what was much more serious, to seek to coalesce the two nationalities. The Portuguese royal family occupied an unchallenged position in the constellation of crowned heads. Afonso's sister was married to the Emperor Frederick III; his aunt Isabel was Duchess of Burgundy; another sister had married Henry of Castile. After the death of his first wife, Afonso dreamed of consolidating his position in the Iberian peninsula by a marriage that would bring the dynasties together. The Portuguese monarch proposed to marry his own niece, Juana, a girl of thirteen and daughter of Henry IV of Castile. The Spanish responded to this idea with the same indignation and resolute determination to prevent a Portuguese king from sitting on their throne as had the Portuguese themselves in rejecting Castilian control at Aljubarrota in the previous century. The defeat at the Battle of Toro on March 1, 1476, assured the throne of Castile to

---

[39] Carvalho, Vasco de, *La Domination portugaise au Maroc 1415–1769*, Lisbon, 1942, p. 21.

the remarkable pair known in history as the *Reyes Católicos*, Ferdinand and Isabel.[40]

Portuguese history, from the accession of the House of Aviz to Afonso V, is filled with solid accomplishments destined to determine permanently the course of the national development. Dom Pedro, who served as regent during the minority of Afonso V, his nephew (1438–1481), was responsible for the *Ordenanzas affonsinas*, a monument of jurisprudence which became the basis of Portuguese law and legal institutions. The royal tradition was now entrenched both in popular tradition and in law. Once more the notion that the Middle Ages, especially this crucial fifteenth century in which the transition from the medieval to the modern is taking place, lacked popular representation in political and social affairs, or that royal absolutism was arbitrary and despotic, is not confirmed by the extraordinary development in Portugal. The gradual consolidation of the crown through historical imperatives was accompanied by the equally significant development of the *Cortes* or parliament which became a basic institution in Portugal. The classical three estates — nobility, clergy, and populace — were represented in the Cortes; each body met separately and one of the primary functions was the determination of taxation. Municipal government was well organized and as in Spain became one of the distinctive features of Iberian institutional life and a very considerable defense against the encroachments of the royal power.

The fifteenth is the determinant century. Portugal had become a full-fledged state, a power of consideration, and was fully conscious of its peculiar Lusitanianism and its mature capacity to carve out a place for itself in the world. It may be said that the lyricism of the Middle Ages; the melancholic, repetitious, and simple melodies that distinguished the abundant poetry of Galicia and Portugal now gave way to a severe and exultant prose, the chronicles of the historians who found more inspiration in the exploits of warriors and crusaders, explorers and adventurers, than in the love affairs of peasant girls and shepherds. History and historical evocation were, in fact, the most original forms of expression during the fifteenth century.[41]

---

[40] Aguado Bleye, Pedro, *Manual de Historia de España, op. cit.*, Vol. I, p. 40.

[41] Le Gentil, G., *La littérature portugaise*, Paris, 1935, p. 17. John I designated

The accession of John II to the throne in 1481 constituted a sort of re-examination of the state of Portugal; a serious and constructive effort to put an end to the confusion of three policies which were being followed simultaneously and with only mediocre success in each case: hegemony in Spain, the occupation of Morocco, and the expansion of the discoveries beyond the seas. The new monarch instituted a series of investigations and surveys, to employ a modern term, and sought above all to curb the autonomy of a restless and sometimes avaricious nobility. This was not the first nor was it to be the last time that Portugal was at grips with a serious social crisis, and one that could be solved only by the strongest of measures and the most balanced of judgments. On August 24, 1484, at Setubal, the king witnessed the official slaying of his turbulent brother-in-law, a leader of the conspiracy, and with the death the backbone of rebellion was broken, leaving John free to pursue the work which had been begun at an earlier date by Prince Henry the Navigator. Portugal was on the threshold of very great advances and the energies and will of the nation seemed poised to undertake the mammoth conquest of the misty lands beyond the horizon that were sensed more by intuition than by precise knowledge.

Fernão Lopes as curator of the famous archives of Torre do Tombo and this distinguished historian occupied the post for a thirty-four-year period beginning in 1418. Rodrigues Lapa, M., *Lições de Literatura portuguesa*, Coimbra, 1952, 2 ed., p. 331 seq.

Chapter III

THE PATH OF EMPIRE: PORTUGUESE EXPANSION BEYOND THE SEAS

THE motivation behind the formidable Portuguese expansion over three continents and the many seas is, of course, a complex one and defies oversimplification. There are those who see in the work of Prince Henry in his lonely outpost at Sagres, the *Sacrum Promontorium,* from which he pursued his scientific researches and awaited anxiously the constant news from the seamen at his service, the direct result of the wave of hostility to the Prince after the unfortunate expedition against Tangier. There was, to be sure, in his character a divine flame, an uncontrollable impulse that led him to devote years to the trying task of breaking through the barriers of ignorance and superstition that cut off the southern hemisphere from the knowledge of Europe. There was, too, a strong religious motive, for during the fifteenth as well as the sixteenth centuries we are constantly aware of the emphasis laid on the propagation of the faith by those who were also interested in spices and in slaves. The mixture of motives is quite natural, indeed inevitable, and forms a backdrop to the extraordinary accomplishments that flowed from the vigilance and study at Sagres.

The Portuguese were a combination of intrepidity, scientific caution, and crusading zeal. The recognition of this convergence of sentiments gives the clue to the capacity of this small nation to carry out a program of conquest, spiritual and material, which far surpasses its meager resources.[1]

[1] In Chapter XXIX of the first volume of his *Historia do descobrimento e*

The scientific antecedents of the Portuguese discoveries attest to the very great influence of Portuguese work in this field, not only in that country but all over Europe.[2] It is not my intention in these pages to retell in detail the moving and dramatic story of how the first Portuguese navigators crept down the coast of Africa, defying the traditions and old wives' tales of centuries, or of how they finally managed to circumnavigate the continent and press on to the spice-rich and palm-covered lands of the Orient. It is important, however, in fixing the character of Portuguese history and the nature of its people to outline these achievements within the framework of the background of Portugal today.

A fascinating subject is the "presence" of Africa in the consciousness of Europe during the long centuries that culminated in the Turkish advance over the eastern Mediterranean and the cutting off of the normal route between the West and the Orient that for so long had led through the Middle East. Abyssinia constituted in many ways the major target of European interest in the mysterious lands that lay beyond the Islamic barrier and far over the vast sand stretches of North Africa. Abyssinia had become Christian in the third century and had, in fact, remained a Christian oasis in a world that was gradually swallowed up by Islam or fringed on the south by paganism. With the occupation of Egypt by the Arabs in the middle of the seventh century and the conversion of that once-Christian center into a Moslem stronghold, Abyssinia passed into the category of a legend. There is little doubt that Prince Henry and, long after his death, King Manuel were both obsessed by the desire to establish contact with the fabulous Prester John. The keen interest in the West in establishing relations with Oriental or African Christians was the natural reaction to the harassment of Islam and the hope that in some form a contact would be established that would provide helpful allies on the other side of the Islamic world, so to speak, and thus squeeze the enemy

conquista da India, Fernão Lopes de Castanheda quotes Francisco de Almeida in a letter to his son Lourenço, in which he, first and foremost, was fighting out on the fringes of the world for the "fé católica e por sua honra," that is, for the Catholic faith and his own honor. This perhaps summarizes the matter as effectively as anything. See the excellent treatment of this question in Hernani Cidade, *A literatura portuguesa e a expansão ultramarina*, Lisbon, 1953, Vol. I.

[2] This question has been exhaustively treated in Armando Cortesão, *Cartografia e cartógrafos portugueses dos séculos XV e XVI*, Lisbon, 1935, two volumes.

between two fires. The existence of old Christian communities on the Malabar coast, the Nestorians in other parts of Asia, and, above all, of the Christian community of Abyssinia formed a part of this hope. Since Abyssinia could no longer be reached via Egypt and, indeed, the eastern Mediterranean itself was alive with Moslem ships, the only alternative seemed to be to try in another direction, and that direction obviously was eastward from the north or west of Africa. As early as the twelfth century the news had spread over Europe that the legendary Prester John was, in fact, a reality and had communicated with the Pope. Although no practical consequences were derived from what seemed to have been something of a hoax, the idea persisted that back behind the fastnesses of Africa a great Christian prince reigned and that it would be of very considerable utility to get in touch with him.[3]

But to return to the progress of Portuguese exploration. The initial step in the process was, quite naturally, the discovery or, to be more accurate, the rediscovery of the islands that lay not too far from Portugal proper, the Azores, Madeira, and, farther south, the Canaries. These island groups have passed in and out of European knowledge numerous times and it would not be proper, perhaps, to attribute their finding to the Portuguese, but rather their effective colonization. The elder Pliny speaks of one existence of the Canaries lying close off the coast of West Africa: and both Plutarch and Ptolemy refer to them as the "Fortunate Isles." In the twelfth century, Arab navigators visited them, in all probability, and toward 1334 a French vessel reached them, driven there by a gale. The Portuguese were interested although no formal claim to possession took place and it was a Norman, Jean de Béthencourt, who secured the title of King of the Canaries from Castile, although they ultimately passed under definitive Spanish sovereignty and do not form, therefore, a part of the chronicle of Portuguese overseas accomplishments.[4]

The Azores were apparently within the ken of the Carthaginians for assortments of their coins have been found in the islands. Their existence appears on maps of 1351 and 1375 and it is presumed that they may have been the mythical St. Brendan Islands. In all probability, they were rediscovered by Portuguese vessels

[3] The story is colorfully told in Paul Herrmann, *Conquest by Man* (translated from the German by Michael Bullokc), New York, 1954, Parts 10 and 11.

[4] Colenbrander, H. T., *Koloniale Geschiedenis*, 'S-Gravenhage, 1925, Vol. I, pp. 14–15.

returning to the homeland after attempts to round Cape Bojador on the African coast. The formal discovery has been attributed to Gonzalo Velho Cabral who, in 1431, was instructed by Prince Henry to sail westward in search of these islands which were logically assumed to exist there.[5] Colonization followed very quickly and within the same century the population had so increased as to make them an important territory economically.

The Madeira Islands became a Portuguese outpost at a very early date after the rediscovery by João Gonçalves Zarco, who sighted Porto Santo in 1418. An Italian map of 1351 depicts the Madeira group quite plainly and has led to the assumption that Genoese navigators had perhaps visited the islands during the fourteenth century. Since the territory was uninhabited, Prince Henry made haste, in collaboration with the Order of Christ, to send out settlers and establish his own claim firmly. Even at this early period, when claims and counterclaims were still ill-defined, the first evidence of Hispano-Portuguese rivalry was already taking place. The dispute over the Canaries had been a most acrimonious one in which Prince Henry had not been able to make good his contention before the Pope and the Spanish court that these islands properly belonged to Portugal. This was certainly one of the many reasons why the Portuguese were so eager to establish themselves securely on the northwest coast of Africa and thus dominate the sea lanes from the Iberian peninsula southward along the African coast.

The next step in the process of conquering Africa geographically was to round Cape Bojador and move on to Cape Verde. We are now approaching Black Africa, distinct and separate from the northern part of the continent, and infinitely more shrouded in mystery for the men of the fifteenth century than the lands along the southern coast of the Mediterranean.[6]

---

[5] A handy one-volume treatment is Peres, Damião, *Descobrimentos portugueses*, Porto, 1943, which covers Portuguese maritime expansion from the Canaries, Madeira, and Cape Verde to the later efforts to find the northwest passage and the possible circumnavigation of Europe and Asia via the Arctic of David Melguero in the seventeenth century. The slow crawl down the African west coast has merited, obviously, an immense bibliography. Magalhães Godinho, Vitorino, *Documentos sobre a expansão portuguesa*, Lisbon, 1945, two volumes; Blake, John William, *Europeans in West Africa, 1450–1560*, London, 1942; Hakluyt Society, 2nd series, two volumes; and by the same author, *European Beginnings in West Africa, 1454–1578*, London, 1937. Prestage, Edgar, *The Portuguese Pioneers*, London, 1933, gives a survey of the expeditions.

[6] "Awareness of a kingdom of the blacks had, of course, existed in Europe

The scientific exploration of the African west coast was a singularly uninviting business. The long stretches of desert, the sparse and nomadic population, and the absence of visible wealth might well have discouraged anyone less intent on the objective in mind than Prince Henry. Adventure and a minimum of booty seem to have impelled numerous Portuguese to proceed southward, but for a long period of time they were psychologically obstructed around Cape Bojador by the terror that was inspired by the legends and traditions of antiquity with regard to sailing farther southward. In spite of repeated disappointment at achieving so little in pertinent knowledge of the area, Henry sent out Gil Eannes in 1433 to demonstrate that it was possible to go beyond Bojador. On a second try he succeeded and proved to have made one of the most considerable advances in the history of navigation by demonstrating that it was quite possible to sail southward beyond the arbitrary, invisible line that ignorance had placed as the outward limit of navigability.

The first explorers made a cautious attempt to move inland a few discreet leagues and seek out such inhabitants as they might encounter. They returned to Portugal, having met a small band, with no captives but with the ineffable satisfaction of having breached the barrier and demonstrated the practicability of further navigation down the long African coast. Some years later the Portuguese brought back the first captives from these expeditions and proved to an astonished Europe that black men actually existed as a race and not as an exotic aberration among normally dark-skinned peoples. In 1444 a voyage under the direction of Nuno Tristão pushed further south and saw for the first time the land of the real Negroes, far beyond the territories of the Islamized Moors.

Between 1445 and 1448, caravel after caravel sailed out of Portugal bent on expanding the thin knowledge already acquired and pushing the known frontier farther and farther south. It is an epic of high adventure, lonely and tormented expectation, fruitless

---

long before. The peoples of North Africa had been trading across the Sahara from the beginning of recorded history, and Herodotus, writing in the fourth century B.C. pieced together a tolerable geography of Negroland. The Portuguese were not even the first people to find their way there by sea. A modest 1,700 years earlier, the Carthaginians sent a gentleman named Hanno with sixty ships, each of fifty oars, to explore, colonise and trade with the Atlantic coast of Africa" (Evans, Harold, *Men in the Tropics*, London, 1949, p. 3).

incursions inland, and loss of precious lives, including more than one of Prince Henry's most trusted lieutenants. The remarkable thing is that the material gain in all this was scarcely commensurate with the effort and cost. Prince Henry was plunged in debt and although the scientific results were more than adequate to satisfy his inquiring mind, it was doubtful that his nation would tolerate such indefinite expenditure simply to ascertain the character of the African continent.

For seven years, from 1448 to 1455, there is a strange silence in the old chronicles about new explorations. Internal difficulties and commitments closer to home may well explain the suspension of the African operation pending a more favorable time. Castile had challenged Portuguese pre-eminence in the field and had laid vigorous claims to much of the land that the Portuguese were opening up to European knowledge. The decision of Pope Nicholas V in 1455 granting priority to Portugal may well have been the reason for the new impetus that the work of discovery received.

The second act in this drama opens with the voyage of a Venetian at the service of Portugal, Cadamosto, who has left us, among other things, one of the most colorful and detailed accounts of the peoples and cultures encountered in Africa. Cadamosto has given us a mixture of accuracy and fantasy that has intrigued the historians of this period ever since. Did he find the Cape Verde Islands or not? Do his descriptions fit the known topography of this archipelago or were they found by some later mariner, perhaps one Diogo Gomes, a close associate of Prince Henry and whose name crops up now and again as one of the probable discoverers of these islands.[7] Another Italian, this time a Genoese, Antoniotto Usodimare, joined up with Cadamosto and the two claimed to have traveled far beyond the African bend until they came to vast forest lands and gigantic river mouths which would indicate that they had reached the Guinea coast and the Gambia River.

---

[7] "Descobrimento de Cabo Verde," in *Portugal em Africa*, Lisbon, May–June, 1956, Vol. XIII, No. 75, pp. 131–140; Peres, Damião, *História dos descobrimentos portugueses, op. cit.*, p. 129 *seq.*; Mendes Corrêa, Antonio, *Ultramar portugues: Ilhas de Cabo Verde*, Lisboa, 1954, p. 121 *seq.*; *Viagens de Luis de Cadamosto e Pedro de Sintra*, Academia Portuguesa da Historia, Lisboa, 1948.

The scene now moves back to Morocco for, simultaneously with the lengthening shadow of Portuguese influence and the increase in knowledge of the coast of Africa, the pressing business of holding the line against the Moslem became a matter of the most crucial moment. This is the time of the fall of Constantinople and the sense of consternation that gripped the Christian world. The exhortations of the Roman pontiffs, notably Nicholas V and Calixtus III, did not go unheeded in Portugal which conceived its national mission as that of the sword and shield of Christendom against the rising wave of the infidel. The Portuguese settled for a new campaign nearer home and, in 1458, occupied the stronghold of Alcacer-Seguer after a long siege. The humiliation of Tangier continued to haunt the national memory and in 1463 and 1464 two expeditions were organized against this strategic citadel of Islam on the tip of Morocco. Both attempts failed, but Portuguese obstinacy did not fail before the task which became the major preoccupation of Afonso V who, in 1471, embarked once more with a huge fleet and thirty thousand troops. After taking the fortress of Arzila, Tangier fell with scarcely a blow.

The Portuguese empire was now firmly established on the Moroccan coast with four splendid anchors: Ceuta, Alcacer-Seguer, Tangier, and Arzila. The reigning monarch, as we have noted, acquired the title of "The African," and added to his dignities, which already included the resounding one of King of Portugal and Master of Ceuta and Alcacer in Africa, that of King of Portugal and the Algarves and overseas Africa. The progress of the Portuguese, which culminated in 1516 with the foundation of Mazagan and Agadir, produced a violent reaction with Morocco; a combination of xenophobia and Islamic fanaticism which arose under the direction of the new dynasty of *Sharifs*, known as the Sa'adi dynasty, an aristocracy more or less descended from the Prophet and originating in the Atlas Mountains. They established themselves first in Marrakech and set out on a *jihad* or Holy War against the Portuguese and especially against the more Berberized Moors who were judged responsible for the presence of the Christian conquerors in so many parts of the country.[8]

On Thursday, November 13, 1460, Prince Henry died and was buried in the town of Lagos. A great and honorable career had

---

[8] Cambon, Henri, *Histoire du Maroc*, Paris, 1952, pp. 40–41.

come to an end and, with his passing, Portugal lost an inestimable servant, a noble man of science, and a Christian prince of undisputed talent and utter devotion. The chronicler Zurara and the historian Barros have heaped high praise on the Prince, calling him "a stern master of himself," a man of great wisdom and authority, and constant in adversity as well as humble in prosperity.[9] He endowed studies at the University, constructed his academy at Sagres, and was generous in contributing to churches and chapels all over the land. Although no charts or geographical works produced at Sagres have come down to us, and even the ruins existing in that area are of uncertain connection with Henry and his contemporaries, the evidence is abundant from the commentaries of the writers of the times and in the progress of cartography that Henry inspired not only adventure and exploration but the soundest scientific study of the problems posed by a rapidly and disconcertingly expanding world. There was an element of secrecy surrounding much of the activity, both in the laboratories at Sagres and in the field. The Portuguese were not at all keen that their work and its results be heralded abroad as an invitation to adventurers and competitors from everywhere in Europe. The result is a spotted and inadequate coverage of what is plainly one of the most intensely dramatic periods in the history of the advancement of man's knowledge of the world in which he has been placed.

The royal House of Aviz was distinguished above all else for a passion for continuity and a persistence in the face of all sorts of adversity. The Moroccan adventure, now that Portugal held key positions from the Mediterranean clear around to the Atlantic, was a costly and trying business. It cost men and money and absorbed a far larger portion of the national revenue than could logically be devoted to this enterprise which was more glorious than consequential and more flattering to the national prestige than to the national purse. The constant attacks spearheaded by revived Moorish nationalism, if it can be called that, pressed the Portuguese more and more harshly and they began to drop back from fort after fort and strong place after strong place. In 1541 the Moors took Agadir, and in 1547, Alcacer-Seguer and Arzila, and the shrinking Portuguese dominions in Morocco remained a shadowy claim, at least

[9] The tomb of Prince Henry in the Capela Real at Batalha Abbey bears the inscription, which strikes one as peculiarly appropriate, "talent de bien fere."

until far into the eighteenth century when the last place, Mazagan, fell.

Portugal had at this time a population of perhaps a million people, so that it was unlikely, after Henry's death and deprived of the driving zeal that he had evidenced, that the nation could carry on in the same tenacious and unrelenting spirit. There was a hiatus; a period of recovery from the overstretched ambitions of the first half of the fifteenth century. It is one of the psychological characteristics of the two Iberian peoples that their whole history has been distinguished by a series of "spurts and starts," to be followed by a sort of inertia or lethargy, the work of exhaustion after an effort that, from any but a spiritual point of view, far surpassed their material means to perform. The epic of Portuguese conquest is quite simply the story of a small people who, through sheer pluck and abundant zeal, managed to perform a job that far outstripped its capacity to follow up permanently. That the Portuguese empire lasted as long as it did and, indeed, that it exists today as the third most considerable of the empires in the contemporary world, is testimony to a remarkable wisdom and foresight, a fuller knowledge of which is not entirely useless in a century such as ours in which not only the fact of European occupation and government of non-European peoples is challenged, but the whole intention and purpose that prompted the action originally is brought into question. But more of this later, when we have occasion to examine the Portuguese possessions beyond the seas as they appear in our own day.

Only the briefest reference need be made to the voyages of Diogo Cão, the first of which took place in 1482 and which took him and his men to the Congo and a short distance up from its mouth. The accelerated pace at which Portuguese expansion was now moving is well attested by the two voyages of Cão and the multiple contacts established with the Negro peoples in and about the Congo. This was more than merely groping for some slight light in the darkness of geographically unknown lands; it was rapidly taking on the appearance of formal claims. John II undertook to open up trade with the interior of Africa, sending out several emissaries, among them Rodrigo Reinel, Pedro de Evora, and Gonçalo Eannes, to establish trading stations at appropriate places. One João Afonso de Aveiro returned from Africa in 1486 with pepper, a number of Africans, and news that a great monarch lived far inland from the coast and bore the na Ogané. The ill-concealed hope that sooner or later some h the existence of Prester John would turn up now soared.

The opening up of the route to the Far East via the Ca was unquestionably made possible by the untiring desire of the Portuguese to locate the powerful Christian prince in farthest Africa and with his assistance squeeze Islam from two sides in a gigantic pincer movement. The court now designated Pero de Corvilhão and Afonso de Paiva to take up the search, and elaborate scientific and personal preparations preceded this mission. In this case, however, it was not around Africa that they traveled but across the Mediterranean, toward Egypt and hence to Goa in India. For years Corvilhão wandered about the East and, among other things, made the pilgrimage to Mecca in disguise.[10] In 1493 he reached Abyssinia and his travels ended abruptly since for the next thirty-odd years he remained in that land until discovered by a later expedition of his countrymen.[11]

Corvilhão was the first Portuguese to set foot on the soil of India and the first to actually enter and settle down in the land

---

[10] Hogarth, David George, *The Penetration of Arabia*, London, 1904, p. 31. In Kiernan, R. H., *L'Exploration de l'Arabie* (French translation by Charles Mourey), Paris, 1938, pp. 51–52, a reference is made to the remarkable travels of Corvilhão: "Via Egypt, the Red Sea, he reached Calicut, the Persian Gulf and Sofala. After sending home the information his sovereign had requested—together with some hints regarding the sea route to India, Covilham entered Abyssinia."

[11] The fascination that strange and exotic lands have always exerted on the Portuguese mind is certainly one of the basic national traits. The cosmopolitanism and world-embracing curiosity of the Portuguese is no better illustrated than in this capacity to become identified with the most diametrically different races and peoples; this ability to merge, so to speak, into the spiritual and ethnic backgrounds of other nationalities and cultures. The accomplishment of Corvilhão is one of many. In modern times, Portugal has produced a galaxy of first-rate travel writers and penetrating observers of other civilizations. The tradition as regards the Far East goes back to such literary monuments as that of Fernão Mendez Pinto. Marques Pereira reinitiated this trend in the middle nineteenth century and the most extraordinary of the writers in this field was undoubtedly Wenceslau de Morais (1854–1929), whose various books on Japan and Japanese life revealed him as completely identified as it is possible for a European to be with the character and way of life of that country. Figueiredo, Fidelino de, *História literaria de Portugal*, Coimbra, 1944, pp. 428–429. "Equally popular in Portugal and worthy of publicity elsewhere is the best in the literature inspired by the Far East, which was a source of so rich and abundant a literature in the Golden Age" (Rossi, Giuseppe Carlo, *Storia della letteratura portoghese*, Florence, 1953, p. 275).

of Prester John. He was a precursor of the Portuguese influence in Abyssinia that was to last for a century or more and may, perhaps, be considered in a still broader sense as responsible for saving Ethiopia for Christianity, thanks to his efforts as a forerunner of the Portuguese Jesuits of the sixteenth century who found their way to that remote land.

Abyssinia was faced, in the late fifteenth and early sixteenth centuries, with the gravest of dangers, springing from the penetration of Islam and the difficulty because of isolation in defending effectively its Christian institutions, cut off as they were from the common trunk of the Catholic Church. Gestures were made toward Europe in much the same way as Portugal was seeking to establish contact from the West. It was clear to many Abyssinians that union with the Church of Rome was perhaps the only policy that would produce the desired end of an alliance.[12] The successful expeditions of Bartolomé Diaz and Vasco da Gama, when the continent of Africa was rounded and the Red Sea made penetrable from the south, made Ethiopia far less inaccessible and, above all, made possible the coming of the Jesuits, whose labors were to be of supreme importance in the saving of Abyssinia from total engulfment in the vast sea of Islam.[13]

It was Bartolomé Diaz who was destined to discover the Cape of Good Hope and prepare the way for the exploit of Vasco da Gama in reaching the Indies. We hear of him prior to 1486 as traveling the Guinea coast and engaging in the ivory trade in the west of Africa. At the service of John II, he departed from Lisbon with three ships, the purpose of which was to continue the work so promisingly begun by Diogo Cão, who had reached

[12] Sabelli, Luca del, *Storia di Abissinia*, Rome, 1936, Vol. II, p. 116.

[13] *Ibid.*, Vol. II, p. 163 *seq.* The foundation of the Ethiopian College in Rome in 1539 and the constant encouragement given the missions in that country by the Holy See attest to the great importance attached to the maintenance of Abyssinia within the Christian orbit. Edward Gibbon pays homage to the remarkable work of the Portuguese Jesuits in saying that "Encompassed on all sides by the enemies of their religion, the Ethiopians slept nearly a thousand years . . . they were awakened by the Portuguese" (*The History of the Decline and Fall of the Roman Empire*, London, 1887, Vol. VI, p. 64). The same historian pays tribute to the work of the Society of Jesus in the remark that "Ethiopia was saved by four hundred and fifty Portuguese . . ." (*ibid.*, p. 65). J. Spencer Trimingham, *Islam in Ethiopia*, Oxford, 1952, p. 76 *seq.*, treats the presence of the Portuguese under the title "The conflict of Christianity and Islam."

at the farthest point a spot on the coast of what is now the former German territory of Southwest Africa. At what is presently Lüderitz Bay, Diaz erected a pillar, as was the Portuguese wont, and moved onward down the African coast. Diaz rounded the Cape and pushed up the other side to halfway between the Cape and Port Elizabeth before turning back. He had demonstrated that Africa did have an end and that it was possible to navigate southward and hence into the Indian Ocean. With the letters from Corvilhão, who, in his travels, had reached the Zanzibar coast as far south as Sofala, the problem of the ocean route around Africa was solved and it was now merely a question of actually establishing communication as a normal thing. It was Vasco da Gama who was to achieve this very great triumph.

Vasco da Gama was born the same year in which Prince Henry died and symbolizes better than any other personality the ultimate success of the dreams and hopes that had gradually been made reality through the tenacity of the Infante. King Manuel, called the Fortunate, came to the throne in 1495 at the age of twenty-six and with his authority over the homeland he inherited equally the tradition and the policy of overseas exploration, especially the pursuance of the effort to discover a route to India. The Royal Council was early convoked to debate the matter, and opinions were divided between those who feared that the ventures envisaged would exhaust the strength of Portugal or, what was much worse, provoke the bitter rivalry and formidable jealously of other European states, particularly Venice. In a word, it was already keenly sensed that Portugal might, in the best of conditions and at considerable sacrifice, pursue the conquest of lands and markets over the seas because with them came spices, drugs, and other forms of wealth. But, should this active policy arouse the hostility of European states more favorably placed, strategically, on the continent and force the Portuguese, perhaps, to defend their suzerainty in Africa or in Asia by a struggle in Europe, this double task was plainly beyond the capacity of the nation. Portugal was quite disposed to avoid all commitments and complications in Europe, as long as Europe was willing to allow the Portuguese to follow their flair for overseas expansion more or less unhampered. Spain learned this lesson very early, for one of the great challenges of the age of

Charles V and Philip II was precisely the harmonizing of obligations overseas with the integrity of an empire in Europe itself.[14]

Vasco da Gama had fought in the wars against Castile and had already revealed himself an able and courageous mariner. On July 9, 1497, the little fleet of four vessels sailed down the Tagus. Four months later he cast anchor in St. Helena Bay, South Africa — and then quickly rounded the cape and proceeded up the coast by the present Mozambique toward Mombasa. The accounts of this voyage are fully available and there is no more moving experience than the reading of João de Barros, in his *Décadas* as he describes the vicissitudes and constant difficulties as they moved slowly up the east coast of Africa and sought by ruse, display of cordiality and threats to persuade the chieftains with whom he came in contact to provide pilots and assistance on the way to India.[15] For the first time the Portuguese were leaving behind the primtive peoples of tropical Africa and were coming in touch with the Islamic civilization on the east coast, where the conditions of life and general atmosphere were quite different both from the desert communities of the north and the inhabitants of Black Africa from the Sahara southward.[16]

The Sultan of Mozambique promised aid and received the visitors with outward evidences of cordiality. The Portuguese were delighted for they were now in a region where there was talk of Prester John

[14] The intensity of this conflict and its embarrassments were numerous: which was to take precedence? The Holy Roman Empire or the overseas territories? Chudoba, Bohdan, *Spain the Empire, 1519–1643*, Chicago, 1952, p. 14; Tritsch, Walther, *Charles Quint*, Paris, 1947, p. 220. An extraordinarily penetrating analysis of this and the kindred problem of Charles and the empire is found in Ramón Menéndez Pidal, *Idea imperial de Carlos V*, Madrid, 1940, p. 34. Spain was always faced by Europe and its problems. Portugal, by disassociation from the continent concerned itself with carrying Europe overseas. This is one of the basic reasons for the divergence in history of the two Iberian peoples. "There is no unity of destiny between the two Iberian nations. There might have been if Portugal had been merely the territory in the peninsula. But it was not: it was on the seas and on three other continents" (Giménez Caballero, E., *Amor a Portugal*, Madrid, 1949, p. 142).

[15] An easily available text of the *Décadas* is the edition of Antonio Baião in the Sá da Costa collection of Portuguese classics, Lisbon, 1945, four volumes.

[16] Of special interest is, of course, the so-called *Roteiro* or journal of the voyage which was published in the past century for the first time and received the original title of *Relação da viagem que fez à India em o ano de 1497*. Of importance is the *Diário de viagem de Vasco da Gama*, with a critical study by Admiral Gago Coutinho, Lisbon, 1945, two volumes.

and of India, the two mirages that had sustained their enthusiasm for so many decades.

Disappointment and near disaster beset the Portuguese at Mombasa where they were tricked and preyed upon by the Moslems. But, in the long run, they managed to get off and after running up the coast a distance, they set out across the open sea for India, arriving there twenty-three days later. The goal had been attained; the real *Indias* and not the fake ones of Columbus had been reached, and here indeed to the dazzled eyes of the weary and cautious Portuguese was a land of milk and honey and of wonders beyond belief.

The moment they set foot in Calicut, a new era was ushered in for India and for the world. It was the opening line in the drama of relations between East and West that was being played out in a crescendo of sound and fury that could not have been foreseen on that May day, about four hundred and fifty years ago, when Da Gama completed what must be ever considered as one of the major achievements of mankind. For Portugal, it was the beginning of a new and exciting experience in contact with an alien and essentially different way of life. It was to bring forth the best thought and instincts in the Portuguese race in the effort to harmonize the conceptions of Europe and especially of Christian Europe with the exigencies of coexistence with the civilized and advanced peoples of India. Suddenly, in the space of a few years, the Portuguese had been handed the problem of dealing with Moors in Morocco and Mauretania; with black Africans of every degree of material and spiritual culture; with Islamized natives of the east coast; and, finally, with India. The Portuguese who made these contacts were rude sailors and professional navigators, more given to the problems of nautical science than to the subtleties of human relations. Yet it was their task to forge the link that was to constitute European relations with Africa and Asia for nearly five centuries. An Indian diplomat and historian sees in the arrival of Vasco da Gama the opening of the age that closed with the British retirement from India — in other words, the age of imperialism and colonialism, in the sense that this term is interpreted in India.[17]

[17] Panikkar, K. M., *Asia and western domination*, London, 1953, p. 11. A striking commentary on how great was the Portuguese task in India and how small the band of men engaged in doing it, is in Danvers, F. C., *The Portuguese*

Certainly the period initiated by Da Gama demonstrated one vital thing above all others: that European sea power and command of the sea lanes could control and determine the destiny of the Asiatic land mass. It was the definitive and dramatic triumph of sea power as exercised by a nation that was limited in resources and lacking in the man power for a large continental role in history. In the second place, it represented the imposition or, at least, the acceptance of an economic life based on international trade rather than on what had been the traditional form of Indian economic life — local production, subsistence farming, and internal commerce. The mastery of the sea was to give Portugal an influence, a prestige, and an actual domination in the affairs of Asia quite incompatible from a purely objective point of view, with the role of Portugal in European affairs. It was not only sea power as such, but sea power in the Atlantic that for the next hundred years was to dominate Asia. The power that controlled the Atlantic was destined to control the Indian and Pacific Oceans. This was an Iberian task for a century until the challenge of Great Britain ended that pre-eminence forever.[18]

The state of India at the moment was propitious for the first contact. Mogul power had not yet triumphed over large areas of the south as was to be the case later under Akbar and the Portuguese found a seriously disrupted political scene and a willingness to deal with the strangers that was in sharp contrast to the conflict and tension in many parts of Africa.[19] The Moslem traders who were in virtual control of the commerce of this part of India were far less tender in their reception and naturally were unwilling to

---

in India, London, 1894, Vol. I, p. 37. Also, Whiteway, R. W., *The Rise of the Portuguese Power in India, 1497–1550*, London, 1899.

[18] See, Spate, O. H. K., *India and Pakistan. A General and Regional Geography*, London, 1954, p. 158 seq.

[19] Nehru, Jawaharlal, *The discovery of India*, London, 1951, third edition, p. 238. Mr. Nehru suggests certain considerations which confirm the statement made about the clash of a landlocked authority with a maritime power. Even later when Portuguese power was consolidated and India was stronger under Akbar, "it was obvious that however powerful Akbar might be on land, the Portuguese were masters of the sea. It is not difficult to understand that a continental power did not attach much importance to sea power, although, as a matter of fact, India's greatness and importance in the past had been partly due to her control of the sea routes."

tolerate the intervention of this new force which upset their monopoly.[20]

Da Gama's first visit was scientifically successful although from the commercial and especially the diplomatic points of view he had achieved precious little. His return to Lisbon demonstrated that the sea route to India was eminently feasible and that the products of India, cinnamon, cloves, ginger, pepper, and countless other things, were all as sensational as they had been depicted and as Portuguese impatience had conceived them. The enthusiasm aroused in Portugal may well be imagined, for here lay the open road to untold wealth, to fabulous fortune if the Portuguese had but the energy and the vision to seize so rare an opportunity. A second expedition was soon under way, under the leadership of Pedro Alvares Cabral, with specific instructions to establish what was sometimes known in English as "factories" on the Malabar coast — that is, trading posts and what, in more modern parlance, may be called a bridgehead for both economic and later spiritual penetration.

In was on April 22, 1500, that Alvares Cabral, sailing the South Atlantic much farther to the west than Vasco da Gama had gone, sighted land, and it was a week later that the navigator took possession of this unknown territory in the name of Portugal, and, since his business was elsewhere, he did not linger, but took on water and dubbed the new-found land Terra da Vera Cruz.[21] The discovery of Brazil is lacking in the dramatic quality of the arrival

[20] The Moors, both natives of that region and foreigners, who were in Calicut at the time for reasons of the spice trade, which they controlled, — when they realized that the mission of Vasco da Gama was precisely trade in that product, *ficaram mui tristes* (were much saddened). Barros, *Décadas*, Vol. I, p. 65.

[21] The main source for a knowledge of this event is the letter to the King of Portugal written by Vaz de Caminha, scribe of the fleet. Full text in Carlos Malheiro Dias, editor, *História da colonisação portuguesa do Brasil*, Porto, 1924–1926, 3 vols., Vol. II, pp. 84–99. Capistrano de Abreu, J., *O descobrimento do Brasil*, Rio de Janeiro, 1929. See also in English, the letter of Vaz de Caminha, in *Portuguese Voyages, 1498–1662*. Edited by C. D. Ley in the Everyman's Library, New York and London, 1947, pp. 41–59.

The polemic has been noisy regarding the priority of the discovery of Brazil. There is the claim that Vespucci saw it first and there is a school that holds that the Portuguese were fully aware of its existence before Cabral. Robert Southey, in his *History of Brazil*, London, 1822, Part I, p. 3, credits Vicente Yañez Pinzón with having seen the coast of Brazil first in 1499–1500. See also Cortesão, Jaime, *A expedição de Pedro Alvares Cabral*, Lisbon, 1922.

in India: as history, it is in a measure "less beautiful than that of the mother country, and less splendid than that of the Portuguese in Asia, but it is not less important than either."[22] The vast country was discovered, if we are to accept the common version, by chance, and was left largely to chance for a long time afterward.

The Western hemisphere had, of course, been disposed of in a sense by the papal bulls of 1493 and the Treaty of Tordesillas in 1494, but with frontiers still uncertain in 1500 and only a vague knowledge of the precise contours of the American land mass, Portugal was not overenthusiastic about this fortuitous landing that had occurred and which seemed to be more of a delay than anything else.[23]

Brazil did not appear excessively promising even to as benevolent an observer as Vaz Caminha, who insists in writing to his sovereign that "for all that, the best fruit that could be gathered hence would be, it seems to me, the salvation of these people."[24] His description of "these people" was not likely to arouse any very deep emotion in the breasts of those who read his chronicle. It appeared very clearly to be a vast and intricate land inhabited as far as one could see by howling savages whose nudity and barbarism might well inspire the pity of the missionary but hardly the avarice of the merchant. Nevertheless the crown could not reconcile itself to the idea of doing nothing about Brazil. The Brazilian bulge was a natural midway point on the route to India via the Cape and even if its utilization was not indispensable, its occupation by an alien and, especially, a hostile power would complicate immeasurably the traffic Portugal was bent on developing. The news of the riches of Mexico and Peru had infiltrated Europe and the Portuguese were not impervious to some sentiment of envy. Brazil might be a steppingstone to wealth of that kind, once more ambitious exploration of its interior was carried out. All in all, Portugal was forced by the imperatives of its own *Grossepolitik* to envisage the settlement of Brazil as part of its claim to territory in America

---

[22] Southey, *op. cit.*, p. 1.

[23] A further matter of some moment to historians is whether Alvares Cabral came upon Brazil quite by accident and, secondly, precisely where did he land. Da Rocha Pombo, Jose Francisco, *Historia do Brasil*, Rio de Janeiro, 1905, Vol. I, p. 167 *seq.* Capistrano de Abreu, *Capítulos de história colonial*, Rio de Janeiro, 1934, pp. 22–33.

[24] *Portuguese Voyages, op. cit.*, p. 59.

under the Treaty of Tordesillas. Brazil was, in a very real sense, the result of international rivalries.[25]

The Orient was destined to be a vast emporium and a source of incalculable commercial benefit for Portugal.[26] From the economic point of view the Asiatic trade was the beginning of what may be called the "oceanic cycle" in the evolution of Portugal in particular and Europe in general. Overland routes were gradually abandoned and replaced by maritime transport as more desirable. The cost of ship construction and the need for sturdy and durable vessels for the long haul to India placed a new burden on Portuguese ingenuity and science. In order to make the months-long voyages economically worthwhile, the product that was brought back must be of high marketable value and relatively easy to transport. From 1497 to 1612, the period during which the Portuguese spice monopoly may be said to have lasted, the statistics show that 806 vessels departed from Lisbon. Of these only 425 returned; 92 were lost, shipwrecked, or burned; 4 fell into enemy hands; and 285 were unable to make the return journey from India. Even the best built vessel could withstand, with difficulty, not more than ten voyages and most of them were incapacitated after two. The man power involved was staggering for the small Portuguese population. Each year some 2500 to 3000 men sailed for the Orient — sailors, soldiers, merchants, and passengers. Frequently a third of this number succumbed.[27]

In 1501 the crown sent out an expedition to explore the coast line and two years later a fleet of six vessels arrived, about whose work we have only the sketchiest idea. The problem of occupying the new land became pressing, for the French were already looking with covetous eyes on the vast unpopulated area. The Oriental commercial enterprise was based on the monopoly of the crown

---

[25] Calmon, Pedro, *História da civilização brasileira*, São Paulo, 1937, 3 ed., p. 19.

[26] The second voyage of Vasco da Gama, for example, brought in products to the value of a million ducats for an expenditure of about 200,000. See Calmon, Pedro, *História social do Brasil*, São Paulo, 1937, 2 ed., p. 12. This same historian notes that the opening up of the Orient via Lisbon prolonged the Middle Ages, socially speaking, in the East while the occupation of Brazil, a modern colonizing project on an agrarian basis initiated a new stage which belongs to the modern age (*ibid*., p. 13).

[27] Simonsen, Roberto C., *História económica do Brasil*, São Paulo, 1937, Vol. I, p. 77.

with very little participation of private interests. Obviously in that part of the world there was no question of occupying open territory in order to resist the counterclaims of other and equally energetic nations. In Brazil it was soon clear that Portugal was quite unable to supply the man power or the money, for that matter, to establish a series of military and administrative posts up and down the extensive coast line. It was necessary to improvise a new policy which was to distinguish the colonization of Brazil: the system of grants to private individuals of *capitanias hereditarias* or captaincies, which carried the obligation of exploitation and occupation by colonists.[28]

But suppose we turn again to events in India before considering the opening up of Brazil in 1530, when the period of colonization as an effective policy is begun. The reaction against the Portuguese in Calicut led Vasco da Gama in 1502 to head a second expedition which bombarded the city and strengthened the "factories" that had been set up at Cochin and Cananore.[29]

In 1503, a Portuguese squadron arrived in India and left a garrison under the command of Duarte Pacheco which became embroiled very soon in war with the local *zamorim* or ruler and managed, with great good fortune, to administer to him a smashing defeat. The fame of the Portuguese grew and their influence spread. By 1507 they had fortified Cochin and set themselves up on the island of Socotra. The Portuguese had restored direct contact with India for the first time since the seventh century and they were well on their way toward dealing a deathblow to almost every Moslem interest in the Middle East. The Mameluke Sultan of Egypt had prospered mightily from the transit trade in Eastern products that for a long time had necessarily passed through his lands. The Red Sea merchants at Jidda, as well as other points in the Levant, were sorely tried by this brash new Western European competitor who not only traded with India but gave every indication of settling down for the long haul. The Portuguese harassed Moslem ships on principle, be they merchant or pilgrims

---

[28] Magalhães, Basilio de, *Expansão geográphica do Brasil colonial*, São Paulo, 1935, 2 ed., p. 18.

[29] The epic of the first journey of Vasco da Gama has been immortalized, of course, in the classic *Lusiads* of Luis de Camões. Here the great bard has sung the glories of this expedition and of the Lusitanian people. It is not without importance that the greatest literary creation of the Portuguese should be an epic poem and one that is basically geographical and historical in content.

on their way to Mecca. The crusade against the crescent was a handy by-product of the rich commerce with the East, and the result was a violent hostility on the part of every Moslem state in the East.[30]

The demands of strategy as well as the expanding commerce dictated the fateful decision to form a *government* in India instead of a series of precarious trading stations. In the *Instrucções*, given by Dom Manuel to Alvares Cabral, we find clearly and precisely indicated the objectives set up by the Portuguese for their venture in the Far East: permanent commercial contacts with the major sources of production and markets; a definitive political structure that would assure Portuguese sovereignty in those areas of principal interest; the propagation of the faith; and finally the transplanation of the institutions and customs of the mother country to the new province to be created in India.[31] The examination of the foundation of the Portuguese state of India as well as the principles that inspired it are of fundamental importance, not only in grasping the nature of Portuguese colonization, which is unique, but as a basis for the understanding of the present-day controversy between the Indian Union and Portugal over Goa, Damão and Diu. The accusation of Portuguese "colonialism" in Goa and nearby territories that the New Delhi government has made and the counterclaim of Lisbon that Goa is an overseas province and not a "colony" in the classical sense of the word constitute the essence of the problem that divides the two countries. In a word, the study of how Portugal came to be in India at all and what policy she followed in setting up her area of control there, form an essential part of the background for the interpretation of the positions of the contending parties today. At the same time, the analysis, super-

---

[30] A brief treatment of this phase in Sir George Dunbar, *A History of India From the Earliest Times to Nineteen Thirty-Nine*, London, 1949, Vol. I, p. 150 *seq.*, "The Portuguese." "Towards the end of the period certain international factors began to contribute to the poverty and misery of the land. In 1497, the Portuguese navigator Vasco da Gama found his way around the Cape of Good Hope. This event was of vital importance in the history of the Syro-Egyptian kingdom. Not only did attacks from the Portuguese and other European fleets become frequent on the Moslem ships in the Red Sea and Indian waters but gradually most of the traffic in spices and other tropical products of India and Arabia were diverted from Syrian and Egyptian ports," Hitti, Philip K., *History of the Arabs From the Earliest Times to the Present*, London and New York, 1951, pp. 696–697.

[31] Gonçalves Pereira, Armando, *India portuguesa*, Lisbon, 1953, p. 58.

ficial as it must be by the dictates of space, of the Portuguese racial policy in India, sheds a very considerable light on one of the most significant — perhaps the most significant of all — aspects of Portugal's overseas administration. In these pages we shall have occasion, time and again, to return to the subject of Portuguese biracialism, or interracialism, as the more accurate term may be, for it is part of the whole concept of relations with alien and non-European peoples. The Portuguese set a definite pattern of conduct on this score, and what is more important, conceived of this pattern as something toward which it was necessary to strive if the full fruits of European-Asiatic and African collaboration were to be realized.

The Portuguese "plan" if it can be called such for the peopling of its territories in Africa and India and encouraging the formation of a substratum of mixed bloods can only be compared in its audacity and dramatic simplicity with the policy of the Arabs in their expansion in the world. Just as Islam was carried to the far corners of the world by a race which was limited in numbers and incapable of colonizing in the strict sense of the word, the only recourse was assimilation with those with whom it came in contact and their "incorporation" into a new ethnic and spiritual framework. Gilberto Freyre, the distinguished Brazilian writer and sociologist to whom we are all indebted for so many suggestive studies, has stressed this point as one of the distinctive features of the Portuguese style or manner in its overseas experiments.[32]

The first viceroy or governor of the Indian territory was Francisco

[32] Freyre, Gilberto, *Um brasileiro em terras portuguesas*, Lisbon, 1953, p. 39; also in his *Adventura e Rotina*, Lisbon. It is plain that the salient characteristic of the Portuguese was racial miscegenation. "The originality of Portuguese colonization is the tendency toward assimilation and the mixture of races . . ." (Deschamps, Hubert, *La fin des empires coloniaux*, Paris, 1950, p. 22). The capacity of the Islamic peoples to incorporate elements of other races simply on the basis of their acceptance of the tenets of Islam itself has always constituted one of the most formidable advantages of the religion of the Koran in its crusade for adherents. The absence of racism, and the point is almost trite, in Islam, finds its counterpart in the Christian world in the Portuguese experience. See Bühler, J., and André, P. J., *Ce que devient l'Islam devant le monde moderne*, Paris, 1952, p. 223. Louis Gardet in his *La cité musulmane*, Paris, 1954, p. 31 *seq.*, under the title of "Egalitarian theocracy," develops the main ideas in Islamic society on this and related points. Alphonse Gouilly in *L'Islam dans l'Afrique Occidentale Française*, Paris, 1952, points out that "Islam excels at incorporating the vanquished into the Islamic community itself and tolerating their institutions" (p. 43).

de Almeida. This extraordinary personality, destined to open up the epic of India for Portugal and to lose his life on the way home at the hands of the Hottentots in West Africa, was sent out with very specific instructions from the monarch. The purpose of the new regime was not the conquest of India, but a twofold one, along far more modest lines: to strike down the Turks and Arabs who had long held the trade monopoly in the Indian Ocean and channel this lucrative commerce toward Europe.[33] In the four years that he served in this capacity (1505–1509) he laid the foundations for the Portuguese state in India. Although trade was the main preoccupation of the crown at the moment, Almeida had a far larger vision of his task than the development of commercial contacts. The normal procedure up to that time had been to establish a foothold, deal with the native rulers in harmony if possible, and avoid commitments of an aggressive nature. Almeida was not of this mind. Instead, he proceeded to erect new forts and expand Portuguese influence; he intervened in local disputes and sent out expeditions up and down the coast from his base at Cochin. The Viceroy's son was as remarkable as his father. Young Lourenço d'Almeida visited Ceylon, discovered the Maldive Islands and devoted a good deal of his time and energies to harassing the Moslems wherever they were to be found, losing his life, finally, at the hands of the Egyptians in 1508. The Viceroy wreaked a terrible punishment on the Moslem in the defeat off Diu, which destroyed totally and irreparably their capacity to challenge Portuguese maritime supremacy.

In 1509, Afonso de Albuquerque arrived to take over the government as successor to Almeida and to usher in the most brilliant period of Portuguese power and prestige in the East.[34] Albuquerque is the central figure in this expansion; the presiding genius in every way, for his imagination, skill, intrepid courage and political vision were responsible, not only for the maintenance of the modest holdings in India, but for the diffusion of Portuguese influence far across Asia to China, Japan, Malacca, and the islands of Malaisia.

[33] Introduction by Castro e Almeida, Virginia de, *Chroniques de Garcia de Resende, João de Barros, Damião de Goes, Gaspar Correa, Fernão Lopes de Castanheda, L'empire portugais d'Orient, Francisco d'Almeida, premier vice-roi de l'Inde*, Brussels, 1940, p. 15.

[34] Professor Hitti suggests that the name Albuquerque may well be Arabic, *abu-al-qurq*, "sandal maker" (*History of the Arabs, op. cit.*, p. 697).

Albuquerque was responsible primarily for what became the major contribution to imperial thought at the time: his conception of an all-Asia strategy and his insistence on the Lusitanization of the Portuguese holdings in India. This statesman demonstrated a sense of grand strategy that far surpassed the more pedestrian achievements and ideas of his predecessors and contemporaries. Almeida had been convinced that the extension of Portuguese influence into the Red Sea and the Straits of Malacca was calculated to weaken the national position and was therefore undesirable. Albuquerque did not partake of these hesitations. His purpose was control of the Indian Ocean and the development of an irresistible power that would be respected from the Red Sea to that of China. Even with Goa in his hands after 1510, as the major basis of Portuguese authority, the danger still existed of Moslem commercial activity in Bengal, Burma, Sumatra, the Spice Islands, Siam, and China. If the Portuguese could hold the mouth of the Red Sea and strike a blow at Moslem influence in Malacca, the assurance of primacy would be attained.[35] It was a grandiose scheme that involved economic domination as well as a very keen sense of the religious implications, since Malacca was the basis or springboard from which Islam penetrated Indonesia.[36]

The first expeditions eastward were crowned with considerable success. Even before the definitive occupation of Goa, Francisco Serrão and Diogo Lopes de Sequeira anchored off the city of Malacca where a factory was founded. There was some discussion regarding the abandonment of Goa, but Albuquerque was determined to retain this position for it had the inestimable advantage of an excellent location, plus the fact that it made it possible to assure from it the necessary protection of shipping in the whole area. Albuquerque insisted on seeing things for himself: he visited Malacca and then returned to the region of the Persian Gulf and Aden, where in 1513 he attacked the city without capturing it and destroyed such Moslem ships as he found in the harbor. Albuquerque

[35] Hall, D. G. E., *A History of Southeast Asia*, London, 1955, p. 198.

[36] The importance of the Portuguese from the Christian point of view as well as the purely mercantile is indicated in a Moslem publication, Khan Dahadur, *Ahsanullah, History of the Muslim World*, Calcutta, 1930, p. 576. "Before the advent of the Portuguese in the 15th century, the Arabs had free and unrestricted trade with the whole of the East and the faith of Islam was preached from Arabia to Sumatra."

had grasped one absolutely fundamental fact of Indian affairs and that was the bitter hostility between Hindu and Moslem and the fact that the former would much prefer European rule and leadership to Moslem if they had any real choice in the matter. The viceroy took full advantage of the disputes and hostility that divided the local princes and chieftains and, exactly as did the British at a later date, he depended in large part on local usage and the village system to maintain Portuguese power.[37]

Albuquerque displayed his usual talent and boundless energy in the capture of Malacca and in the negotiations carried on with the various sovereigns in the area under conquest. Ambassadors were sent to Burma and to Siam and an expedition set out for the distant Moluccas where clove, nutmeg, and mace were products which might readily tempt the traders. The Portuguese after years of intrigue and fighting dislodged the Sultan of Molucca from Bintang and forced the sovereign to move to Johore where he continued to harass and aggravate their commerce. Borneo became the new center of Islamic penetration from which missionaries and traders sought to avoid contact with the Portuguese and carry on their activities in the islands.

The situation of the Portuguese was complicated by the circumnavigation of the globe by Magellan and the institution of Spanish sovereignty in the Philippines. The other Iberian state also became an Asiatic power and a rival of Portugal in the prosperous trade of the Far East, so that the latter was now faced by the formidable combination of Spain's intrusion; the hostility of the sultanates of the Malay area and the vast distance over which her merchants, missionaries, and administrators were operating.[38]

---

[37] The "plan" of Albuquerque consisted of the following principles:

1. The political occupation of the area and not merely the commercial exploitation;
2. Make Goa a prolongation of the home country in every way, especially spiritually, culturally, and institutionally;
3. Facilitate the marriage of his soldiers with native women, providing land for such married couples;
4. Contribute in every way to the expansion of the Christian faith;
5. Maintain local usages except those in direct contradiction to Christian morality.

(Pereira Gonçalves, *India portuguesa*, *op. cit.*, p. 91.)

[38] The solid accomplishments of the Portuguese may be seen in the remarkable spread of their language. Portuguese became the one European language to gain the universal character of a *lingua franca* in the Far East. "The Portu-

As has been indicated, the propagation of the Christian faith was one of the major preoccupations of the Portuguese crown and ample provision was made for this work in connection with the establishments to which reference has already been made. The origins of Christianity in India have been traced, as everyone knows, to Thomas the Apostle, for it is supposed that in going forth to preach the Gospel, Thomas reached the Malabar coast via Parthia and northwest India. The success of the Apostle in this lonely mission among a Hindu people, whose facility of syncretism made the propagation of Christianity infinitely difficult, has been attributed by the successors of those who founded the faith in that area to the saintly life and numerous miracles which carried infinite conviction.[39] Until the fourth century of our era, little is known of the Christian community in Malabar. At that time a momentous event occurred which changed the fortunes of the struggling Christian community very substantially: a considerable Syrian migration which increased the prestige and influence of the Malabar Church.[40] Cut off from direct contact for centuries with

---

guese language spread to every part of India and the East and for over a century was the *lingua franca* of Europeans in the East Indies" (Meile, Pierre, *Histoire de l'Inde*, Paris, 1951, p. 55). "The years between 1500 and 1550 witnessed, in Portugal as in Spain, the transition from the linguistic conditions of the Middle Ages to those of the adult and imperial tongue" (Entwistle, William James, *The Spanish Language*, *op. cit.*, p. 294). Portuguese in relatively pure or dialectal forms exists in many parts of the Far East to this day. Entwistle speaks of "Indo-Portuguese" for India and of the peculiarities of the language as used by the Chinese of Macau (*ibid.*, p. 313 *seq.*). The philologist, Leite de Vasconcelos, writes of Indo-Portuguese as divided into such dialects as that of Diu, Damão, and others of the north coast; the Goese dialect, and those of Mangalor, Cananor, Mahé Cochin, and Coromandel. In Ceylon there is a definite Portuguese, and Malay has in turn exerted influence on the Portuguese that has remained in Java, and especially Singapore. The Portuguese of Timor in the archipelago of Indonesia is still another linguistic variation. All of these are in use today and serve the needs of an appreciable non-European population. This contrasts with the absence of such cultural influence on the part of the Dutch in their East Indian possessions. See Vasconcelos, Leite de, *Esquisse d'une dialectologie portugaise*, Paris, 1901, pp. 29–30. Also Mendonça, Renato, *O portugues do Brasil: origens, evolução, tendencias*, Rio de Janeiro, 1935, Chapter II, entitled "Geography of the Portuguese Language."

[39] Thomas, P., *Christians and Christianity in India and Pakistan*, London, 1954, p. 14. Also, Musset, Henri, *Histoire du Christianisme spécialement en Orient*, Harissa, Lebanon, 1948, Vol. I, p. 41.

[40] Hitti, Philip K., *History of Syria*, London, 1951, p. 518: "Members of the Syrian rite in India acquired the name of Christians of St. Thomas. . . . Christian immigrants from Baghdad and other Moslem cities reinforced in the eighth and ninth centuries this community."

the Western Church, schismatic in their doctrine and with a rite that was peculiar to the Malabar, this isolated segment of Christianity was not brought into the orbit of the common Christianity until the arrival of the Portuguese. The relations were at first cordial between the European Christians and the Syrians, both ignorant in many ways of the usages and attitudes of the other. But it is with the arrival of the Franciscans and Dominicans and later the Jesuits that Christianity moves forward, not merely as an obscure community on the fringes of Indian life, but as a compact, cohesive *nationality* of mixed Portuguese and Indian blood that professes the same doctrine and practices the same liturgy as in Europe.

An extremely important aspect of the missionary work of Portugal both in Africa and in the Far East is the juridical recognition by the Holy See of royal intervention in matters which are primarily ecclesiastical. This is the problem of the royal patronage, in Portuguese *padroado,* which plays a very large role in the question of Goa and will demand some slight reference in later pages. Martin V, on April 4, 1418, declared that privileged position of the Portuguese crown in all places that should be taken from the Moslems.[41]

In a series of papal documents, the right of the Portuguese to the presentation of ecclesiastical candidates is recognized, especially in that of Leo X, in 1514, in which it is specifically stated that the monarch shall have the right of presentation for ecclesiastical benefits in all lands acquired over the past two years and those which may be acquired in the future.[42] The problem involving the

[41] Alves da Cunha, M., *Portugal: a sua accão missionária,* Lisbon, 1929, p. 6. In the papal bull, *Sane charissimus,* the Portuguese campaign in Africa was deemed a crusade and the Pope enjoined every aid and support in wresting the lands of the Moslems from their control. Eugene IV blessed the endeavors of Dom Duarte and Afonso V in like manner in the bulls of 1436 and 1443. Oliveira, Miguel de, *História ecclesiástica de Portugal,* Lisboa, 1948, p. 196. The publication of Coutinho, B. X., *L'idee de croisade au Portugal au XVième siècle,* Louvain, 1946, treats of the crusade in connection with the Portuguese expansion overseas. The Agência Geral do Ultramar has published innumerable volumes of primary importance on the overseas areas. A vast collection of source material on the missions is in Brásio, Antonio de, *Monumenta Missionária Africana* in process of publication.

[42] Oliveira, *op. cit.,* pp. 198–199. Also Silva Rego, António da, *O Padroado portugues do Oriente, Esboço histórico,* Lisbon, 1940. The patronage in the case of Portugal included: presentation for benefices including the episcopal; preservation and repair of churches, monasteries, and sanctuaries; furnishing of religious houses with all that was necessary for their operation, the building of such houses and churches as necessary; maintenance of the clergy. There is no

padroado was to arise in later years when the question came up as to precisely what territories were envisaged when the grant of privilege was made to the crown? Did it include those areas originally under Portuguese control or even the entire Far East? The Holy See quite naturally sent out missionaries later to areas that were not Portuguese and therefore was not bound to take into consideration agreements or accords that had been made with Portugal. But more of this dispute later. Sterile as it may seem and arid as the discussion strikes one, it is a fundamental point that has its place in the present controversy regarding Goa, since one of the elements in this difficulty is the religious, that is to say, to what degree the matter can be considered as bound up with the vital interests of the Catholic Church in India. Suffice it to say at this point that the whole system of the royal patronage, in the case of Portugal as well as of Spain, was a natural, inevitable outcome of the circumstances that prevailed at the time of the reconquest against the Moslems and during the long period of expansion overseas. The two Iberian nations were the only ones that had the fleets to carry out this kind of exploration. They were equipped, insofar as anyone was equipped, to deal with the indigenous peoples that they found. The civil arm was responsible for the establishment of towns, the defense of the national interests, and the security of its territory. Quite obviously, since one of the motivations in the enterprise was the expansion of the faith, the State collaborated in every way with the Church in the achievement of the purely spiritual objectives involved. It would be improper to treat this subject in the light of the twentieth century or to consider that the strict separation of Church and State is a *sine qua non* to all effective work of the Church itself. In the sixteenth century the close identification of the Church and State, especially in a country like Portugal was so natural and logical that it would have been an aberration to conceive of anything else.

The organization ecclesiastically of the Portuguese world followed very quickly the events we have been outlining. Ceuta was already

---

mention of missions in the Portuguese patronage in contrast with that of Spain. This is explained by the difference in colonizing methods of the two countries: Spain penetrated and began the work of conversion among the pagans at once; Portugal set up bases and then turned them into regular dioceses and from this worked outward at a slower rhythm.

the seat of a bishop in 1420, followed by the rest of Morocco and then the Azores. Goa was established as a diocese in 1534 and raised to the dignity of an archdiocese in 1557 with two suffragan jurisdictions, Cochin and Malacca. Long before the end of the century, this authority was extended over the islands of the East Indies, to Japan, and to China, thus completing the definition of the spiritual sphere of influence staked out for the Portuguese. The Portuguese missionaries overseas had already begun activity as early as 1466 in Cape Verde and the Guinea coast under the Franciscans. The first church was erected in the Congo in 1491 — Carmelites and Dominicans followed. The Jesuits were the first to work in Angola, which was destined to become Portugal's most important holding on the west coast of Africa, and in Mozambique, on the east, the Franciscans began operations by the beginning of the sixteenth century.

Mission action in the Far East is, of course, linked with the glorious name of St. Francis Xavier. This Spanish nobleman, at the service of the Church in the territories which Portugal had opened to the spread of the faith, reached Goa on May 6, 1542, and from that day until his lonely death within sight of the China mainland, his name was inseparably bound up with Goa and Portuguese India. The intensity of feeling for St. Francis and the symbol that he represents for Catholic Goa is impossible to exaggerate.[43] Goa at the time was well on the way to becoming a cosmopolitan focal point of the entire Far East. Its streets teemed with Hindus, Moslems, Christians, and peoples attracted from far and wide by the growing prosperity of the emporium. St. Francis Xavier was not particularly impressed by the mundane character of the city nor was he attracted by the idea of serving exclusively the European element established there. The opportunities for spiritual conquest were limitless with the vast hinterland of India behind and still farther on the immensity of China and the islands.[44]

---

[43] "De Sanchão a Malaca e Goa" in *Boletim Ecclesiástico da Arquidiocese de Goa*, Saligão, Portuguese India, April, 1955, No. 10, p. 433 *seq.*

[44] The saint's appreciation of the attitude of the Portuguese was expressed in one of his letters which I transcribe in Xavier's own Spanish:

"Los que a estas partes por solo amor y serviçio de Dios nuestro Señor vinieren para acrescentar el numero de los fieles y límites de la sancta Yglesia, madre nuestra — pues ay tanta dispossición en esta tierra — hallarán todo favor y ayuda necessaria en los portogueses desta tierra con mucha abastança, y serán

The tribulations of St. Francis on the Indian coast, among the fisherfolk, and with the obstinate blindness of those whom he would convince have been told again and again. Very early in his career the great missionary was faced by a familiar problem, one that crops up in areas where political control is accompanied by the spread of Christianity. This is simply the fact that an easy and comprehensible connection was established between Portuguese control and government, in the India of the sixteenth century, and the Catholic faith as professed by these particular Europeans. To become a Christian was to become automatically a Portuguese: the civil authorities were not adverse to so considering the Indian who passed over to Christianity and the association became stronger as time went on. In a word, the indigenous or non-European character of the Christian faith was submerged in the face of a political reality. The incident of the massacre of the several hundred fishermen at Manar, who had become Christian, because their king feared that their conversion was the entering wedge for Portuguese influence, illustrates perfectly this very serious problem.[45]

Portugal led the way in the tentative opening up of China in the early sixteenth century. Two years after the capture of Malacca by Afonso de Albuquerque, Jorge Alvares journeyed to China. The Portuguese had been in contact with the Chinese at Malacca and in 1517 Fernão Peres de Andrade, accompanied by the naturalist, Tomé Pires, journeyed to China for the express purpose of establishing relations with the emperor and securing a concession for Portuguese interests at Canton.[46]

---

dellos recibidos con mucha charidad y amor, por ser la nación portoguesa tan amiga de su ley y desseosa de ver estas partes de infieles convertidas a la fee de Christo nuestro Redemptor. . . ."

(De Sá, Artur Basilio, *Documentação para a história das missões do Padroado português do Oriente*, Lisboa, 1954, Vol. I, p. 418.)

"Those who may come to these parts solely out of love of God to increase the number of faithful and the frontiers of Mother Church . . . will find every favor and all aid on the part of the local Portuguese and will be received by them with charity and love since the Portuguese nation is obedient to his law and desirous of seeing these people converted to the faith of Christ our Redeemer."

[45] Thomas, *Christianity in India and Pakistan, op. cit.*, pp. 57–58.

[46] Lobo, Pedro José, see *Bases e processos da economia de Macau*, Macao, 1953, p. 2. Also see the excellent chronology of the history of Macao in Gomes, Luis G., *Efemérides da história de Macau*, Macao, 1954, and Boxer, Charles R., *Fidalgos in the Far East, 1550–1770*, The Hague, 1948.

By 1557 the Portuguese possessed three trading centers near Canton in the south of China: Shang Chuan, Langpokau and Macao itself. The first two were ultimately abandoned and Macao remained as the primary center of all activity in the area. This outpost of the empire in China was not subject, as was the rest of the Portuguese world during the centuries that followed the first explorations and discoveries, to some of the more severe economic shocks that took place, such as the cheaper production of sugar in the West Indies and the exhaustion of Brazilian gold. The expulsion of the Jesuits from Japan in 1639 was a definite setback and reduced the importance of Macao as a vital way station between India, Malacca, and the Japanese islands. Trade with China itself maintained the colony, but the establishment of the British close by at Hong-Kong in 1841 deprived Macao of the glory and opulence that had been its peculiar characteristic during the centuries of greatness.[47]

But it was in the religious order that Macao gained its greatest significance. "Macao, by virtue of its ecclesiastical history alone, is the earliest stronghold of Catholicism in the Orient."[48] By 1563, the first regularly established priest resided in Macao and from then on the colony developed rapidly, both politically and religiously. The fact that within a few years of the foundation nearly a thousand Portuguese had settled on this tiny territory near Canton inspired the Lisbon government to formalize its relations and erect the diocese.[49] The Jesuit Father Cardim, writing in 1646, describes Macao:

> Macau is distinguished by its very fine buildings and is rich by reason of the commerce that moves into its port day and night. It is

[47] Braga, J., *The Western Pioneers and Their Discovery of Macao*, Macao, 1949, pp. 102–105.

[48] Brunt, M. Hugo, "An Architectural Survey of the Jesuit Church of St. Paul's, Macao," in *Journal of Oriental Studies*, University of Hong Kong, Hong Kong, Vol. I, No. 2, July, 1954, p. 2. See also Fergusson, Donald, *Letters From Portuguese Captives in Canton Written in 1534 and 1536 With An Introduction on Portuguese Intercourse with China in the First Half of the Sixteenth Century*, Bombay, 1901. Teixeira, Manuel, *Macau e a sua diocese*, Macao, 1940, 2 vols.

[49] "Macau, Mãe das missões no Extremo Oriente," Arnáiz, Eusebio, C.SS.R., in *Boletim Ecclesiástico da diocese de Macau*, Macao, February, 1956, No. 622, p. 104 seq. Also, the article by Father Thomas Uyttenbroeck under the title, "Macao — Mother of Missions" in *Mission Bulletin*, Hong Kong, Vol. VI, No. 10, December, 1954, p. 919 seq.

> held in great renown throughout the Orient as the emporium of gold, silver, silks, pearls, all manner of drugs, spices and perfumes from China, Japan, Tonkin, Cochin China, Cambodia, Macassar and Solor. But above all it is distinguished as the head of Christiandom in the East.[50]

Macao was originally ceded to the Portuguese as a reward for their assistance to the Chinese in ridding the area of pirates, but the formal cession of the colony was not made until 1887. Macao was the only part of the Portuguese world, incidentally, where, in 1580, when Portugal ceased to be independent and passed under Spanish rule, the national flag was never hauled down.

The thread of the story of Portuguese India may be taken up again briefly to indicate how the successors of Afonso de Albuquerque consolidated their holdings in Goa and immediately adjacent territory and assured Portuguese control at such strategic spots as Diu, which they had long coveted as particularly significant for the trade and defense of the northwest shores of India. Hence the explanation of how today Portugal holds these several unconnected pieces of territory which, in the sixteenth century, served as the basis for her operations all over the Indian Ocean.

Portugal's motives in this complex project, the barest outlines of which have been suggested, were, of course, often contradictory. It is not always possible, in the case of enterprises of this kind, to separate the noble from the base or the disinterested from the sordid. Gain and glory were naturally present and if we have insisted on the role of the spread of the Gospel, it is because this was undoubtedly a vital and possibly the most vital element of all. Portuguese thought in the sixteenth century was indistinguishable from its religious sentiment. There was no rupture, no break between one and the other, and, as has been stated, the secular and the spiritual marched hand in hand. Portugal achieved universality through her dedication to the propagation of the faith through the missions.[51]

---

[50] Cardim, *Relazione della provincia del Giappone*, Paris, 1646.

[51] This thought is emphasized in a comment of *Osservatore Romano*, Vatican City, December 18, 1955, with reference to the introduction of the study of missiology in the Overseas Institute in Lisbon: "It was missionary expansion that launched Portugal on the road to universality."

A Portuguese writer has commented, "We do not wish to advance the notion of a spiritual crusade as the sole or even the primary aim of our policy at all times. More than once, in our relations with individuals of other continents, we failed in the respect due to human personality" (Andrade, Antonio Alberto de, *Many races — One Nation*, Lisbon, 1954, p. 5).

It was Afonso de Albuquerque in India who initiated the policy of encouraging mixed marriages between the Portuguese and the natives.[52]

Not only was intermarriage encouraged as the surest guarantee of future stability, but the person of color was not restricted in his aspirations. Henrique Dias, a hero of the Portuguese restoration in Pernambuco in Brazil, was rewarded by designation as a *fidalgo*, or member of the king's household, in 1638 and in 1657 was made a commander of the Portuguese armed forces.[53] No more eloquent testimony to this idea of miscegenation as the basis of a social order can be found than a much later piece of Portuguese legislation which is the royal ordinance of 1755. In this ordinance the monarch imparts specific instructions that "considering how fitting it is that my royal domains in America should be populated and that intercourse with the Indians through marriage may contribute to this end, I am pleased to declare that my vassals of this kingdom and of America who marry Indians there shall in no way be dishonored, rather shall they be worthy of my royal attention. . . ."[54] In an ordinance of 1761 addressed to Portuguese India, the king refers to the "pious laws and customs that have united my vassals with the mother country from the earliest times" and proceeds then to declare that Portuguese citizens of India, regardless of race or condition, are to be considered absolutely equal to

---

[52] Andrade, *op. cit.*, p. 6. A most important phase of this policy was the transportation of Portuguese women to India for the purpose of creating a new Portugal of mixed blood in that region. "In most historical works that refer to our colonization, India and Brazil, I note that as a rule, the role of the Portuguese women who went out as colonizers is relegated to a very secondary place in spite of their enormous contribution to the creation of a new Portugal overseas" (Correia, Germano, *História da colonização portuguesa na India*, Lisboa, 1950, Vol. II, p. 4). This work in several huge volumes is a detailed study of the original immigrants and the families descended from them in Portuguese India and demonstrates beyond any doubt that the occupation of India was far from merely a commercial enterprise or military venture and that it was literally a transplantation by Portugal of its own people for the purpose of forging a new society that was to be Indo-Portuguese in blood and Portuguese in speech and culture. This is a vital point in connection with the controversy over Goa today, because the Goese are palpably not Indians in the ordinary sense, but what must be called Indo-Portuguese, which is not the same thing at all. See the same author's *Os luso-descendentes da India*, Nova Goa, 1921.

[53] Frazão de Vasconcelos, *Henrique Dias, herói da Restauração de Pernambuco*, Lisbon, 1940, p. 11.

[54] *Collecção das leys, decretos e alvarás, que comprehende o feliz reinado del Rei Fidelíssimo D. José I nosso Senhor*, Lisbon, Vol. I, 1771.

those born and bred in Europe. "It is recommended to the viceroys of the said state as well as to the ministers and officials that they give preference to such natives of the respective territories as show themselves apt in examinations for honors, dignities, employments, posts and offices, on pain of My considering Myself very ill served by the contrary."[55]

The opening up of Asia by the Portuguese was, in brief, the story of indomitable men who individually were responsible for most that was accomplished. Great governors and conquerors as well as administrators of the type of Francisco de Almeida, Afonso de Albuquerque, Nuno da Cunha, and João de Castro; military heroes of the caliber of Duarte Pacheco, Antonio de Silveira, and João de Mascarenhas were matched in every case by adventurers and explorers of the category of Duarte Coelho and Mendes Pinto.

The examination of Portugal as a world power in the sixteenth century and its subsequent falling off would be incomplete were we to include no mention, although very brief, of the formal establishment of Portuguese control in Africa. We have already noted the general outline of how the Portuguese crept down the African coast, rounded the Cape in a burst of intrepidity, and then pushed on to Asia. Once attained, it was India that absorbed the attention and interest of kings and businessmen. Africa was not, however, totally neglected and the foundations were laid for the present empire there.

Until the Portuguese reached the Gold Coast of West Africa, they had not achieved any solid purpose, economically. The gold of the Gold Coast came from Ashanti and adjacent districts which was one of the sources of supply for the trans-Saharan gold trade.[56] The domination of this coast and its precious metal had the particularly attractive feature of cutting off the Arabs in North Africa from their supply and at the same time assuring themselves of funds and resources for the costly exterprise of reaching India. Once the latter was attained, it was natural that West Africa should be neglected. In the first place trade was rudimentary in this region, and the vast forests made its development far more arduous than in the urbanized and effete East. There was little temptation to

[55] Quoted in de Andrade, Alberto, *op. cit.*, p. 34.

[56] Fage, J. D., *An Introduction to the History of West Africa*, Cambridge, 1955, p. 47.

penetrate far inland and the Portuguese were prone to regard most spots along the coast as convenient ports for the journey out to India. Moreover, in penetrating the hinterland of the African bulge and the Gulf of Guinea, there was an excellent chance of running into the Moslem traders who moved in those parts.[57] It was John II who proposed that Portugal have a permanent settlement on the Guinea coast and so ordained that São Jorge de Mina be founded in 1482.

Portuguese influence north of the Senegal was ever slight; south of that line, however, and especially from the conveniently based Cape Verde Islands, they exerted a very real mercantile and later religious influence on the mainland, and in their early establishment on the island of Fernando Po, that bears the name of one of the captains who charted this span of coast, there was developed in agriculture and general social structure a system very similar to what was later to become the West Indies.

The west coast of Africa was infinitely less attractive than the East or even America and the development on Fernando Po was not undertaken elsewhere. "West Africa, the first fruit of the age of discovery and the nearest to the new continents, was the last to be developed. It became a reservoir of labour for America."[58] The ever curious Lusitanians did in all certainty penetrate inland to rather considerable distances and there is the off chance that around 1565 they reached Timbuctu. On the Gold Coast, so active had trade become that by the early sixteenth century traders were sending home to Lisbon gold to the equivalent of one tenth of the world's gold supply at the time.[59] On some parts of the coast, the rough surf, the shoals, and other obstructions discouraged active trade and when there was nothing much there in any event, the Portuguese were prone to pass it up. The trading Post at Gwato, the port for the African kingdom of Benin, was maintained for thirty years as a most profitable enterprise.

It was natural that the slave trade, of which we shall say more shortly, should encourage permanent settlements in such islands

[57] On the significance of Arab and especially Moslem colonization and expansion in Africa — a neglected aspect of the influences on the continent, see Meynier, O., *l'Afrique noire*, Paris, 1921, Chapter IV, p. 116 *seq.*, entitled "The Arab Colonization of Black Africa."

[58] Pedler, F. J., *West Africa*, London, 1951, p. 55.

[59] Fage, *op. cit.*, p. 54.

as São Tomé, Príncipe, and Fernando Po. The former two of these islands are still Portuguese today and form one of the African overseas provinces. The islands were easily defendable; unlikely to merit the covetousness of Dutch, French, or British, and a most handy assembly point for slaves to be transferred to Brazil.

Farther south the Portuguese asserted, from the end of the fifteenth century, general claims over the whole coast line and very particularly that which extended southward from the mouth of the Congo River. Gonçalo de Sousa was dispatched on a mission to the ruler of the area, Mwani Congo, in 1490, and soon thereafter the first missionaries entered the country. A cathedral was erected in the newly baptized town of São Salvador in 1534. In general the national interest was more concentrated on the southern part of the territory, now Angola, than the north and it was perhaps because of the wild accounts of its vast silver wealth that originally attracted occupants. An African chieftain, one N'Gola, ruled in what is now Angola and to him as Portuguese ambassador went Paulo Dias de Novais, grandson of Bartolomé Dias, while missionaries accompanied the mission in the hope of repeating what had been accomplished in the Congo when the indigenous king had been converted to the Christian faith. N'Gola was a tougher adversary and kept the Portuguese prisoners for six years, when they were released and returned home, whence they took the most fabulous tales of the riches to be found in this land in South Africa. In 1575 Novaes returned as governor general to what was to be known as the "Kingdom of Sebaste" and with him went a group of Jesuit priests for the evangelization of this remote land.

The spiritual conquest of Angola, if we may employ the term, was nothing as promising as the Congo, for in the latter region, as had been indicated, the conversion occurred in 1491 and almost immediately relations were established with the Holy See via the Portuguese court. Portugal was specifically made responsible for the religious surveillance of the great Congo territory. One of the most remarkable testimonies to Portuguese diligence in this regard was the fact that by 1518, a Negro Congolese bishop presided over the spiritual destinies of his people. This was D. Henrique, son of the Congo king Affonso, born in 1495 in what is today the lower Belgian Congo. He was sent to Lisbon early in the sixteenth century, made his studies, was ordained, and eventually consecrated bishop.[60] The Portuguese government was generous in supporting the entire ecclesiastical organization and clergy in this huge territory.[61] From the foundation of Benguela in 1617 to date, the sovereignty of Portugal over the coast line as far north as Ambriz, has been undisputed save for the period from 1640 to 1648 when the Dutch made serious efforts to land forces and expel the Portuguese. The colony did not enjoy, during the earlier centuries, any considerable development on its own and was dependent in large part on the slave trade with Brazil, which was the source, as already indicated, of the very real prosperity of much of West Africa. The natural resources were neglected badly in favor of the human.

Curiously enough, the tip of Africa attracted the Portuguese considerably less and what was later to become the seat of a Dutch settlement and then British and finally the Union of South Africa was passed up by the mariners and tradesmen out of Lisbon who much preferred the coasts of Mozambique for rest and recuperation on the long journey to India. This was perhaps due in part to the unfortunate death of Viceroy Almeida, at Table Bay in 1510, at the hands of the Hottentots and the fact that the Bantu tribes of the east coast were more amenable and less warlike than the aborigines at the end of the continent. The problems faced in the colonization of Mozambique were diametrically opposite of those encountered in Angola. In the latter, native rulers offered resistance but, thanks to the rapidity of the Portuguese penetration and the effects of Christianization, the reaction was short-lived and European rule became fixed very quickly. In the east the major factor with which to contend was the extension of Arab-Moslem influence far down the African coast. Ever since the tenth century, the Arabs and the Islamized local inhabitants had been influential as far as Sofala, which is in the general latitude of the present city of Mozambique in the northern part of the province. It is a truism of European expansion that the problems faced in areas of peoples untouched by Islam are radically different from those who have

---

[60] See Alves da Cunha, Manuel, "Os primeiros bispos negros," in *Boletim da diocese de Angola e Congo*, Luanda, Angola, 1939, Vol. V, pp. 158–175. Also the excellent account in Cuvelier, J., and Jadin, L., *L'Ancien Congo d'après les archives romaines (1518–1640)*, Brussels, 1954, p. 37 *seq*.

[61] Jadin, L., "Rapport sur les recherches aux archives d'Angola," in *Bulletin de l'Institut royal colonial belge*, Brussels, 1953.

either been Islamized or at least submitted to contact with that religion. The Mozambique coast in the early years of the sixteenth century was an area in which Moslem influence was preponderant and which in turn exerted a very powerful effect on the local aboriginal population.[62]

By 1510 the Portuguese had managed to secure the port of Mozambique and dominate to a very real extent the various sultanates up and down the coast. The period was most trying and the constant assaults of the Moors, as they were called, that is to say, the Arabs and Islamized natives, made life for the handful of Portuguese colonizers extremely precarious.[63] The search for the so-called "land of gold" led the early explorers to fan out from Sofala, while farther south, Lourenço Marques opened up trade around Delagoa Bay, thus marking the southernmost limit of Portuguese expansion. Other expeditions, especially that of Francisco Barreto and Vasco Fernandez Homem pushed far into the interior in the effort to locate gold in abundance, only to return disappointed at the paucity of the precious metal. The development of Mozambique was slow, in part because of the interest in India and, toward the end of the century, because of the political union of Portugal with Spain during which time Spanish international interests prevailed over those of Portugal. The Jesuits from 1560 onward and later the Dominicans did yeoman work in the exploration and evangelization of Mozambique, and this colony, like the rest of the Portuguese world, suffered the almost irreparable blow that was dealt in 1767 with the expulsion of the Society of Jesus.

This hasty survey of the formation or genesis of the Portuguese empire indicates very clearly certain basic or salient features that can well be underlined once more. The empire was the work of a tiny nation that not only exhausted its resources in the effort to stretch its lines across the world, but went far beyond the normal capacity. The story of the rise, apogee, and decline of this empire is the story of the economic cycles through which the Portuguese race passed. The nation began in the corner of Europe

[62] Oliveira Boléo, *Moçambique*, Lisbon, 1951, p. 165. Reference is made in this general study of Mozambique to the fact that the "war against the white man was incited principally by the Moslems."

[63] The details of this period from 1498 to 1530 in Lobato, Alexandre, *A expansão portuguesa em Moçambique de 1498 a 1530*, Lisbon, 1954.

as a modest agrarian monarchy, whose people lived close to the soil and whose prosperity such as it was depended on the exploitation of the land and the product of the soil.[64] The second cycle began with the opening up of the African coasts and the initiation of the slave trade, and the first commerce with that continent. The establishment of Portuguese India is the third and what Lucio de Azevedo calls the "Indian and the pepper cycle." Each of these stages or periods involves not only a different type of product and a distinct form of economic exploitation but implies some very definite modifications in the structure of the economic and social life of Portugal itself.

The shift from the purely agricultural to an economic order that depended on navigation and overseas trade for its subsistence was in itself a fundamental change in Portuguese life. The landed aristocracy declined in importance or urbanized itself in order to profit from the new tendency. There grew up in Lisbon, Porto, and the other Portuguese cities a new class of men whose interests were essentially mercantile and imperial with only a minimum of concern for those elements of the national life which had been the basis of Portuguese society since the days of Afonso Henriques.

The experience in India was followed, not in strict chronological order, to be sure, by the first "gold cycle" — that is, the gold from Mina on the Guinea coast, and from Sofala in Mozambique. Then came the "sugar empire," that is, the period during which sugar was one of the major products. This was true of the settlements in Madeira, in the Cape Verde Islands, and, above all, in Brazil where sugar and tobacco became the two basic products of the new economy that was coming into being. And finally came the epoch of gold and diamonds with the discovery of these two products in Brazil.

In most of the standard texts, the Portuguese empire is treated as an institution that reached its point of maximum development during the sixteenth century and then went into decline. Territorially, the empire has remained down to the present time much what it was at the end of the initial period of colonization, since Portugal never held any appreciable part of India; there was nothing comparable to the vast area called British India. In Malacca and the

---

[64] The indispensable work dealing with the series of "cycles" or transformations is de Azevedo, J. Lucio, *Epocas de Portugal económico. Esboços de história,* Lisbon, 1929.

Malay territories the Portuguese never laid claim to more than a few stations or factories here and there with no pretension to the setting up of a formal imperial government whereas in Africa, Portugal came through the trials of the sixteenth century and the formidable international rivalries of the later ones, especially with the British and the Dutch, in fairly good shape. The decline insofar as it occurred was in monopoly control of trade and, above all, in exclusiveness of influence. With the appearance of European rivals in the Far East and in Africa, Portugal was no longer able to do more than maintain what she had and suffer the loss of the prestige that she had gained from being for so many years the sole European influence in the area. For a long time, the Portuguese found it necessary to expend fortune and energy in preventing the Dutch in particular from seizing their property in Brazil, in India, in the Indonesian islands and in Africa.

Oliveira Martins, with that skepticism so typical of the Portuguese in dealing with their own affairs, writes bitingly of how the national prestige declined in India: "Begun in anarchy, the occupation of India from the beginning to the end was anarchical. The maritime and commercial policy of Francisco de Almeida, the empire of Afonso de Albuquerque, and the competent government of João de Castro all proved equally impotent in organizing effectively the Portuguese empire in the Orient."[65] The specific causes assigned by the historian to this incapacity to organize the Indian empire properly were as follows: the influence of the Renaissance and the prevalence of the "new thought" in the Europe of the sixteenth century which revolutionized human habits, mental and otherwise, exalted the individual and anarchized society in general. Portugal, claims Oliveira Martins, was not entirely free of this stigma. In addition there were all the enervating influences of the East and of Africa: the climate, the sensuality of the customs, the tendency to luxury, and the inability to resist on the part of the Portuguese themselves in the light of their more superficial than real adherence to Catholic belief and practice. Moreover, the Portuguese temper was simply not adapted to the patient labor of analysis and exploitation of the economy of these regions, as was the Dutch. Portugal displayed a gigantic burst of enthusiasm and energy and then collapsed into a sort of lethargy that was to endure

[65] Martins, Oliveira, *op. cit.*, p. 296.

until her claims had been overridden by stronger and more aggressive rivals.[66]

Rather than seek the causes of this crisis in the character of the people or in the national temperament, it seems more reasonable to note that a series of political circumstances combined toward the end of the sixteenth century to produce these effects. During the early part of the reign of Sebastian, divisions and conflicts within the court led to neglect of the defenses in India. The defeat of Portugal in Africa, to which we shall refer shortly and the tragedy of Dom Sebastian conspired to weaken Portuguese authority at its source. Then came the union with Spain and for sixty years Portugal was subordinated to the larger neighboring country; Spanish interests dominated and Portugal was dragged into every conflict in which the Spanish were involved.[67]

But overshadowing these considerations is a point which it seems to me to merit more than passing attention and that is the significance of this experiment in Africa and especially in Asia in establishing what the French call the "dialogue" between East and West. We are supremely conscious in this mid-twentieth century of the importance — the absolute urgency, indeed — of contact between Europe and what may be called, for the sake of a better term, non-Europe, spiritually and intellectually. It is no longer a matter of tea out of China or pepper out of India, but of the capacity of the European, and I include in this expression the inhabitants of America, to understand the thought and the sensibility of Asiatics and Africans. Portugal was the first European nation to undertake this delicate mission and it may be worthwhile to take note rapidly of how these two continents influenced the Portuguese way of life and what impact they had on the *mores* and the attitudes of a European people before whose eyes a vast and intriguing new world opened up.

The point deserves to be re-emphasized that the Portuguese approached this problem under the influence of their century-long struggle *against* Islam. There was, unquestionably, a psychological barrier, an intellectual obstruction that had to be overcome before the spiritual and cultural elements of these strange and heretofore

---

[66] *Ibid.*, p. 298.

[67] Schaefer, Henrique, *Historia de Portugal desde a fundação da monarchia até a revolução de 1820* (Portuguese translation from the German), Porto, 1898, Vol. IV, p. 173.

hostile civilizations could be appraised properly. Even more than the Spanish, the Portuguese had been conditioned to militancy against the Moslem. It began during the five centuries of struggle in the peninsula itself; it continued during the efforts to seize and retain Morocco and it continued in the waters of the Red Sea, the Indian Ocean, and the Persian Gulf. Spain, after all, fought the Moor to a standstill in 1492 and freed the nation's soil from his presence, and, aside from occasional encounters such as Lepanto, the Spanish turned their efforts westward and to a more limited degree in the non-Moslem Far East. The Portuguese, on the other hand, by virtue of this ceaseless engagement, maintained what Hernani Cidade calls their military "formation" and medieval spirit of crusade.[68]

This survey of the empire — and let it be understood once more that Portugal is quite incomprehensible if divorced from these territories overseas — would be more than normally inadequate were we not to devote a few pages at least to the consolidation of the colony in Brazil after the first ephemeral contact by Cabral and the somewhat disappointing reaction of the discoverers. Brazil is the largest, the most challenging, and the most impressive of all Portuguese ventures beyond the seas. Here the Lusitanian genius flowered in all of its splendor and demonstrated in a laboratory of social experimentation precisely how the Portuguese projected themselves beyond their borders and with what ultimate results. For Portugal created a race in Brazil. It built a society so novel by what can only be called an act of deliberate conception. It guided this new society for three hundred years until the burden became intolerable and events in Europe provoked by Bonaparte provided the only reasonable solution: the separation of the giant colony from the motherland that had given it birth.

The history of Brazil does not properly belong to this account of Portugal except during the period when the two were part of the same domain and owed allegiance to the same crowned head. In order to understand more perfectly how Portugal acted, it may be useful to suggest, first, a brief note on how Lisbon proposed to organize and govern this half continent to which it fell heir after 1500 and, second, how it proposed to populate these

[68] Cidade, Hernani, *A literatura portuguesa e a expansão ultramarina*, *op. cit.*, p. 13.

limitless forest wastes where the indigenous population was woefully inadequate to anything like the exploitation of its resources. In no other case, not even that of India, is the Portuguese character so eloquently depicted as in this great adventure of forging a new social order. In the Far East, the most that the Portuguese could do was to graft their own species on to the stock of those already there. It was a molding together on the basis of the ancient ethnic elements that already peopled India and China. In Brazil, the Indian was limited in number and the Portuguese did not have a surplus population that could be transplanted in any great number. The result was that a third element was introduced, the African, and Brazil was the wedding of American Indian, European Portuguese, and African black in a range of proportions and varieties. The story of how this came about and what it means is very definitely a part of the analysis of what Portugal was and by the same logic what it is today, for Brazil represents, let me repeat once again, the tangible evidence of Portuguese handiwork in this field.

The broad outline of how Brazil was blocked out by the Portuguese as their own preserve need not detain us for more than a few lines. It was plain after 1500 that the Portuguese were faced by something very different from what they had encountered in Africa. Just as the Spanish in the case of their first contacts with the Antilles brought to their activity the experience of the Canaries and the limited tropical knowledge they had acquired, so the Portuguese were prompted in Brazil to think in terms of what they knew from Africa. But Brazil was not Africa. And, for almost an entire century, from 1500 to well after 1570, the relations in Brazil were those of Europeans with Indians, for large contingents of Negroes did not begin to arrive until the last two decades of the sixteenth century.[69]

As has been suggested, Brazil offered a very special challenge to Portuguese ingenuity. It was not populated with an openly hostile, organized force such as Moorish Africa; it did not have any appreciable number of handy islands off the coast to serve as a springboard or an anchor as did Madeira, Cape Verde, and the islands off the west coast of Africa. Nevertheless, the system of

---

[69] See "Introduction" in Marchant, Alexander, *From Barter to Slavery. The Economic Relations of Portuguese and Indians in the Settlement of Brazil, 1500–1580*, Baltimore, 1942, pp. 13–27.

donatários had already been set up and worked to satisfaction. It was to be applied later to Brazil on a very extensive scale. A handful of Portuguese lived in an incalculably large area among a people more numerous than themselves and better adapted in some ways to the milieu than themselves. Therefore, the natural thing was to adopt those of the Indian practices that seemed desirable and made life a little more bearable.[70] In housing, dress, food, and other forms of daily living, they "went native," so to speak, for the simple reason that the Portuguese have always seemed to believe that a Brazilian Indian knew better how to live in Brazil than the recent arrival from Alentejo and by the same token the Angolan was probably aware of more effective ways of making a living in his own territory than was a settler fresh from Braga or Bragança. Colonial Brazil went through various stages before its course became more or less definitely fixed toward 1580:

I. From 1500 to about 1533 during which the Portuguese were principally interested in brazilwood or tradesmen on the coast.
II. The second from 1533 to 1549 with proprietary landlords seeking to settle colonies and develop agriculture.
III. 1549 to the end of the century. The French threat led to the sending out of more settlers, and with them came the establishments and the setting up of a formal government under a royal governor.[71]

The problem of cultural contact and the possibility of the Europeanization of the natives was implicit in the comments of Vaz de Caminha in his famous letter.[72] The arrival of Martim Affonso de Souza in Brazil in 1534 opened up the era of the *donatários* or proprietary landowners, which was essentially the policy of the crown to encourage individuals to assume the responsibility for the settlement and the defense of territory that the state itself was incapable of doing.[73] John III decided on the need for setting up a central government, and it was in 1548 that the new regime was instituted, with a civil and military administration and the usual

[70] De Varnhagen, Francisco Adolfo, *História geral do Brazil,* Rio de Janeiro, 1926, Vol. I, pp. 264–277.
[71] Marchant, *op. cit.,* pp. 23–24.
[72] Sousa Pinto, Manoel de, *Pero Vaz de Caminha e a carta do "achamento" do Brasil,* Lisboa, 1934; Prado, J. F. de Almeida, *Primeiros povoadores do Brasil, 1500–1530,* São Paulo, 1939, 2 ed.
[73] Abreu, Capistrano de, *Descobrimento do Brasil,* Rio de Janeiro, 1929, p. 89.

complement of functionaries and officials. São Salvador de Bahia became the capital city.

The religious welfare of Brazil was by no means neglected as the coming of the Jesuits in 1549 with Tomé de Sousa, the first governor, attests. Three years later the first bishopric was established. The work of the Jesuits is inextricably linked with the name of Manoel de Nóbrega whose personality towers above the entire human landscape of his time and belongs to the very smallish number of the very great missionaries of all times.[74]

The work of Father Nóbrega consisted primarily in bringing a more widely accepted morality into the social life of incipient Brazil where laxity was by no means a rarity. He was equally interested in taming the savages and especially in working out the bases of harmony between the various ethnic groups. Were he living in the twentieth century, we should be bound to speak of him as a specialist in "race relations." He concerned himself with the foundation of towns and in combating the enslavement of the Indians. With a vision that was far ahead of his time, he comprehended the necessity of making European culture and especially the Portuguese language and all that went with it accessible to the Indian. This was not merely a question of teaching a new tongue by rote or of making possible a minimum of communication. It represented a serious effort to devise a scheme whereby the essence of Portuguese culture could become a part of the moral and intellectual life of the aborigines. Father Nóbrega did not solve the problem in his day, nor for that matter has it been solved in ours, for every Hispanic American nation with any appreciable body of Indians retaining their community life is faced by this same task, from Mexico to Guatemala, to Peru, Ecuador, and Bolivia.

What seemed to be the most effective instruments for attaining this desirable end of a fusion or at least a harmonious juxtaposition of a highly developed European tradition and culture and one that was as yet primitive and immature? The twin forces to this end were miscegenation and Christianity, the only two that the Portuguese have ever found to really work.[75] The Portuguese may be accused of many things, as they have been, but there is no gain-

---

[74] De Moraes, José M., *Nóbrega, o primeiro jesuita do Brasil,* Rio de Janeiro, 1940.

[75] Rodrigues, José Honório, *Brasil,* Mexico, 1953, pp. 52–53.

saying their fundamental realism. In the matter of constituting a sound basis for the contact of two different races inhabiting the same territory and in close relations one with the other, they proceeded on the extremely sensible and realistic premise that races never live together without mixing; that racial miscegenation is the rule of life. Ergo, it is far more desirable to channel this inevitable tendency to the end of a rational mixed social order than to berate and deny it and suffer the untold misery of seeking a solution outside the framework of things as they are. The resultant society was not, of course, either an Indian or a Portuguese entity, but a new one that partook of both its parent stocks. But more of this a little later when we shall deal with the great influx of Africans who were to form so formidable a part of the Brazilian population in the making.

Brazil was open territory and the Portuguese began very early to push up and down the coast, establish towns and communities, and then move inland wherever it was physically possible and communication was to be established. It is not strange, if one looks at the map of Brazil, that even to the twentieth century the great land mass should be occupied primarily along the coastal fringes or that the interior, even in our day, should remain immense and plunged in deep shadows. The Atlantic coast affords no large river entrance into the hinterland. Aside from the feeble São Francisco River in the north, the coast is not indented at any point. The French intruders were expelled; Maranhão, in the north, occupied; and Belem do Pará, in the mouth of the Amazon, settled. The latter river was the great artery that led inland and it is to be noted that only a brief time was to pass before the course of this mighty stream was dotted with tiny establishments while the forest areas and tributaries on each side were to remain imperfectly known and less explored down to our day. The Portuguese were forced, during the seventeenth century, to engage in a monumental struggle against the Dutch who not only harassed their trade and attacked their colonies in the East, but actually settled in the region of Pernambuco in Brazil. During a brief period they gave promise of retaining a New Holland on the South American coast.[76] The Dutch occupa-

[76] See Wätjen, Hermann, *Das Holländische Kolonialreich in Brasilien*, The Hague, 1921; Boxer, C. R., *Salvador de Sá and the struggle for Brazil and Angola, 1602–1686*, London, 1952; and Rodrigues, José Honório, and Ribeiro, Joaquim, *Civilização holandesa no Brasil*, São Paulo, 1940.

tion was part of the world-wide bid for maritime power and primacy in the colonial sphere that the United Netherlands made in the seventeenth century. Again the union of Spain and Portugal had submitted the Portuguese to the depredations and attacks of Spain's enemies. The Dutch were active in North America, in Ceylon and the Indies, and their explorers were demonstrating an energy and enterprising spirit comparable to the Portuguese themselves in such figures as Van Diemens and others. Their claims over part of northeast Brazil were relatively short-lived, for Portugal did not yield other than temporarily before this pressure. Ultimately Olinda-Pernambuco which the Hollanders had made the center of their influence and regime was recovered by Portugal.[77]

Expansion went on at a regular rhythm, distinguished primarily by that peculiarly Portuguese institution in Brazil, the *bandeiras*. These were mass movements of population: a combination of *trek*, exploration, *razzia*, and colonization scheme, all rolled into one. The Portuguese were adept at this tactic which was part of the never ending process of pushing backward into open and unsettled territory and of struggling against the Spanish encroachments in lands that Portugal rightfully held to belong to it.

There is no more thrilling story than that of the "frontier in movement," as it has been called, of colonial Brazil. The Portuguese were handicapped, as we have seen, by the absence of navigable streams aside from the Amazon that led into the interior. They were forced to rely on arduous, difficult, and costly overland operations to assert their legal claims to lands that had been assigned them by the Treaty of Tordesillas but which had never been effectively occupied by settlers. Portuguese America was originally colonized in the area between Bahia and Rio de Janeiro. Two great masses of land, in the northeast and north and in the south stretching down to the Rio de la Plata basin, were left to later centuries to be filled in. To prevent the Spanish from taking full advantage of the discovery of the Amazon by Francisco de Orellana, a Portuguese, Pedro Teixeira, undertook to traverse the route in 1539, to lay formal claim to the Amazon valley for the Portuguese. The *bandeirantes* from São Paulo were on the move as early as 1602, and one of their number, Nicolau Barreto, was said to have penetrated as far as the

[77] Geyl, P., *Geschiedenis van de Nederlandse stam, Amsterdam,* 1953, Vol. II, p. 481 *seq.*

Paraguay River and into what is today Bolivia.[78] The invasion of Rio Grande do Sul was initiated in 1635 and with bands of men on the move westward and southward Portugal was rapidly pushing out her land frontiers far beyond the limits that had been fixed at the end of the fifteenth century. From other strategic points in the center and north, similar expeditions were moving inland to create fragile but permanent centers of population.[79] Other *bandeiras*, defined poetically as "a city traveling with its officials and citizens," operated from almost every focal point on the coastland.[80]

Two periods were especially tragic for Portuguese Brazil: the first, the sixty years of Spanish domination that ended in 1640, and the second, the regime of Pombal in Portugal, about which we shall have something to say in a later chapter and which was distinguished largely by the expulsion of the Jesuits and what Gilberto Freyre has called, with so picturesque a substantive, the "Pombalization" of the great colony.

Colonial Brazil with its sugar, diamonds, and the gold of Minas Geraes was a complex organism: Indians and half-breeds, slaves and mulattoes, *bandeirantes* and *grands seigneurs*. Missionaries of the caliber of Manoel de Nóbrega worked diligently. Four years later came another remarkable priest of the Society, José de Anchieta, whose works and deeds might well fill many pages and who taught the Indians Latin while studiously learning Tupi himself![81] In the next century it was Father Antonio Vieira who filled a whole age and brought torrents of light into a Brazil still in the throes of social and ethnic gestation. It was a Portuguese Brazil of gold and the hunt for more gold, of audacious speculation and economic exploitation on the meagerest of investments. Until the last of the eighteenth century and the beginning of the nineteenth, when the shadow of the French eagles were cast over Portugal, lonely settlements on the Guaporé and Tocantins, on the Xingu and the Araguaya, as well as on the rolling plains of Rio Grande and the

[78] Ellis, Alfredo, *O bandeirismo paulista e o recúo do meridiano*, São Paulo, 1934, 2 ed., p. 33.

[79] Vianna, Urbino, *Bandeiras e sertanistas bahianos*, São Paulo, 1935.

[80] d'Altavilla, Jayme, *História da civilisação das Alagoas*, Maceió, Alagoas, 1935, p. 18.

[81] Of Father Anchieta it has been said that "he lived at the end of the world in 1560, protected by miracles, walking on waves and transported by the gift of ubiquity" (de Lima, Jorge, *Anchieta*, Rio de Janeiro, 1934, p. 8).

parched dust bowl of the northwest, attested to the presence of Portugal.

Philip Ainsworth Means calls attention to how the Spanish in Mexico and Peru found themselves in native states strongly organized for war and enjoying a civilization in which they had much to admire and where it was possible to construct what this historian dubs "a bi-racial colonial policy."[82] The Portuguese found themselves in a Brazil where the indigenous races were numerous, sometimes hostile, often nomadic, and extremely primitive and where, in general, the trappings of anything like an advanced material civilization were lacking. They nevertheless undertook, first of all, a "bi-racial" policy and, once this had proved inadequate for the social and economic needs of the expanding colony, they began what may be called, for the lack of a better word, their "triracial policy." It is with particular reference to the African influx into Brazil that a great deal has been written, and so important is the subject and so faithful a reflection of Portuguese attitudes and policy that it would seem proper to summarize in a few pages the essential features of this sociological experiment, the like of which has probably never occurred anywhere in modern times before.

Slavery was definitely not unknown to Western Europe before the fifteenth century and there had been for a considerable time some African influence on Portugal. However, the point of departure for a consideration of the traffic as it affected the Portuguese and their empire may be 1440–1444. Up to that time the slave trade had been largely in the hands of Arabs and the routes out of black Africa were overland. After that date, although the former trade did not dry up, it became the common practice to transport the "black pieces," as they were called, by water.[83] It was at this time too that a new factor was introduced into the institution of slavery, namely that Europeans themselves became not only the beneficiaries but the carriers of slaves from Africa. The discovery of an immense supply of human resources in Africa and the opening up of a relatively underpopulated continent across the Atlantic constituted a coincidence that caused the trade to expand in a way that would never have been conceivable had Europe alone

[82] Means, Philip Ainsworth, *The Spanish Main*, New York, 1935, p. 15.

[83] Saca, José Antonio, *Historia de la esclavitud de la raza africana en el Nuevo Mundo*, Barcelona, 1879, p. 26.

been the destination of the human cargoes from the dark continent. In Zurara's chronicle of the discovery and conquest of Guinea we have reference to the slaves captured on one of these early voyages.[84]

"The market which Portugal and Spain could furnish for negroes must have been speedily saturated and the commerce in negroes have remained but a small part of European commerce, monopolized by the Portuguese, had not the new world discovered a need for labor which the native Indian could not meet."[85] This trade began to take a lively turn almost from the arrival of the Spanish in Hispaniola and of the Portuguese in Brazil. Governor Ovando had instructions when he took office in Hispaniola to introduce slaves and the implication was that even before 1502 there was some traffic in Negroes.[86]

But it is Brazil that interests us particularly in this review of the phenomenon of a multiracial society formed deliberately by the Portuguese settlers with the encouragement and even the insistence of their government.

First of all, however, a word of caution regarding one fact that is basic to all understanding of the Negro in the New World and it is this: the Africans who came to America were not uniform, nor did they all derive from the same areas nor indeed did they all possess a similar cultural background. It is, perhaps, platitudinous to insist that the Negro peoples are no more identical among themselves than are all Europeans or all persons of the Indian races.[87] There were numerous branches of Negroes from different "nations" which varied among themselves as to culture, social experience, and religion. During the age that preceded the discoveries, as well as during that period, the African continent was a "peripheric continent," that is to say, one which received cultural "radiations" from various other parts of the surrounding world: North Africa was not black at all and partook of the Mediterranean civilizations

[84] De Zurara, Gomes Eannes, *The Chronicle of the Discovery and Conquest of Guinea*, London, 1896, translated by C. Raymond Beazley and Edgar Prestage.

[85] Donnan, Elizabeth, *Documents Illustrative of the History of the Slave Trade to America*, Washington, D. C., 1930, Vol. I, p. 14.

[86] Scelle, Georges, *La traité négrière aux Indes de Castille, Contrats et traités d'assiento*, Paris, 1906, Vol. I, p. 122.

[87] In my translation of the text of the late Brazilian Africanist, Arthur Ramos, *The Negro in Brazil*, Washington, D. C., 1939, a summary is suggested of the origins of the Negro population, the impact and contribution to both colonial and modern Brazil.

with which it had had contact since antiquity; East Africa was strongly under the influence of the Arabs, their traders, their religion, and their speech; while much of West Africa and even the central and southern portions of the continent were influenced in turn by the mercantile peoples of Europe, notably the Portuguese.[88]

Africa has always revealed a startlingly large variety of cultural levels and political forms as well as degrees of isolation or of permeability. In some instances we have the impression that until the continent was opened up to contact with Europe, that sheer and unmitigated savagery prevailed with barbarism the exclusive order of the day. Still, no people, no matter how isolated in appearance are immune to some influence from outside and this is true even of prediscovery Africa.[89] As information regarding the Negro past has increased in the period since slave running ceased to be the major preoccupation of the outsider in this continent, it is evident that Black Africa was in many cases highly organized and, according to its lights, socially developed. The kingdoms and empires of Gana, Bambara, and the Sudan, the Haussa states and Bornu as well as those of Angola and among the Zulus provide striking evidence that Negro Africa was no chaos of naked savages given over to the foulest of practices and quite unacquainted with any of the disciplines that are associated with civilized conduct and life.[90] Africa was, and to a very real extent still is, distinguished by the historically decisive characteristic of inaccessibility. In addition, the African population has always been insufficient for the best of economic health.[91]

The Portuguese among other Europeans were in touch with almost every variety of African peoples, from the Hamitic groups in the north to the Sudanese, Bantus, Hottentots, Bushmen, and even the Pygmies of the center. From where did the slaves transplanted to Brazil come? For many years there was considerable confusion on this point since the dealers in human flesh during

---

[88] Weulersse, Jacques, *L'Afrique noire*, Paris, 1934, p. 17.

[89] Paulme, Denise, *Les civilisations africaines*, Paris, 1953, pp. 119–120.

[90] See Labrouret, Henri, *Histoire des noirs d'Afrique*, Paris, 1950; Hardy, G., *Vue générale de l'histoire d'Afrique*, Paris, 1922; Delafosse, *Les noirs de l'Afrique*, Paris, 1922; and Frobenius, Leo, *Kulturgeschichte Afrikas*, Vienna, 1933. A first-rate summary of these background features by Amanke Okafor, "West African Background: an Outline," in *The New West Africa*, London, 1953, p. 20 *seq.* Craft-Johnson, I. C., *African Glory*, New York, 1954.

[91] Macmillan, W. M., *Africa Emergent*, London, 1949, pp. 23, 37.

the centuries when the traffic was in vogue had never been particularly scrupulous about keeping a careful record of the racial or cultural origins of their cargoes. Suffice it that the Negroes were available, reasonably healthy and capable of working, and it was a matter of indifference whether they were of this or that tribe.

The date of the introduction of the first Negroes into Brazil is unknown. In the first sugar mills that functioned in the captaincy of São Vicente, Negro slaves were employed and certain authorities have claimed that slaves arrived with the expedition of Martim Affonso de Souza in 1531.[92] With the expanding importance of sugar cane as one of the major crops in Brazil, the Portuguese crown granted to each mill owner the privilege of introducing 120 slaves each from Guinea and the Island of São Tomé. The arrival of slaves in growing numbers did not fail to occupy the attention of Father Nóbrega who complained of the danger for the city of Bahia.[93] Royal legislation of the sixteenth and seventeenth centuries regulated the traffic and fixed its conditions.

The total number of slaves entering Brazil cannot be fixed with anything like precision. It must be remembered that simultaneously with the introduction of Africans and later, during the seventeenth century when Negro slaves became scarcer, there was also the enslavement of Indians which was one of the more lively by-products, so to speak, of the expeditions of the *bandeirantes* to which we have referred.[94]

It is claimed that at the end of the eighteenth century, out of a total population of 3,250,000, the number of free Negroes were some 406,000 and the slaves, 1,582,000. In the official statistics of 1817–1818 just before independence, there were nearly two million slaves listed in a population that did not reach four million.[95]

---

[92] Varnhagen, *História geral do Brasil, op. cit.* An old work includes mention of this same date, Malheiro, Perdigão, *A escravidão no Brasil*, Rio de Janeiro, 1867, p. 6. Also Ramos, Arthur, *As culturas negras no Novo Mundo*, Rio de Janeiro, 1937, p. 281.

[93] Ramos, *op. cit.*, p. 282.

[94] Leite, Serafim, S.J., *História da Companhia de Jesus no Brasil*, Lisbon and Rio de Janeiro, 1938, Vol. I, p. 251 *seq.* This fundamental study of the Society of Jesus in Brazil calls attention to some of the moral complications involved in this business of slavery. Many of the *bandeirantes* made incursions into Spanish territory to seize Indians, thus combining a most lucrative trade with the expansion of Portuguese claims.

[95] Pierson, Donald, *Negroes in Brazil*, Chicago, 1942, pp. 29–30; De Moraes,

For over three hundred years the slave trade flourished between Africa and Brazil, extending from the small bases on the west coast at the beginning to Angola and Mozambique later, as the demands of an expanding Brazilian economy absorbed more and more manual laborers. The total number over the years has been estimated from three to eighteen millions. The best estimate places the total at perhaps five millions.[96] The regions and ethnic groups from which the slaves came covered a goodly portion of the geography of Africa. There were slaves from the so-called "Mina Coast," and from Angola between 1790 and 1795 over 17,000 Africans were landed. Ships plied between the Brazilian ports of Bahia, Pernambuco, Rio de Janeiro, and Maranhao and the African cities of Luanda, Benguela, and Novo Redondo.[97] Negroes from among the Yorubas, Ewes, Haussas, Fulahs, Mandingas, and Ashantis swelled the number that poured into the colony and many of the slaves were from Islamized Africa, particularly the Sudanese and the Haussas and there seems little doubt that they were not averse to making converts among the fetishist or Aninust Negroes with whom they came in contact in the New World. This fact has a direct bearing on the interpretation of African influence in modern Brazil for vestiges of Moslem culture and practices have been noted in predominantly Negro communities down to the present day.

It was not unknown that slaves were literate and some of them assuredly spoke Arabic.[98] Large batches of Bantus came from southern Africa and especially from Mozambique, landing principally in Maranhão, Rio de Janeiro, and Pernambuco from where they were not infrequently transported to São Paulo and the south. The full story of how the Negro adapted himself to the climate, conditions of life, and culture of the predominant Portuguese element in

---

Evaristo, *A escravidão africana no Brasil*, São Paulo, 1933; and Dornas Filho, João, *A escravidão no Brasil*, Rio de Janeiro, 1939.

[96] Ramos, Arthur, *The Negro in Brazil*, *op. cit.*, p. 6.

[97] Graham, Maria, *Journal of a Voyage to Brazil, 1821–1823*, London, 1824, p. 146. Quoted in Pierson, *op. cit.*, p. 35.

[98] Ramos, *O negro brasileiro*, Rio de Janeiro, 1934, pp. 58–62. These Islamized Negroes who quickly produced a religious syncretism with fetishism were among the most rebellious of all slaves and responsible for many of the slave uprisings that occurred during the colonial period. "The Negro adherents of Mohammed bloodied the streets of the city of Bahia at the beginning of the nineteenth century" (Carneiro, Edison, *Religiões negras*, Rio de Janeiro, 1936, p. 25).

Brazil is as dramatic as any to be found in the annals of social history. Gilberto Freyre has developed more effectively than any contemporary investigator the profundity of this influence and its meaningfulness for the emerging cultural and social pattern of Portuguese America. The predilection of the Portuguese for the darker races was one of the stimuli in the rapid process of miscegenation.[99] The Negro, as the successor of the Indian, was the architect, physically and, to an astonishing degree, culturally of the new Brazil.[100] Sufficient reference has been made in the course of these pages to the absence, insofar as is humanly conceivable of race prejudice among the Portuguese. Freyre insists that "racial purity never influenced or limited the efforts of the Portuguese."[101] This was due certainly in large measure both to historical experience and contact and to the predominance of the Catholic faith among them that did not seek to place barriers in the way of ethnic intermixture.[102]

This did not mean, to be sure, that there was never a reaction or that pride of race did not exist among certain social classes. But taken by and large, the Portuguese generally accepted the facts of life as they were and made no pretense of creating overseas the precise ethnic image of the motherland, settling for what may be called quite frankly the "experimentation of hybridism."[103]

It would be straying far afield to indicate the manner in which the Negro has left his permanent imprint on Brazilian life, or on what may more properly be called the Luso-Afro-American culture that Portugal left to independent Brazil as its most significant heritage. In almost every field of art, music, letters, politics, folk-

---

[99] Freyre, Gilberto, *Casa grande e senzala*, Rio de Janeiro, 1938, p. 7: " . . . in terms of propensity toward miscegenation, no colonizing people among the modern exceeded or even equaled the Portuguese on this point.

[100] Belo, José Maria, *Panorama do Brasil*, Rio de Janeiro, 1936, p. 62: "Among the three human elements that form the basis of the Brazilian population, the Portuguese predominate because they were the most active and competent; the Indian and above all the Negro were the material instrument of their constructive labor."

[101] Freyre, Gilberto, *Uma cultura ameaçada; a luso-brasileira*, Recife, 1940, pp. 43–44.

[102] *Ibid.*, pp. 29–30.

[103] Franco, Affonso Arinos de Mello, *Conceito de civilisação brasileira*, São Paulo, 1936, p. 95. This writer suggests that "the impartial acceptance of these elements in the formation of our national organism — is practically unanimous in all really representative circles of Brazil."

ways and popular customs, language and thought, the Negro has played an important and sometimes a decisive role. Brazil is in the merging of the various racial elements the test case of how Portugal believed in and practiced in reality a policy and a way of life in which the non-European was not merely associated with the predominant culture, but was joined to it intimately and for all time. The Portuguese could have followed no procedure more certain to guarantee the integrity of their territories nor demonstrate more palpably their recognition of the intrinsic values of other cultures and other bloods.[104]

---

[104] A suggestion of the wide influence of the Negro on Portuguese colonial society is evident in the titles of a few of the more noteworthy books on the subject, the following of which we have not had occasion to mention up to now: Rodrigues, Nina, *O animismo fetichista dos negros bahianos*, Rio de Janeiro, 1935, on religion; Freyre, Gilberto, and collaborators, *Novos estudos afro-brasileiros*, Rio de Janeiro, 1937, in the essays of this series we discover how deep the influence from Africa was in such varied matters as music, and even the typical cuisine of modern Brazil; Ramos, Arthur, *O folklore negro do Brasil*, Rio de Janeiro, 1935; Roquette Pinto, E., *Ensaios de anthropologia brasiliana*, São Paulo, 1938; Freyre, Gilberto, *Sobrados e mucambos*, São Paulo, 1936; Querino, Manuel, *Costumes africanos no Brasil*, Rio de Janeiro, 1938; Carneiro, Edison, *Negros bantus*, Rio de Janeiro, 1937; Carneiro, Souza, *Mitos africanos no Brasil*, São Paulo, 1937. In language, a fundamental work is Mendonça, Renato, *O português do Brasil*, Rio de Janeiro, 1936, and, by the same author, *A influência africana no português do Brasil*, São Paulo, 1935. Also Raimundo, Jacques, *A lingua portuguesa no Brasil*, Rio de Janeiro, 1941. Even the influence of the African population on the diseases of Brazil has merited attention, as evidenced in the work of de Freitas, Octavio, *Doenças africanas no Brasil*, São Paulo, 1935.

Chapter IV

STRESS AND STRAIN: THE DECLINE FROM GREATNESS

The gigantic effort of mariners and crusaders gave Portugal an empire; the inherent weaknesses of the nation, especially its limited population and the hazards of international politics placed it on the defensive from the sixteenth century onward. Spain completed its national unity and with the expulsion of the last remnants of the Moors, turned its attention to expansion and through the services of Columbus and Magellan achieved an empire. The Moors in North Africa harassed and besieged the Portuguese garrisons at every point, obliging one after the other to abandon their positions. John III, who came to the throne in 1521, was fully aware not only of the material dangers that beset his domains everywhere but of the moral threat of religious dissension that was no respecter of frontiers or cultures. This was the Europe of the Reformation and the remote Iberian peninsula was not immune to the winds that blew from Wittenberg. Portugal requested the establishment of the Holy Office of the Inquisition — about which a great deal of nonsense has been written — whose basic purpose was to preserve the spiritual unity of the country, sorely pressed by the currents of thought that were running high everywhere from Poland to Scotland. The Inquisition and the introduction of the Society of Jesus contributed effectively to preserving Portugal from the ravages of the religious wars that desolated France and menaced the integrity of so many other European lands. Religious orthodoxy, let it be emphasized, was deemed in this age concomitant with national security, and the terms of the Reform were considered in Portugal to be just as dangerous to the well-being of the body politic as Marxism is in our time in the Western world.

The Jesuits arrived in 1540, and, in addition to their remarkable contribution to the propagation of the faith in territories overseas, they became in many ways the mentors of Portuguese culture, in view of their influential position at the University of Coimbra and in the centers of classical education all over the country. They bolstered a Portugal that might have succumbed to external pressures and internal doubts; they were in a very real sense the architects of the emerging culture of Portuguese America. But the significant trait of this turbulent period is that it was rapidly becoming transformed into an era of defense. Portugal was losing the initiative and henceforth it was largely a matter of conserving what she possessed and staving off the inevitability of retreat.

Four hundred years of Portuguese history, roughly speaking, spread out before us from John III to Manuel, last king of the country, overthrown in 1910. It is a long period of trial and disappointment, of foreign occupation and incursion, of loss and retrenchment, and, what is the most serious of all, of a growing sentiment of futility that gripped the Portuguese people as they lost faith in their own potentialities. How severe this strain was, may be judged from the salient events:

The military defeat and death of Sebastian in North Africa;
The union of the Spanish and Portuguese crowns with the inevitable submergence of the latter within the larger scheme of Hispanic empire;
The Pombal revolution which deformed and disfigured the natural course of Portuguese history;
The earthquake that destroyed Lisbon;
The Napoleonic invasion;
The loss of Brazil with its independence in 1822;
The monarchical stagnation of the rest of the nineteenth century;
The Republican experiment of 1910 and liberalism until the National Revolution of 1926.

It is my purpose in the following pages to review rapidly the broad events that illustrate this process since their understanding lies at the basis of the renovation that came when Dr. Oliveira Salazar left the lecture hall at Coimbra to take up the task of reforming the finances of the nation. The story of Portugal is not merely one of a growing political flabbiness but of moral decay working from within. Nations like individuals are subject to the loss of their will to achieve, even of their will to survive. Nations like individuals run the perpetual risk of losing their soul through betrayal of the vocation for which they have been destined. For long years Portugal failed to perform what may be called the duties or obligations of its station in the world. This moral abdication could not be redressed until an agonizing examination of conscience had taken place and a re-education of the collective will had been accomplished to the end that responsibility replaced lethargy and an unreal escapism that had captured the national mind.

Young Prince Sebastian grew up in an atmosphere of pride and hopefulness. Endowed with a lively imagination, he was fed on the annals of India and Morocco. Not so many years before he ascended the throne, the hard-pressed Portuguese had abandoned several strong places in North Africa: Aguer, Safim, Azamor, Arzila, and Alcacer-Sequer.[1] Sebastian was definitely a throwback to the age of the Crusades and his zeal knew no bounds in matters concerning the extension of the faith among the infidels.[2]

Sebastian burned with religious fervor, national pride, and royal ambition, and the last was not the least of the motivations that led him to dream of expanding Portugal's empire in North Africa, for the Spain of Philip II, his uncle, was no mean stimulus to the sense of emulation of the Portuguese sovereign. The second half of the sixteenth century was a culminating point in Portuguese history. Many of the king's entourage were convinced that the nation needed rest; that it had reached its maximum capacity and that every counsel of common sense dictated that the wisest course was to let well enough alone and retain what had honorably been won. New adventures to an overtaxed and exhausted people could mean nothing but an invitation to calamity. But Sebastian was of another mind. This "posthumous son of the Middle Ages," as he was called by one writer, was the last person to be seduced by the prudence of those who advised moderation.[3]

---

[1] Queiroz Velloso, J. M. de, *D. Sebastião 1554–1578*, Lisbon, 1935, 2 ed., pp. 90–91.

[2] Father Baltasar Teles in his *Chrónica da Companhia de Jesu na Provincia de Portugal* records how the young prince wrote in a Missal that he hoped that the good Fathers would pray that "God keep me chaste and very zealous in spreading his holy faith all over the world."

[3] Dias, Carlos Malheiro, *O Piedoso e o Desejado*, Lisbon, 1925, p. 118. A classical historian writes of Sebastian in this manner: "The courageous spirit and Catholic fervor that moved the heroic Prince breathed valor and faith, but the lack of moderation led to the most disastrous collapse" (Rocha Pitta, Sebastião da, *História de América portuguesa*, Lisbon, 1880, 2 ed., p. 91).

Sebastian sought the aid of Philip II and was received with reservations. The Pope granted a bull proclaiming the proposed Portuguese venture a crusade, which it definitely was, and the Portuguese sovereign proceeded to engage among his forces not only his own subjects but the greatest variety of foreigners. On June 24, 1578, a huge fleet, numbering some five hundred vessels, set out for Africa. All signs seemed propitious that summer for there was civil strife among the Moors and assurances from the discontented factions that aid would be forthcoming to the invading Portuguese. There was some disquietude on the Portuguese side for, in view of the temerity of the king and his love of action, there was fear that with no provision made for the succession in the event of his death, Portugal would fall indeed on evil times since there was no heir to the throne.[4] But this doubt was quickly smothered in the general exaltation that accompanied the fleet and the conviction that with this feat of arms, Portuguese prestige would be restored in all its plenitude.[5]

Whatever military merits Sebastian might have had, he was definitely not possessed of anything like good political sense. The fact that he had announced that after defeating the Moors he proposed to force baptism on every Jew on whom he could lay hands in North Africa did nothing to endear him to the Israelites who had taken refuge in that area and who were quick to make known these sentiments.[6]

At Alcacer-Quibir, the Portuguese and their allies met the Moslems under the dying Abd El-Malik and on that August day in 1578, the flower of Portuguese knighthood was cut down by the onrushing Moors precisely at the moment when, in the exultation of victory, the Christians prepared to rest. In the clash of the battle, Sebastian disappeared, no one knew where nor in what circumstances. The legends multiplied and from that date henceforth the monarch who gave his life on the Moroccan desert for God and country bore the popular name of the *Desejado*, the one

[4] Múrias, Manuel, *A política de Africa de El-Rei D. Sebastião*, Lisbon, 1926, p. 48.

[5] Alessandro Brandano in his *Storia delle guerre di Portogallo*, Venice, 1689, p. 4, notes that if Sebastian were successful in his undertaking, he would be "outstandingly conspicuous and feared by every nation in the world."

[6] Esaguy, José de, *Um relato inédito sobre o desembarque de El-Rei D. Sebastião em Tanger*, Lisbon, 1935, p. 15.

whom his stricken people desired above all else.[7] With this catastrophe, there vanished not only a dream but a great deal of the reality. What dizzy heights Portugal might have scaled had Sebastian triumphed on that summer day in Morocco! With India in her hands, Brazil in full development, the victorious monarch would have been heralded as the leading prince in Christendom and on his return might well have carried out the suggested marriage with the daughter of Philip II. He might, if Providence had so decreed, become what Charles V had never managed to be, the ruler of a united Christian world under the aegis of Lusitania.[8]

Pending the confirmation of Sebastian's death — and there were many in this case as in all analogous cases who persisted in the belief that one day he would return — Cardinal Henrique assumed the duties of chief of state. There was no direct descendant, but no dearth of potential candidates for the vacant throne. There is no need for the coherence of this narrative to examine the aspirants or the basis of their claims. Suffice it to say that among them was Philip of Spain, whose pretension was solidly based on family ties: grandson of Manuel I on the maternal side. For two and a half years, Portugal lived in fear of the outcome of the intrigues around the throne until, on the death of the Cardinal, the Duke of Alba led a Spanish army of occupation and, in December of 1580, Philip himself crossed the frontier at Elvas, received the homage of a certain number of the notables and called for a meeting of the Cortes at Tomar in April next when the dual monarchy would be proclaimed. Portugal had ceased to exist as an independent entity.

The sixty years of Spanish rule constitute a hiatus in the history of Portugal. The national energies and hopes are concentrated on removing the foreign yoke and restoring a national dynasty. Foreign affairs were no longer urgent, for Portuguese policy was now subordinated to Spain and Spain's enemies determined those whom Portugal should engage in combat. The effects were far reaching, as we have noted in the case of Asia and Brazil, for the immense Portuguese empire was open now to countless depredations directed against Philip II and his Spain.

If Portuguese hopes had been interred at Alcacer-Quibir in a

[7] Costa, Brochado, *D. Sebastião o Desejado*, Lisbon, 1941, p. 350.
[8] Ameal, João, *História de Portugal*, Porto, 1940, pp. 353–354.

grandiose gesture of recklessness, a sort of national *hara-kiri* on an epic scale, the legend of King Sebastian sustained national hopes during the long Spanish twilight — a legend that grew and was nourished in the desolation of defeat and the bitterness of deflated pride. If Philip II had the power and prestige, it was the Duchess of Bragança who probably had better legal claims to the throne than did the Spanish monarch. But Portugal in the aftermath of Alcacer-Quibir was in no position to continue the fight for survival after losing the battle for glory.

Portugal was not incorporated or annexed as might be expected. The union was to be purely personal and every guarantee was extended the Portuguese that their autonomy: language, institutions, laws, and even the personnel of their civil service, should be maintained intact and undisturbed by the new regime. Obviously this experience has been interpreted in diametrically opposite ways according to whether one contemplates the situation from the Portuguese or the Spanish side. The claim that all Portugal accepted the situation docilely was very far from the case. There was active opposition under the direction of a remarkable individual, Dom Antonio, prior of Crato, who declared himself king at Santarem. The prior sought to arouse his people in 1580 as they had been in 1385 at the time of John of Aviz, but the times were out of joint and the response was lacking. The French sought to profit from the confusion and support Dom Antonio even to the extent of sending a fleet to aid him in the Azores, only to have it promptly destroyed by the Spanish. Certain sectors of opinion waited for Sebastian to return and set things right.[9]

João Ameal writes of the period of captivity as follows:

> The Phenomenon was inevitable. We ceased to constitute a center of attraction and became a part of the Spanish empire. Whatever may have been the good or the bad intentions and in the case of Philip II it was clearly more astuteness and prudence than genuine respect toward us . . . gradual incorporation was bound to be tried. We were forced to suffer a foreign yoke.[10]

The idea that Philip II dreamed of ultimate identification of the two countries is indicated in many ways for among other projects — and Philip was especially strong on projects — was that

[9] Martins D'Antas, Miguel, *Les faux Dom Sébastien*, Paris, 1866.
[10] Ameal, João, *História de Portugal*, *op. cit.*, p. 375.

of making the Tagus navigable from Lisbon to Toledo and accomplish what the Romans had attempted with a highway from the center of the peninsula to the Atlantic coast, "that is to say, unite horizontally the interior of Spain with the coast of Portugal via Merida, in order to erase the idea that Portugal was a separate territorial unit."[11] The problem cannot be reduced to the simple proportions of bureaucratic control or the fact that Philip respected scrupulously his commitment to name no Spaniard to an administrative post in Portugal. Behind these externals was an idea, which had long germinated in the mind of Philip, and it envisaged the union of the two peninsular people in terms of the world policy of the Habsburg monarchy. The conflict with the Lutheran and Calvinist heresies, plus the evident proximity of a showdown with England engendered in Philip's imagination the vision of the two arms or branches of the Iberian family now joining to create a balance that would tip in favor of Catholic-Mediterranean Europe.[12]

The much desired Iberian union was the one substantial result to which the Spanish could point with pride in the common administration.[13] But all efforts were vain in the face of the dislike of the Portuguese for foreign control of any sort, and Spanish control in particular, and the disastrous consequences to the nations of the common destiny with Spain, as reflected in the crushing defeat of the Armada in which Portugal lost its fleet, along with that of Philip, in 1588.[14] England's seadogs, Hawkins, Drake, and

---

[11] Pemán, José María, *Breve historia de España*, Madrid, 1950, p. 246.

[12] Maura, Duque de, *Grandeza y decadencia de España*, Madrid, n.d., p. 169 *seq.* The text of a lecture delivered at Coimbra under the title, "The Imperial Idea of Philip II": "The prospect of his accession to the throne of Portugal seemed to define in a definite way his destiny. God who writes straight with crooked lines, separated the two peninsular peoples so they simultaneously might devote their different talents to the common task of civilization. Once this objective was attained, it was his task to unite and consolidate them. Spain and Portugal together would build the Atlantic empire."

[13] Ballesteros y Beretta, Antonio, *Historia de España y su influencia en la historia universal*, Barcelona, 1926, Vol. IV, p. 110: "The profitable results of the annexation had been in the first place the accomplishment of Iberian union, the participation of Portuguese counsellors in Spanish affairs and the considerable increase of the territories under the Spanish monarchy."

[14] Crevea, Rafael Altamira y, *Historia de España y de la civilización española*, Barcelona, 1913, Vol. III, pp. 98–99: "But the conduct of Philip was useless in the face of the hostility of the [Portuguese] people, who educated for centuries in the hatred of Spain, opposed the Spanish occupation and were profoundly hurt in their national pride." The French ambassador in Madrid summed the

Frobisher, were free to prey untiringly on Portuguese trade. As of 1581, William of Orange was rid of Spanish control and joined the ranks of the despoilers of the Hispanic-Lusitanian empire. Francis Drake seized the *São Filipe* off the Azores and Burrough, another English hero, or pirate according to the point of view, made one of the richest hauls of all time with the *Madre de Deus*, returning with a fabulous cargo from India. The Count of Cumberland blockaded Lisbon, while the Dutch joined the sport. Cornelius Houtman had initiated the Dutch journeys to the Far East in 1597 and from that date on the "Hollanders in the tropics" became a new chapter in the history of imperial rivalries.[15]

The year in which the Hispanic-Portuguese personal union took place was one of the decisive years in modern history; indeed, it may almost be looked on as the real beginning, the legitimate frontier between the medieval, which culminates in the explosion of the discoveries and conquests, and the modern in which the fundamental lines of political relations are laid down. "It is at this moment and only then, at the time of the conflict with Portugal, that the great struggle for the Atlantic and the domination of the world is joined. Spanish policy turns with every ounce of its strength toward the ocean and western Europe."[16] The year 1580 was, in effect, a crucial moment — one of those turning points when the stream of events that has been harnessed and channeled suddenly breaks out from its course and leads to a completely new orientation. Fifteen hundred and eighty was the year when Philip II began what may properly be called his new policy of aggression after an initial stage during which his claim to fame was that of the presentation of peace. Those who stood with the Spanish king when he listened to those who were called the "peace party," Ruy Gomez and Antonio Pérez, were no longer in favor. Spain — and Portugal necessarily — was now embarked on a program of energetic

situation up by writing that the Portuguese would prefer "to belong to the Devil before belonging to Castille" (Mousset, Albert, *Histoire d'Espagne*, Paris, 1947, p. 223).

[15] "The formation of the Iberian union between 1580 and 1640 opened the Portuguese empire to Dutch activity. In the waters of the Far East the Dutch had completely ruined this empire from the beginning of the seventeenth century, leaving only Macao on the Asiatic Pacific coast" (Hauser, Henri, *La prépondérance espagnole 1599–1660*, Paris, 1933, pp. 423–424).

[16] Braudel, Fernand, *La Méditerranée et le monde méditerranéen à l'époque de Philippe II*, Paris, 1949, p. 1020.

intervention in the affairs of western Europe, which is equivalent to saving the world.

The tragedy of Portugal at this time and in other contingencies of history has been that she was the victim of circumstances and combinations of power over which the nation had no control or even influence. As long as Spain was divided and as long as the unsolved question of the presence of the Moslems remained, the Spanish were no threat. The formation of the world-wide empire of Charles V changed all that and with Philip II it is doubtful if the Portuguese could have retained their independence even if Alcacer-Quibir had not intervened to produce that precise juncture from which the Spanish monarch drew the maximum advantage. The only way in which Portugal could have resisted Spanish penetration and control was by an alliance with its Protestant foes: Calvinist France, England, or the Dutch. In fact the major weakness of the prior of Crato, in his dogged determination to carry on against the Spanish occupier, was that he undertook to return to Portugal on an English ship and toward 1590 entered into negotiations with the Turks. The destruction of Portugal, even more than the defeat of the Armada eight years later, marked the shift in the center of Spanish political gravitation and the ensuing humiliation to which she was submitted. When this center was moved from Madrid to Lisbon and with it the maritime interests of Spain became dominant, the conflict with the English and Dutch was inevitable and in the collapse that followed, Portugal was irrevocably canceled out as a major power in the world.[17]

The opening years of the seventeenth century are a welter of clashing rivalries and ambitions on the part of every European state to join in the scramble for overseas possessions. In addition to the Dutch and English, to whom the most passing reference has been made, the French East India Company dates from 1604; Denmark founded a similar enterprise in 1616 and constructed a fortress at Trangambar and commercial depots on the Malabar Coast.[18] In far-off corners of the world, all but forgotten by their

---

[17] Halecki, Oscar, *The Limits and Divisions of European History*, London and New York, 1950, pp. 158–159.

[18] The full story of Danish adventures in the tropics is fascinating. The company formed by Christian IV was in line with the awakening consciousness in Denmark of the importance of overseas relations. Greenland had been abandoned and was now to be reopened to contact, and the stimulus of the Dutch and others

own people at home, courageous Portuguese pioneers defended the interests of their country unstintingly against Dutch and British. The gallant defense of Amboim by André Furtado de Mendonça was one of the outstanding incidents of this kind. But the Netherlanders, in the seventeenth century, were demonstrating in turn the same energy and disconcerting ubiquity that the Portuguese themselves had revealed during the previous century. Men of the stripe of Van Dieman moved about the Indonesian Islands with the recklessness and daring of the Portuguese. Australia and the remoter portions of the Pacific were brought within their ken, and the *Nederlandse Oost-Indische Compagnie* became one of the leading forces in the Far East in the establishment of a commercial monopoly.[19]

The Spanish regime in Portugal dragged on, suffered rather than supported, tolerated rather than approved. As usual it was European politics in general that conspired to make possible the re-establishment of the national independence. In a way it would be proper to say that the Thirty Years' War was responsible for the separation of Portugal from Spain. The success of the Protestant forces in Central Europe and the prolonged hostilities that ensued between the two religious groups engaged the lively sympathy and support of Philip IV, who had ascended the throne in 1621 and was to live to witness the loss of Portugal. Dependent on his favorite, Gaspar Guzmán de Olivares, Philip IV was incapable of the kind of action that might have made possible the ideal to which he dedicated his life, namely, the increase of the unity of the Spanish empire. The moral fiber of Spain was far from what it had been under Philip II and the will to survival as a world power was becoming rapidly undermined.[20] The hopeless struggle of the exhausted Spanish people against the Lutheran heresy, the penetration of heterodoxy

---

in the Far East excited the curiosity and the desire for participation of the Danes (de Lannoy, Charles, and Vander Linden, Herman, *Histoire de l'Expansion coloniale des peuples européens. Néerlande et Danemark, XVII et XVIII siècles*, Paris and Brussels, 1911, p. 401).

[19] Geyl, P., *Geschiedenis van de Nederlandse stam*, *op. cit.*, p. 478.

[20] An excellent source may be found in the works of José Deleito y Piñuela, dealing with the reign of Philip IV: *El declinar de la monarquía española*, Madrid, 1947; *Sólo Madrid es Corte* (*La capital de dos mundos bajo Felipe IV*), Madrid, 1942; and for the general "climate" of the period in which Portugal regained its independence, by the same author, *La vida religiosa española bajo el cuarto Felipe*, Madrid, 1952.

across the Pyrenees; the rising commercial might of the Low Countries, the antagonism of France and the open hostility of England were apparent by the early years of the seventeenth century. A restless Portugal was unlikely to remain docile under Spanish rule when the circumstances were favorable for throwing off the hated yoke of Castilian control.

The basic reasons for the restoration of independence in Portugal were domestic and foreign simultaneously. The French unquestionably contributed to rousing the Portuguese people to rebellion, for this would appreciably weaken Spain. On the other hand, the latent sentiment of the Portuguese themselves needed precious little to bring it to the surface in an outbreak of patriotic fervor against the foreign intruder. In the face of the recommendation of Olivares to Philip IV that he imitate the example of Richelieu in France and "reduce all the regions of which Spain was composed to a single, homogeneous monarchy under the same laws so as to become the most powerful monarch in the world," it was fairly evident to the Portuguese that the self-control which Philip II had imposed on himself in 1580 was no longer tolerable. Moreover, on the other side of the peninsula, in Catalonia, the *segadors* had descended on Barcelona and rebellion rapidly spread to the entire province. Olivares remained obdurate in the face of Catalan claims and pushed the project for the complete personal union of the Spanish and Portuguese kingdoms in violation of the guarantees of Philip II. In 1635, new taxes had been introduced and it was proposed that Portuguese troops be raised for service against the Catalans and in the Netherlands. On December 1, 1640, the Viceregal Adviser Vasconcelos was killed and the insurgents, who had requested aid from Richelieu, escorted the representative in Portugal of Philip IV, Margaret of Savoy, to the frontier. John of Bragança, a descendant of Dom Manuel, was proclaimed king and quickly recognized by France, Denmark, England, and Sweden. A truce was arranged between Portugal and the Netherlands and the Lisbon government was committed to take no action with reference to Spain without prior consultation with the French.[21]

Portugal was faced by the double challenge of preventing the reoccupation of its territory and defending itself against the Spanish invasion which was deemed certain and, in the second place, re-

[21] Hauser, Henri, *La Préponderance espagnole*, *op. cit.*, pp. 325–326.

establishing the nation as an independent power in the world after sixty years of the suspension of its sovereignty. International politics, and this is to state a platitude, make for some bizarre combinations. Portugal had been crippled by the Dutch while she was under Spanish rule and was now allied with the Netherlands in opposition to Spain and had actually had a Dutch fleet in Lisbon harbor in 1641. But the achievement of the Portuguese in casting out the alien regime incited the colonists in Dutch-held Brazil to do likewise and so we find that during the reign of John IV, Portuguese Brazil was at war with Holland whereas the newly installed Bragança dynasty was allied with the Netherlands in Europe and eager to assure its aid in the event of complications with Spain. The French alliance of 1655 provided some degree of assurance, although it was generally suspected that Portugal would be finished off as soon as Spain could extricate itself from the foreign wars in which it was then involved and give its undivided attention to this uprising on the Atlantic side of the peninsula. There was a great deal of an air of the provisional about the new dynasty and that was no more keenly appreciated than by John IV himself, whose reign had begun in such trying circumstances and, quite frankly, with such slim prospects of enduring.

The problem of Portugal in 1640 was not simply to retrieve an independence that had been lost, but to re-establish it on a basis that would preclude, in the future, a repetition of the crises of 1383 and 1580. It posed a problem in political theory since the act of 1640 was rebellion — violent rebellion — and had been followed by the choosing of a king by those who had been responsible for throwing off the Spanish yoke. The kingship of the Duke of Bragança was recognized by the Cortes of 1641, in which the doctrine on the matter of the royal power, as professed by the school of Suarez, served as the basis for justifying the new regime. In one of the declarations of the Cortes, it was stated plainly that "the royal power of the monarch is in the people and their agencies and from them it will be granted at once."[22]

The Duke of Bragança was faced by the very special difficulty of holding the throne and of cementing its bases in such a manner as to achieve that "legitimacy" of which Guglielmo Ferrero writes as the *sine qua non* of all monarchy, that rock-bottom element of

[22] Ameal, *História de Portugal, op. cit.*, p. 432.

general common consent without which the monarchy and the person of the monarch can never be more than usurpers or, at the worst, despots. It was a delicate problem in political thought that faced the Portugal of 1641. It is possible that what happened then, as enunciated in the principle just quoted, was to have at a much later date — nearly three hundred years later in fact — the most serious repercussions, for if the theory of the popular source of the royal authority served to make John IV's position tenable in 1641, it was also responsible for the excesses of 1910 with the violent reaction against the monarchical institution itself. In a word, John of Bragança had to consolidate his reign — personally, as a family, and as the legitimate successor of the dynasty of Aviz.

It is remarkable that in the midst of this acutely dangerous situation that the Portuguese managed to preserve as much as they did. Salvador Correia de Sá e Benavides, one of the really great men of the sea of all times, reconquered Angola and São Tomé, restoring them to their proper owners. In the Far East the chances of dislodging the Dutch were infinitesimal for distance, lack of man power, paucity of resources, and the heavy toll that had been taken of Portuguese ships, all conspired to make that impossible.

In the peninsula, it was to take twenty-five years and an interminable series of skirmishes and battles between the Spanish and the Portuguese before peace could be brought about. Death took the king and with his decease came another regency on behalf of Affonso VI. The Queen Mother was one of those strong-willed women who appear on the scene of history every now and then in the Iberian peninsula and give the lie to the notion that in these Mediterranean lands women rarely play a role of any consideration in politics. Portugal's strength depended, under Luiza de Gusmão, on the kind of foreign alliances she and her counselors could devise, and for sheer complexity it would be difficult to find a combination more elaborate or, in the long run, more effective. The problem of an alliance is to secure a maximum of security at the price of a minimum of contradictory commitment. To form such ties with England, France, and Holland simultaneously, where the three powers were periodically at war with one another, represented a danger of involvement in which the sole beneficiary would be Spain, then burning for vengeance for the affront of the restoration of 1640.

It was to England that the Portuguese turned, as they have so many times in their long history: not to the England of the ancient alliance of the fourteenth century but to the new, Protestantized England, fresh from civil war, and in which the revival of the Portuguese arrangement was less likely to meet with the popular and official approval that it had in centuries past. It was proposed that the newly restored Charles II marry Catherine of Bragança. The results of the marriage contract were conceived as eminently favorable to all parties: Charles would get a wife and a dowry and perhaps some choice bits of Portuguese territory in the Orient which would be a factor of some moment in the advancement of English interests. Portugal could count on the veterans of the civil war in case of emergency. The French were willing to go along, since it cost them nothing anyhow, and made the probability of any intervention on their part in a peninsular war less likely.

On the last day of May, 1662, the marriage took place and so was restored the policy of close relations with England that had been a cornerstone of the diplomacy of the Aviz dynasty. The price for the alliance was high in terms of territorial concessions for Tangier was given up and the English were granted wide privileges in the lucrative India trade and the chance for a foothold on Ceylon. The dim design of the future British India was shaping up at this date and it was the product, quite literally, of Portugal's dire necessity to provide the armor for the defense of its integrity in Europe. War continued on the frontier and in Lisbon intrigue reached a new high level with French and English interests vying for supremacy and a "peace party," eager for a settlement with Spain, very much in evidence. The marriage of the weak and, by this time, debauched Affonso to the granddaughter of Henry IV of France contributed to making things anything but boring in the Portuguese court which had become, in some ways, one of the major centers of European politics. A French princess on the throne of Portugal and a Portuguese queen in England could scarcely simplify matters or make the task of peace with Madrid any easier.

But peace did come with Spain, and Portugal paid for it by losing Ceuta. Fortunately the nation also managed to lose Affonso in the process, for, out of his degeneracy and the breakup of his marriage and ultimate retirement, Portugal regained some degree at least of its national composure. It was Dom Pedro, a younger brother of Affonso, who became regent and ultimately king under the title of Pedro II. A sober, natural administrator, he managed to perform the impossible: restore prosperity to an exhausted nation, abstain from interference in Spain, and keep on excellent terms with both France and England. This miracle of political prestidigitation paid off in first-rate dividends. The process of the revival of independent Portugal begun in 1640 was now completed and another cycle in the national history was about to begin.

When Charles II of Spain passed away without a successor, the way was open for the practical demonstration of the rivalry of Austria and France, since both the emperor, in the first case, and the king, in the second, were married to daughters of Philip IV. Louis XIV transferred the claims to the Spanish throne to his grandson, the Duke of Anjou, and it was with his installation in Madrid that the Bourbon chapter of Spanish history opens. Fear ran through Europe at what appeared to be the wiping out of the Pyrenees as a frontier. The Grand Alliance of England, Holland, and Austria was formed in the early autumn of 1701. The lines were drawn for the gigantic tug of arms over the Spanish succession.[23]

Portugal could not do other than recognize Philip V as successor of Charles II in Spain. But if the Spanish danger as such was removed, the still greater one of the French was now very much present. It was evident from the moment that the Duke of Anjou took the crown as Philip V that France conceived of Spain as a protectorate and that, if technically the crowns were separate, French influence in the conduct of Spanish diplomacy and commerce was to be predominant. The French were granted privileges in Africa; their ships entered the slave trade and, in Flanders, French influence was beginning to prevail. For the Portuguese, a French king on the throne in Madrid conjured up the specter once more of another occupation and a long period of foreign rule. Yet, oddly enough, Portugal had signed an accord with France recognizing Philip V in return for the assurance of protection against that precise eventuality. *Quis custodiet custodes?*

The Portuguese appreciated that it was far more prudent to renew in practice as well as spirit the ties with England for there could

---

[23] Deschanel, Louis Paul, *Histoire de la politique extérieure de la France, 806–1936*, Paris, 1936, p. 108. The expression of Louis XIV became famous, "Il n'y a plus de Pyrénées."

be little doubt that the new dynasty in Madrid was casting covetous glances toward Lisbon. Cardinal Portocarrero, who was high in the esteem of Philip V, referred to Pedro II of Portugal invariably as the "rebel Duke of Bragança." In 1703 the Treaty of Methuen was signed between Portugal and England, placing the Portuguese definitely on the side of the Grand Alliance. In this case, as a century later during the era of Bonaparte, Portugal was caught on the horns of an insoluble dilemma, the result of her geographical position and the overseas interests of the country: between the naval power of England and the continental or land-mass power of France. The ideal of neutrality was then difficult and became even more difficult later for a nation that occupies one of the most strategic spots on the map of Europe. By entering the pact in 1703, Portugal committed itself to "impede the common danger for Europe and maintain the rights to the throne of Spain of the most august House of Habsburg."[24]

The relations with England were not limited to the political or even to the military, because the Treaty of Methuen represents a considerable shift in the economic position of Portugal. This may be taken as the approximate date of what has often been called the British domination of Portugal. English textiles were to enter Portugal in return for Portuguese wines and, if this were to remain an effective arrangement, Portugal was doomed to continue as an agricultural country dependent on English industry for manufactured products.[25] It was the commencement of the steady influx into Portugal of British capital, enterprises and even residents until Porto, in particular, became famous for the number of English

---

[24] Ferreira Borges de Castro, José, *Collecção de tratados, convenções, contractos, e actos públicos celebrados entre a Coroa de Portugal e as mais potencias*, Lisbon, 1856, Vol. II, p. 163.

[25] Guedes, Marques, A *Aliança inglesa. Notas de história diplomática 1383–1943, op. cit.*, p. 312 *seq.* In these pages is discussed the advantages and disadvantages to Portugal of Methuen and the significance of the treaty from the commercial point of view. A German historian notes that, in 1703, "Portugal freed itself from French political and cultural influence but at the same time became dependent culturally on England, a position which the country has occupied more or less down to the present day" (Diercks, Gustav, *Portugiesische Geschichte*, Berlin, 1927, p. 128).

It was popularly said that the treaty had converted Portuguese grain lands into vineyards and that bread had been sacrificed for wine (Osório de Andrade, Gilberto, *Os fundamentos da neutralidade portuguesa*, Lisbon, n.d., p. 148).

businessmen who were established there as wine merchants and shippers.[26]

The allied armies under a combined English-Portuguese command entered Spain and in 1706 actually took Madrid, only to find themselves faced by that indomitable, fierce spirit of independence that the Spanish invariably oppose to those who would take their lands. The Portuguese, with English aid, assured their own survival and this in itself was no small accomplishment in the war years that ended finally in 1713. From the point of view of its world-wide interests, this period of severe losses in Asia pushed the Portuguese to a much more intense development of their Brazilian colony. The center of activity shifted very definitely to the New World and from the imperial angle, it was Portuguese America which was to play the leading role during the ensuing century down to separation in 1822.

The eighteenth century, as has been implied by the previous remarks, is the "English century" for Portugal and entailed participation by the Portuguese in the innumerable wars in which Britain was engaged.

The succeeding monarchs tended toward personal rule; Brazilian gold kept them from bankruptcy and the English alliance gave the country a sense of protection. It was an age without heroism. There was no moment of dramatic grandeur, no repetition, as in the sixteenth century, of those magnificent, costly, illogical gestures that branded the Portuguese the world's greatest adventurers. The most striking feature is the product of absolutism in the person of the Marquis de Pombal. His regime is of the very first importance in the history of Portuguese thought and institutions and deserves a more than passing description as the culminating feature of the century.

It was during the reign of King José, from 1750 to 1777, that Sebastião José de Carvalho e Melo, better known by his title of Marquis of Pombal, ruled Portugal. The extraordinary feature of this case was that Pombal — and we use the more familiar title rather than his own name — was fifty years of age before he was given office and had enjoyed no particular consideration under José's

26 This particular segment of Portuguese national life has merited some attention from its men of letters. One of the best known popular novels in Portugal is *Uma familia inglesa* by Julio Diniz.

predecessor. A word as to his life before rising to the top in Portuguese administrative circles. Pombal began his professional career in diplomacy, representing Portugal as special ambassador in London in 1738, where he remained until 1745.

Pombal's earlier career gave extremely little insight into his later activity and prestige. Son of an obscure country squire from the area near Coimbra, he had neither the social condition nor the influence, to all appearances, to achieve anything particularly notable in a country where royal favor was very hard to come by and the number of notables enjoying it painfully limited. By eloping with one Teresa Noronha of a noble and exclusive family, Pombal caused a minor scandal, brought notice to himself, and became, by his marriage to the widow, related to almost every noble family in the realm.[27]

With his wife's money and a small inheritance of his own, he obtained appointment six years later to a post in London and was launched on what at that moment did not look like much more than a fairly routine diplomatic career. We have already made mention of the close relations with England that had been built up and culminated in the Treaty of Methuen. There had been an accord in 1642, immediately after the Restoration, and under Cromwell's Protectorate a further treaty had been signed in 1654 that prepared the way for those later ones, to which some attention has been given.[28] To what degree we may attribute the ideas of Pombal to his London experience is difficult to say. The dates of his residence there are certainly significant, for it was a time when the religious zeal of the civil war years had ebbed and England had settled down to a complacent Protestantism and to making money. The vulgar fervor, as it was called, of the Wesleyans, founded in 1737, had not yet disturbed, to any serious degree, the religious indifference of the classes that esteemed themselves as counting in the country. Pombal came straight out of the semi-Oriental society of Portugal into the mercantile, skeptical atmosphere of London in the years approaching the mid-eighteenth century. He undoubtedly experienced a sense of personal liberation in this environment and, at the same time, he was undoubtedly pricked

[27] In English one of the handiest biographies of Pombal is that of Cheke, Marcus, *Dictator of Portugal, Marquis of Pombal*, London, 1938.
[28] *Ibid.*, p. 20.

by envy at the rising power of England and the far less effective role that his own country was playing. He managed, however, to measure fairly accurately the precise character of this curious alliance between Protestant and Catholic: an empire of the past and one that was on the threshhold of the future; between an agrarian, backward economy and one that was not far from the Industrial Revolution. As later dictator of Portugal, this experience in London stood him in good stead and served him as an excellent backdrop to many of his own policies. One thing stands out with pristine clarity and that is that Pombal became in his thinking very much the *homo economicus;* it was economic development that seemed to him to hold the key to everything and to the aspect of Portuguese life to which he was to devote his greatest energies.[29]

On the conclusion of his mission to London he spent some time trying to devise a scheme for the creation of a Portuguese East India Company along lines similar to those that had led to the various private companies of England operating in the Far East. In the midst of these cerebrations about the economic exploitations of the East, he was assigned to Vienna on a new diplomatic mission. His situation in 1745 was far from brilliant. His status was somewhat vague and his fellow diplomats were less than helpful in advancing his mission and he was given no grant for financial maintenance while in Vienna. He complained constantly that the only recourse was to retire to Soure from which he came and hope to avoid his more persistent creditors. His wife died in Lisbon and Pombal was presumably far from overcome by the loss. At least we may assume so, for he promptly married a lady in waiting of the Dowager Empress Cristina, with a pedigree that dated from the twelfth century. Pombal himself could hardly have been considered even by a lady in waiting with a galaxy of ancestors as an extraordinary match. He was pushing fifty, penniless, unlikely to have much of a career at home, and rheumatic. Let it be added for what historical value it may have that the first two children of the marriage were given the names of Adam and Eve. What mystical significance this nomenclature may have is impossible to ascertain. Conceivably Pombal had some vague idea that he

---

[29] D'Azevedo, J. Lucio, *O Marquês de Pombal e a sua época,* Rio de Janeiro-Lisbon-Porto, 1922, p. 42.

was initiating life *ab novo*; a prefiguration of his regime that was to transform Portugal so radically.[30]

He was recalled home as Minister of Foreign Affairs in 1750, and within months of this designation King John died and José ascended the throne as his successor. The general situation of Portugal was definitely not promising. Her credit was low; the finances in a deplorable state in spite of Brazilian gold; and the prestige of the nation abroad extremely low. There is no generally accepted version of how Pombal managed to get complete control of the State in his hands in a relatively short time. Several circumstances combined to produce this result: the fact that his own wife and the queen were fellow nationals; that King José, a man of vast ideas and limited ability in carrying them out, needed a strong arm as executive of his proposals; and the desire of the monarch to choose someone who was less involved in court intrigue than the rest — and Pombal fitted this need nicely since he had spent so much time outside the country. The situation of the new minister became particularly solid after the devastating Lisbon earthquake of November 1, 1775. This terrible calamity that has been so often described had one important effect on the aspirations of Pombal; it furnished him with an admirable point of departure for the new regime. The fact that Lisbon had to be rebuilt, and that the population which had suffered the effects of the quake was in a state of mind where anything in the way of reconstruction sounded plausible, made it just that much easier, in the light of this psychological attitude toward rebuilding, to go far beyond the mere restoration of the city.[31]

But it is in the economic order that Pombal stands out as a planner, for he belongs to the tradition of Sully and Colbert in the grandiose projects that formed in his mind and which, in many cases, he sought to put into effect. But in the realization of these schemes for the enrichment of the nation there was an strong element of dehumanization, that is, of conceiving of in-

[30] D'Azevedo, *op. cit.*, p. 57.

[31] A first-rate account of the Lisbon earthquake, not merely as a shattering physical phenomenon but as an event that provoked a continent-wide spiritual reaction and a vast amount of repentance is Kendrick, T. D., *The Lisbon Earthquake*, London, 1956. The effect of the destruction of Lisbon was staggering on contemporary thought and ended, as the author suggests, "the age of optimism."

dustry as a technical challenge that had nothing to do with the human qualities of the workers. The important thing in Pombal's program was to increase industrial output; the welfare of those who lived by industry as its toilers was of quite secondary importance. On the commercial side, Pombal's policy was strongly nationalistic and consisted in aiding national shipping in order to reduce dependence on foreign and especially British markets and, at the same time, maintain the monopoly for Portuguese interests in such enterprises as the Companhia do Grão Pará in Brazil.[32]

It would be a wearisome business to dwell in detail on the numerous economic projects that Pombal carried out, or their effect on the general life of the country. There was, in everything that he did, an air of paternalism that was associated distinctly with the driving idea behind the Pombalian reform in general: the complete establishment of royal absolutism. It was enlightened despotism tinged with the liberalism and the *Illustration* of the century that gives the era of Pombal its peculiar flavor. Pombal's dictatorship — and it was a dictatorship in the modern sense of the word — used every device with which we are accustomed to associate the more contemporary experiments in the same direction.[33]

To what extent, for instance, was the conspiracy of 1758 a bit of flummery on the part of Pombal? Presumedly the king was fired upon as he returned from amorous dalliance late at night and, after a few days of speculation, a number of the nobility were arrested, as well as members of the Society of Jesus, for complicity. Pombal recognized, as do all proper dictators, that the full absolutism to which he aspired was out of the question until those forces within the nation, that operated more or less independently, were liquidated. The nobility was one of them and, of course, the Jesuits were one of the others. The whole matter smacks strangely of the Reichstag fire in the halcyon days of the National Socialists in Germany. The trial and execution of the accused were accomplished with a rapidity that left the nation gasping.

[32] "In the mind of Pombal, the whole difficulty arose not from the treaties; the oppressive one of 1654 and the more clever one of 1703 but from the lack of ocean going bottoms" (Azevedo, J. Lucio de, *Epocas de Portugal económico*, *op. cit.*, p. 446).

[33] "At a time when the fate of Europe is largely in the hands of Dictators, it is interesting to examine the career of a Dictator who in many respects may be regarded as the prototype of such rulers, and who was famous only a century and a half ago" (Cheke, *op. cit.*, p. vii).

But the epic struggle in the story of the dictatorship was with the Church. This is no strange or perplexing feature of the Pombal regime for the twentieth century has long since accustomed us to recognize that religious institutions, if deeply and authentically rooted in the soil and heart of a nation, are the most impervious to the pressures that the dictatorial state exerts against them. Pombal was not merely opposed to the Church because there were Jesuits within it, but to the Catholic Church itself. His addiction to total royal supremacy was, in itself, a position plainly hostile to the exercise of any real authority by the Church. It was not Pombal's purpose to lay low a powerful and overwhelmingly influential Church in the name of civil authority, but to assert the supremacy of the latter with the submission of the Church. Pombal was a curious combination of ideas: Anglican, Jansenist, Josephist, and the political conceptions favorable to absolutism that were floating about in the atmosphere of Germany of the time.

Even in pre-Pombalian Portugal, especially after the Restoration in 1640, there were any number of influences favorable to these theories of the primacy of the civil over the spiritual. Regalism, as it is called, was advanced by a Spanish author, Gabriel Pereira de Castro, in his *De manu regia*, published in 1640. The absence of relations between the Holy See and Portugal during this period and after the Restoration, plus the prestige of the France of Louis XIV and the absolutism of John V, all combined to create a climate that may be dubbed, for the sake of a better word, as definitely "anti-Roman" in certain sectors of Portuguese public opinion.[34] In the statutes drawn up for the universities we find one of the best statements of Pombal's ideas in this and related matters. Reference

[34] An excellent summary of Jansenism in Portugal and the consequences of the teachings of Pereira is to be found in that mine of information that is the *Historia de los heterodoxos españoles* of Marcelino Menéndez y Pelayo (Buenos Aires, 1945, Vol. VI, Chapter II, under the title "The Regalist Jansenism in the XVIII Century," p. 143 *seq.*). Menéndez y Pelayo calls attention to previous conflicts in Portugal between certain prelates and Rome: "Benedict XIII (1724–1730) was unable to maintain peace with John V who demanded in the rudest fashion that the Pope raise to the dignity of Cardinal the Nuncio Bichi, then retired in Lisbon. The College of Cardinals protested. John was irritated; recalled all Portuguese resident in Rome; broke relations with the Holy See and forbade the Portuguese convents to send their accustomed contributions to Rome" (p. 148). Pereira is the best example of the doctrinaire approach to these matters and Menéndez calls Pombal, quite rightly, "the sanguinary executor of Pereira's theology" (p. 148).

is made in these texts to the "liberties of the Lusitanian Church" and, since nationalism and absolutism are not far removed, it was proposed that Canon Law reflect the "peculiar character of the Portuguese nation."[35] At the time that relations with the Holy See had been broken (1728) it was provided by law that no bull, letter, or other communication from the Vatican should be made public in Portugal without royal permission and this restriction was enacted into permanent law in 1765.

The position of the Jesuits in the Portugal of the Restoration was one of very considerable prestige. The Society had given solid support to the national cause and the Restoration and enjoyed a great deal of popular support. But there were powerful currents running against them and Pombal, with that rare sense of timing which is an essential characteristic of the competent dictator, was fully aware of it.[36]

One of the alleged causes of the persecution for which Pombal must assume personal responsibility is a situation in South America. By reason of an agreement between Portugal and Spain, several missions with some 30,000 inhabitants were to be transferred from the sovereignty of one country to the other. This involved the famous Jesuit missions of Paraguay.[37] The fact that in this transfer human beings were involved made very little impression on so astute a statesman as Pombal. The upshot was the wild rebellion of some 30,000 Indians who had no intention of being moved from spot to spot like so many chessmen.[38] The Portuguese minister placed

[35] Oliveira, Miguel de, *História eclesiástica de Portugal*, *op. cit.*, p. 297.

[36] Salvador de Madariaga, with his usual urbane treatment of historical matters relating to the Iberian world, sums the situation up excellently: "A whole series of forces were converging on the Society. The Jansenists or nationalist Catholics hated them for their ultramontanism and as instruments of papal authority. In those days the number of Jansenist priests and bishops in France, Spain, Portugal, Naples and even Rome, was legion. The philosophers attacked them as the vanguard of the Catholic Church. The general trend of the century toward free thought and political liberty saw in them a bulwark of reaction . . ." (*Cuadro histórico de las Indias*, Buenos Aires, 1950, p. 759).

[37] The Portuguese were to give up the colony of Sacramento on the La Plata River "situated as it was almost in front of Buenos Aires" and were to receive in return a number of missions in the region of Uruguay. The classic work in English on the Jesuit missions is R. B. Cunninghame Graham, *A Vanished Arcadia, Being Some Account of the Jesuits in Paraguay, 1607 to 1767*, London, 1901. The description of the reaction to Pombal's proposal is contained on page 236 *seq.*

[38] Cunninghame Graham remarks that "indifference to the feelings of others

the entire responsibility for this unfortunate situation on the Society of Jesus whose missions were involved and the incident in the far-off Paraguay country was the opening gun in a full-scale persecution of the Jesuits which was to have the most far-reaching repercussions both in America and Europe and, very particularly, consequences of the most tragic sort for Portugal itself.[39]

A primary factor in the dispute was the policy of Pombal to cut off commercial activity on the part of the missions, especially since the formation of the new mercantile enterprise, Companhia do Grão Pará. Without trade relations for the marketing of the mission products, it was obviously impossible for the Jesuit "reductions," as they were called, to survive. Systematically, with the kind of persistence we find among the governments of the popular democracies in eastern Europe today, Pombal assigned to the Jesuits the cause of the most improbable events and built up a case against them to justify the draconian measures his regime proposed to take against them. A small riot in Porto in 1757 against a wine exporting company was seized upon by Pombal as an excuse to accuse the Jesuits of complicity. In 1757 the new laws in Brazil providing for the "liberation" of the Indians and the extinction of the missions came into effect. The former missionaries could remain in charge of parishes, but the actual government of the indigenous population passed out of their hands into that of the State. Pombal worked on the Holy See to prove that the Jesuits were engaged in illicit trade and responsible for innumerable acts against the State. From then on to the final *dénouement* in this drama in 1767, the Jesuits were subjected to every conceivable vexation and calumny. The *Dedução Cronológica*, written by Pombal himself, appeared in 1767 and attributed to the Society every evil that had beset Portugal since the reign of John III.[40]

Pombal's barrage was not directed against the Jesuits only. Reli

---

is perhaps the greatest proof a public man can give of his attachment to the State" (*ibid.*, p. 237).

[39] This affair in Paraguay has been celebrated in one of the most famous literary pieces of the colonial epoch, the *Uruguay* of José Basilio de Gama, an ex-Jesuit. "In order to prove his complete break with the Jesuits, he published *Uruguay* in 1769, in which he did not spare the Society from the most savage attacks, as men and as colonizers. He was violent to the point of rank injustice" (Carvalho, Ronald de, *Pequena historia da literatura brasileira*, Rio de Janeiro 1935, 5 ed., p. 152).

[40] Oliveira, Miguel de, *História eclesiástica de Portugal*, *op. cit.*, p. 302.

gious institutions of other communities and the secular clergy were equally the target of his misguided zeal to extirpate from the soil of Portugal every rival to the supremacy of the royal power. One of the victims was Miguel da Anunciação, Bishop of Coimbra, who suffered imprisonment for more than eight years because of a pastoral in which he had called attention to the danger of certain books contrary to morals which the censor had allowed to circulate. Years later, when Pombal was no longer in power, he was to receive from this same bishop his blessing and a few words of comfort.[41] Pombal even used the Inquisition, which was to exist in Portugal until 1821, for the purposes of his policy.

Pombal has been praised by those who conceive of his regime as a period of enlightenment for his educational reforms and for the elimination from Portuguese academic life of the medieval "obscurantism" which was supposedly its principal feature. The expulsion of the Jesuits left a formidable gap in Portuguese education, for they directed, at the time of the persecution, twenty-four colleges and some seventeen residences and other centers. In 1772 the new university statutes were promulgated, the principal purpose of which was to stimulate Encyclopedism as the basis of the new orientation and eradicate all traces of the hated Society of Jesus. The books that the Jesuits had employed by preference were burned and every effort was made to encourage an academic tradition diametrically opposed to theirs. Theology suffered as one might expect while the natural sciences were encouraged in every way. The Pombal reforms in this sense left some important and perhaps even valuable contributions, but the sum total was a dreary, fragile, and unimpressive improvisation from which Portugal has not yet entirely recovered.

The purpose behind all this was not to raise the intellectual level of the country but to encourage a middle class whose primary interests would be the practical disciplines and especially trade. It was a means of combating the influence of the landed aristocracy and of providing a counterbalance against the nobility, the only social class capable of forming an opposition. In other words, Pombal aspired at creating a social foundation for the structure of the new state. When José died in 1777, Pombal was not

[41] De Saldanha Oliveira e Sousa, João, *O Marques de Pombal, Sua vida e morte cristã*, Lisbon, 1934, p. 172.

destined to survive him, and at his advanced age of seventy-seven retirement seemed the proper conclusion of this remarkable career.

The peculiar vagaries of his reform program can be observed in no more effective way than in his attitude toward slavery. The minister was responsible for the abolition of slavery in Portugal by the decree of May 25, 1773, by which the grandsons of slaves and all born after that date were to be free. But in Brazil, where slavery was infinitely more important and economically necessary according to the opinion of the day, Pombal took no steps at all to end Negro servitude. Pombal was possessed of boundless energy — most dictators are, in fact — and was concerned with everything from the style of architecture in the new Lisbon to the accounting in public offices. He interested himself in the reform of the army but it was to the economic development of the country that he devoted his principal attention. But in this field, as in others, the Portugal he believed himself to be inaugurating was quite unreal and very much the figment of his own imagination. Mr. Marcus Cheke in his excellent book on Pombal, to which I have referred, sums the situation up admirably.

In June, 1775, the Marquis de Pombal prepared a longish memorandum for the king in which he made a series of "secret observations" on the state of Portugal. This document is the best source for knowing what Pombal himself claimed to have done during his long service to the monarch. It is plain that the dictator was quite convinced that he had inaugurated a Golden Age for the Portuguese people. In the somewhat ornate style of the time, Pombal calls attention to how popular education has spread, and for every civil post requiring a clerk there are regiments of competent applicants; how manufacturing has increased so that Portugal no longer depends on the foreign market for necessary products; how architecture has progressed and flourished in an elaborate building program; how the progress of literature has been most encouraging, as "exemplified by the multitude of works in prose and in verse . . . with an elegance of style worthy of the age of Demosthenes, Homer, Tully, Virgil and Horace."[42]

And, finally, Pombal quoted with deep satisfaction the prosperous state of the country and the wealth that had been created. Was there any reality in all this? Precious little, as any honest

[42] Cheke, *Dictator of Portugal*, *op. cit.*, p. 236 seq.

appraisal of the Pombal period demonstrates. Manufacturing had been encouraged under artificial conditions and the products sold at ruinous prices. Foreign trade was choked with obstructions that only a dictatorial regime can conceive when the imagination in matters bureaucratic is allowed to run wild. The government extended its protection to every field of productive activity and therefore created the impression that this production was actually wealth. The only conclusion to which one can rightfully come is that this child of his age, who thought that if one imprisoned Jesuits he advanced culture and that if the State decreed that an industry should be established it necessarily reflected economic progress, had undertaken to lead Portugal in the way that historically was not her rightful one. Pombal, in a very real sense, represented a detour in Portuguese history and it was to take considerable time before the nation could recover from this Encyclopedist indoctrination and get back on its feet.[43]

Internationally, Pombal led into some curious contradictions. His zeal for the introduction of French ideas did not extend to the introduction of French politics and he remained loyal to the implications of the Anglo-Portuguese alliance even to the extent of joining England in war with France. "The position of Portugal in the years before the French Revolution was, as it generally is in times of peace, one of compromise between the maritimist and the militarist Great Powers."[44] The intellectual winds that had blown from France and that had seemed so bracing to many in those years of the mid-eighteenth century were now to be transformed into storm clouds of the first magnitude. The French Revolution and the Napoleonic era were to bring changes of the greatest moment to Portugal, remote as the country seemed to be from the main vortex of European power politics.

Portugal was torn between remaining loyal to the English commitment under the most trying of circumstances or of succumbing to the continentalism of the French. Since Europe was experiencing a gigantic realignment of forces, it was but natural that a small state with no decisive voice in the direction of events should

[43] Marcus Cheke concludes in this way: "It is evident that the Secret Observations were a ghastly masquerade planned to flatter the King and perhaps to cheat posterity" (*ibid.*, p. 241).

[44] Young, George, *Portugal Old and Young. A Historical Study*, London, 1917, p. 203.

find it inordinately difficult to wend its way through the Europe of 1790 to 1815.

The French Revolution had in its day an influence on European thought and action that was fundamentally divisive and was at the bottom of the great cleavage between conservative and progressive, liberal and reactionary that was to be the most outstanding feature of Portuguese politics for the next century. Portuguese opinion, especially in intellectual circles, was largely favorable to the ideas that had contributed to the germination of the Revolution. Rousseau was in vogue and republicanism exerted its appeal among those who followed events abroad. On the conservative side were ranged officialdom and the bureaucracy that Pombal had created and which was still intact, the landed class and nobility and the mass of peasantry, attached to that traditionalism which makes this class in every nation a source of stability. On the other side were the urban, professional classes, the middle class, and, to some extent, the artisans and others of the *petite bourgeoisie.* The liberals or progressives were prone to be ardently pro-French, according to their interpretation of what was transpiring in France while the conservatives, by the same token, tended more and more to identify their antirevolutionary sentiments with England and therefore became the pro-English party or group.[45]

The proclamation of the French republic aggravated this division of opinion and made the governments elsewhere in Europe, that up to that time had been relatively tolerant, more keenly aware of the danger of an expansionist republicanism from France. All across the continent measures were taken to protect monarchical institutions and French citizens found themselves embarrassed or expelled in Spain and Portugal. The Portuguese government expelled the French ambassador and prepared to send troops to aid the Spanish in the invasion of Roussillon. The war policy of Godoy in Madrid, into which Portugal was plunged, envisaged the invasion of France and possibly the placing of Louis XVII on a French throne in one of the border provinces under Spanish pro-

[45] The division might be expressed another way, by the sympathy of the liberals of the France that was emerging as republican and liberal and the one that still remained on the defensive in the person of the monarchists and especially the *émigrés,* the traditionalist France. Bessand-Massenet, P., *Des deux France 1799–1804,* Paris, 1949, describes within France this "drama of conflict of conscience" which divided men so irreconcilably.

tection.[46] The invasion of the French forces in 1794 ended this dream and led straight to the Treaty of Basel in July of 1795. The treaty not only ended the expedition into France but placed Spain on the French side in the general conflict. Portugal was deserted and forced to seek terms with the pro-French element at home. Moreover France itself had entered the Treaty of San Ildefonso for the partition of Portugal. Portugal was terrified at this *volte-face* and the revival of the danger of invasion and promptly catapulted over into the English camp. The tugging and pulling between the French and the English parties within the country ended in large measure in 1800 when Bonaparte assumed the direction of French affairs and the Revolution became not the attractive ideological experiment that it had been conceived, but a militarist, antinational imperialism in which revolutionarism was the driving force. The Portuguese people at this juncture were divided between the hope of civil liberty if the principles of the French Revolution prevailed and the fear of losing their political independence if France, where these principles were presumedly nurtured, managed to triumph. It was another of those embarrassing dilemmas that have faced the Portuguese at so many points in their history. The pressure then began on Portugal from the new ruler of France and every advantage was offered for entry into the continental system. When Portugal refused, Spanish forces invaded her territory, in what has been called, by one French historian, "*une sorte de guerre entre le Portugal et l'Espagne*."[47] In spite of the crushing defeat of the Portuguese and their considerable losses, the English retaliated by seizing Madeira and Goa. The result was that all hopes of maintaining a dignified neutrality were lost for while seeking to do so, both sides considered themselves fully justified in plundering Portugal of its possessions.

The story of the Napoleonic period as regards Portugal is the gradual transformation of the imperial conflict that placed France against Britain from a political into an economic struggle. Politics can be altered readily and governments can commit themselves to anti- or even non-national policies, but the dictates of economics

---

[46] Sorel, Albert, *L'Europe et la Révolution française*, Paris, 1892, Vol. IV, p. 144.

[47] Driault, Edouard, *Napoléon et l'Europe. La politique extérieure du Premier Consul, 1800–1803*, Paris, 1910, p. 109.

are harder to modify. The basic fact, in the early part of the nineteenth century, was that Portugal belonged to the British bloc and that France had nothing to offer in place of the ties that bound the Iberian country economically to England.

During the great period of the Napoleonic empire, from 1802 to 1807, the French emperor had had little time to devote to such secondary affairs as Portugal. The Iberian peninsula remained, however, a very definite preoccupation in the construction of the French imperial system, for as long as this so-called "colony" of England remained outside the restrictions that the French had imposed, just so long Europe itself was open in the rear and a danger to the policy of destroying British trade. At Tilsit, Napoleon had decided to conquer Portugal and on his return to Paris he proceeded to organize the expeditionary corps. To reach Portugal it was obviously necessary to traverse Spain. As early as 1806, Godoy, the Prince of Peace, as he was designated, had insinuated his willingness to accept compensation in Portugal and, at this late date, to repeat more or less what the counts of Burgundy had done in centuries before. After the great victory of Jena, Godoy, who had hesitated for a long time whether to support France or Britain, decided for the French alliance and revived the Portuguese project. By the Treaty of Fontainebleau of October 27, 1807, Portugal was to be divided into three parts; the Algarve or south for Godoy; the north for the queen of Etruria, and Lisbon to be reserved for whatever future Napoleon might envisage for it.[48]

In November, 1807, a purely French force crossed the frontier and in forced marches headed for Portugal. Spanish assistance, as always in these cases, was more theoretical than real, and the French army suffered the greatest privations in its invasion. The Portuguese made no resistance at all, so rapid was Junot's advance and so unexpected the occupation. The inertia of the royal family surpassed all belief: King John was a hopeless dullard and Queen Maria Francisca was incurably mad, while most of the court were eager to take advantage of the presence in the harbor of English

---

[48] Lefebre, Georges, *Napoléon*, Paris, 1935, p. 250; La Cases, *Mémorial de Ste. Hélène*, Paris, 1948, Vol. I, p. 785. In the famous memoirs of Napoleon from Saint Helena, the former emperor described the ambitions of Godoy and his hope of creating in the Algarve a separate kingdom to which he might retire on the conclusion of the war. See also Fugier, André, *Napoléon et l'Espagne, 1799–1808*, Paris, 1930, Vol. II, p. 200 *seq.*

ships to make an escape. The Portuguese anticlericals, Pombalists, and liberals in general welcomed the French as liberators and saw in them the artisans of a gigantic house cleaning that was to put an end to the corruption of the Braganças. The Sebastianists — that is to say, those who were still awaiting the appearance of the royal Messias in the person of the king who had been defeated at Alcacer-Quibir and who expected him to return in 1808 — were no less inclined to get rid of the Braganças as a preparation of the way for the legitimate monarch.

The Portuguese had made overtures to Britain for assistance and had gone in for a spot of conscience-examining before giving up the national territory. But for the time being Britain was unable to do anything and French domination had its day.[49]

Napoleon had declared categorically that "The House of Bragança has ceased to rule," and in spite of this clear statement, the royal family was led to undertake negotiations at the last moment in the hope of arriving at some sort of understanding. Lord Strankford, the British ambassador, remained close to Lisbon on one of His Majesty's ships anchored in the harbor, and it is recounted that as the French army approached, the ambassador spent his time with the Portuguese prince seeking to convince him that Napoleon could not really last. When the topic became somewhat boring they discussed Portuguese literature since the ambassador had a scholar's knowledge of this field.[50]

Junot became president of the Council of Regency and it was soon very evident that what shreds of Portuguese were to be

---

[49] Varenne Alberic, *Quand la France occupait l'Europe,* Paris, 1948, p. 244. An excellent chapter on Portugal under French domination. As sources for the situation of Portugal in the face of the French invasions: de Oliveira Lima, Manuel, *Dom João VI no Brasil,* Rio de Janeiro, 1908, 2 vols. This is the classical study of the period by one of Brazil's greatest historians. De Moraes Leite Velho, B. T. *Estudo histórico das relações diplomáticas e políticas entre a França e Portugal,* Lisbon, 1895; Acursio das Neves, J., *História geral da invasão dos franceses em Portugal e da restauração deste reino,* Lisbon, 1810–1811, 5 vols.; Pandía Calogeras, João, *A política exterior do Imperio,* Rio de Janeiro, 1927. The best known memoirs of the period are, perhaps, those of Beckford, William, *Memoirs,* London, 1859, 2 vols.

[50] Junot set himself up on the shores of the Tagus as though he expected to end his days there. ". . . nevertheless the Lisbon population talked too constantly of the coming English invasion for the French supreme commander to remain totally ignorant of a danger that grew every day" (Varenne, *Quand la France occupait l'Europe, op. cit.,* p. 255).

retained were shadowy in the extreme and that the rule was now French. Napoleon realized very early that it was impossible to rule Portugal from Paris and therefore he was obliged to depend entirely on Junot for local administration. The latter did little to conceal his aspirations to the Portuguese throne and in the seeking of this post he made concessions to the local inhabitants and in many ways favored national institutions.

The Portuguese were not misled, for French conduct in the provinces revealed them as conquerors and the feeling was as strong as, if not stronger than, in the days of the Spanish regime. Events in the neighboring country were fast accumulating to produce the formidable explosion of 1808 in which the Spanish people, as one man, rose against the French, in what was often called, in Paris, "*guerre de brigandage*," but which was interpreted in Spain as the great patriotic war against the insufferable invader and his fictitious regime.[51] When this occurred, the Portuguese masses rose courageously against the foreign yoke. Liberty, equality, and fraternity meant nothing to the hardy peasantry of Alentejo or Tras-os-Montes; what they fully understood was that a host of foreigners had descended on their land and they did not propose to tolerate the situation any longer, once the Spanish were on the march and a chance of success existed. In August, 1808, a British expeditionary force landed and the partnership in arms of the Iberian peoples and the English led to the successful conclusion of the Peninsular War.[52] On August 1, Wellesley, brother of the future Duke of Wellington, landed with 13,000 men at the mouth of the Mondego. Junot was defeated at Vimeiro and on the thirtieth of the month signed an agreement known as the Convention of Sintra, which provided that the 25,000 French in Portugal should be allowed to depart for France together with the Portuguese nationals who had become deeply compromised with them. Lisbon was thereby liberated without fighting and the road to Madrid open for the advancing British forces.

As the hostile forces drained away, Portugal was seen as devastated. The exigencies of war had led the government to abdicate and those

---

[51] Oman, C. W. C., *History of the Peninsular War*, Oxford, 1902–1930, 7 vols.

[52] Grandmaison, Geoffrey de, *L'Espagne et Napoléon, 1804–1809*, Paris 1908, Vol. I, p. 276.

who remained had delivered national affairs over into the hands of the English. The "colonial" status of Portugal, about which so many Portuguese had complained for decades, was now fairly close to becoming a reality. The difference between the state of Spain and that of Portugal was striking. The former was equally the victim of the most ferocious of wars and the French were very far from tender to the Spanish towns and villages that fell to them. But there had always remained in Spain a healthy tradition of local self-government that all the efforts of the Bourbons for over a hundred years had not quite managed to suppress. When the uprising came, it was of a people who found leadership in the municipal councils and local entities that still carried on the glorious traditions of the Middle Ages. In Portugal, this was not the case. Pombal among others had done the job well and Portuguese local institutions, which are inevitably a source of opposition to dictators and to arbitrary national policies, had withered and died in the general movement toward absolutist centralism. The monarchy was gone for the moment in the person of the monarch. Who, then, in a demoralized Portugal, which was slowly coming out of the catacombs of occupation and systematic exploitation, could assume the role of national leader? The old alignments of pro-French and pro-British, which in themselves indicated to what degree Portugal had fallen in the scale of national pride, were no longer pertinent divisions. The pro-French were discredited because of the outrages of the French themselves, and the pro-British were very quickly equally unpopular because of the irksome character of the rule of Beresford and Stewart and the general reluctance to exchange one foreign domination for another. This was precisely what seemed to be the case in that interval between the peninsular uprising and the Congress of Vienna.

The British themselves were perhaps responsible in part — unconsciously responsible to be sure — for the situation that ensued. It was no simple matter to transfer to national organisms the management of Portuguese affairs and hope that somehow in the muddled condition of the land that a parliamentary system would emerge and that the politically inclined groups in existence would ultimately coalesce into proper conservative and liberal parties. If it is difficult and unbecoming for a victorious power to occupy the territory of a vanquished country and govern it, it is infinitely more difficult for an allied country to conduct the affairs of a state that has collaborated in a recent war. The United States is highly aware of this truism in the relations with the Republic of Korea after 1950 and those that have prevailed with the Nationalist Chinese government in Taiwan since the triumph of the communist cause on the China mainland. Comradeship in arms is no guarantee of solidarity afterward and this was exactly what was happening in Anglo-Portuguese relations after the successful conclusion of the peninsular campaign.[53]

The Congress of Vienna assembled for the declared purpose of unscrambling the confused political omelet that Napoleon had made of the map of Europe and restoring kingdoms and principalities in the names of the legitimacy that had been invoked. Portugal was not represented at the preliminary meetings in Paris after the abdication of Bonaparte; Great Britain undertook to represent Portuguese interests in these preliminary deliberations. The Portuguese did send three representatives to Vienna who acted on the basis of instructions received from the king in Rio de Janeiro. It was in the name of His Royal Highness, the Prince Regent of Portugal and Brazil, that the nation's delegates demanded two things primarily: the restitution to Portugal of the territory of Olivença that had been taken from it and handed over to Spain, and the rectification of the territorial claims with France in South America concerning the area of the Guianas. It must be noted that the British representation did not devote itself with what could be called excessive ardor in defending the cause of Portugal or its territorial claims.[54]

---

[53] Richard Ford, the classical travel guide to Spain, comments with what we may consider as oversimplification on this matter when he wrote: "These English fed and led Portingals, faced and beat back even the French. What greater honour could they desire? Now that they have neither English beef, pay nor leaders, they and their country are truly beggarly inefficient and *hors de combat* and yet this paltry port-wine kingdom, which in a week would become either a Spanish or a French province, except backed by the alliance of England, out-Herods even her neighbour in scandalous violation of treaties, ingratitude and contumely towards her best and only ally" (*Handbook for Travellers in Spain and Readers at Home*, London, 1845, p. 526).

[54] De Queiroz Veloso, J. M., *Como perdemos Olivença*, Lisbon, 1932, p. 114. On this and kindred points regarding Portugal at Vienna, see Brazão, Eduardo, *História diplomática de Portugal*, Lisbon, 1933, Vol. II. The little town of Olivença has been termed a sort of Portuguese Gibraltar in Spain. It is still an issue as is attested by the comment of a Portuguese ambassador in London. "Por-

Fundamentally the integrity of Portugal, aside from Olivença, was recognized. In addition the slave trade was declared inhuman and it was abolished by France, Spain, Holland, and Sweden, and promised to be abolished by Portugal.[55] Since the full nature of the negotiations were known in Portugal, it was unlikely that the regency under British direction could possibly endure unless, of course, the London government was prepared to use force and more force and this was an extremely improbable policy. In 1818 the plot and execution of Gomes Pereira Freire de Andrade e Castro, to give him his complete name, shook Portugal to its foundations. This soldier had served in Algiers against the pirates in 1784, then went to Russia four years later to fight the Turks, and toward the end of the century saw service on behalf of Portugal in Roussillon. In 1808 he departed for France to head the Portuguese Legion at Napoleon's orders and returned to Portugal in 1815. He was the ideal type of ex-military man with a long career behind him to find adjustment to the life of a British-controlled Portugal excessively galling. The execution of the general and ten of his colleagues terminated once and for all any prospect of peaceful collaboration between English and Portuguese. In 1818 Porto and Lisbon rose in rebellion; a constitutional assembly was convoked and in the next few years, under the auspices of what was still called the French party, a new political structure for the country was adopted.

The year 1820 was, to be sure, a critical one in all Europe of the past century. In conventional historical terms it represents one of the first of the waves of hostility to the settlement of Vienna and the spirit which is frequently associated with the name of Prince Metternich. The triumph of the liberal revolution on Spain had instant repercussions across the frontier and from the moment that Ferdinand VII swore to uphold the constitution of 1812,

---

tugal has never seriously raised the matter," the Portuguese ambassador to the Court of St. James himself told me, "in order not to disturb relations with Spain, which, as is generally known, could hardly be improved" (footnote in Cole, S. F. A., *Franco of Spain,* London, 1955, p. 215). There exists in Portugal today an organization known as "Grupo dos amigos de Olivença" who maintain interest in this tiny *terra irredenta* and who publish a review called *Olivença* to focus attention on Portuguese claims.

[55] Grant, A. J., and Temperley, Harold, *Europe in the Nineteenth and Twentieth Centuries, 1789–1939,* London and New York, 1948, 5 ed., p. 117.

temporarily abandoned in 1814, Spain became a hotbed of political agitation, with ramifications that reached into every corner of the peninsula.[56] José María de Pando, minister to Lisbon, was an active agent in the cause of constitutional liberalism and it was not long before close contact was established with the Portuguese liberals.[57] There is little doubt that the old aspiration of certain sectors in Spain for the union of the peninsula was still lively, for there was information available that a united Iberia was projected with the capital in Lisbon.[58] There was a suggestion afloat that the peninsula might well be federalized and Portugal divided into Lusitania Ulterior and Lusitania Citerior. This sounds suspiciously like most of the liberal programs in Spain, both in the past century and the present, in which regionalism and federalism play a very large part.

The story of what happened in Portugal involves some attention to what was happening in Brazil across the way. As of 1806, the royal family had fled to the colony and there had set up the combined government of Portugal and Brazil, an almost unique case in historical annals in which the colony became the focal point from which administrative claims were made to the homeland.

The dominant royal figure during this period is the Prince of Brazil, regent of Portugal at the time in view of the condition of the king, and later to become John VI. Although some thought had been given to the possibility of a transfer of the royal authority and therefore of the court to America, the Treaty of Fontainebleau which carved up Portugal and would probably later have included the empire, and declared the House of Bragança deposed, removed all theoretical aspects of the matter, and made it a very practical reality: a reality that was even more acute when Junot entered Portugal with the invading French.[59]

The transfer was placed under British direction and it must be

---

[56] Peres, Damião, *História de Portugal, op. cit.*, Vol. VII. p. 44 *seq.*

[57] Soriano, Luz, *História da guerra civil*, Lisbon, 1866, Vol. I, p. 405. "The same club that instructed M. Onis to stir up rebellion in Naples, has now passed on similar instructions to Pando to bring revolution to Portugal" (letter from Antonio Saldanha da Gama, Portuguese minister in Madrid, to his colleague, Marques da Marialva in Paris).

[58] Soriano, *op. cit.*, pp. 403–404.

[59] An extremely handy short account with full bibliographical notes of this period when the Portuguese court found its way to Brazil is contained in Lacombe Jacobina, Américo, *Brasil*, Mexico, 1956.

confessed that Britain did not fare badly in the compensation for this service. The Portuguese opened the Brazilian ports to British commerce and made other concessions of importance. The major problem was, however, the adjustment of the royal family to Brazil and, what was even more trying, of Brazil to the royal family.[60] The regent continued to employ this title until the death of his demented mother, Queen Mary, in 1816 when he assumed that of John VI, King of Portugal, although residing in Brazil. Something like 15,000 persons accompanied the court on its transatlantic trek, a unique case of migration of individuals of such category in the whole history of America.[61]

With the conclusion of the Congress of Vienna, it was necessary to normalize this extraordinary situation and Brazil was raised to the category of a kingdom.[62] If John VI himself plays a leading role in this drama, especially in the light of the heritage of disease and insanity that afflicted his immediate predecessors, an even more remarkable personage on the scene was Carlota Joaquina, Queen of Portugal, and one of the fascinating women in the whole of Portuguese or any other history.[63] She was the daughter of King Charles IV of Spain and Queen Maria Luisa of Parma and was married in 1785 to the eighteen-year-old Prince John of Portugal. The new princess was physically unattractive from all descriptions but blessed with a lively intelligence, the fruits of which were to be noted a little later. Life in the dismal Portuguese court of the last part of the eighteenth and early part of the nineteenth centuries could not have been any bed of roses for a high-spirited girl eager to use her knowledge and talents to some good end.

It may not be amiss, simply as a matter of picking up the thread and making the story coherent, to note in passing the decay of the royal family down to the time that we find them in Brazil. It is an important fact not only in the history of the Bragança

---

[60] Armitage, John, *The History of Brazil*, London, 1836, Vol. I, p. 13 *seq.* Armitage's history is a continuation of that of Southey and takes the story from the arrival of the royal family in March, 1808 to 1831.

[61] Norton, Luís, *A corte de Portugal no Brasil*, São Paulo, 1938.

[62] Oliveira Lima, *Dom João VI no Brasil* (*op. cit.*, Vol. I, p. 17) considers John VI as the genuine founder of the Brazilian nation and the initiator of the process that was to culminate in its independence a few years later.

[63] A popular biography of John VI is that of Calmon, Pedro, *O Rei do Brasil*, Rio de Janeiro, 1935. For Carlota Joaquina in English, Cheke, Marcus, *Carlota Joaquina, Queen of Portugal*, London, 1947.

family, but in the prestige of the throne in Portugal itself. John V had died in 1750, after a reign whose financial prodigality has already been mentioned as one of the wonders of the age. Under his successor, Joseph I, Pombal achieved his ambitious program, to the detriment of king and country.

His reign lasted twenty-seven years and he was succeeded by Queen Maria I, his daughter, whose devotion to the Church was unceasing and who spent her life in the effort to undo the work of Pombal and make amends for his persecution of religion. As the years passed, her mind became unhinged. It was the young John, heir to Maria, and his wife Carlota who were to achieve a somewhat more normal court in far-off Rio de Janeiro. Their progeny were destined to play a role in the history of several countries: Pedro as emperor of Brazil; Carlos in the Carlist wars in Spain; and, finally, Dom Miguel. John was the second son and it was through the death of the heir, Joseph, that John and Carlota were in line for the succession. Carlota has gone down in history as vindictive, energetic, and having an immense flair for political intrigue which took a variety of forms, from trying to get her husband declared insane and herself made regent, to the revival of the idea of uniting the crowns of Spain and Portugal.

The history of how Brazil became independent is a facet of the larger story at which we have already hinted of the disappointment of the Portuguese at the results of Vienna. An additional factor was the absence of the king, who had left the country to drift without him, and the sentiments regarding the Holy Alliance during the critical years that followed the peace of 1815. Just as in the rest of Europe, liberalism flowered because of the efforts of the major powers to maintain legitimacy by force, if need be, so in Portugal, where that force was obvious and visible in the British occupants, liberalism tended to become associated with nationalism.[64]

In Brazil there developed a current of thought openly favorable to the liberal-constitutional pretensions in Portugal but which, a little later, was to run into the absence in the mother country of any particular sympathy for the political partnership of the two countries such as was envisaged by Brazilians as a consequence of

[64] Viana, António, *Apontamentos para a história diplomática contemporânea*, Lisbon, 1901, Vol. I, "A Revolução de 1820 e o Congresso de Verona."

the elevation of the colony to the level of a kingdom. Brazilian delegates attended the Portuguese Cortes in Lisbon and in general it is accurate to say that almost to the end there was no overwhelming sentiment in the American colony for separatism; this came about only when it was evident that equality of treatment and position was impossible.

The striking originality of Brazilian independence was that it was directed by Dom Pedro, son of John VI, and in collaboration with the Portuguese royal family itself.[65] The revolution of 1820 had wrought profound changes at home and on April 22, 1821, John VI departed for Lisbon leaving Dom Pedro as Regent of Brazil. Independence was now only a matter of time. It was not to be the work of revolutionaries or political incendiaries but a transformation from the top in full accord with the rational conviction of the regent that the time for separation had come. José Bonifacio de Andrada e Silva, the patriarch of Brazilian independence, was, in his personality and action, fairly symbolic of this essentially bloodless separation. Aside from the revolt of 1817, Brazil came into independence as smoothly as could reasonably be expected, retaining the monarchical institutions and, above all, the continuity of tradition from Portugal.

Portuguese America, in contrast with Spanish America, achieved independent existence without breaking with the past and this is one of the basic explanations why the territorial integrity and the relative tranquillity of the nineteenth century in Brazil was possible. There was no doctrinaire transformation on the basis of an unreal and quixotic dedication to republicanism. The same Bragança dynasty continued to rule with no basic perturbation of institutional life. It could scarcely have been planned better.

John VI had little stomach for ruling Portugal as a constitutional monarch along lines pleasing to Westminster. Moreover, Carlota and Miguel were opposed to the constitution and to any form of liberalism, preferring, during the difficult period when these ideas held sway, to exert their influence in the way of a return to the absolutist traditions of the past. The nineteenth century in Portugal is not a period of glory nor does heroism flourish in the midst of

---

[65] In the correspondence of Dom Pedro with his father, there is ample evidence of his intentions and sentiments (*Cartas dirigidas a S. M. o Senhor D. João VI Pelo Príncipe Real o Senhor D. Pedro de Alcântara*, Lisbon, 1822).

intrigue and jockeying for power. I shall not attempt in these pages more than the merest summary for the full story is intricate and dreary.

The years immediately following 1820, the constitution and the concern of the Holy Alliance, were ones during which the clash of liberals and absolutists continued until the accession of Miguel in 1826, who threw overboard most of the constitutional ideas and proposed to govern as an absolutist. The liberals expected Canning to help them in the struggle with the new authoritarianism. They were mistaken, for this was still the era of Metternich. The daughter of Pedro, Maria da Gloria, had been proclaimed Queen prior to Miguel's accession and her ousting opened the way for one of the dynastic rivalries which occur so constantly in the history of Portugal.

Few monarchs have been judged more severely or from a more radically different point of view than Dom Miguel. Obviously, the problem rests in part on the interpretation of terms. In using the word "liberal" we are prone to assume that of necessity whatever is done in the name of this vague doctrine is more decent and humanitarian than that which is executed by conservatives. We are conditioned in the twentieth century to accept liberal as more noble than conservative, republican as better than monarchical, and progressive as superior to reactionary. The conservatism of Dom Miguel was not exclusively reactionary in the ordinary sense of the word. To be sure, he proposed to preserve and defend what he conceived as the traditions of Portugal, but above all to liberate the nation from the yoke of foreign control. "The reign of Miguel is a short one but one that has left a deep impression in history: dignity, love of country. The sovereign was elevated to the throne by the will of the nation and the force of law."[66]

This short reign was characterized by a permanent civil war — a preview of what was to become, during the century, endemic in Portugal. The liberal *émigrés* agitated from every vantage point; and at one time actually undertook an expedition against the mainland from the Azores. When Louis Philippe was placed on the throne of France through the revolution of 1830, the Portuguese liberals found a new support and in the forward-looking, Masonic atmosphere of the Paris of 1830, political refugees from every

[66] Ameal, *História de Portugal, op. cit.*, p. 657.

corner of Europe found the conditions ideal for plotting their particular cause.[67] Pedro, first emperor of Brazil, was deeply and irrevocably involved in the defense of the interests of his daughter, excluded from the Portuguese throne by the alleged usurpation of her uncle, Miguel. The complicated problem of the Portuguese succession, which Pedro hoped to solve by the marriage of uncle and niece, need not detain us here.[68] The conflict of interests between Dom Pedro in Brazil and Dom Miguel in Portugal completed the effective separation of the two countries more than any other single event in their history. In 1831, Pedro abdicated in Brazil and left for Europe to take up the cause of his daughter who still bore the title, Queen of Portugal, and could count on support in the Azores. The former emperor landed in Portugal in 1832 at the head of an army and installed his forces in Porto. British troops entered from Algarve and in a month Portugal was handed over to Maria II as queen. The combination of the Spain of Maria Cristina, the France of Louis Philippe, and the England of Palmerston was too great for Miguel who left for exile in 1834. From this date onward the Portuguese monarchy declines in prestige and vigor; the course of events resembles strangely the one in France, from the reign of Charles X to the disaster of the second Napoleon in 1870. National unity is a thing of the past and the way is open now for the party struggle which was destined to desolate the land for almost a century until the reaction set in in 1926. Maria occupied the throne, thanks to her father's intervention from abroad and the bayonettes of British troops. This was not the most auspicious beginning for a glorious reign. The dreary panorama of civil war, pronunciamentos, and mob violence reads like the obituary of a once proud and heroic people. The litany of revolution runs somewhat as follows:

1836. The September revolution, in which the military and populace impose a restoration of the Constitution of 1822.[69]
In November of the same year, the queen and her supporters undertook a reaction.

---

[67] "Paris became a center of international action" (Lefebre, G., Pouthas, Ch. H., and Baumont, M., *Histoire de la France*, Paris, 1950, Vol. II, p. 228).

[68] Oliveira Lima, *Dom Pedro e Dom Miguel. A querela da sucessão*, São Paulo, 1925 and *D. Miguel no trono*, Coimbra, 1933.

[69] For this and subsequent events, see Peres, Damião, *História de Portugal*, *op. cit.*, Vol. VII, p. 253 *seq.*

1837. A new struggle between the so-called "Septembrists" and "Chartists."
1838. Promulgation of a new constitution as a compromise among the parties involved.
1839. The regime of Antonio Bernardo da Costa Cabral, distinguished by many elements of dictatorship.
1846. Revolt against Costa Cabral and his exile.

The Portugal of the mid-nineteenth century was an incredible chaos in which national political forces struggled for supremacy and the rest of Europe intervened more or less openly. A British fleet under Maitland entered the Tagus and a Spanish army crossed the frontier, presumedly for the purpose of restoring order, and the situation at this point was not dissimilar to that of certain of the Hispanic-American republics during the first decades of the twentieth century in which it became almost monotonous for governments to collapse, anarchy to prevail, and foreign intervention to follow as an inevitable consequence. Maria II died in 1853 and during the minority of the heir, her husband, Ferdinand of Coburg, served as regent. The queen had demonstrated remarkable stamina during these long years of political convulsion and military *coups*. Her son, Pedro V, belongs definitely to the romantic period, not only by reason of chronology but by temperament. In 1861 his brother Luis succeeded the young monarch who died prematurely at the age of twenty-four. The only solid accomplishment of this period was an agreement that has been called in Portuguese *rotativismo* whereby the government alternated in the hands of two of the major political parties. For twenty-eight years of his reign, Portugal slid farther and farther down the scale of misery, poverty, and political impotence. Alexandre Herculano at the end of his own life, faced by the spectacle of his country in so dire a situation, compared it to a body in the final agony.

Strangely enough when desolation characterized the national scene in Europe, there was a resurgence of interest in the overseas empire and a rekindling of the old fervor that had marked the great Portuguese adventure of previous centuries. Statesmen of the type of Sá Bandeira, Andrade Corvo, Luciano Cordeiro, and others gave intelligent attention to the problems of the territories in Africa and Asia. It was the age of Livingstone, Brazza, and Stanley whose penetration of Africa was to lead to a new political orientation of that continent. Suddenly Portugal was to be faced with the presence of British, French, Germans, and Belgians on a continent where heretofore she had wielded almost the sole European influence — all these others now constituting the gravest threat to the primacy of Portuguese occupation. Portugal was obliged to look to its own defenses, and it is testimony to the sagacity of the men of the time that they managed to save the empire from disintegration at a moment when the concerted forces of the rest of Europe looked upon the Lusitanian colonies as proper spheres of expansion. Portuguese efforts were stimulated by the scramble for Africa which was clearly in the offing. Andrade Corvo and Bernardino Antonio Gomes formed the *Commissão Geográphica Africana*, and between 1877 and 1882 several expeditions were launched, while in 1884, two outstanding Portuguese explorers, Augusto Cardoso and Serpa Pinto, pushed back the frontiers of Portuguese influence in the Angola area.[70]

But the difficulties were not always surmountable or even soluble by appeal to the past. Belgium and Portugal were involved in the most serious litigation regarding the Congo, which was destined to be the main topic at the conference provoked by Germany in 1884 and 1885. The activities of Cecil Rhodes culminated in the extention of British influence into the interior of Africa toward the Congo, thus splitting Angola from Mozambique.[71]

Portugal was incited to take action in its own territories to pacify the native peoples in a state of more or less permanent revolt and give tangible evidence that its rule was not a mere fiction that dated back to Vasco da Gama and had no further reality. African exploration received a remarkable spurt in the 1890's; in Angola under Artur de Paiva, Mario de Sousa Dias, Massano de Amorim, Teixeira Moutinho, João de Almeida, and many others.[72] On the Mozambique side, similar enterprises were undertaken under Caldas Xavier, Eduardo Costa, and the extraordinary Mousinho de Al-

[70] De Serpa Pinto, Carlota, *A vida breve e ardente de Serpa Pinto*, Lisbon 1937. An excellent summary on Portuguese Africa during the second half of the last century by Professor Manuel Lopes de Almeida in Peres, *História de Portugal*, *op. cit.*, Volume VII, pp. 563–606.

[71] The British ultimatum of 1889 made perfectly clear that Portugal was to be deprived of territory linking its possessions on the two oceans.

[72] The bibliography is obviously extensive for this and related points. One of the most interesting sources for Angola, for example, is the works of Gastão Sousa Dias: *Artur de Paiva*, Lisbon, 1938; *Como Serpa Pinto atravessou a Africa*, Lisbon, 1944; *Jornadas heroicas de Artur de Paiva*, Lisbon, 1949; and Galvão Henrique, *História do nosso Tempo*, Lisbon, 1931.

buquerque, who, between 1895 and 1896, carried on a series of colonial wars that pacified vast sections of the interior of the colony.

Portugal was pressed by the Belgians, the French, and, what was the most aggravating of all, by their own British allies. In view of the growing threat of conflict with the Boers in South Africa, the British government sought to accommodate the Germans as much as possible and in 1898 signed a secret agreement to provide for the eventual dismemberment of the Portuguese empire in Africa: Angola to fall to Germany and Mozambique to Great Britain. This was to happen in the event — which both great powers considered more or less probable — that the Portuguese government would find itself unable in the not distant future to maintain the integrity of its possessions. Its financial difficulties were cited as the basic cause for this rapid disintegration of its dominions beyond the seas.[73]

But internally Portugal was still far from capable of the necessary reaction. The commencement of the reign of Charles I in 1889 was distinguished by profound agitation, resulting from the British pressure in the colonial world and which was interpreted in Portugal as the gravest affront to the national sovereignty. The fever of patriotism that gripped the country was exploited by the republicans, who were now of some influence, in the abortive revolution of January, 1891. The significance of this event was not great, but it was destined to have the most profound repercussions for this was the first time that a movement had been launched which was an attack on the throne itself.[74]

The older parties had become, by this time, totally discredited and Portugal was crying for a renewal of its spirit and for a leadership capable of galvanizing the country into action. Oliveira Martins, the historian, launched what was known as the *Vida Nova* which aspired to grouping those who were eager for a reaffirmation of authority and for a reform of the public administration. Charles I stands out in the midst of this descent toward the abyss for his abnegation and keen desire to save the nation. In the international

[73] Baumont, Maurice, *L'Essor industriel et l'Impérialisme colonial, (1878–1904)*, Paris, 1937, p. 266. Schwarze, Fritz, *Das deutsch-englische Abkommen über die portugiesischen Kolonien vom 30 August 1898*, Göttingen, 1931.

[74] Coelho, Manuel Maria, "A revolta de 31 de Janeiro de 1891," in *História do regime republicano em Portugal*, Lisbon, 1930. Directed by Luis de Montalvor, Vol. I, p. 339.

field there is definite improvement. The Treaty of Windsor with Britain in 1899 rectified, to a certain extent, the effects of the ultimatum and allayed the fear in Portugal that London was planning to let its ally down. The king, cognizant of the precipitation with which events were moving, turned the government over to João Franco, who became virtually dictator of Portugal. But the forces of disorder and anarchy were far more powerful than supposed. In 1908 a revolution broke out while the royal family was at Vila Viçosa. On February 1, however, the king and the crown prince were murdered. The Council of State in panic dismissed Franco and literally abdicated in the face of the opposition in a series of events that recalls vividly the course in Spain in 1931 when the monarchy fell and anarchy became the rule; the monarchy revealing its incapacity to control the situation which threatened its existence. The Portuguese monarchy was felled on the day that it showed a total inability to react against the policy of terrorism that had been instituted against it. Manuel II succeeded to the throne to rule for exactly a year and a half, or, more accurately, to preside over the demise of the traditional regime. In October of 1910, the Republic was proclaimed and, aside from a handful of loyal supporters who fought to the last to impede this manifestation of ineptitude, inefficiency, and mob rule, there was little opposition.

How did the Republic manage to succeed in a land where republicanism was unknown and where little in the way of a tradition existed in which it might be nurtured? It may be useful to describe rapidly the broad lines of Portuguese republicanism since the problem is basic to the study of the present regime in the country, and explain how it has come about that the Revolution of 1926, which brought Dr. Oliveira Salazar into the government, did not then and has not since then proposed to change the structure of the state itself.

The origins of republicanism as a political ideal are to be found ultimately in the gradual transformation of the intellectual climate of Portugal from the French Revolution onward. The penetration of romanticism around 1825 and the political turmoil to which we have made reference meant that a great many of the men of letters became ardent adherents of the new currents of thought elsewhere in Europe. The isolation of Portugal was somewhat broken down by the exiles who spent part of their lives abroad and absorbed by this experience ideas which were alien to the national traditionalism. Men of the caliber of Almeida Garrett, Alexandre Herculano, and António Feliciano de Castilho symbolize this new Portugal of the mid-nineteenth century. The advent in letters of the period of realism, extending from 1870 to 1900, roughly, is enormously significant in terms of an accentuation of the national pessimism. If the Portuguese are somewhat prone to pessimism in the best of circumstances, the new school of letters which gave tone and direction to the thinking of the country during the last decades of the nineteenth century aggravated this tendency. It is a fascinating period from the point of view of ideas and the undisputed talent of many of its representatives. It is the period of the extraordinary lyricist, Antero de Quental, whose haunting verse is scarcely surpassed in any modern literature and who ended his life a suicide. It is the age of Teófilo Braga, whose influence in education and letters was fundamental and who represented the purest of Positivism with an impact that took years to wear off. His fecundity was almost alarming as year after year he poured forth books in every field of human activity. Pessimism becomes even more acute in the group known in the annals of Portuguese literary history as the *vencidos da vida* (the vanquished by life) and to which belonged Eça de Queiroz, Oliveira Martins, Ramalho Ortigão, and others. The attitude in many cases of the men of letters was skeptical of the current political scene, somewhat cynical as in the case of Eça, or simply depressed as in that of Herculano who spent the last years of his life in complete retirement, disillusioned by the course of events.

A definition of terms is necessary quite plainly if we are to speak of "republicanism" and "liberalism" in the Portugal of the nineteenth and twentieth centuries. Republicanism was, first of all, a vague conception without any concrete manifestation until much later although many of the conspiracies of the earlier part of the past century were republican in character.[75]

At the time of the Cortes in 1821, when constitutional reform was the principal topic, the English political philosopher Jeremy

---

[75] Arriaga, José de, *História da revolução de 1820*, Lisbon, 1886, p. 650. An account is given here of the antecedents of the revolt of 1818 and how Fernandes Tomás, the leader, was intrigued and charmed by his reading of the constitution of Bolivia which he considered as the most appropriate for Portugal.

Bentham addressed a communication (June 5, 1821) in which he praised the efforts of the assembly for devising a system comparable only to that of the United States.

The reality, was, however, that up to 1848 republicanism was limited strictly to the sporadic and even to the purely anecdotal, for there was no organized movement that could be designated by this term. During the period of Miguel, republicanism was synonymous with liberalism, and was an emotional appeal rather than a party program. Antonio Feliciano de Castilho translated, in 1846, some of Lamennais and in his preface writes in a language that has a definite Jacobite flavor. The Revolution of 1848 in France resounded throughout Europe and with its successful conclusion, republicanism received a considerable impetus. In Portugal the first newspaper of this tendency appeared under the title of *A República*. In the initial issue, the appeal to republicanism ran as follows:

> Republic. A government in conformity with nature? A government based on equality? A government of liberty without license? A government of love among all men? A government of angels? Republic! The name is vain if it remains nothing but a name. Does Portugal want a Republic? We reply that the nation does. . . .[76]

The republican movement was the heir of liberal monarchism and was indebted for its growth more to external circumstances than to developments within Portugal. The party, if we may use the term, was born after the French Revolution of 1848 and disappeared with the proclamation of the empire. It reappeared in 1873 when Spain experimented with its first republican regime and collapsed at the same time as the Spanish one did. In 1876 it revived once more, largely because of the defeat of Napoleon III and the establishment of the Third French Republic.[77] The events of 1848 really raised no more than an echo in far-off Portugal and it took thirty years for the attitudes that prospered in the France that liquidated Louis Philippe to travel the distance that separates Paris from Lisbon.

The fact that Portuguese republicanism was so inseparably bound up with what happened elsewhere leads one to reflect on the degree

---

[76] April 25, 1848, reproduced in *História do regime republicano em Portugal*, *op. cit.*, Vol. I, p. 214.

[77] Lopes, Arthur Ribeiro, *Histoire de la république portugaise*, Paris, 1939, p. 67.

that this political doctrine may be considered as an authentic expression of the Portuguese mind at all. As in the case of Spain, there is something artificial and fictitious about the republicanism that flourished in Portugal. Spain's tragedy, both in 1873 and in 1931, was that the republic was foisted on a nation in which there were almost literally no republicans. In Portugal, the same kind of *intelligentsia*, the same restricted intellectual leadership and the same professional aspirants to political power constituted the basic nucleus out of which republicanism sprang. It may be repeated once more that the change of regime of 1908–1910 was not the fruit of a slow transformation of the national mentality, but the seizure of power at a moment when the monarchy was reduced to the most pathetic impotence. What was particularly evident, and this was entirely to the honor of Portugal, was that Portuguese society was not propitious for engendering its own revoluntionary ideology; the best that it could do was to adapt that which had originated abroad. The Portuguese people have always demonstrated a sound basis of common sense, and the general atmosphere of the land has been singularly unaccommodating to general ideas of social revolution. The formative process consisted of the new intellectual tone to which we have referred. A vague, nonviolent Proudhonism invaded certain spirits: "Kantian rationalism was the mold in which the natural tendencies of Herculano found their expression."[78] The mid-nineteenth century was an era filled with generous and in most cases quite unrealizable ideas. Federalism and Iberian unity were topics that acquired a certain actuality and revealed perhaps more than anything else the romantic tendency of the period.[79] Henriquez Nogueira was the most outstanding of the leaders of this federationist idea to which, together with federalism went most of the social ideas of the time, derived in abundance from Louis Blanc, Fourier, and the numerous social experiments going on in France.

The idea of organizing the working classes took form in two enterprises, the *Associação dos Operários* and the *Centro Promotor dos Melhoramentos das Classes Laboriosas*. The latter institution was not at all revolutionary until after 1872 when Marxism penetrated Portugal. Intellectually the last part of the nineteenth cen-

[78] Oliveira Martins, *Portugal contemporáneo*, *op. cit.*, Vol. II, p. 308.

[79] Palmeirim, L. A., *Portugal e os seus detractores*, Lisbon 1877; Ribeiro, Rafael, *O iberismo dos monárquicos*, Lisbon, 1930.

tury was a period when such writers as Antero de Quental amplified his activity from the purely academic to the practical and became a revolutionary militant.[80] The Spanish revolution of 1868 aroused boundless enthusiasm in him and he wrote warmly of the "revolutionary mission" and employed other of the conventional phrases of the extreme left.[81] Hegel, Michelet, and Proudhon had formed his mind and he was now talking glibly of the accomplished mission of the bourgeoisie and the need for instituting the social revolution once the political had been achieved. The task of the middle class was to bring about political freedom and the industrial order. Once this task had been completed, it was the mission of militant socialism to erect the "structure of equality and justice." This was the essence of contemporary socialism.[82] Socialism was above all the doctrine of natural evolution; the social expression of biological evolutionism. "The thought of Oliveira Martins differed from marxism and collectivism and tended to compare more with the doctrine of Proudhon in a fusion of the Middle Class and the proletariat in a new social class."[83]

Socialists and the ordinary run of republicans did not see eye to eye on one important point: to the former, the supreme necessity was an economic revolution, whereas the latter inclined to the conviction that the primary task at hand was the political. Teófilo Braga was led to exclaim that "socialism is a deterrent to the political reorganization of the country . . . for the socialists consider the republic as simply a political formula of the middle class conservatives."[84]

One of the essential consequences of this propaganda was the attempt to re-evaluate the whole of Portuguese history. The nation had lived for generations in the belief that the discoveries and conquests of the sixteenth century had represented its apex of glory and that it was to this past of achievement that the nationality should look for inspiration and self-confidence. Oliveira Martins

---

[80] The great poet collaborated in such periodicals as the *República federal* and *Pensamento social*. In 1872, more or less, he entered into contacts with the representatives of the Spanish section of the Internationale and in the same year aided in the foundation of the Portuguese branch of the International Workers Association.

[81] Quental, Antero de, "Pensamento social," in *Prosas*, Coimbra, 1931.

[82] *Ibid.* Article, "O que é a Internacional," in *Prosas*, Vol. II, pp. 172–173.

[83] *Regime republicano em Portugal, op. cit.*, Vol. I, p. 246.

[84] Braga, Teófilo, *História das idéias republicanas*, Lisbon, p. 315.

attacked this idea furiously, denouncing the discoveries as an inept age of monumental stupidity and the occupation of the Orient as a record of murder, rapine, robbery, and sacrilege. Eça de Queiroz, in a polemic that caused a sensation, insisted that a patriotism that does not recognize historical truth is a patriotism lacking a sound basis and can be construed purely as an archaeological survival.[85]

The more eloquent of Portuguese liberal spokesmen searched abroad for examples to justify their assertions and found in Switzerland the most perfect example of the federalistic state. Carrilho Videira wrote that "no unified republic has endured up to this time unless supported periodically by terror which invariably ends in dictatorship."[86] In 1873 the Central Federal Republican Committee of Lisbon issued its program of principles which is an excellent summary of the status of republican thought up to that time. This program included two federal capitals, Lisbon and Porto; complete equality of the two sexes; guarantee of the right to freedom of speech, work, credit, and property; elimination of all restriction to the marriage contract since this is simply an arrangement between men and women and should suffer no interference; direct elections; constitution of a federal parliament; abolition of the army; free education; and a host of labor clauses which were to protect women and children.[87] This text reflects perfectly the exultant thought that characterized Portuguese republicanism; in fact, the same rhetoric that distinguished the republicanism of Spain as well. The comparison with the Spanish experience is valid, for Portugal was going through the same evolution as the sister nation, and destined in many ways to suffer identical deceptions. A comparison of the articles of the proposed document of 1873 and the Spanish republican constitution both of the first and the second republics is instructive. Federalism presided prominently over the gestation of both constitutions and the experience of 1931 in Spain demonstrated eloquently that a federalist system, no matter how theoretically sound, was, in the case of these traditionally unitarian nations, the forerunner of complete disintegration and separatism.

Republicanism was not limited to literary circles but began

[85] Ribeiro Lopes, *Histoire de la république portugaise*, *op. cit.*, p. 80.

[86] *Regime republicano*, *op. cit.*, p. 252.

[87] Published in the journal, *Rebate*, Lisbon, No. 1, 1873. Reproduced entirely in *Regime republicano*, Vol. I, p. 251.

to infiltrate downward among the classes that heretofore had been untouched by its propaganda or were too obtuse to appreciate the blessings of its doctrine. In 1879 a federal center was inaugurated and a republican club organized under the presidency of Oliveira Marreca. The journal, *Trinta Diabos* increased its circulation considerably and made a much greater impact on public opinion. The celebration in 1880 of the third centenary of Camões and the humiliations suffered by Portugal in Africa awakened a new zeal that was quickly converted in criticism of the regime that had led Portugal to this sorry pass. In 1884 two republican deputies were elected to the Chambers and, in positions of importance in the administration and especially in the academic world, republican figures were more prominent. The striking analogy between what was happening in Portugal at this time and the evolution of Spanish republicanism is again evident.

The monarchists attempted to meet this challenge by various political movements in defense of the regime, or at least the principle of monarchical continuity. The very fact that monarchism was forced to have recourse to the stratagems of partisan politics demonstrated the degree of bankruptcy which it had reached. A sound monarchism does not depend on parties since the institutional superstructure of the state is above the contingencies of day-by-day politics. The British monarchy would be on the way out if the Labour Party were opposed not merely to the Conservatives as a *party* but to the existence of the crown as the basic premise or assumption on which the whole operation of the state depended. When the point had been reached in Portugal that the monarchy was fighting for its life on the same plane as the republican movement which was seeking to unhorse it — then there was little doubt that its days were definitely numbered.

The essential feature of republicanism was the degree to which the movement grasped every source of national indignation to further its own ends, or to express it as does the brilliant Spanish historian of Republican Portugal, Jesús Pabón, "to use patriotism against the country."[88] The ability of republicanism to seize power must be understood against the background of the action of four

[88] Pabón, Jesús, *La revolución portuguesa*, Madrid, 1941, Vol. I, p. 15. The expression in the original is far more graphic: "*emplear el patriotismo contra la Patria.*"

deputies who occupied seats in the Chambers during the last years of the monarchy: Antonio José de Almeida, Alfonso Costa, Alexander Braga, and João de Menezes. The latter was especially addicted to harangues to the working class in which republican propaganda was adroitly mixed with appeals to the class struggle. Each of these deputies, in his own right and in his contacts with specific sectors of public opinion, contributed powerfully to sowing the seeds of dissension and antagonism to the monarchy. Irony, cynicism, blunt attacks, and conspiracy all went into the complex ingredients from which the Portuguese republic was distilled. But republicanism needed a personality that would inspire confidence among those to whom a change of regimen was a detestable thing full of unsuspected dangers and risks both at home and abroad. It was Bernardino Machado who provided this front, in much the same way as the calm prestige and apparent tranquillity of Aniceto Alcalá Zamora in the Spain of 1931 seemed to constitute a guarantee that the vociferous extremism of some of the propagandists was in reality nothing but window dressing and the republicans were in fact honorable gentlemen who would disturb the established order as little as possible. In other words, once the intellectual atmosphere had been prepared and the leadership in letters and the arts had been won over to the antimonarchical cause, the next task was to make the movement popularly respectable, to give it a front and to make it seem just another party of the government. If republicanism did triumph it would be no more than the abandonment of office by the king and the accession of a president, who would have the particular virtue of not remaining on the scene beyond a fixed period of time.

Machado was of Brazilian origin and had been professor at Coimbra University and minister of the crown. He was wealthy, had an admirably large family, and looked very much like a benevolent patriarch. His own thought on the matter of the advent of the republic was "that it is necessary that the republican party become a government party." The ideal would be to bring about a peaceful revolution with republicans in ministerial posts from which vantage point they could ease the monarch out with the minimum of scandal.[89] In July, 1903, Machado made a public profession of his republicanism and expectation was enormous that

[89] Brandão, Raúl, *Memórias*, Lisbon, 1925, p. 154.

this former minister of the monarchy would deliver a sensational declaration to account for his change of political affiliation. His ideas were as confused as his personality was elastic and courteous. He was capable of praising anarchism and eulogizing the Bishop of Coimbra in the same breath and no one seemed inclined to hold him to account for the flagrant contradiction.[90]

In any well-conceived plot against the established political order in the so-called Latin countries, the religious question is bound to come to the surface sooner or later. Portuguese republicanism was intimately connected with this phase of the national life. "The campaign of threats and hatred of religion and the Church that the republican leaders promoted with tireless zeal at the end of the monarchical period made it plain what the republican revolution would be like once it triumphed."[91] On February 17, 1901, nine years before the proclamation of the republic, an outbreak of antireligious sentiment led to the stoning of the Catholic paper A *Palavra* and to insults to the clergy, accompanied by the demand for the suppression of the religious communities. The immediate enemy as always was the Society of Jesus, a reminder of the Pombal period when the Society had been the target of the persecution. Freemasonry, which wielded considerable influence in this Portugal in disintegration, entered the fray and demanded that the communities be eliminated.[92]

There seems to be little doubt that Freemasonry assumed the direction of much of the plotting against the monarchy and, even though its membership may have been inadequate for the task of overthrowing the existing institutions, its collaboration was of inestimable importance in furthering the atmosphere of disorder and growing anarchy.[93]

There were, of course, contrary forces, which realized fully the

---

[90] Machado, Bernardino, *Da monarchia para a república*, Coimbra, 1912, p. 232.

[91] Lourenço, Joaquim Maria, *Situação jurídica da Igreja em Portugal*, Coimbra, 1943, 2 ed., p. 95.

[92] Santos, Machado, *A revolução portuguesa*, Lisbon, 1919, p. 16.

[93] Poncins, L. de, *La F. M. d'après ses documents secrets*, Paris, 1934. See also, by the same writer, in Spanish translation, *Oliveira Salazar y el Nuevo Portugal*, San Sebastián, 1937. Bernardino Machado himself was a militant Mason, as he testifies in his book, *Da monarchia para a república*, *op. cit.*, p. 166. The head of Portuguese Masonry, Sebastião de Magalhães Lima, was a fervent republican and *Deus ex machina* of many of the events that prepared the way for the change. Magalhães, Lima, *Episodios da minha vida*, Lisbon, 1927.

disasters toward which Portugal was moving. The conflict as far back as 1876 when the supporters of the monarchy had divided between those who supported the constitution granted by the king as against a constitution emanating from popular choice, brought into existence the so-called *regenerador* group and the *progresista*, the latter inclined toward accommodation with the tendencies of the day. The system whereby the groups alternated in power converted them into instruments of policy and not of principle. In the long run the *regeneradores* supported the dictatorship of João Franco; the *progresistas* became more and more identified with the disorder itself.[94] The strength of monarchism, insofar as it may be said to have had any in the grim days before 1910, was in a certain number of individual personalities.

José Luciano de Castro was for years the most outstanding figure of the *progresistas*, that is, the liberal monarchists or left wing of the party that supported the established order but with grave reservations. He served at intervals as minister of state from 1869 on, but when the crisis came with the collapse of the dictatorship he was incapable of action in the same way as were the befuddled and terrified monarchists in the Spain of April, 1931, when none of them, save possibly the Count of Romanones, were capable of facing the contingency of the moment with a minimum of dignity.[95]

And so, in the midst of financial difficulties which were almost insoluble; in the gnawing fear that the colonies in Africa might be ignominiously lost, in the vicious and irresponsible attacks of a press that knew no limits and no decorum, in the terrible aftermath of the assassination of Dom Carlos and the frantic effort of Dom Manuel to bring order out of chaos, the republic was ushered in. The analysis of the circumstances of how this came about precisely is not easy because the abundant literature regarding it is filled with eulogies and calumnies, with attack and counterattack. As in other cases in which a multisecular institution has collapsed, the first impression of the establishment of the republic in Portugal is: How could this happen for so little apparent cause? How could a monarchy that had centuries behind it topple so irrevocably in so short a space of time? "The Republic came in; the

---

[94] Pabón, Jesús, *op. cit.*, p. 44 *seq.*
[95] *Cartas d'el Rei D. Carlos a José Luciano de Castro*, Lisbon, 1927.

monarchy went out. That was the entire story."[96] The advent of the republic was not a pitched battle in which one side won, but the ultimate step in a gradual, inevitable process. When Teixeira de Sousa, head of the "regeneradores" took over power in the last days of the monarchy, it was already too late to oppose any effective action at the onrush of republicanism. His ideas of thwarting republican designs consisted of outliberalizing the most extreme in terms of policy proposals and, if this attitude failed, to use force. Neither measure could possibly be effective in 1910.[97] Within hours, on October 5, 1910, and with a minimum of gunplay, the republic was proclaimed and Dom Manuel, with the members of his immediate family, slipped away into exile. The Portuguese people received this change with total indifference.[98] And so this melancholy page of Portuguese history was concluded. The grandeur of the monarchy in the period of its greatness had given way to hesitation and doubt; the monarchy had lost faith in itself, and, what was far more serious, the monarchists had lost faith in the monarchy.

It is my intention in the next few pages to recount as succinctly as possible the vicissitudes of the republic from its inauguration in the midst of the delirious enthusiasm of its supporters until sixteen years later, in the face of unending crisis and financial insolvency, the leaders of the republic appealed to a university professor in Coimbra to assume the gigantic task of rescuing the country from the follies of its governors.

Republicanism in Latin Europe, and very particularly this special brand of republicanism that carries with it the label of "liberal," tends to be implacable with its foes and, in the name of freedom, generally manages to suppress whatever remnants of it that still

---

[96] Pabón, *op. cit.*, p. 103.

[97] De Sousa, Teixeira, *Para a história da revolução*, Lisbon, p. 181.

[98] "On October 5, 1910, the republic was proclaimed in Lisbon. The majority of the population accepted the new state of affairs with perfect indifference, while the wildest enthusiasm overcame the partisans of the movement" (Guyomard, George, *La dictature militaire au Portugal. Impressions d'un français retour de Lisbonne*, Paris, 1927, p. 5). "The extraordinary success of the revolution is explainable by the attitude of the royalists who did not even try to defend it. There has even been talk of complicity on the part of the last monarchical government. What is certain is that the majority of the political figures of the former dynastic parties made every haste to express their support of the republic." (Marvaud, Angel, *Le Portugal et ses colonies*, Paris, 1912, p. 52).

subsist. Brito Camacho, one of the three republican leaders to whom we have referred, stated on the assumption of power by his party:

> The men who are called to organize the republic must be implacable with the discredited servants of the monarchy who in the responsible posts they have occupied are the cause of the major crimes of the late regime.[99]

One Portuguese writer has summarized the period from 1908 to 1921, that is, from the two years of republican agitation preceding the fall of the monarchy until the crisis of 1921, as one in which twenty-two revolutions were hatched. The balance sheet, if we may call it such, of republican instability may be summed up as follows:

SUCCESSFUL REVOLUTIONS:

- October 5, 1910. Establishment of the Republic
- May 14, 1915. Movement against the government of Pimenta de Castro
- December 5, 1917. Revolution against the government of Costa Norton de Matos
- October 19, 1921. Revolution against the government of Antonio Granjo

UNSUCCESSFUL REVOLUTIONS:

- April 27, 1913. Revolt against government of Alfonso Costa
- December 13, 1916. Movement of Machado Santos against government of Alfonso Costa Norton de Matos
- January 8, 1918. Naval forces against Sidónio Paes
- January 28, 1908. Republicans revolt against João Franco
- October 12, 1918. Rebellion against the government of Sidónio Paes
- January 17, 1919. Rebellion in Santarem and Lisbon
- October 19, 1921. Revolt against the government of Ginestal Machado

COUPS D'ETAT AND MINOR REBELLIONS:

This includes a whole series of movements, many of them monarchical in character, from September 29, 1911, to May 21, 1921.[100]

Obviously in this listing of disturbances of a political nature no mention is made of the minor disorders: strikes, riots, attacks of political personalities, and persecutions of every kind. The number

[99] Quoted in Nunes, Leopoldo, *Carmona, estudo biográfico*, Lisbon, 1942, p. 42.

[100] Sá Pereira, Consigliere, *A noite sangrenta*. Lisbon, 1924, pp. 178–179.

was infinite and in the pages of *O Século* of Lisbon (February 7, 1934) an attempt was made to draw up a comprehensive list of this kind of incident that contributed to the anarchy of the republican period. The result showed something like seventeen incidents of a fairly grave character in 1911; nineteen in 1912; thirteen in 1913; eighteen in 1914; twenty in 1915; and twenty-three in 1919. From 1911 to 1927, occurrences of a violent nature, most of them politically inspired, reach the respectable figure of 208.[101]

Three times under the republic, dictatorship was installed as the response to anarchy. The broad periods of the republic are as follows:

I. From October 5, 1910, to May 14, 1915
Afonso Costa is the leading figure, as Justice minister in the first provisional government and then as President of the Council of Ministers. General Pimenta de Castro sought through a personal dictatorship to put an end to the confusion.

II. May 14, 1915, to December 14, 1918
After the second provisional presidency of Teófilo Braga, Bernardino Machado became president of the republic. The dictatorship of Sidónio Paes ends this regime and in turn Sidónio Paes is assassinated.

III. December 14, 1918, to April 27, 1928
Presidents come and go. Teixeira Gomes, Bernardino Machado and others. Antonio José de Almeida is the only one to complete his term of office. The rebellion of Gomes da Costa leads to the dictatorship of General Carmona. On April 27, 1928, Dr. Oliveira Salazar took over definitely the finance ministry and from this date on, the fortunes of Portugal change radically.[102]

It would be a dreary business indeed to follow the tortuous evolution of the first eighteen years of republicanism and I have no intention of doing so, since the main points that have been raised indicate the character of the new regime and the reasons that explain the overwhelming necessity in 1926–1928 for a reorientation to save the country from ruin. But before undertaking an examination of the National Revolution, as it is called, it may be convenient to point out some of the features of republican administration up to that time which motivated this change.

As has been indicated, it was plain that the new republican regime was to follow a policy of extreme rigor with the Church and the

[101] Pabón, *op. cit.*, pp. 112–113.

[102] The outline of broad divisions corresponds to that suggested by Jesús Pabón, *op. cit.*, pp. 113–114.

religious communities. Within three days of the proclamation of the republic, on October 8, 1910, the Minister of Justice, Afonso Costa, put into effect the decrees of Pombal against the Jesuits and those of 1834 against the other religious orders. Every foreign member of a religious community was expelled and every member of Portuguese nationality was obliged by law to lead a secular life and abandon the convent or monastery.

That these measures were not the product of the passions of the moment is amply demonstrated by the fact that a year later, in the republican constitution of 1911, the same provisions are included against the Church and the orders.[103] In addition to these specific efforts to destroy religious life, a whole series of ordinances and other pieces of legislation aim at the secularization of Portuguese society. In view of the importance of the restoration of religion in the Portugal of the present regime, it is significant to note to what degree the country had been systematically shorn of its Catholic character and to what extent the secularist republic of the first eighteen years had gone in the avowed effort to make the nation as little Catholic as possible. It is against this background of the destruction of the Catholic customs, practices, and ultimately the faith of the Portuguese people that must be set the miracle of Fatima in 1917 and the providential accession to power of Oliveira Salazar eleven years later.

The process of dechristianization may be summarized in the following manner, by noting the principal regulations or laws that were put into effect:

October 18, 1910: Abolition of all religious oaths

October 22, 1910: All religious instruction in the schools was abolished[104]

October 23, 1910: Abolition of the Faculty of Theology of the University of Coimbra; a faculty that had existed since the foundation of the university in 1290

November 14, 1910: Decree abolishing the chair of Canon Law in the Faculty of Law

[103] Lourenço, Joaquim, *op. cit.*, p. 95 *seq.*, with full text of the various laws and decrees and the constitutional provision, Article 3, part 12.

[104] The justification of the elimination of religious instruction in the schools is particularly interesting. The purpose was "to satisfy the liberal spirit and the republican aspirations of the Portuguese people. . . . The teaching of dogma is incompatible with sound pedagogical principles." Article 3 notes that religious instruction is out of keeping with the democratic hopes of Portugal (*ibid.*, p. 99).

October 26, 1910: Elimination of Holy Days as far as public observance was concerned
February 28, 1911: In all official correspondence and documents, no reference was to be made to the Christian era
November 28, 1910: The armed forces were forbidden to take part in any religious ceremony
November 3, 1910: Civil divorce provided.[105]

Against these and numerous other provisions, the Portuguese bishops protested vigorously, especially in the Collective Pastoral of December 24, 1910. Bishop Sebastião de Vasconcelos of Beja was removed from his episcopal office by the government and sent into exile for his pains.[106]

His Holiness, Pope Pius X in the encyclical *Jamdudum in Lusitania* of May 24, 1911, stated that "since the establishment of the republican government, there began to be promulgated measures that evidence an open hatred of the Church. . . . In a fanatical desire to secularize the civil organization and leave no trace of religion in public acts, the religious feast days were eliminated, divorce established and religious instruction removed from the schools."[107]

But the culmination of this process was the law providing for the separation of Church and State of April 20, 1911. For eight centuries the Portuguese State and Church had been united; united, that is, in the Catholic sense which does not imply fusion or the absence of a frontier between the two authorities in matters of jurisdiction.[108] Even in the period of great tension, although cordial collaboration was certainly lacking, the juridical principle that the Church was the predominating religious force in the country was not abandoned until the republicans brought about the separation. What goes by the name of "Separation" was in fact anything but that. Instead of leaving the Church to its own devices,

[105] On December 25, 1910 — and the date was perhaps chosen deliberately — it was announced that "the marriage contract is purely civil and is presumed permanent, unless severed by divorce" (*ibid.*, p. 107).

[106] Almeida, Fortunato de, *História da Igreja em Portugal*, Coimbra, 1910, Vol. IV, p. 69 *seq.*

[107] Lourenço, Joaquim Maria, *op. cit.*, pp. 125–126.

[108] This is no place to enter upon the intricate question of "union of Church and State." The comment of Heinrich A. Rommen, *The State in Catholic Thought*, St. Louis and London, 1947, p. 593, will serve in the case of Portugal: "So we have to distinguish the Catholic type of a friendly cooperation between Church and Christian state in a legal form from the full union as it has existed in England since the break with Rome."

the State moved in on strictly ecclesiastical activities and invaded the proper sphere of the Church to such a degree as to exert a literal tyranny over it. That persecution and ultimate extinction and not simply separation was envisaged is clear both from the text of the law itself and from the explanations provided at the time of its passage by such political figures as the Minister of Justice, Afonso Costa, who stated in a speech at Porto in defense of the new arrangement, "that Catholicism would become extinct in Portugal within two or three generations."[109]

The law of separation was a thoroughgoing effort to destroy the Catholic Church as a moral and legal personality in the life of the nation. Catholicism was reduced to the same level as every other religious belief and the Church lost all claim to its traditional juridical status. The Church lost all claims to its own property, and the churches, chapels, and everything else that belonged to it passed to the State. This is one of the most sweeping cases of expropriation by the State that one can find in contemporary history, comparable, perhaps, to what transpired in Mexico in the application of the legal and constitutional restrictions on the freedom of property holding by the Church or its ministers. In order to prevent the freedom of communication of the hierarchy with Rome and with the faithful, Article 181 provided that under no circumstances should any bull, pastoral, or other letter of the Holy See or of the bishops themselves be read or made public unless approved by the government. In other words, the State proposed the most rigorous censorship on the normal communications between ecclesiastical authorities. In Article 184, the State arrogated to itself the right to intervene in the seminaries, name the professors, and determine what textbooks should be used. Every effort was made by legal means to make impossible seminary studies and especially those preparatory for theology.

In addition to the reaction of the bishops, the effectiveness of the application of these regulations and restrictions depended in large measure on the attitude of the local functionaries themselves.

---

[109] *Diario do Governo*, Lisbon, April 21, 1911; da Silva, M. D. Coelho, *Dez meses de governo do Bispado do Porto*, Porto, 1912, p. 28. Magalhães Lima, a leading Freemason in Lausanne, Switzerland declared that the Portuguese republic "has accomplished in the destruction of clericalism what it has taken others years to do" (*De la monarchie á la république laïque*, Lausanne, 1912, pp. 18–25). Also Lourenço, Joaquim Maria, *op. cit.*, p. 130.

In many localities the law was virtually a dead letter, whereas in others, where anticlerical zeal was the order of the day, the law was applied in all its details. The Holy See condemned the form of separation that had taken place in Portugal and protested against the violence that had been employed against the clergy. Little by little, Catholic opinion that had been completely demoralized by the events of 1910 began to coalesce in associations and organizations and later political groups, whose purpose was to combat the anti-religious policy of the government.

In December of 1917, as indicated in the summary a few pages back of the history of the republic, a revolutionary movement under the leadership of Sidónio Paes broke out, the purpose of which was to restore justice and decency in the commonplace rhetoric of the day. Sidónio Paes is one of the most intriguing personalities in contemporary Portuguese history. An artillery officer, he later abandoned the military career for a professorship in mathematics at Coimbra, where he was a student of Bernardino Machado, whom he was destined to oust from the presidency in 1917. He was a republican, a Mason, a deputy, and a minister, and nothing indicated, in 1917, that he represented anything more than the most routine type of careerism under the new republican dispensation. He had represented Portugal in Berlin and had left Germany when the war came and Portugal was slowly pulled into the allied camp. Sidónio Paes was capable of making a revolution but not of governing and he became, oddly enough, the "man on horseback" of the Revolution of 1917. By one of those rarities of metamorphosis, Sidónio Paes created the impression of dignity and charm, which were elements the republic badly lacked.[110] One of the initial acts of Sidónio Paes was to abrogate the laws against the various members of the hierarchy that had been decreed in the name of the separation of Church and State.[111] On January 3, 1918, the president dissolved the commission for the execution of the separation of Church and State which had been charged with the responsibility of putting these measures into effect.

Although the modification of many of the measures gave satisfaction to Catholic opinion, the regime of Sidónio Paes was very far from a formal reversal of this policy. One of the principal de-

[110] Costa, Cunha e, *A Igreja católica e Sidónio Paes*, Coimbra, 1921.
[111] *Ibid.*, p. 124.

mands by Catholics was that relations with the Holy See be normalized. By decree on July 10, 1918, the Portuguese legation accredited to the Vatican was re-established and Monsignor Locatelli was named Apostolic Nuncio in Lisbon.[112]

Although the decisions of Sidónio Paes did not entirely satisfy the demands of the Catholics, it was a substantial step forward toward the normalization of relations and a hiatus, at least, in the frenzied war that the republic had initiated against the Church.[113] In spite of the assassination of Sidónio Paes the mitigation of the legislation remained the law and even the missions in the colonial areas were somewhat protected from that date onward. The law of separation had obstructed seriously the work of the missions in Africa and Asia, since State aid had been withdrawn and the effectiveness of their work was left entirely to the initiative of private enterprise and the charity of the Portuguese Catholics themselves. Another consequence of the relaxing of the Catholic character of the Portuguese State was the introduction of Protestant missions into the overseas territories, which dated from the Berlin Conference of 1885 and responded to the insistence of the foreign powers which equated Protestant mission activity with liberalism.

Once the Holy See had been recognized, the more violent phase of Catholic opposition disappeared, for it was no longer legitimate for Catholic organizations to oppose the established regime with the latent purpose of bringing about a change. One of the first creations of the hierarchy was the *Centro Católico*. Regarding its work, we may perhaps cite the words of Dr. Oliveira Salazar, at the time professor at Coimbra University:

> The purpose of the *Centro Católico* in obedience to the directives of the Holy See is to sacrifice for the moment their political revindications as regards the regime and unite for political action in conformity with the constitution for the purpose of securing a recognition of the rights and liberties of the Church.[114]

The attitude of Catholics toward the republic was one of political prudence. While accepting the regime *de facto*, the objective of the *Centro* was to bring about the re-establishment of harmonious relations without committing itself to the basic question of the regime

---

[112] Brandão, Raul, *Vale de Josafat*, Lisbon, 1933, p. 98.
[113] Costa, Cunha e, *op. cit.*, p. 138; Lourenço, Joaquim Maria, *op. cit.*, p. 210.
[114] Salazar, Oliveira, *Centro Católico português*, Coimbra, 1922, p. 38.

per se.[115] Unfortunately the Catholic Center was unable to rally the forces of Catholicism in the country on a large scale and many Catholics either refused their adherence or actually rejected the movement's validity. The result was a serious weakening of Catholic opinion in the political field. The reaction in public opinion was healthy. In 1922, a provision was presented to the parliament to undo the evil that had been perpetrated in 1910 and allow religious instruction in the schools in conformity with the views of the overwhelming majority of the Portuguese people.[116] In February of 1926 the parliament paid public homage to the person of the Supreme Pontiff, Pius XI, and the then president, Bernardino Machado, was able to announce that the peace that had been established with the Vatican was a guarantee that never again should a religious-civil conflict arise in Portugal.[117] And so it was that on the eve of the national revolution, Portugal had progressed to the point where the doctrinaire anticlericalism of the first sixteen years no longer produced a substantial echo. It was now evident that anti-Catholicism was an ineffective and disastrous national policy which could have no other results than to lead the nation to sterile and exhausting dissension.

In this way, year after year the republic made its confused, turbulent way toward the final stage which was the admission of total impotency. The participation of Portugal in World War I was an inglorious affair, largely the result of the English alliance and the feeling of pro-Allied sentiment in the land. It did not contribute, to be sure, to the strengthening of the internal institutions. But before we leave the republic and its somber history of violence and assassination together with fiscal and economic degeneration, it may be useful, in order to complete the picture, to refer briefly to the development in public opinion of a sentiment

[115] *Ibid.*, p. 53.

[116] João Paulo Freite interviewed a number of leaders for the *Diario de Noticias* of Lisbon and published the results of the survey (January 13, 1923). Raúl Brandão asserted that "All education should be religious." Guerra Junqueira, the literary figure, stated that "In the organization of Portugal as in all properly organized societies, the most important function is the religious. We should grant the Church the liberty and the necessary means for carrying out its mission integrally. Portugal is today the only country where the barbarous practice prevails of prohibiting in the schools all religious instruction" (*ibid.*, January 26, 1923).

[117] *Novidades*, Lisbon, February 7, 1926.

of restoration which, in most cases, took the form of monarchism. The term that covers this tendency is generally that of "Portuguese integralism."

The nation had definitely not abdicated its dream of greatness nor were all the citizenry content with the bumbling, inefficient governments that succeeded one another monotonously. Deep down in the national consciousness was a sentiment of rebellion, of holy indignation at the turpitude of those who were running public affairs and a grim determination to put things right and return the country to the path that had once, in what now seemed the dim past, led it to great heights of prestige. It is not easy to summarize this sentiment which for a long time was ill-defined and consisted primarily of a bitter sense of frustration at the manner in which the monarchy had been overturned. It is a period of profound disenchantment from which the vigorous policy of Salazar was to rescue the people. It may be compared in its corrosive effects with the nineteenth century to which we have alluded when the Portuguese were more than ready to relinquish any pretense of playing a role in the world. Logically, the remedy was not simply a return to monarchy. No convinced monarchists were ready to assume that the restoration pure and simple of the state of affairs of 1910 would bring happiness and well-being, for it was obvious to all that the monarchy, at the time of its fall, had suffered from certain irremediable defects. It was a new monarchism which developed, convinced that the principle was sound if applied properly and if the national institutions that supported the crown were of the healthy, sound kind that the times demanded.[118] Anti-revolutionary sentiment has a long history in Portugal and a host of able spokesmen had represented in letters and the press the belief that monarchy with its stability and traditionalism represented the only firm basis for the national life.[119]

No solution on the purely sentimental plane was valid for the

[118] Preto, Rolão, *Para além da guerra*, Lisbon, 1942, p. 31. "The disquietude of people is quickly converted into despair. The monarchy was dead and the republic was stillborn." There were many who doubted that the monarchy could be restored effectively. "The monarchy could live as long as it imitated the republic; that is to say, in so far as it was willing to sign its own death warrant" (Raposo, Hipólito, *Dois nacionalismos*, Lisbon, 1929, pp. 16–17).

[119] See Campos, Fernando, *O pensamento contra-revolucionário em Portugal*, Lisbon, 1933, 2 vols. This author treats particularly of the nineteenth century and those who dealt with the problem from the traditionalist point of view.

desperate situation after 1910. Merely to appeal to the past and sigh for its restoration was a form of escapism. The monarchist leaders realized this fully. The sentimental protest was against the men who had made the republic; the intellectual protest was against the republican ideology itself.[120] Antonio Sardinha, a student at Coimbra in the days of the republic's first excesses, was the nucleus of what was to become Portuguese integralism or nationalism.[121] There were monarchist uprisings and even a considerable body of exiles who from Galicia and other strategic points hoped to regain the motherland for the cause. In 1913 a group of these young idealists founded the review *Alma portuguesa* where for the first time the expression "*integralismo lusitano*" appeared.[122]

The outstanding personality of this current of thought was undoubtedly António Sardinha. He was born in Monforte de Alentejo in 1887 and after graduating from Coimbra, following the traditional intellectual process of almost every Portuguese since the Middle Ages, he was, on the conclusion of his studies in 1911, a republican. His conversion, which was both political and religious, occurred in 1912 and from that date onward he was destined to become one of the most eloquent voices in Portugal against the conception of the State and its mission as conceived by the republicans. João do Amaral has noted how, in 1910, there was no organized movement favorable to traditionalism and that gradually, almost without effort, the disillusioned and those depressed with the shoddiness of the republic began to recapitulate.[123] In April of 1914 the first issue of *Nação portuguesa* was published and with it a statement of the principles that guided the new movement: an organic monarchy, that was to be traditionalist and antiparliamentarian. It must be noted, however, that the movement did not aspire to become simply another political party, whose number was already legion, but to create a sentiment that would surpass the contingencies of politics.[124]

---

[120] Sardinha, Antonio, *Processo dum Rei*, Porto, 1937, p. 90.

[121] De Almeida Braga, Louis, *Sob o pendão real*, Lisbon, 1942, p. 414.

[122] Ramos Ascensão, *O integralismo lusitano*, Lisbon, 1943, p. 24. Also Ameal, João, *Panorama do nacionalismo português*, Lisbon, 1932. As a traditionalist view of Portuguese history, Múrias, Manuel, *Portugal: Império*, Lisbon, 1939.

[123] Amaral, João do, *Aqui d'El-Rei*, Lisbon, No. 1, February, 1941.

[124] Botelho, Alfonso, *El integralismo portugués*, Madrid, 1953, p. 11. "Its founders wanted only to comprehend and defend the nation. For this reason

One of the hardy perennials on the Portuguese political scene was the "Iberian question," that is, the problem of the possible union with Spain. The monarchists suffered from the accusation that the monarchy had been fundamentally favorable to union and that the partisans of the restoration were secretly convinced that the intervention of Spain would further their cause. The allegedly antinational character of monarchism was one of the principal arguments against its validity. The result was that integralism devoted a great deal of its energies to demonstrating what must be a self-evident proposition for anyone reasonably objective in his judgment, that Portugal is not Spain and that its claim to an independent existence is supported by every consideration of culture and history. There seems little doubt that there were affinities between Portuguese integralism and *Action française* in France and that Maurras exerted an unquestioned influence on the thought of this generation of Portuguese who were seeking a reaffirmation of authority and traditionalism. There is in the thought of Sardinha and his collaborators a powerful element of hope; a hope that Portugal would return to its days of greatness; a hope that a new Sebastian would enter the mouth of the Tagus to restore the glories of empire.

It would be unfair to assume that on the republican side there were no serious efforts to introduce reform and make of the new organization of the State an effective and honorable institution. Men of the caliber of António Sergio, Minister of Education under President Teixeira Gomes, was one of the founders of the review *Seara Nova* in 1921 which had, as its program, aimed at a fundamental intellectual revolution; the improvement of bureaucratic competence and a moral cleansing of the climate of government. In the pages of António Sergio, are numerous critiques of integralism and considerations regarding the democratic processes as they operated in Portugal.[125]

What then was the situation of the republic on the eve of the new revolution that was impending? A review of the political and administrative conditions need hardly be undertaken again for it

---

the initial concern was not to launch a new political program, effective only in the field of practical politics, but to recreate the atmosphere and climate of the national life." Also Vide, Fernão da, *O pensamento integralista*, Lisbon, 1923.

[125] Sergio, António, *Ensaios*, Lisbon, 1936. In several volumes. See particularly Volume III, p. 264 seq.

is evident from previous comments that this was little short of disastrous. On the financial side, the state of affairs was chaotic. This was not entirely the work of the republic, for financial depression had set in long before, in the days of the monarchy.[126]

In 1923, Dr. António José de Almeida completed his term of office, the first of the presidents of Portugal to do so, and his successor was Texeira de Gomes, former ambassador in London. The first indication of rebellion against the stagnation of this period was the unsuccessful uprising of March 5, 1925. On April 18 of the same year a second movement was launched by a group of the military with no better luck and on July 19, a third led by one Captain Mendes Cabeçadas fared the same way. The military men involved in these subversive movements were all brought to trial and took advantage of the situation to denounce the political leadership of the country. Several of them were acquitted and were thus able later to participate in the National Revolution of May 28, 1926. At the end of 1925 Bernardino Machado was elected president and cabinet crisis followed cabinet crisis with five new governments in the course of that single year. Portugal was the scene at this time of a major financial scandal in the form of a counterfeiting plot in which Portuguese banknotes manufactured fraudulently in London were passed off in Portugal through a new bank, the Angola e Metrópoli. Inflation caused by the inpouring of fake banknotes added to the trials of the national economy.

The movement of May, 1926, which is the point of departure for the renovation of Portugal and ultimately for the establishment of the *Estado Novo,* was military in character and started in the north under the direction of General Gomes da Costa, who had guided Portugal's military forces during World War I. The story of how this revolution was spectacularly successful and led to the opening of the new era of Oliveira Salazar is the topic of the next chapter.

---

[126] Marvaud, Angel, *Le portugal et ses colonies, op. cit.,* p. 76. "The deplorable state of Portuguese finances was the consequence of an accumulation of constant deficits in relation to the budget."

Chapter V

THE NATIONAL REVOLUTION.

ANTÓNIO OLIVEIRA SALAZAR, THE MAN

THE National Revolution was launched at Braga where General Gomes da Costa issued a proclamation in which he analyzed the state of affairs in the country and appealed to his fellow countrymen to enter the struggle for national dignity and honor.[1] The immediate purpose of this clarion call to arms and to victory was to rid the country of the Democratic party, which was then in power, and restore something like sanity in public life. The words, "liberty, honor and dignity," were bandied about freely and it was clear that once more, as in the past, the army had taken into its hands the salvation of the nation. The conception behind the movement was basically one of "moral insurrection" to cauterize the running sores of corruption and greed that had infected the whole body politic. The story of the actual conspiracy is confused, as events of this sort are likely to be. It reminds one a bit of the immediate background of the eighteenth of July, 1936, in Spain when the air was full of charges and countercharges and the universal belief that something was about to happen without any precise information as to what. Some of the officers involved had been in the thing

[1] The supercharged atmosphere of scandal, suspicion, and hopelessness was echoed by António María da Silva when he wrote in the *Diario de Lisboa* (May 26, 1926) that "I do not wish to deny that there is plotting. I have confidence in the army and in the navy." A detailed account of the conspiracy and the events of May 28 in Pabón, *op. cit.*, p. 219 seq.

from the beginning. Some, like Gomes da Costa himself, entered the plot only a few days before it broke and General Carmona, later to be president of the republic, became involved after the blow had been delivered.[2]

The difficulty seemed to be that the movement was perfectly clear as to what to do on May 28 but not at all sure what to do on the subsequent days when government would have to be managed and administration provided. Opposition was merely nominal, for the government in power lacked all will to survive.[3] The absence of a political doctrine to give content and substance to the movement was the primary characteristic.[4] The army officers in Braga had worked out a plan of action for the moment of victory that involved "the formation of a national ministry above and beyond political parties within the framework of the republic for the purpose of restoring honesty and decency in public administration."[5] Between May 28 and May 31, the whole country had risen in arms and the central government in Lisbon capitulated. Dr. Bernardino Machado resigned as president and all powers, including all ministries, were turned over to Mendes Cabeçadas. The revolution had triumphed all along the line with scarcely a single casualty. The events of this decisive moment in Portuguese history strike one as singularly lacking in heroism and as one of the more dull revolutions in history. In spite of the absence of dramatic moments, the twenty-eighth of May marks a remarkable stage in the recent history of Portugal. The complete unity of the army was a factor of the greatest importance and with the army, the entire population. The astonishing thing was that in the course of the five days there appeared nowhere the slightest appreciable support of the regime against which the revolution had risen. The wonder was that someone had not pushed it over long before that.

On June 4, the new government was installed, consisting of a triumvirate: Mendes Cabeçadas, Gomes da Costa and Carmona,

---

[2] Costa, Gomes da, *Memorias*, Lisbon, 1930, p. 238. Also Paxeco, Oscar, *Os que arrancarram em 28 de maio*, Lisbon, 1937, pp. 44–45.

[3] Nunes, Leopoldo, *Carmona. Estudo biográfico*, *op. cit.*, p. 122.

[4] Pimenta, Alfredo, *Nas vésperas do Estado novo*, Porto, 1937, p. 30. "The personal and military qualities of General Gomes da Costa are not brought into question. They are evident and undebatable. What was lacking was a specific political program and a sound organic doctrine."

[5] Reproduced in Pabón, *op. cit.*, Vol. II, p. 222.

the latter in charge of foreign affairs. The other ministerial posts were distributed about, and that of finance was under the direction of Dr. António Oliveira Salazar. In this modest way, the National Revolution, which had started out as a simple house-cleaning operation to rid the nation of the administrative rubbish which had accumulated and bring new blood to the management of public affairs, was now on the threshold of one of the most audacious and far-reaching transformations in the whole history of the nation. And this transformation was attached to the name of the last of the new ministers who succeeded to power.

It was plain from the beginning that the provisional government could scarcely be expected to appreciate the immensity of the task that the national regeneration demanded: the responsible leaders were far more wedded to reform than to reformation and saw the situation more or less in the light of the liberalism that had prevailed for so many decades. But even the new revolution was doomed to suffer the same handicaps as the preceding regimes: the basic instability that was the curse of Portuguese government. "In little more than a month of the National Revolution, a great many men had occupied posts in the new regime who had scarcely had time, so short was their period of service, to take care of even the routine matters of their office."[6]

In was in June of 1926 that Professor Salazar of the University of Coimbra was asked to take over the finance ministry. Antonio Ferro, to whom we are indebted for two excellent volumes on Dr. Salazar, as well as other works of inestimable value on contemporary Portugal, has told the story of this first appearance, and the details of it have long since become a part of the historical folklore of the nation. General Gomes da Costa and a group of his supporters were waiting at the airport of Amadora on June 6, 1926, when the general, within a week of his triumphal conduct of the revolution, was asked as to some of his ministerial appointments. "The new government is the best we can find at a moment like this. The Minister of Finance is to be a certain Salazar from Coimbra. Everyone speaks very highly of him. Do you happen to know him?"[7] No one seemed to know him for he had been

[6] Nunes, Leopoldo, *Carmona*, *op. cit.*, p. 131.

[7] Ferro, António, *Salazar, o homem e a sua obra*, Lisbon, 1935, 3 ed., p. 3. This book exists in English translation under the title *Salazar. Portugal and her leader*, London, 1939.

turned up by some of the military during the course of the recent revolution and from his reputation at the university seemed quite the man for the uninviting job of trying to bring order out of the chaos of national finances. Salazar spent less than a week on the job in 1926, just long enough, says Antonio Ferro, "to leave a faint trail of hope."

From the moment that he had gone down from the university to Lisbon to undertake the ungrateful task, Salazar had made it plain that unless he were given liberty of action it would be impossible to carry on. He was fearful from the first of the "fragility" of the situation, and especially the unceasing *coups d'état* that made sustained work impossible and were an invitation for ministers to do well for themselves in the short time they enjoyed the prerogatives of office. The story is told, that may or may not be apocryphal, that after a few days in office and after insisting uncompromisingly on the strictest economy and the severest measures of retrenchment, Salazar was entirely aware that these proposals were unpalatable to his colleagues and that the probability of his lasting on the job were slim in the extreme. The story goes that one morning he called his own office and heard a strange voice on the other end of the line. When he asked who was speaking, he was informed that it was the Minister of Finance. "Oh," he said quietly, "I was under the impression that I was Minister of Finance." He hung up the receiver and took the night train back to Coimbra.[8]

The chronic instability continued as before. In the space of a few months, Portugal had the government of Cabeçadas, followed by a triumvirate, after which several ministers resigned and a new government was produced with the military more heavily represented. The army expressed its lack of confidence in Gomes da Costa and by July the victorious commander of the bloodless campaign which was the revolution of May 28 was no longer in

---

[8] Egerton, F. C. C., *Salazar, Rebuilder of Portugal,* London, 1943, p. 114. The same anecdote is recounted in Dr. E. Brongersma's introduction to *Dr. Antonio de Oliveira Salazar, Minister-President van Portugal. Corporatief Portugal,* Hilversum, 1941, p. 17. "Three days were sufficient for the new minister (precisely as one contact in 1918 was enough for Marshal Lyautey to realize his total disagreement with our parliament) to realize his authority was quite insufficient to rehabilitate the finances of the country" (Schreiber, Emile, *Le Portugal de Salazar,* Paris, 1938, p. 25).

power. General Carmona had taken his place.[9] On July 9, 1926, General Carmona consolidated his new government, and in the delicate post of finance minister he placed General Sinel de Cordes. The regime may be considered as the "dictatorship" of Carmona and was to last until April, 1928. In November, 1926, Carmona had been designated as provisional president of the republic. It was in 1928 that the definitive consolidation took place with the combination Carmona-Salazar in power.

General Carmona is given far too little credit in the study of contemporary Portugal, since the figure of Salazar looms so large on the landscape and tends to obscure everyone else around him. The new president was by no means a genius nor did he have the impulsive audacity of Gomes da Costa, his predecessor. Carmona was a gentleman, a profoundly honest man, and deeply conscious of the task before him and of his own limitations. In innumerable declarations he insisted that his government was not made up of supermen, but that it was motivated by excellent intentions and had as its fundamental purpose to get to work and make the machinery of State operate. The two problems that faced the country between 1926 and 1928 were: first, the chronic political disorder and the absence of the habit of living politically without violence; and second, the financial disorder which had brought the country to the brink of absolute disaster.[10] These months were not free from counterrevolutionary activity and the longer the regime retained power the more frequent became these manifestations of opposition. In September, 1926, a plot against the State was discovered under the leadership of Colonel João de Almeida; in January, 1927, another conspiracy was uncovered with the explosion of a bomb; in February of the same year, the most serious attempt to overthrow the regime occurred. In both the north of the country and in Lisbon this rebellion took on the proportions of a minor civil war and for three days open battles went on between the supporters of the government and the rebels.[11] The events of this month were the most serious of all the challenges laid down to

[9] Nunes, Leopoldo, A *ditadura militar Dois anos de história política contemporánea*, Lisbon, 1928, 2 ed., p. 88.

[10] Corte-Real, João Afonso, *O Chefe do Estado*, Lisbon, 1941.

[11] Pabón, *op. cit.*, Vol. II, pp. 238–239; Costa, Sousa, *Heróis desconhecidos. Lisboa revolucionaria*, Lisbon, 1935, p. 300 *seq.*

the revolution of May 28, and for a long time afterward, in spite of victory, the cause of profound disquietude on the part of the Carmona government.

If the fight against anarchy had been won at least temporarily, the struggle for financial survival was another thing entirely. The regime could not postpone the inevitable; it was indispensable that a solution be found for the state of penury of the national treasury.[12]

The country lived in a state of chronic deficit, and since many of the republican parties believed in their own propaganda and remained in power too short a time to come to grips with the problem, the preference was for vague assurances that all was well and to hope for the best. Year after year the indebtedness mounted to fantastic proportions for a poor and ill-developed country. "The deficits between 1893 and 1910 were covered principally by increasing the floating debt through the issuance of bank bills by the treasury and loans from the Bank of Portugal to the state.[13] The figures themselves are somewhat deceptive, but in general terms it is possible to fix with accuracy the trend of Portuguese finances up to the time that Dr. Salazar assumed office in 1928. From the sum of twenty-five thousand *contos* (a thousand *escudos* constitute a *conto*) in 1914–1915, the annual deficit grew steadily, until it reached 501,000 in 1922–1923 and 642,000 in 1926–1927. There was no effort to eliminate the deficits; the most that was undertaken was to liquidate the previous ones, so that the problem was attacked not in its causes but in its effect. Inflation was increased by a constant flow of paper money. Living costs on the eve of the Salazar regime were about thirty times what they had been in 1914. The deficit curve in the national budget is in itself instructive as an illustration of the frustrated administration that preceded the revolution:

The following table, expressed in thousands of *contos* gives a graphic picture of the steady rise in the deficit:

[12] A fundamental work on this problem is that of Correia, Araujo, *Portugal económico e financeiro*, Lisbon, 1938, 2 vols.

[13] *Ibid.*, Vol. I, p. 15; Lewandowski, Maurice, "Une expérience de redressement — M. Oliveira Salazar" in *Revue des Deux mondes*, Paris, June 1, 1934, p. 521. This observer who deals with the financial regeneration of the country places the deficit at 600,000,000 *escudos*.

1910–1911	0.3	1918–1919	115
1911–1912	6	1920–1921	188
1914–1915	25	1922–1923	501
1915–1916	38	1926–1927	642[14]
1916–1917	50		

The statistics for indebtedness and for the increase of currency show exactly the same type of spiral increase. In the comparison of expenditures between the last parliamentary regime and the dictatorship of 1927, it is evident that the increase was enormous, estimated in something like 233,600 *contos*.[15] A very large increase was to be noted in the budgets of the various defense ministries and agencies; a reflection of the anxiety of the government to assure its own permanence in power. The dilemma facing a revolutionary government such as that of 1926–1927 in a country like Portugal is terrifying and as near insoluble as any problem that can be imagined. Obviously, the first task is to reduce the budget and cut expenses to a minimum. On the other hand the forces that work against this simple solution are numerous. Those who have adhered to the victorious movement expect to be rewarded and it is not through curbing the budget and reducing radically the administrative personnel that these hundreds of office seekers will be satisfied. At the same time, the new regime is tempted to stimulate economic development and point to a program of construction and social advancement to justify itself. This costs money and is not always compatible with serious reductions in expenditure. There is always the danger of political turmoil and the repetition of revolution, as we have noted during the first two years of the Carmona dictatorship. This demands large expenditures for the army and the navy and the periods of disorder constitute, in a negative way, a severe loss for the nation through economic paralyzation and the stoppage of work. All in all, the best will in the world was inadequate to the task of providing a solution to the central problem of all: the economic and financial health of Portugal.

Some efforts were made in this direction before Salazar took over in 1928. Sinel de Cordes, as finance minister, undertook to

---

[14] *A obra de Salazar na pasta das finanças. 27 de abril de 1928 a 28 de agosto de 1940*, Lisbon, 1941, p. 15. This excellent study of the work of Salazar in the financial ministry opens with a short but succinct examination of the financial status of the country on the eve of the new regime.

[15] Leal, Cunha, *A obra intangivel do Dr. Oliveira Salazar*, Lisbon, 1950, p. 22.

work on the British debt which terminated in the agreement of December 31, 1926.[16] The next step was to throw the country more or less on the mercy of the League of Nations and seek financial consolation in Geneva. This had already been done in several cases: Austria, Hungary, and Bulgaria between 1923 and 1926. The Portuguese government proposed a similar arrangement for bailing the country out economically in the autumn of 1927, following which a commission of the League visited Portugal, reported favorably on the loan, and proposed the machinery for putting the money to work. This included inquiry into the financial state of the nation and the Bank of Portugal, in other words, international control of Portuguese finances. The arrangement was rejected out of hand by Portuguese public opinion and Ivens Ferraz, who had been charged with the mission, was acclaimed by a people who considered their integrity and honor saved by the refusal to become a financial charge of the international organization.[17]

If honor was saved, the finances were still precisely where they were before, if not worse. On April 15, 1928, General Oscar Carmona was proclaimed president of the republic and in his official pronouncement he declared that the permanent secretary of finances would be a man of the highest competence in whom the whole nation could have the greatest confidence. Duarte Pacheco, Minister of Public Instruction, was given the task of persuading Dr. Oliveira Salazar to undertake once more, and in very different conditions, the ungrateful job of putting the financial house in order.[18]

---

[16] Pabón, *op. cit.*, p. 248.

[17] Pabón, *op. cit.*, Vol. I, p. 250; Derrick, Michael, *The Portugal of Salazar*, London, 1938, p. 48. "General Ivens Ferraz conducted himself with honor in refusing in the name of the country the humiliating clause of international inspection of our finances" (Ameal, João de, *História de Portugal, op. cit.*, p. 786). See also the excellent study of Gilles, P., *Le redressement financier au Portugal*, Paris, 1938, p. 26.

[18] Dr. Salazar himself has described his own emotions on this occasion. Christine Garnier, a French journalist, has published her *Vacances avec Salazar*, Paris, 1952, p. 63, which consist of a series of interviews on men and events since 1926. "I know that right after the revolution . . . you came into office in spite of yourself . . . I would like to know what your sentiments were the day Duarte Pacheco arrived in Coimbra for the purpose of taking you back to Lisbon." Salazar's reply is enormously revealing of the man's temperament: "I hesitated all night. I did not know if I should accept the proposition that was made me. I was terribly depressed at the idea of leaving the University. I was fully aware of the distance between the man of study and the man of action. And then, I was afraid." Mlle. Garnier was astonished at this reply and asked

Salazar had left no considerable mark on national affairs during the few days he had been minister in 1926. During the first months of 1928, however, the Lisbon daily, *Novidades*, had published a series of his articles in which he dealt with the urgent financial reform and suggested certain lines of action aimed at achieving this objective. On April 27, 1928, he entered upon his new duties, and he was insistent above all on independence from interested influence. In his acceptance speech, made with a complete absence of fanfare and theatricals, Salazar, who was thirty-nine years old on the twenty-eighth of that month, insisted that he was assuming the new responsibilities solely because of the dictates of conscience and out of duty to the country and that no commitments of friendship obligated him in the discharge of his appointed task. Thin, pallid, dressed in the conventional black of the Portuguese professional man, Salazar took the oath of office. In his own words: "The new Minister of Finance is a modest person. His health is somewhat precarious although he is never ill. He has a limited capacity for work, but labors tirelessly."[19]

Of all the strong men of twentieth-century Europe, Salazar is unquestionably the least personalized of them all. In that legion of reformers, mystics, military swashbucklers, and megalomaniacs who have occupied the stage since World War I, Salazar fits into no conventional classification; indeed, he defies all facile generalizations. He has something of the grim determination to rebuild a ruined land of Kemal Ataturk; something of the mystical conviction in the destiny of his own people of Francisco Franco, a profound attachment to Catholicism that is comparable to that of Dollfuss or Monsignor Seipel, but none of the strident histrionics of a Mussolini and much less the hysteria of a Hitler. Salazar left his university classes reluctantly and has never pretended to want anything better than a modest academic career. He has never indulged in mass oratory nor does he go in for flattery of the mob. He had no party when he came to power; no organization behind him, no *Bewegung* on which he rode to the zenith of authority. He did not develop, prior to 1928, an elaborate doctrine

---

why. "Naturally I was afraid," Salazar said. "I foresaw the possibility of failure. Imagine if I did not succeed in putting the finances in shape, what would my students at the University think of me?"

[19] Salazar, *Discursos e notas políticas*, Coimbra, 1937, Vol. I, p. 3.

nor did he stage a march on Lisbon. There was no propaganda and there were no balcony scenes.

Austerity is the only word to describe the extraordinary manner in which the savior of Portugal has lived for the past twenty-five years. It is well known that university salaries at Coimbra do not encourage sybaritism. The minister of finance and, later, president of the Council of Ministers has retained for a quarter of a century the keen sense of propriety and a modest way of life that does not exceed that of any comfortably established civil servant. He has never married and when the State proposed that he receive, at its expense, house, furnishings, and domestic service, he refused everything but the house — and a modest one at that. Once when he suffered a broken leg, he insisted on paying the hospital charges himself. While in Lisbon, he resides in a three-room flat which he has himself furnished according to his taste. "When I leave office, I shall turn out my pockets and shake the dust from them for I do not want to take even that with me."[20]

With a modest salary, the Portuguese "dictator," so called, is hardly equipped for the more fantastic extravagances. In the excellent pages that Christine Garnier has given us, we get an insight into the personal delicacy, the devotion to friends, and the discreet charity of Dr. Salazar. We see plainly enough that here is a man to whom the pomp and glory of high office have meant little or nothing, and who has retained, like a religious in his cell, an unfailing sense of proportion and dedication to the job at hand.

Salazar came into the government not because he was a Catholic but because he was an economist, and it is as a professor of political economy that we must consider him fundamentally. His speeches, while fairly numerous over the years, are all directed at specific problems and specific situations. He is no orator, nor does he seek to *épater le bourgeois* by any display of oratorical pyrotechnics. He is by all odds the least *visible* of the outstanding public figures of our day, and his love of retirement has become proverbial. Contact with his people has never implied a vulgar manifestation of political self-seeking nor a will to win popularity through dazzling promises. Salazar has never promised Portugal anything but hard work, rectitude, tenacity, and the kind of daily homework in economics that he imposed on his students at Coimbra.

---

[20] Garnier, Christine, *Vacances avec Salazar*, *op. cit.*, p. 146.

Salazar is first and foremost an extremely competent housekeeper and he has conceived of Portugal as a *ménage* which was in dire need of being put in order lest it fall apart.[21]

This solitary figure, whose serenity of view and excellence of judgment has given Portugal a new lease on life, has always conceived of his mission as a heavy cross which it has been his lot to bear. In a preface to another volume of the speeches, the Portuguese statesman expresses the melancholy that has maintained him for years far from Coimbra:

> Ten years ago I was obliged to abandon that priesthood which is the teaching career and to carry a heavy cross along most difficult paths. And many times in the midst of anxieties, responsibilities, and difficulties, I find myself alone and in order to carry on must depend on three basic things: my conscience, my will power and the learning that I absorbed at my university.[22]

"Salazar carries his responsibility of office like the Christian his cross" are the words of the distinguished Swiss historian Gonzague de Reynold, who has written one of the most delightful and illuminating books of our time on Portugal.[23]

António de Oliveira Salazar was born in 1889 at Vimeiro, not far from Santa Comba in the upper Beira. His father, António Oliveira, was of most modest circumstances and worked on a nearby farm. His parents brought up the one son and four daughters and by dint of hard labor managed to bring together enough capital to purchase a small piece of land and set up an inn at Santa Comba.[24] It is not without significance that one of Salazar's sisters,

[21] In the preface of one of the volumes of his collected addresses, Salazar writes as follows: "As I am one of the heads of government who talks the least, it takes time for me to organize the material for a volume of speeches. This (1943) is the third in fifteen years, that is to say, one volume for each five years of my government" (Oliveira Salazar, *Discursos e notas políticas 1938–1943*, *op. cit.*, Vol. III, p. v). Salazar himself has said of his austere life, "I owe to Providence the grace of poverty; devoid of goods of value, very little binds me to the wheel of fortune. Not that I ever missed not having lucrative posts, riches, ostentations. And to earn my daily bread on the modest scale to which I have accustomed myself and in which I can live, I have not to enmesh myself in the tangle of business or in embarrassing commitments. I am an independent man" (speech delivered at Porto to the National Union, January 7, 1949; text in *My Deposition*, Lisbon, 1949, p. 6).

[22] Salazar, *Discursos 1935–37*, Coimbra, 1937, Vol. II, pp. xxi–xxii.

[23] Reynold, Gonzague de, *Portugal*, *op. cit.*, p. 268.

[24] Couto, João Xavier do Carmo, *O homem que rehabilitou Portugal*, Lisbon, 1940, p. 9; Derrick, *op. cit.*, p. 51 seq. Christine Garnier introduces her biography of Salazar under the title, "*L'Ecolier de Vimeiro*," *op. cit.*, p. 32 seq.

Marta, taught elementary school at Vimeiro for more than forty years and when she received Christine Garnier, in the modest dwelling where the family had been brought up, her comment was that her illustrious brother was "still as kind and as patient as when he was a child."[25] Certainly in this typical peasant background, composed of an endless struggle to buy a small piece of land and a house, the future minister of finance acquired a keen, practical knowledge of the virtues of economy.

Salazar began his instruction under the direction of one José Duarte, who received, in his modest dwelling, a number of the children of the vicinity. One can easily imagine these rudimentary rural schools, where the teacher is scarcely more advanced in learning than the pupils and where the maximum is some small knowledge of writing, arithmetic, and reading. António Salazar began life in that hard school of poverty and frugality which has been the lot of the Portuguese peasantry for centuries. He sprang from the solid stock that gave the world the discoverers, and conquerors of Africa, Brazil, and the East. After that he studied with Father João Pimentel at Viseu and in 1901 he passed on to the local seminary where he spent the next eight years, but did not accept ordination at the end of that period. It was not unusual, in the Portugal of the time, to do the full philosophy and theology courses in a seminary without taking orders at the conclusion. There was perhaps something in the idea that, since it was the custom for families to destine their sons to the priesthood, Salazar had undertaken his studies without any very definitely fixed vocation. Those of his former comrades who have written or spoken of those far-off days, describe him as rigorous in carrying out the rules and as distinguished by a great deal of prudence which was one of the reasons for the delay in turning his talents to action.[26] Above all, he has retained the ascetic quality of life which he developed at a very early age. For a time he taught in the Via Sacra College — history, letters, and mathematics and then, almost to a day with the proclamation of the republic, entered Coimbra as a student.

Salazar studied law and gave lessons to lyceum students over a period of four years. For fifteen years, as student and later as pro-

---

[25] Garnier, *op. cit.*, p. 34.

[26] Garnier, Christine, *op. cit.*, p. 44 *seq.*, in quoting Mario de Figueiredo, a leading parliamentarian and former classmate of the president of the Council.

fessor, he lived in the same residence with a priest by the name of Manuel Gonçalves Cerejeira, whose ecclesiastical career is a strange duplication of the civil career of Salazar: Coimbra student, professor of history, and finally member of the hierarchy and Cardinal Patriarch of Lisbon. Salazar became identified during his student days with an organization known as the C.A.D.C. (Centro Académico de Democracia Cristã). During the period from the murder of King Carlos until the proclamation of the republic, Coimbra was one of the centers of agitation and among the students the contradictory currents of thought of the time were particularly rampant. The portraits of the former monarchs were torn down in *Capelos*, the academic hall, and the reaction against the professors of theology was virulent. The association of Christian democracy was an effort on the part of a number of serious-minded students and professors to re-establish the proper kind of moral climate for the regeneration of the country. Salazar wrote for its journal, *Imparcial*, and spoke frequently on its behalf. He became a lecturer in political economy before receiving the doctorate and was very soon installed as a regular teaching member of the institution. A year after entering upon these duties, Salazar was suspended, along with three other professors, accused of monarchical propaganda and general obstructionism in the republicanization of the Law Faculty. In the elections of July, 1921, he was a candidate for the Catholic Center for Guimarães and sat in parliament for a very brief period of time, only to renounce this particular phase of public life to return to the university.

These were the formative years for the young professor and embryonic political leader. A time was spent in the study of the social encyclicals of Leo XIII and the writings of those who represented Catholic social thought at the time: Le Play, de Mun, Tour du Pin, and others. He was attracted by the ideas of the restoration as espoused by the integralists and was, in part, an architect of the Center Party which would, in Portugal, have reflected Catholic thought in politics and economics in much the same way as the various parties of Christian inspiration have operated in Austria, Italy, Germany, Belgium, Holland, and elsewhere. But he was first and last a professor of economy and a specialist in problems of finance and public administration.

In his office as finance minister, he proceeded calmly and with no regard for the expectation that filled the atmosphere to apply to the problems of the country the simple principles that seemed to work in all matters of revenue and expenditure: addition, subtraction, multiplication, and division.[27]

He was addicted to what has been called a "terrifying silence" in his manipulation of state figures. In a country where rhetoric was both cheap and abundant, where speeches preceded action and promises, accomplishment, Salazar was a grotesque personality, a weird contradiction about whom people speculated and argued. The only difficulty was that no one could argue with him for he shunned all discussion and indulged in no collective daydreaming. His hermitlike existence precluded any criticism of his personal life, and there was so little material on which to base a criticism of his policy that in course of time public opinion became accustomed to this enigmatic miracle-worker and it was not many years before he entered the stream of national consciousness as part of the Portuguese scene: an impassive, ever vigilant, ever devoted defender of its integrity.[28]

António Ferro describes how in arranging his "conversations" with the minister he was assaulted by the fear that he was dealing with a cold aloof man, whose impenetrability would ward off anything in the way of confidences and whose notorious diffidence would make the give and take of dialogue out of the question. Then came the "sigh of silent relief that Salazar is not at all the formidable and stand-offish personage that I had been led to believe him."[29]

One of the most pronounced manifestations of Salazar's sense of reality was his refusal to bow to the dictates of the traditional party organization that had plagued Portugal for many years. Political parties in Portugal, as we have noted from the examination of the historical background, had never been programs of action or of constructive realization. They had been camarillas centered around individual personalities and more often than not reflected little more than the presidential aspirations of the individual who had

[27] Ferro, António, *Salazar. Portugal and her leader, op. cit.*, p. 114.

[28] Andrade, José Gonçalves de, *Doutor Oliveira Salazar o seu tempo e a sua obra*, Porto, 1937, p. 24. "Salazar's fire is entirely within him and does not make him communicative. People would like to hear him more frequently if his duties permitted."

[29] *Ibid.*, p. 125.

created them. Party politics became an endless jockeying for advantage and a promise of compensation for support. They were not, in any real sense of the word, mass movements, for the great bulk of the population remained singularly indifferent on the assumption, which was probably correct, that a change of party was merely a change of the personnel that was running the country and that little could be expected in terms of a basic reorientation. Salazar realized that to govern meant to avoid the pitfalls of this kind of particularism, that he must achieve certain objectives above and beyond the exigencies of the immediate. It was in the irregular functioning of the public services that the cause of political disorder was to be found and these deficiencies in turn were caused by other disorders of a moral kind. Political parties exercised a *de facto* sovereignty over the nation, but sedition was considered as a normal weapon for change, and conspiracy had long since become a procedure to which such parties had recourse when elections were no longer susceptible of manipulation. "The presidency of the republic had neither prestige nor stability. Parliament offered a permanent spectacle of disharmony, confusion, legislative incapacity, of obstructive tactics, shocking the country with its methods and the paltriness of its achievements."[30] Salazar's problem, as we shall have occasion to note in the discussion of the Corporate State, was to provide the machinery for an adequate representation of opinion and eliminate as deleterious to the national life and utterly incompatible with its social and economic well-being the classic interplay of partisanship and party politics.[31]

Salazar has never taken a single step that could be construed as destructive of the republic; on the contrary he has maintained the institution of 1910 as the framework of the reform and as the foundation of the superstructure of the *Estado Novo*. Many accused him, in the initial stages, of aspiring to high position himself and of using the confusion of the 1926–1928 period as a steppingstone. He has consistently refused to accept candidacy for the presidency and, while holding many of the ministerial positions and sometimes

---

[30] Salazar, António de Oliveira, *Doctrine and Action. Internal and Foreign Policy of the New Portugal, 1928–1939*, London, 1939, translated by Robert Edgar Broughton, p. 70. A fundamental book for the English reader dealing with Salazar's own ideas on politics and social policy.

[31] Anselmo, Manuel, *As ideas sociais e filosóficas do Estado Novo*, Porto, 1934, p. 29.

several simultaneously, he has maintained a careful separation of the functions of President of the Council of Ministers and that of President of the Republic. His own answer to this problem was that he much preferred to remain in a post where his action would be beneficial and from which he could retire when he chose rather than in the presidency, from which such retirement would be conducive to a grave crisis in the supreme direction of the state.[32]

The monarchists have fared no better under the Salazar dispensation, although there were many who suspected that he had come into power as the gravedigger of the republic itself. The dictatorship, as he has himself often stated, "was fashioned against all party spirit and not merely against the republic parties."[33] Salazar made it plain that while he could not ask convinced royalists to abandon their ideas, he did not expect their collaboration in the administration to be used as a vantage point for subverting the State itself. In other words, Portugal was worth more than any of its parties and the form of the State was less vital than the existence of the nation itself.

Dr. António de Oliveira Salazar cannot be described in a biography. As a matter of fact, it is astonishing how few biographies as such have been written of him for his life contains almost nothing of the dramatic. There is no buildup of frustration and dire want in a war-depressed Austria, as in the case of Adolph Hitler, followed by entrance into partisan politics and the gradual capture of a party machine. There is no socialist youth and a long period of clandestine propaganda and flight from country to country as in the case of Mussolini. There is no outstanding military career, of service in Morocco, in the peninsula, and in the guidance of the destinies of the army as in the case of Franco. Salazar simply does not fall into any category. He is called dictatorial, authoritarian, fascist, and clerical. None of the terms have any meaning in his case. He has created something that is deeply rooted in the peculiarities of the Portuguese milieu; an authentic, national thing, that has taken on certain characteristics commonly associated with other nations, but which does not partake in the least of their essence.

Salazar is a Catholic and thinks as a Catholic. As Michael Der-

[32] Garnier, Christine, *op. cit.*, p. 70.
[33] Ferro, *Salazar, op. cit.*, p. 130.

rick, in his able study of the Salazar regime, remarks: "it might have been expected that the government of Portugal would soon become (in the usual but offensive phrase) 'priest ridden.'" But nothing of the kind has happened. Salazar has kept Church and State quite apart.[34] Even on the personal plane, Salazar in public life has maintained a distance which may be considered a distinction between himself and Cardinal Cerejeira, in spite of the many years in which they were associated at Coimbra.[35] The details of the relations of the modern Portuguese State with the Church reflects once more the *sui generis* character of the present regime and the impossibility of reducing its constituent elements to any easily definable dimensions. It is a definitely "spiritualistic" conception of the State in which Catholicism is recognized as the religious tradition in its history and practice. Separation has not, however, been removed and the Concordat of 1940 which regulates the relations serves as the legal basis of the relations, more about which will be said in a later discussion.

---

[34] Derrick, Michael, *op. cit.*, p. 56. "Portugal," Salazar has stated, "was born within the shadow of the Church and the Catholic religion was, from the beginning, a formative element of the nation's soul and a dominant feature of the character of the Portuguese people" (*My Deposition, op. cit.*, p. 19).

[35] Christine Garnier describes her conversation with Cardinal Cerejeira in which he notes that since Dr. Salazar's arrival in power, their relations have been limited to one meeting a year of a purely protocol type (*Vacances avec Salazar, op. cit.*, p. 187).

Chapter VI

SALAZAR AND THE *ESTADO NOVO*: CORPORATIVISM

UNDER the above caption, I propose to examine some of the features of the modern Portuguese State as it has evolved during the thirty years since the name of Oliveira Salazar has been associated with it. It is not easy to disengage, from the mass of details regarding financial reconstruction, constitutional reform, and, in general, the economic and political resurgence of Portugal, those points which graphically and pointedly emphasize the way in which the *Estado Novo*, or New State as it is called, is distinguished from its liberal predecessors. We find the principles on which the new Portugal is founded in the addresses of Salazar, from the first, on April 27, 1928, entitled "Conditions for Financial Reform," down to the later ones in the period of rehabilitation and the war years. It may be useful to assess these general guideposts which form the scaffolding for the emerging state.[1]

The doctrinal side, distinct from the administrative, finds expression among the early statements in the address delivered at army headquarters on June 9, 1928, where, in speaking to the officers, that is, to many of those who had been responsible for the national revolution two years earlier, Dr. Salazar stressed the problems facing the nation according to their importance and acuteness. "The situation in Portugal today is bad and is felt in every sphere of life." The minister made no effort to gloss over or conceal the depth of the tragedy. Nor did he offer any facile palliatives as a solution.

---

[1] Oliveira Salazar, *Discursos, op. cit.*, Coimbra, 1935, Vol. I, for the years, 1928–1934. Dr. Salazar, with the delicate irony which is often his characteristic, excuses himself in the preface of the first volume by noting that "Since I do not have that irresistible vocation of the men of my race to speak and to write, all tasks of this nature are the result of the duty of my office" (p. x).

Salazar has always been distinguished by never underestimating the problem nor exaggerating the accomplishments of his own administration in solving them. "This situation is the result of four fundamental problems: the financial, the economic, the social, and the political. I have suggested them in this order and the choice is not arbitrary."[2] Since the various national problems cannot be solved simultaneously, it is necessary to begin some place and that place is the financial situation which Salazar characterizes, as usual, as one of chronic deficit; a deficit which has attained the proportions of a venerable national institution. An unstable currency has long impeded the prosperity of the country and the process of devaluating and degrading the currency by the easy issuance of money, has made "the State the great enemy of the national economy." The solution of the social problem and the inequalities and injustices that come from permanent maladjustment of the finances, depends on the distribution of wealth and an increase in production. But even though the political stability of the nation is essential in this composite of forces, Salazar refused, in 1928, to express himself definitely on that point since, for the moment, "everything is subordinate to the balancing of the public accounts."[3]

A preview of the New State is to be found in the speech of October 21, 1929, in which Salazar defines the general orientation that will be required if the end that has been established is reached. "In an administrative system in which lack of sincerity and clarity were evident, the first requirement is a *policy of truth*. In a social order in which rights were competitive and unaccompanied by equivalent duties, the crying need is a *policy of sacrifice*. And in a nation divided against itself by groups and clashing interests which threatened its unity, the main need is a *national policy*."[4]

In this address, Salazar refers to the "dictatorship" and makes clear the responsibilities of this form of government toward the governed as well as that of the governed toward their government. A dictatorship may not be subject to the whims of public opinion nor shift and change in accordance with the way this opinion moves, but if it is a responsible institution, it must be scrupulously honest with the people, and inform them fully of the nature of

---

[2] *Discursos*, Vol. I, pp., 11–12.
[3] *Ibid.*, p. 17.
[4] *Ibid.*, p. 23.

the problems facing them. The very fact that a dictatorship generally has at its disposal a greater force than other regimes imposes on it a very special duty of perfect sincerity.

It was in 1930 that Salazar delivered some of the basic pronouncements that form the foundation of the new state. On May 28, it was stated that the reform of the constitution and the political institutions was under way. Salazar noted that there were several positions of opinion in the country regarding the dictatorship and that it was necessary to analyze them. One current of thought insisted that the dictatorship had nothing to do with politics and had been instituted solely for the purpose of bringing about a badly needed administrative reform. Another school held that the dictatorship was itself the solution of the political problem. Salazar was disinclined to accept this last theory, for the dictatorship was a political formula but not the definitive solution of the problem itself. Moreover, dictatorships have a habit of considering themselves permanent and, as the Portuguese minister underscored, "It is not a good thing to propose eternity to oneself."[5] The third proposition, namely, that the dictatorship should contribute to the solution of the political problem, seems the most logical position to take, and it is through the rational reorganization of the State that this will be accomplished.

The statement of principles of what is termed the National Union gives us a clear idea of the political philosophy of the dictatorship in general and of Dr. Salazar in particular.[6]

The year 1930 was one of world-wide economic dislocation, and, with the existence for the preceding eight years of fascism in Italy and the events in Austria and elsewhere, the political or institutional crisis was equally evident. Dr. Salazar was perfectly aware of the strong currents that were running in the world: the crisis of individualism, socialism, and parliamentarianism. Nationalism and anti-individualism were fast developing "into extreme doctrines or into open or disguised dictatorships — always abnormal even when justified by the necessity of the moment."[7] In the midst of this confusion, it was necessary to think through a system that would pre-

---

[5] *Ibid.*, p. 64.

[6] In Salazar, *Doctrine and Action*, *op. cit.*, p. 89 *seq.*; the English text of this address is available.

[7] *Discursos*, Vol. I, p. 71.

serve order and tranquillity, give the state the necessary authority to co-ordinate and operate — in a word, to find a formula for equilibrium that met the peculiar needs of the nation.

The dictatorship that came from the revolution four years before was not, Salazar insisted, a "barrack-room plot" nor the triumph of a military clique bent on power. It responded to the deepest yearning of the Portuguese people for an end to the convulsions and tension under which they had lived for too long a time. The fundamental principles of the New Order are fairly simple and can be given exactly as Salazar himself gave them to his own people in 1930: The first reality is the independent existence of the Portuguese nation with its overseas possessions. The nation is more than the individual and more than any collection of individuals and it is more than any party. These obvious and natural principles, as Salazar calls them, that is, the doctrine of the common good, might seem superfluous. But the obvious is often the most neglected and bears reiteration from time to time.

The Portuguese nationality in the modern world rests on certain very sound bases: its frontiers are as old as any in Europe and have never been extended at the expense of anyone else. This places Portugal outside the sphere of competitive conquests and revenges and increases the nation's moral force in the community of nations. The Portuguese in centuries gone by crossed the oceans to carry their civilization to vast areas. In the twentieth-century nationalism there is no element of conquest, expansion, or desire to dislodge others from their rightful possessions. At no time has Portugal laid a single claim to that which has not been its rightful patrimony for centuries. This, Salazar has emphasized, is the source of Portugal's legitimate pride and in the healthy nationalism that inspires the work of the new regime.

The "crisis of the modern State" is one of the dominant features of our age. The extreme views of an impotent State versus the deified one have dominated the age in which fascism and its concomitants, as well as communism, have prevailed in so many lands. The new Portugal sought to steer a passage between these two tricky shoals: "Both these extreme views must be confronted by a State that is strong, but moderated by principles of morality, by the rights of the people, and by individual guarantees and liberties, which are the principal requirements of a social community."[8]

In every reference to the consolidation of the State, the new leader laid stress on morality and moral right. Force was not to preside in this process of revival and even since the memorable date when these principles were enunciated as the basis of the New State, Salazar has always retained that keen sense of balance and of persuasion. Never in his long career has the professor from Coimbra crammed ideas down people's gullets or forced his fellow citizens into some arbitrary mold that seemed to him proper. He urges, expostulates, and usually convinces. He does not overwhelm by audacity and much less does he threaten. He has the bland confidence of the man who is delivering a lecture about a subject that he knows perfectly well he understands far better than anyone listening to him. His serenity carries its own conviction. And the results are there for everyone to see. He recognized long ago, just as he does now, that there is a very real danger of creating empty institutions that sound very good when orated about or even in blueprint stage, but somehow lack the human fire that makes things work. There is an inner urge that must come from ideas freely accepted by people who realize that what is proposed is very much the best thing. The study of Salazar's record will, I am confident, show that he has done this.

Two dangers loom particularly large in the mind of Portugal's leader: class warfare and party politics which run wild. The extreme left has stimulated the first, and parliamentary liberalism, especially as practiced in certain areas, has managed to make the latter reasonably obnoxious. In July of 1953, twenty-three years after the pronouncements of which I have been writing, Salazar stated that "the time has come to rekindle the fires of old and to continue on our way. . . . Only through corporativism can we avoid the most appalling class warfare and a trend toward party politics."

The State is the visible instrument of this co-ordination and strength. The nation, as has been emphasized, is the entire people and not a part. On this point the Portuguese regime has been adamant, rejecting the racist basis of National Socialist Germany,

[8] *Doctrine and Action, op. cit.*, p. 97.

the classist basis of the Soviet Union, or the party basis of fascist Italy. The State is not at the service of a party nor is a party to be confused with the State, no matter how vital its function may be in the body politic. Salazar has declared formally that the Portuguese State wants peace, is disposed to every form of legitimate collaboration in the international order, rejects wars of ambition, is favorable to arbitration. The State must be sufficiently strong so as to have no need for recourse to violence.

The next principle is the strengthening of the executive arm of the State. The weakness of the executive, and this is perhaps an indirect reference to certain specific situations both then and now, is generally the characteristic of regimes under the influence of liberal individualism, socialism, party conflict, and the worse disorders and impotencies of the parliamentary system. While a balance of power is desirable, "what we cannot admit is that the legislative chamber should have the right of choosing and dismissing ministers, and of obstructing public life."[9]

The head of the State must be able to execute and to administer and to be independent — as independent, certainly, as the legislative branch. The experience of Portugal has been an apparent inability to harmonize the two jurisdictions. Either the executive has prevailed totally with the subsequent elimination of the legislative, or the latter has taken over and the executive reduced to a mere figurehead. Moreover, the most unfortunate thing of all has been the tendency to operate outside the constitution whenever the fundamental document became a hindrance to government. The previous Portuguese constitutions were often excellent charters that were suspended whenever it happened to be convenient or whenever a *coup d'état* made the practical applications of their articles impossible. The country needs a realistic constitution that is theoretically sound and pragmatically workable; that can be applied organically and not mechanically; and that will reflect the *pays réel* as against the ideal situation which exists only in the imagination of the drafters of the constitution.

The next essential is social co-ordination, that is, the nation within the State. Political liberalism of the nineteenth century produced the "citizen," that is, an individual personality who, endowed with political attributes, apparently operated in space with little or no

[9] *Ibid.*, p. 100.

regard to the attachments that made him the kind of human being we know him to be, identified with family, class, profession, culture, and other interests. The citizen is not merely an elector who votes; he is a person who functions within a framework of institutional life that cannot be disassociated from his activity as a segment of the nation. The basis of all social structure is the family, insists Salazar, "the irreducible social cell, the casual nucleus of the parish, of the municipality and therefore of the nation: the family is, accordingly, by nature, the first organic political element of the constitutional state."[10] The family and the moral and economic corporations, as they are called, form the basis for the organization of the national life, and we see already in 1930 the outline if not the full details of the proposed Corporate system with which the name of Salazar is so definitely linked. "It is our intention to establish the social and corporative State in close correlation with the natural constitution of society."[11] We shall have occasion to deal more in detail with with this aspect of the problem when treating of the corporate State proper and how it is organized and how it functions. Basic to all progress, political and social, is a well-ordered economy and every effort must be made spontaneously or through State encouragement to bring about the creation of units and agencies, based on the natural composition of society to the end that every effort may be bent to the achievement of the common good.

Salazar himself admits that he anticipated criticism because he had spoken very little about democracy and the sovereignty of the people and a great deal about duty and work and sacrifice.[12] Un-

[10] *Ibid.*, p. 101.

[11] *Ibid.*, p. 103.

[12] Salazar has always been perfectly conscious of the criticism of his regime abroad with the charges of dictatorship, fascism, and the rest of the usual epithets. He expresses himself as encouraged, however, when "one notes the existence of an understanding of our way of doing things, of the relativity of political institutions and therefore of the legitimacy which our own offers, non-arbitrary authority, representation without parliamentarianism, liberties which need not be called democratic in order to make them effective. But one cannot forget that most western countries are governed better or worse under institutions of another type and that world public opinion appears to have certain prejudices against us" (speech of July 10, 1953, in *Portugal. Bulletin of Political, Economic and Cultural Information*, Lisbon, July–August, 1953, p. 12). The political side is best summed up as "the *indispensable* authority combined with the *possible* liberty" (Fonseca, J. Dinis de, "La experiencia política portuguesa, in *Panorama político de la Europa actual,* Madrid, 1953, p. 102).

fortunately, since he does not indulge in flattery, it was necessary to say some very plain and even harsh things, and to emphasize those aspects of the national rehabilitation which are indispensable if Portugal is to survive.

These are the ideas, sketched in the most superficial manner, that underlie Salazar's thinking. Where do they come from? They come from traditional Christian thought first of all and, to anyone familiar with the social encyclicals of the Popes, the terms and even the phrases are quite recognizable.[13] Everything he has to say breathes the Christian concept of society and the place of the individual and, especially, the family. The vital thing, it seems to me, is not to dissect the origins of Salazar's thought, interesting as that process may be, but to grasp how he went about putting these generalities into practice. In all doctrine, there always comes a moment which can be excruciatingly embarrassing — of making the transition from the theoretical to the practical and of putting to work in a specific environment and for a specific people those principles which, as a general expression of conviction, are admittedly universal truths. Certainly Salazar got many of his corporative ideas from the Catholic sociology that propounded them as a possible solution of the social problem. His universality of view is definitely of a Christian order for, in spite of his intense nationalism and his pride in Portugal as a human entity, there is never, in all of Salazar's utterances, the slightest note of chauvinism or of xenophobia. He does not love his own country more because he hates another more violently. He is Portuguese to the core in hope and aspiration and devotion. But he belongs to the wider community of mankind in conceiving of the role of his own country in the broad community of peoples.

Salazar was never one to acknowledge that there was any intrinsic identification between his system and that of the totalitarian countries of the 1930's. To be sure there were casual points of contact: the authoritarianism and, in the Italian case, the corporativism. But

---

[13] An excellent summary of the principles is contained in Egerton, *Salazar, Rebuilder of Portugal*, *op. cit.*, p. 157 *seq.* As to its Christian character, it has been said that "Portuguese corporativism is undoubtedly the most authentic and most Christian form" (Azpiazu, Joaquín, S.J., *The Corporate State*, St. Louis and London, 1951, p. 260). The *Semaines sociales de France* at Angers in 1935 devoted attention to the problem of corporate organization. See *L'Organisation corporative*, Lyon, 1936, p. 174 *seq.*, for Portugal.

Salazar's arrangement was very much *sui generis* and did not depend in the least on what was happening elsewhere.

This brings us to the constitution of Portugal as drafted and adopted in 1933, some months after Dr. Oliveira Salazar became prime minister, thus amplifying his functions from the more limited ones of minister of finance. The new system that was initiated through financial reform and retrenchment in 1928 and formalized in the constitution in 1933 is looked upon as essentially a liberation of the State from the impotency to which creeping anarchy had condemned it; the Portuguese people as the principal victims of the confusion and degeneration of institutional life that preceded the revolution. The social and political constitution of 1933 reflects the thinking of the regime a few years after its inception and for the sake of clarity it may be helpful to summarize its main features and purpose.[14]

Marcelo Caetano, one of the architects of the corporate State, has defined it as "an ideal form of good economic organization because it constitutes a kind of self-government in each branch of production. . . . Corporativism is a movement whereby the State seeks to lead the citizens to mutual understanding as regards their common interests by means of agreements, to which it gives legal sanctions. Each guild, each syndicate, is an autonomous association, with both legislative and executive functions."[15] The State is there to maintain a co-ordinating control in the national interest, else each of these entities would tend to relapse into a kind of feudal dispersion. The world economic depression was in full swing and, only a few days before, the drastic monetary policy of the Roosevelt administration had been announced in Washington. It was definitely a moment of economic anxiety, and one can imagine the expectation with which the words of Portugal's wizard of finance were heard by a hopeful people. Salazar took one conception after another of those that have prevailed in the economic field and demolished them as insufficient for the national needs:

---

[14] One of the most solid studies of the corporative State is Pereira dos Santos, *Un Etat corporatif: La Constitution Sociale et Politique portugaise*, Paris, 1935. This study, which was a doctoral thesis, tends to be theoretical but is useful for a detailed exposition of the thought and theory of the constitution.

[15] Caetano, Marcelo, Preface to the volume of Cotta, Freppel, *Economic Planning in Corporative Portugal*, London, 1937, p. x.

> The policy of powerful cartels, the policy of formidable trusts, the policy of high wages, the policy of super-production, the policy of super-abundant credit, the policy of artificial valuations, the policy of huge public expenditures, the policy of excessive consumption, the policy of exclusivist nationalisms, the policy of the police state that does nothing and the policy of the State-producer that pretends to do everything.[16]

Was this the moment for a small State, "this little Portuguese house," as Salazar called it, to go about seeking for remedies of evils that seem world wide and far beyond its capacity to do anything about? The concept of wealth itself, said Salazar, had been adulterated and the worker as the producer of wealth shorn of his human dignity. "We disassociate the worker from the natural background of his profession and we leave him alone with no discipline of association. Then we consent to his association on another basis which instead of for productive purposes is against someone or something."[17] Craft unions gave way to industrial or class unions for the purpose of combating the State, the natural protector of the social order, the employer, or even fellow workers. The State passed from a stage of indifference and passivity to this economic development to one of overactive, bureaucratized intervention.

The remedy was not a revival of medieval guild associations, but of a corporative society, to reconcile the opposing interests in capitalist society. Salazar's analysis was in nowise different from that of Pope Leo XIII and in general his thought runs along the lines proposed by the Church. Portuguese corporations, as they had existed up to 1834, had been abolished by law, and society had lost all recollection of the system as it prevailed until the period of Pombal and the aftermath of Bonaparte.[18] The re-establishment of the corporations may be said to begin with the Constitution of 1933 which declares, in Article V, that the nation is "a unitary and corporative republic, founded upon the equality of all its citizens before the law, on the free access of all classes to the benefits of civilization and on the participation of all the elements that

---

16 Salazar, *Discursos, op. cit.*, Vol. I, p. 188.

17 *Ibid.*, p. 191.

18 Reference has already been made to the representative system of the Middle Ages and the "house of the Twenty-Four," a forerunner of the modern Corporate Chamber. See Caetano, Marcelo, *Lições de Direito Corporativo*, Lisbon, 1935, p. 34 seq.

make up the nation in the administrative activity and in the enactment of its laws."[19] The question of the human person is followed at once in the fundamental charter by a longish reference to the family and its defense, because the three elements that make up the structure of Portuguese society as conceived in this document are the individual, the family, and the corporation.[20] Title II, Article 8, for instance, defines the rights of citizens in considerable detail and constitutes an admirable bill of rights with the emphasis on the social and economic point of view, instead of on political rights as we are accustomed to think of them. Besides these political rights there are also the natural rights which spring from man's nature as a creature of God and those that are socially granted according to the contingencies of time and place, a distinction that is useful in judging of the character of the Portuguese constitution and the place given in the text to human rights.

Article 16 makes it the duty of the State to authorize " . . . all corporative, collective, intellectual or economic bodies, and to promote and assist their formation." Article 20 provides that "in the corporate organization all branches of the nation's activities shall be represented through their association in the corporative organizations and it shall be their duty to participate in the election of town councils and provincial boards and the constitution of the Corporative Chamber." Title VIII is entirely social and economic and provides in considerable detail for the functioning of the New State and especially for the role of the government itself in the carrying out of these precepts. The corporations, incidentally, are not merely economic in the industrial or agricultural sense but also scientific, literary and artistic (Articles 16–18). The new economic order is to operate toward attaining "a maximum of production and socially useful wealth and at the same time the establishment of a collective existence which will result in the authority for the State and justice for the citizenry."[21]

The State is to regulate economic activity only on the national level, and it shall not intervene directly in the management of private economic undertakings except when it actually finances

[19] *Political Constitution of the Portuguese Republic, op. cit.*, p. 5.
[20] Egerton, *Salazar, Rebuilder of Portugal, op. cit.*, p. 199.
[21] Belaúnde, César H., *Organización profesional corporativa,* Buenos Aires, 1953, p. 226 seq.

them or for the purpose of securing a larger measure of social benefit that would otherwise be impossible. Small industry is recognized and it need hardly be stressed that the constitution affirms vigorously the justice of private property and, by the same token, private enterprise.

If this system of corporative bodies is the basis of the economically productive life of the country, in the political sphere, these organisms, plus the families and the local groups, such as parishes and municipalities, form the basis of representation. The national representation is assured by a National Assembly of 120 deputies elected by direct suffrage and the Corporative Chamber made up of representatives of the local corporations. The Chamber functions in a consultative capacity and must be called upon by the National Assembly and may be consulted by the government itself for this purpose.

The executive power, about which Salazar had been so critical, is centered in a president elected for seven years and who has been given substantial authority, including the foremost one of designating the head of the government, that is, the president of the Council of Ministers, who is not responsible to either the National Assembly or the Corporative Chamber. A Council of State, consisting of the president of the Council of Ministers and several other functionaries such as the chairman of the National Assembly, of the Corporative Chamber, and of the Supreme Court, forms a consultative body to the president in terms of his own functions.[22]

As important as the constitution in the setting up of the corporate state is the Statute of Labor, promulgated on September 23, 1933. Obviously, in spite of the reminiscence of the medieval guilds and craft associations, the Portuguese corporate State has never pretended to reintroduce or resuscitate these ancient institutions. " . . . the modern corporative organization differs fundamentally from the old guild system of arts and trades, by the fact that the former one represented in a single organization all the productive elements, whereas the modern, by virtue of the profound difference between employer and worker (a technical, economic, and social difference) the basis of the structure must be dualistic."[23]

---

[22] Caetano, Marcelo, *L'Organisation politique portugaise*, Lisbon, n.d.

[23] Leite, João Pinto da Costa, *A doutrina corporativa em Portugal*, Lisbon, 1936, p. 125. The complete text with commentary in Costa, Augusto da, *A Nação corporativa. Textos legais, comentados e justificados*, Lisbon, 1934, 2 ed.

This is literally a charter for the economic life of the country. The State is not the producer but the regulator of production and the guarantee that it shall serve the common good. Capital is fully recognized in its legitimate role and work is declared to be a social function that must be guaranteed with a living wage. Employer associations and workers' unions are invited to work out matters of mutual interest in collective contracts which, in turn, are approved by the corporations and the State. Strikes and lockouts are illegal and in the event of conflict between capital and labor, arbitration commissions and boards are provided for. The principal corporative entities are the employers' associations on one side and the workers on the other. Each is fully recognized before the law, and it is competent to represent the interests of its members in all cases. Only one guild or association may function for each professional or trade group. The great problem of corporativism, as Salazar himself has admitted, was to create a state of mind that would admit of its potentialities and exploit them advantageously without the machinery so created degenerating into simply another government bureaucracy. Suppose we examine now how this corporativism has been set up. I realize that these last pages have been shockingly dull, devoted as they have been to matters which are singularly unexciting. A description of the elaborate operation of the corporate State would not, I am afraid, be much more intriguing. It may be useful, however, to indicate the general outline and nothing else.

The principle of the thing is crystal clear: the citizen in a corporatively organized community belongs first and foremost to those groups which are his by nature or by his profession. A man is born into a family and a village; he is part of a social cosmos, both large and small, but he is not born a socialist or a free trader or a republican or a monarchist. The normal play of political parties places a premium on an aspect of human life which is accidental and arbitrary and provides the means for association along lines which easily exclude the vital connections of the individual. If an organization can be provided that allows the citizen to express himself through the medium of his group association and in terms of his basic family and professional interests, the resultant is a far more authentic thing than if heterogeneous groups, for diverse reasons, associate to form a political party, whose fundamental aim is to attain power and control others. This may be an oversimplification, but I think it represents essentially the idea behind corporativism. We are so formidably conditioned to thinking in terms of parliaments and congresses, political parties and platforms that it does not come easy to imagine a system in which none of this apparatus exists. Nevertheless, it is important to bear in mind that men can express their convictions on matters vital to them and attain an effective participation in public affairs through other channels than the ordinary ones to which we are accustomed.

Salazar has constantly emphasized that he does not want the State to do the job of the corporations but that, as the corporative spirit permeates the nation, it shall be the task of the associations themselves to function as autonomously as possible. Obviously all this takes time and even today, thirty years afterward, there is still a long way to go before the transformation can be considered as achieved. There is always the danger, of which many have warned, that corporativism become simply a blueprint for a sort of ideal society to be put into effect willy-nilly, regardless of human nature or conviction. Portugal in this respect has undertaken to follow a line considerably different from that of fascist Italy where the intervention of the State was much greater.

The supreme direction, so to speak, of corporativism consists of (1) the agencies that promote, control, and develop the individual corporations, and (2) the agency through which the corporations in turn influence and guide legislation and the national economy. Under the first category, we have the Undersecretary of State of Corporations and Social Providence and the specific ministry of the government, such as Agriculture, Commerce and Industry, and, under the second category, the Corporative Chamber which, functioning with the National Assembly, is the supreme authority.

In the actual setting up of the corporations, the basic idea is, as has been stressed, the professional group, that is, all those who contribute directly to the same process of production; and in establishing the corporation, the purpose is to harmonize these interests within the enterprise. The employer class is organized in *gremios*, along the lines of the same principle and we therefore have such corporate groups as *The National Confederation of Wheat Producers*, *The Confederation of Wine Producers*, and innumerable others. For the rural area where the agricultural class offers certain difficulties of organization, the corporate State has created the *Casas do Povo*, the principal responsibility, for which, during the initial years, belonged to Dr. Teotónio Pereira.[24] The corporate State seeks to create what is called a "hierarchy of functions" rather than a hierarchy of classes. There is, of course, a delicate problem of terminology since it would be misleading to use the words "Trade union" to designate these associations, which are not in defense of special interest groups at all, but co-operative associations. The Portuguese use of the words "syndicate" and "syndicalism" which again in English usage is likely to be somewhat confusing. The ordinary corporation numbers over a hundred members, at least, and there is not more than one for each district into which the country is divided.

Article XII of the Statutes of Labor imposes specific duties on the corporations. They are expected to enter into labor contracts, set up providential societies for their members, care for the unemployed, and maintain schools for technical and professional training, plus a number of forms of social aid. The aim here is to achieve what has been called the *corporativisme d'association* as against the simple *corporativisme d'état*, or State control. It is true that the employers' organizations were fostered by State intervention which was explainable by the fact that many of the producers' interests involve such matters as foreign markets, trade relations, and duties over which the State and the State only has control. This was singularly true of such groups as those selling sardines, wine, and cork abroad.

Has this theoretical structure been faithfully translated into reality? The process is still going on and Salazar would be the last to assume that the job was done for all time. The Portuguese system has sought organic growth and in contrast with the Italian experiment under fascism, what has been happening in Portugal may be called "integral corporativism," that is, one in which autonomous groups with their own rights represent not only the economic forces of the nation, but the cultural, social, and religious.[25]

---

[24] Cabrita, Henrique, A *Ordem corporativa*, Lisbon, 1934, p. 19. An absolutely fundamental book on the building of the corporate State and which I have followed in preparing these notes is Brongersma, E., *De opbouw van een Corporatieven Staat*, Utrecht, 1941. In 589 pages this volume traces in abundant detail the structure and development of the new Portugal.

[25] Cotta, *op. cit.*, p. 23.

There is still a long way to go and in the commemorations of the thirty years of the Salazar regime, a considerable discussion ensued regarding the achievements in the corporative as well as in other fields. The most striking feature is the apparent desire of the State to relinquish certain of its functions and especially of its controls so that the supreme and ultimate authority of the corporations may be autonomous.

Salazar himself has been the first to admit the deficiencies of the regime and its weaknesses. "Close study of the regime will reveal immediately two important failings: the suspension of corporative evolution and the quasi non-existence of political indoctrination."[26] The development of the regime was distinguished by a spirit of almost academic patience. In his address of October 20, 1949, Salazar noted:

> One thing on which I have not come to a definite decision is the future of the National Assembly. The Chamber of Corporations . . . is much more representative of various interests within the Nation than the Assembly is. . . . At the moment I do not see clearly whether this organ should be constituted in the way that we are now adopting, whether it should emanate from the Chamber of Corporations itself — whether it should be permanent or subject to review from time to time. . . . Let us trust that time will help us find a solution.[27]

In the balance sheet of progress in Portugal, one of the most frequently voiced criticisms is the excessive prudence of the regime, the caution with which it proceeds on every matter. Portuguese collaboration in the Organization for European Economic Cooperation has been distinguished by this same spirit. It has been commented that the careful reflection and unhurried judgments of Salazar are both the guarantee of the present system and a problem as to the succession.

Dr. Marcelo Caetano, in whom some see the successor of Salazar, proclaimed that Portugal already had a complete and authentic corporative organization, whereas Salazar had insisted that one of

[26] Address to the National Union, July 10, 1953. In *Portugal, Bulletin of Political, Economic and Cultural Information*, Lisbon, July–August, 1953, Nos. 180–181, p. 12. The excellent Portuguese review, *Brotéria* (Lisbon, Vol. LXII, No. 5, 1956, p. 545) notes that "it is an open secret that the intervention of the members of the unions and the *gremios* in their professional life, has been practically nil." Article by Marques, Henrique, "O corporativismo em marcha."

[27] *Reforming the Constitution. Another Step Toward Defining and Consolidating the Regime*, Lisbon, 1949. In English translation, p. 11.

the major problems was the suspension of the evolution toward corporativism.[28] There have been doubts and hesitations about what to do and how to do it. Thirty years after initiating the new economic order, there is a considerable amount of soul searching and divergencies of judgment which are, in the long run, a far greater guarantee of the durability of the regime than the insensate mouthings of "Il duce a sempre regione" that was the motto of fascist Italy. At a conference of the National Union Party on June 2, 1956, Dr. Marcelo Caetano revised his thought and stressed the need for a revision and revamping of the present organization, both political and economic. There was criticism of many features of present policy and some 440 resolutions touching every phase of the national life were introduced for discussion. "What Salazar appears to be planning is the establishment of political machinery that would inherit some of the executive powers now vested in himself."[29] The proposal has been made for the creation of six corporations to coordinate and channel on a national scale all activities connected with agriculture, industry, transport, commerce, tourism, banking, insurance, fishing, and canning. A text of a bill was presented to the National Assembly to the end that the guilds and syndicates elect their representatives directly to the Corporate Chamber. "Officials said the ultimate aim of the government was to give the Corporative Chamber that is to be formed final deliberative powers. Its decisions on all matters affecting the interests of the corporations would be binding."[30]

The Economist of London, in a special survey of Portugal, poses the problem this way:

> Does Professor Salazar's insistence on the corporative theory despite his failure to complete the structure he designed over twenty years ago, disqualify him from earning praise as a pragmatist? It is hard to find anyone in Portugal today who believes that the network of employers guilds (gremios) and that trade unions created before the war will ever be crowned, as the theory demands, by the blending of the two elements into vertical corporations, one for each industry

[28] "Le régime portugais a trente ans" in *Le Monde*, Paris, May 30, 1956.

[29] *The New York Times*, June 27, 1956. Report of Camille Cianfarra on the party congress — "One of the major complaints heard among both opponents and supporters of the Government is that the Premier's policies have tended to strengthen the grip of the upper classes on Portugal's economy and resources."

[30] *Ibid.*, June 26, 1956.

or activity, and the convening of a genuine Corporative Chamber representing these bodies.[31]

This is still the major problem in a regime that the same distinguished journal calls "the quiet phenomenon."

In this survey of the *Estado Novo* and the concrete achievements of the Salazar regime, the economic revival and financial rehabilitation naturally loom as the most important. I propose in the next few pages to summarize rapidly some of the major economic advances, the nature of the financial miracle, and something of the social legislation that the Salazar government has sponsored. Since none of this can be divorced from politics, it may be useful as a concluding remark to refer to the political forces at work in the country over the past few years.

Salazar has never entertained the slightest illusion as regards the potentialities of Portugal from the economic point of view. The country is poor and the most that it can expect, in the light of present circumstances, is to achieve a degree of well-being that is modest and dignified.[32] Certain basic economic facts of life will explain why the individual income in Portugal is still one of the lowest in Europe. About 50 per cent of the population depends on agriculture, another 15 per cent on fishing, while industry as such does not absorb much more than 12 to 15 per cent. The lack of certain fundamental industrial raw materials, such as coal and oil in quantity, are factors that must be taken into account in the examination of the Portuguese scene. Wine production, which suffered considerably during the war when the markets were cut off, has begun to revive. Cork still remains one of the most important national products, with Portugal producing for export half of all the cork in the world. Cereals are produced in a quantity barely sufficient to cover the national consumption. Fishing has always been a mainstay of the Portuguese economy and continues to play this vital role in its existence. Industrial planning plays a very important part in the general program of Dr. Salazar. As early as May, 1944, a bill for the development and reorganization of industry was discussed for the general industrial reorientation of the country.[33]

[31] *The Economist*, London, April 17, 1954, p. 237.

[32] An excellent survey of Portugal's economics in *L'Evolution économique du Portugal*, Documentation Française, Paris, May 13, 1949.

[33] *Portugal. Overseas Economic Surveys. November, 1948*, London, 1949, His Majesty's Stationery Office, p. 15.

These measures envisaged an intensification of industry along every line from metal refining to wood distillation and the development of hydroelectric facilities. Further schemes for port expansion, reafforestation, and the development of uncultivated land within the country were proposed. Vigilant neutrality during the war years left its effect for Portugal in the period immediately following the end of hostilities. In prewar years, Portugal's trade showed an adverse visible balance of trade to the tune of nearly 900 million *escudos*. From 1941 to 1943 the competitive demand boosted the export of certain of her products. Then came the tightening and in the postwar period the necessary adjustment with larger imports and lower exports.[34] The social question is intimately related to the economic. The Portuguese birth rate continues to be high and the population increase steady.[35] The social service that has been developed by the *Estado Novo* is extensive and varied. In 1940 there was created an Undersecretaryship of State for social assistance, and a series of measures for improvement in this domain were initiated. It would be impossible in the space of these summary annotations on the Portuguese social system to do more than simply call attention to the elaborate program of the regime for the social amelioration of the people. There is protection for the family in terms of the family allowance against accidents in work and sickness and disease that are the consequence of working conditions or in the course of duty.[36] The system of social security includes the various institutions which have been created to care for the different classes of the population: the *Casas do Povo*, to which reference has been made, and the *Casa dos Pescadores*, which is the equivalent for the fishermen. In each case these institutions are charged with putting into effect obligatory insurance and other forms of protection for the class to whose interests they are dedicated. From 1935 onward, a similar protection has been extended to employees in commerce and to industrial workers. In June, 1946, a federation of units under the name of *Socio-Medical Services* was created and embraced the whole field of medical aid to the needy;

[34] *Portugal. Review of Commercial Conditions*, London, 1945, His Majesty's Stationery Office, p. 25.

[35] Article, "Portugal's Growing Birth Rate" in *Portugal Bulletin of Political, Economic and Cultural Information*, Lisbon, January 31, 1947.

[36] A fairly detailed statement of the provisions of the social legislation in *A B C do seguro social*, Lisbon, 1949.

improved health and sanitation and instruction in hygiene. The pension system, which is also a part of the Portuguese social service legislation, is extensive to all classes and normally operates at the age of 65. Ever since the initial measures taken in 1933, the program of cheap housing, especially for the less privileged sectors of the population, has been moving forward with encouraging speed. Social Assistance Savings Banks have contributed to encouraging thrift among their members.

Education as such has by no means been neglected. Portugal's illiteracy rate has always been high and was calculated, in the 1920's as three out of four. "It would be idle to contend that any real progress had been made in dealing with the problem of illiteracy until shortly after the present government came into power."[37]

But to return to the economic side of the picture. Most industries in the country are family concerns run by their proprietors. Heavy industry is rare and, aside from such enterprises as the Companhia União Fabril which produces fertilizers, copper sulfate, and other chemicals, the lack of iron and coal has been a basic impediment.

But in every field of economic endeavor there is a marked improvement. Electric power, in millions of kilowatts increased from 942 in 1950 to 1380 in 1953. The capacity of power stations moved from 345 to 694 over the same period of time. Shipbuilding and repairing, engineering and the metal industries, cotton spinning and weaving, and a host of other industries, such as rayon, linens, carpets, wool, chemicals, rubber, paper, glass, and so on have been increased in terms of their capacity. The government's six-year development plan for 1952–1958, approved by law in December, 1952, contemplates an expenditure of 7,701.8 millions of *escudos* in metropolitan Portugal and 6,000 millions in the overseas territories. The plan is a continuation of the eight-year program initiated originally in 1944. The plan's main aims for continental Portugal were to develop agriculture, to increase hydroelectric power, to provide a sound foundation for the basic industries, including a new iron and steel industry — to improve communications and to extend technical edu-

[37] *Portugal. Overseas Economic Surveys, op. cit.*, p. 66. The educational statistics for recent years are as follows: the census of 1940 showed 47.5 per cent of the population over seven years of age as able to read and write; that of 1950, 59.6 per cent. In 1944–1945 there were 10,079 primary schools with 528,109 pupils; in 1952–1953 the number of such schools was 13,355 with 726,498 pupils (*Statesman's Yearbook*, 1947, p. 1174, and *ibid.*, 1955, p. 1329).

cation. Budgetary contributions would cover approximately a third of the entire expenditure. In 1953 a loan of seventeen million dollars was obtained from the Export-Import Bank of Washington. In 1953, Salazar referred to the "dead end" of some of the economic projects and the pressing need for a revitalization.[38]

The most spectacular aspect of Portugal's economic revival has been, as we have had occasion to refer to many times in these pages, financial reconstruction and stabilization and the fact that Salazar has brought the country out of the red after the decades of chaotic financial conditions. In his acceptance of April 27, 1928, the new minister laid down the conditions under which he would undertake the job. They were as follows:

I. Each ministry shall limit its expenditures and organize its services within the strict limits laid down by the Finance Ministry.
II. Measures taken by other ministries involving expenditures shall be first submitted to the Ministry of Finance.
III. The Ministry of Finance shall be authorized to veto any item that it does not consider indispensable.
IV. The Ministry of Finance will collaborate with the other ministries as to means of reducing expenditures so that the services may be all organized along uniform lines.

There is nothing very exciting about four principles like this nor do they lend themselves to oratory. They are the bedrock, however, of the National Revolution and everything that has happened since 1928 is explained because Salazar has seen to it that these premises have remained in force and observed by the other government agencies.[39]

On May 14, Salazar issued an order of seven points to assure the equilibrium of the budget. The decree of March 27, 1929, completed the reform of the budgetary operations and set up the General Intendency of the Budget. The first national budget prepared under Salazar's guidance showed a credit balance of 1,576 *contos*. When the accounts were all in, it was shown that the credit balance was 274,953 *contos*; a spectacular figure that probably did more to assure Salazar's permanency than anything else.

Taxes were increased by over 200 thousand *contos* and from that date on Portugal has never had anything but a balanced budget

[38] McVittie, W. W., *Portugal. Economic and Commercial Conditions in Portugal*, Overseas Economic Surveys, London, 1955, pp. 3–4.
[39] Salazar, *Discursos, op. cit.*, Vol. I, pp. 4–5.

with a goodly margin on the credit side. Year by year Salazar attacked the problem from every angle. New boards and commissions to care for taxes, credit operations, the state debt, and other problems were set up. The liquidation of the public debt was a source of very special attention and in 1935 the system of industrial taxation was remodeled and the National Statistical Institute founded; the urban property tax was reformed and the salary scale of civil servants carefully revised. In 1936 the form of taxation applicable to the corporative organizations was worked out.

Among other things the new regime stabilized the Portuguese currency, the *escudo*, so that today it ranks with the dollar and the Swiss franc as one of the steadiest, soundest currencies in the world. Currency fluctuations were no longer a matter of irregularities in the treasury or incapacity to pay, but depended on general economic conditions at home and abroad. For a long time the *escudo* was at a par with the pound sterling, but so great was the inflation during World War I that it was quoted at 157 to the pound. On December 5, 1931, Salazar launched a currency reform and although Portugal tried to return to the gold standard this proved a short-lived experiment. After World War II, the *escudo* regained a certain independence and its value became fixed in relation both to the pound and to the dollar.

The margin of credit has decreased in more recent years in view of the larger expenditures for all sorts of projects in economic improvement as well as military and defense spending. The 1953 budget, for example, provided for a revenue of 6,363.9 millions and expenditures of 6,351.8. For 1954 it was 7,075.9 for revenues and 7,061.3 for expenditures.

The Portuguese economy has been governed by what has been called the "classical" rules of finance and political economy, with the result that this sick nation of thirty years ago is presently in good economic health.

A final word on the political evolution of Portugal over the past few years and the present status of political activity. That there is opposition to the Salazar regime is, of course, natural. There are extreme monarchists who would like to get rid of the republic and there are the elements of the left who would like to get rid of Salazar. There are those who have criticized his regime as "fascist" and point to the Portuguese Legion and the organization of young people called the *Mocidade portuguesa* as evidence of a predilection for Mussolini-like agencies of pressure. The existence of the National Union as the single dominant party has failed to please a great many politicians or at least those who have aspired to the kind of partisan strife in the land that would make a political career profitable. Presidential elections were held on February 13, 1949. For three consecutive terms, General Carmona had been returned handsomely and without challenge. This time an opposition candidate appeared in the person of General Norton de Matos, a former colonial administrator and diplomat. The support he received came from some of the vestiges of the old political parties of the days before 1926. General Norton de Matos announced his candidacy in July, 1948, and demanded certain reforms such as the lifting of the censorship and freedom of meeting.[40] General Carmona was renominated by the National Union. Many of the restrictions were lifted but General Norton later withdrew his name from the lists. The opposition was a loose coalition with no program of a substantial kind. General Norton made the mistake of saluting the communists as "patriots" and there was no assurance forthcoming that the Church would not suffer the persecution it had experienced in the early days of the republic. It was definitely proved that the opposition to Salazar reposed on a very fragile basis and that if the gates were thrown wide open to political expression there was a good chance that the anarchical forces that had ruined the country before might return to power.[41]

I have mentioned the word "censorship" and this requires a further word of explanation. There is censorship in Portugal and there has been for years. Its severity is mitigated by the natural character of the Portuguese themselves who have no particular national talent for harshness and, much less, Teutonic thoroughness. Salazar has believed censorship necessary to avoid the dangers of demagoguery. It takes a long time for a nation to come out of the valley of darkness through which Portugal had walked for countless years. The virulent, uninhibited nature of the old Portguese press with its penchant for calumny of the most outrageous sort was

[40] Matos, Norton de, *Os dois primeiros meses da minha candidatura a presidencia da República*, Lisbon, 1948.

[41] Salazar stated his own position in several speeches, among them *Para que os surdos ouçam e os proprios cegos vejam*, Lisbon, 1951 (address in the Sports Palace in Lisbon, July 19, 1951).

considered outmoded and undesirable and the present curb as the sanest way of re-educating a people to responsibility in public utterance.[42]

The death of General Carmona on April 18, 1951, was the first break in the continuity of the regime since its inception. The opposition this time consisted first of one Ruy Luis Gomes who refused to repudiate communism — thereby not endearing himself particularly either to the government or public opinion. The other, Manuel Carlos de Quintão Meireles, Foreign Minister under the regime in 1928–1929, withdrew because the conditions under which the elections were to be held did not please him. The candidate of the National Union, General Craveiro Lopes, was presented and elected.[43]

In conclusion, what shall we say in summing up the activities of Dr. Oliveira Salazar and his regime? The record speaks eloquently for itself in every sphere. His sagacious, scholarly touch has transformed every aspect of national life. Presiding over it all is his acute sense of tradition and continuity and, especially, his contempt for the shoddiness of many of the so-called "liberal" programs and measures of the day. He has restored the dignity of work and

---

[42] Eugene Bagger in an excellent series on Portugal for the N.C.W.C. News Service (Washington, D. C.) treats in one article of censorship: "The upholders of the regime say that 'press censorship does not annul freedom of expression but insures that it shall be exercised in accordance with truth and justice. . . . It is the duty of the State to prevent attacks on the common good. They would say further that whenever a newspaper represents Soviet Russia as a people's democracy and worker's paradise, and denounces the United States for war-mongering, it attempts to poison the people's minds" (November 22, 1948). The fact that there is outspoken comment in Portugal regarding the problem is evident in the remarks of Norberto Lopes, director of the *Diario de Lisboa* who joined with the editors of the *Diario Ilustrado* in May, 1957, to insist that "the time has come to examine the problem of freedom of the press in Portugal." He demanded that a free press be restored in order for the newspapers and reviews to fulfill their proper function. *Le Monde* (Paris, May 25, 1957).

[43] General Francisco Higino Craveiro Lopes is a personality in his own right. Born in 1894, he attended cavalry school and later took part in the Mozambique campaign against Germany in World War I. In 1918 he was in the air force on the western front in France. In 1929 he was aide-de-camp to his father as governor general of Portuguese India and remained there for nine years. He became an air force commander on return and in 1944 was commander of the Portuguese Legion, formed originally in 1936 to fight in Spain as volunteers. From 1945 to 1949 he was a deputy to the National Assembly.

constant effort to his people.[44] The question has been raised as to the secret of Salazar's success. It may well be his sense of the moral content of political life and the fundamental moral conviction that he brings to the task at hand.[45] The eminent Spanish intellectual, Gregorio Marañón, has called Salazar "one of the most eminent personalities of our time; a professor not within university walls but in Portuguese life."[46] The distinguished Belgian academician, Marcel de Corte, in saluting Salazar for his qualities and for his salvation of Portugal, complains that "parties can have leaders and revolutionaries can have chieftains, but our age denies to nations the right to leadership that it readily concedes to any organized band. . . . Salazar has achieved what the dynasties of the past secured by continuity and permanency . . . his success is unique."[47] His Holiness, Pope Pius XII, hailed Salazar as "a government leader who has won the affection of his people . . . and the respect and esteem of the world."[48]

---

[44] Bernard Noël in a series of articles in *Le Figaro* (Paris, July 12, 16, 18 and 21, 1953) speaks of the Portuguese as "busy beavers," with a mania for construction.

[45] This idea is emphasized in *Revista Latina* (Rome, April–May, 1953) in commemorating the twenty-fifth anniversary of the Portuguese regime.

[46] *Diario de la Marina*, Habana, Cuba, October 30, 1940.

[47] *La Libre Belgique*, Brussels, April 20, 1953.

[48] Reply of His Holiness Pope Pius XII to the Portuguese ambassador to the Holy See, October 20, 1940, in *Anuário Católico de Portugal*, Lisbon, 1947, p. 27.

Chapter VII

PORTUGAL AND THE EMPIRE: A CONTEMPORARY SURVEY

THE Portuguese colonies, officially known as the overseas provinces since the approval of the Colonial Act of 1933, constitute today the third largest empire in the world and, in terms of stability and attachment to the European homeland, the most pacific. And what is most remarkable is that this small nation is "the only European power that has retained its position in the world and, in the crises that have afflicted the colonial states since 1890, has not lost one single inch of territory. Where the French, Spanish, British and Americans have been forced to leave, Portugal remains."[1] The Portuguese imperial world is of major interest to us today for a number of specific reasons: (1) because it is enormous and potentially capable of great economic development, (2) because it gives no sign of unrest or disturbance of the type that prevails in the French and British colonial territories, and (3) because Portugal is working out devices that may prove an effective solution to the greatest challenge of our time, that is, the capacity of the white man to work out a harmonious basis of intelligence and collaboration with the colored races.[2]

Sufficient attention has perhaps already been given in the pages devoted to the imperial expansion of Portugal to appreciate the Portuguese racial attitude and the absence of anything remotely smacking of the *Herrenvolk* among them. I have no intention of presenting here a panegyric of Portuguese rule or of suggesting that it is uniformly enlightened. There have been blunders, mis-

[1] "Il colonialismo portoghese," in *Eurafrica*, Rome, July–August, 1955, p. 10.

[2] Lobato, Alexandre, "Problemas do nosso Ultramar," in *Lusitania*, Lisbon, July, 1948. The author speaks of a "Portuguese position or solution" in colonial matters that departs from the formulae of the other imperial powers.

takes, inefficiency, and all that normally falls to the lot of human beings in an enterprise that has covered five centuries and involved almost every corner of the earth. Miss Mary H. Kingsley, that remarkable woman who wrote such extraordinary books on West Africa, has commented that "I have seen too much of the Portuguese in Africa to believe that they would, in a wholesale way, be cruel to natives."[3]

This chapter does not propose to deal with the history of the African and Asiatic provinces nor give a detailed account of the internal development of each. It is limited to a general statement of the status, the evolution, and the present situation of each of the overseas territories with a few comments as to some of the major problems that face them. We can begin, perhaps, most effectively to make this survey by beginning with the Cape Verde Islands, and proceed systematically down the West African coast, around the cape to Mozambique and then to Asia.[4]

CAPE VERDE

The province of Cape Verde consists of ten islands and five islets, administered from the capital of Praia. All the islands are of volcanic origin and the climate varies, in spite of the small area involved, between the tropical and the more moderate, comparable to Madeira and the Canaries. The islands were unpopulated at the time of the Portuguese occupation so that they constitute a perfect example of Portuguese colonization. The population, according to the census of 1950, was 147,328 in all, and divided among 3034 whites, 101 of mixed blood, and 42,000 Negroes. The agricultural products of the archipelago include corn, a basic crop, sisal, and sugar cane. Coffee is cultivated to a considerable extent. The industrial

---

[3] Kingsley, Mary H., *Travels in West Africa*, London, 1904, p. 42. This observant Englishwoman also notes that the natives of the Kru coast were of a mind that "God made white man and God made black man, but dem debil make Portuguee" (*ibid.*, p. 41).

[4] No effort is made to provide anything near an exhaustive bibliography, for the literature on the Portuguese possessions is immense. See Jakob, E. G., *Das Portugiesische Kolonialreich*, Leipzig, 1940; the *Boletim da Agência Geral do Ultramar*, published monthly; and the *Anuário Estatistico do Ultramar* provide information on overseas progress. An excellent summary of Portuguese colonial theory is contained in Silva Cunha, J. M. da, *O sistema português de política indigena* (*Subsidios para o seu estudo*), Coimbra, 1953, with abundant bibliography.

development has been modest and is largely restricted to operations that stem from the cultivation of cane sugar. The extraction of salt is also one of the major sources of income. The islands have always played an important role as a natural stopping place on the route to Africa and to America, and the ports of São Vicente and of Praia, which have undergone improvement in recent years, receive the bulk of transatlantic shipping that makes use of their facilities. It is a vital link for the Portuguese themselves in the run between Lisbon and the ports of Angola and Mozambique. Cape Verde has been included in the six-year development plan of the Portuguese government, due to reach its conclusion in 1958, to the extent of 112 million *escudos* for such improvements as afforestation, scientific stock breeding, communications and transportation, especially airports, and expansion of the exploitation of the natural resources.[5] The smallness of the islands is one of the impediments to greater economic vitality. The largest of the group, São Thiago, has an area of 350 square miles and 63,000 people, while some of the smaller islands, such as Maio, have 70 square miles, and Brava has only 23. The latter has the special feature of a female population that far outnumbers the male because of the tendency of the latter to migrate, at a fairly early age, to America.[6]

PORTUGUESE GUINEA

On the continent of Africa, the northernmost Portuguese province is Portuguese Guinea, which became a separate colony in 1879. It is entirely surrounded, on the land side, by French West Africa and the frontiers were fixed by the Convention of 1886 and by a further treaty on frontiers in 1906. Its coast line is highly indented and so numerous are the deep-water canals which penetrate far inland that it has been compared — the proportions strictly regarded,

[5] *Portugal. Overseas Economic Surveys*, London, June, 1954, p. 106.

[6] An excellent survey, now a little out of date, is *L'Empire Colonial portugais*, Paris, May, 1949. This publication is one of the series "La Documentation Française" issued by the French Ministry of Finance and Economic Affairs. Each area is presented succinctly with the principal facts. The distinguished Portuguese anthropologist, Dr. António Mendes Corrêa in his *Ultramar português: Ilhas de Cabo Verde*, Lisbon, 1954, p. 137, notes that "The Cape Verde Islands constitute one of the most fascinating and important natural laboratories for anthropology and ethnography in the world." The convergence of races on the islands and the high degree to which racial crossing has been carried make of the islands a synthesis of Portugal overseas.

of course — with the fjords of Norway.[7] Together with the adjacent archipelago of Bijagoz and the island of Bolama, the area of the province is 13,948 square miles, and the population totals 510,777, of whom only 2263 are Europeans and less than 5000 are mulattoes. The rest, almost to a man, are African natives. One reporter who has given us his impressions recently states that Bissau, the capital town, is far more European than Dakar and that the number of mulattoes was considerable.[8]

The indigenous population is divided between Moslem Negroes of the interior and the non-Moslem on the coast, and, aside from the race called Funali, almost all are engaged in agriculture. Native resistance did not end until well into the twentieth century and the province cannot be said today to have even begun systematic development.[9] The natural productivity of the province is great and, in addition to rice which is one of the principal crops, experiments have demonstrated that tobacco, sisal, cotton, and sugar cane can be grown with success. Stock raising has developed to a relatively high point and constitutes one of the most promising sources of the economic advancement of the territory. Here, as elsewhere in the Portuguese world, lack of capital for investment has always been a factor of major importance in the slowness with which economic and social progress has come, and in spite of the vastly improved conditions, Portugal is still a poor country and incapable of the massive improvement schemes that would transform the still primitive economy of such places as Guinea.[10]

---

[7] Vasconcelos, Ernesto de, *As colónias*, Lisbon, 1929, p. 14.

[8] Meeker, Oden, *Report on Africa*, New York, 1954, p. 224.

[9] Barreto, J., *História da Guiné*, Lisbon, 1938. On the native population, Carreira, A., *Mandingas da Guiné Portuguesa*, Lisbon, 1947; Simões, L., *Babel negra, etnografia, arte e cultura dos indigenas da Guiné*, Porto, 1935; de Carvalho Viegas, Luis António, *Guiné Portuguesa*, Lisbon, 1936, Vol. I; Mendes Correia, A. A., *Raças do Imperio*, Porto, 1943; Santos Lima, Augusto J., *Organização económica e social dos Bijagós*, Lisbon, 1947. Especially to be recommended for its accuracy, vision, and penetrating conclusions is Teixeira da Mota, A., *Guiné Portuguesa*, Lisbon, 1954, 2 vols.

[10] A splendid source for Portuguese Guinea is the *Boletim Cultural da Guiné portuguesa* published at Bissau for the *Centro de Estudos da Guiné Portuguesa*. This society for scientific research and publication can be proud of this excellently edited and printed bulletin that is now running to some ten volumes and contains articles and studies on every phase of Guinea life, including in each issue information regarding the financial status of the province. The growing interest of Portugal in the rational development of its African territories is no better illustrated than in the enormous expansion of scientific work in Africa.

The Portuguese, nevertheless, have managed to give the native peoples a dignity and a self-respect that slipshod administration in the past and insufficient budgets have not been able to effect.[11] Although industry is almost entirely on a home basis and represents little in the sum total, commerce has been reasonably active and the province, within modest proportions, may be said to have enjoyed prosperity over the past years. In 1927, imports totaled over 34 million *escudos* and exports around the same figure. In 1950, the province exported over 127 million *escudos'* worth of its products. The budget has remained somewhat unbalanced, due to expenditures for development schemes and other types of improvement. The third quarter of 1953, for example, the total receipts for the provincial government were a little over 14 million *escudos* and the expenditures for that same period, 19 million.[12]

Much of this is under the direction of the remarkable organization known as the *Junta das Missões geográficas e de Investigações coloniais* of Lisbon. See the work *Occupação cientifica do Ultramar português*, Lisbon, 1950, which discusses in detail the legislation and projects for all sorts of scientific expeditions and work in the various overseas areas. This is perhaps as good a place as any to mention the indispensable publications of the *Agencia Geral de Ultramar* which cannot be overlooked by anyone seriously interested in the study of the Portuguese empire.

[11] "That they (the Portuguese) were not unduly hard taskmasters is a conclusion borne out by the self-respect and independence of many tribes in modern Portuguese territory. . . . the truth is that Portugal has never had the resources in men and material either for large social enterprise or for close and continuous administration" (Macmillan, W. M., *Africa Emergent, op. cit.*, pp. 93–94).

[12] *Boletim Cultural da Guiné portuguesa*, Bissau, January, 1954, No. 33, Vol. IX, p. 228. Ignorance of Portuguese Africa is appalling even among those who ought to know better. The extraordinary blind spot that prevails regarding these territories extends to every type of expert or quasi-expert on African affairs. In many of the current popular books on Africa, especially in the United States, one gets the impression that there is virtually nothing written on these possessions and that the Portuguese have sought to keep them out of sight of inquisitive foreigners. As an illustration of the absurdities that circulate regarding the Portuguese world, we may take the case of Portuguese Guinea. John Gunther dismisses the area pithily by calling it "this shabby, moribund fragment of territory" (*Inside Africa, op. cit.*, p. 598). L. Dudley Stamp in his authoritative volume *Africa, a Study in Tropical Development*, New York, 1953, devotes two pages to Guinea and a half page to Angola. This distinguished British scholar writes about Portuguese Guinea in the following vein: "Most of the people are Mandingas or Fulani, little touched by either Mohammedanism or Christianity, who are of course agriculturalists and pastoralists" (p. 288). He continues by saying that "The Portuguese are a mere handful mainly officials. Such trade as there is — is in the hands of French and Belgians." The province has been presented as a sloppy little backwash where somnolent Portuguese tyrannize over untutored blacks. A telling reply to this ignorance is provided by Michael

SÃO TOMÉ AND PRÍNCIPE

As we move southward and around the bulge of West Africa, we come to the islands of São Tomé and Príncipe, sitting almost on the Equator in the midst of the Gulf of Guinea, about 125 miles off the mainland. The total area of the islands is 964 square miles, and the population in 1950 was estimated at a little over 60,000 with a small minority of perhaps 1200 Europeans. The islands produce cacao, coffee, coconut, copra, palm oil, cinchona, and a dozen other tropical products. Angola and Mozambique have contributed to the populating of the islands and today the two form a separate province of Portugal, according to the legislation laid down in 1951 for the provincial status of each one of these areas. The islands used to have a plantation system that provoked the protests of the missionaries and was notorious up and down the African coast. Oden Meeker, who devotes a few amusing pages to São Tomé and Príncipe, describes them as under a paternalistic regime that keeps things in perfect order and that the forced labor for public works and the like "did not seem an intolerable burden."[13] It is fairly plain that so tiny a province cannot be economically portentous. Yet in 1952 the revenue topped a good 50 million *escudos* and exports pushed a healthy 200 million for the same year. Nineteen or twenty elementary schools and a technical institution for more advanced training seem to satisfy the needs of this very small population. To São Tomé and Príncipe is attached that remarkable

---

Crowder, "Progress in Portuguese Guinea," in *African World*, London, August, 1956. Mr. Crowder points out that on almost every count Professor Stamp is wrong. One third of the natives of Guinea are Moslems and as for the handful of Portuguese, there is in fact a considerable white minority in proportion to the total population. He adds: "The whole country is linked up by one of the best communications systems in Africa. There are 29 air strips in the territory. 1,860 miles of road, of which 1,200 are open all the year round, make movement around the colony very easy." He insists equally that the "standard of administration is high" and that "medical progress has been considerable." Mr. Crowder concludes that "Today Portuguese Guinea is one of Portugal's best administered provinces and is entering on a promising new era of its history. Even the staid *Encyclopædia Britannica* notes that "more than 2000 miles of roads have been built since 1940" (Vol. 18, p. 289, 1952 ed.).

[13] Meeker, *op. cit.*, p. 219. Inso, Egydio, *As ilhas de S. Tomé e Príncipe*, São Tomé, 1922. This province is treated in some detail, although not always with scrupulous accuracy in Galvão, Henerique, and Selvagem, Carlos, *Império ultramarino portuguȇs*, Lisbon, 1951, Vol. II, p. 180 *seq.*

little enclave called São João Batista de Ajudá, with a tiny strip of land about it, near Quidak in French Dahomey.

Although administratively a part of Angola, there is another Portuguese enclave, but in this case of considerably larger proportions, that is called Cabinda. It lies just north of the mouth of the Congo River and touches French Equatorial Africa and the Belgian Congo on the land side, with a coast line of some 93 miles and an extension inland of about 70. The town of Cabinda was formerly a prominent slave mart and remains today an export center for palm oil, nuts, and other produce of the Congo basin. The population is about 50,000 and is made up largely of a native race called the Cabindas, who have long been famed for their intelligence and enterprise, both as mariners and traders. The area is attached to the province of Angola as one of its districts.

ANGOLA

In coming to Angola, we reach one of the two principal Portuguese territories in all Africa and one whose importance as a possible area of absorption of European immigrants is considerable.[14] The coast line of Angola stretches for a thousand miles from the Belgian Congo on the north to Southwest Africa below covering over 481,000 square miles. The tropical and subtropical climate is affected by various factors which make it a promising land for colonization from abroad: the altitude of the interior and the highlands that are temperate in climate; the latitude south of the Equator and the Benguela current, an offspring of the Antarctic stream, that modifies considerably the degree of heat. The present population is placed at 3,738,010 inhabitants, and in contrast with many European possessions in Africa, there are a fairly large number of urban centers with the resultant distribution of population:

---

[14] Delgado, R., *História de Angola*, Lisbon, 1948; Santos, A. C. Valdes Thomas dos, *Perspectivas económicas de Angola*, Lisbon, 1949. The government of Angola publishes *A Voz de Angola*, issued by the Office for Economic Affairs in Luanda, a fortnightly. The *Boletim Oficial* (Luanda) is equally useful for month-by-month developments. The *Mensário Administrativo* summarizes developments in the administrative field. See also Lefebre, Gabriel, *L'Angola, son histoire, son économie* (Liège, 1947), and the best general survey in English: Egerton, F. Clement C., *Angola in perspective. Endeavour and achievement in Portuguese West Africa* (London, 1957).

Luanda, Benguela, Lobito, Nova Lisboa, Sã de Bandeira, and others.[15]

The population of Angola, which in the early part of the century had been grossly overestimated, has been demonstrated to be extremely small for the territory and of slow growth. The various causes of this demographic stagnation are: dynastic wars of the tribes, slavery, alcoholism, and disease.[16] The native races in Angola have long followed the classical Portuguese system of admitting to the enjoyment of the privileges, as well as the obligations, of civilization, that is, European civilization, those who by education and effort achieve a certain level. The number in this case has been estimated at about 25,000 natives who are considered *assimilados* and perhaps 24,000 mixed bloods who belong to the same category.[17] The promotion of the integration of the races has not progressed as far or as happily as might be wished and as he has always been in the background of the Portuguese mind from the days when Africa was first reached. The tendency toward miscegenation seems to have slowed up considerably in Angola, perhaps because of the 80,000 whites who have settled down there. Justino Teixeira, an

[15] *Anuario Commercial e industrial de Angola*, Luanda, 1955, p. v. The distribution of white and colored population in the principal Angolan cities is indicative to some extent of the degree of European penetration:

	1940		*1950*	
City	*Total*	*White*	*Total*	*White*
Luanda	61,028	8,944	141,722	20,710
Nova Lisboa	16,288	3,214	28,297	4,756
Malange	5,299	865	9,473	1,592
Lobito	13,592	1,616	23,897	4,074
Benguela	14,243	1,461	14,690	3,346
Silva Porto	4,671	663	8,840	1,229
Sã da Bandeira	8,521	1,189	11,657	6,204
Mocamedes	4,926	2,165	8,576	3,545
Total	128,568	20,117	247,152	45,456

Angola, province portugaise en Afrique, supplement of the review, *La Revue Française*, Paris, No. 45, 1953.

[16] A. C. Valdez Santos, Thomas dos, *Angola, coração do império*, Lisbon, 1945, p. 27.

[17] There has been a great deal of discussion pro and con by foreign writers interested in Africa on the value of Portugal's system of *assimilados*. The arrangement has nothing to do with race or color. It is simply a recognition that a bush Negro cannot very well be expected to pass immediately and with no transition in time from the jungle to the drawing room. See Belchior, Manuel Dias, *Compreendamos os negros* (Lisbon, 1951), which is a first-rate study of the problem of how to deal with the administration of large indigenous areas and how to achieve the integration and especially the collaboration of European and African. The author is an administrator in Mozambique. See *Provincia de Angola-Recenseamento Geral da População*, Luanda, 1955, Vol. IV and Vol. V.

engineer in Angola, has studied this extremely interesting facet of life in the province and has come to certain definite conclusions. In the examination of interracial marriages between young white men and Africans, it is to be noted that a large percentage prefer women of mixed blood and light color. The mulattoes, on the other hand, in general marry among themselves, tending to stabilize this third element of society. Among the natives, 95 per cent of the marriages are with persons of their own race and only 5 with mulattoes. There seem to be no cases of whites married to full-blooded Africans.[18]

Another peculiarity of the population of Angola is that the term "white" and "European" are not synonymous. The number of creoles, or persons of white blood born in the province, is now so large that in certain areas of the south they outnumber the Portuguese from Portugal. In no part of tropical Africa does a comparable situation exist.[19]

This phenomenon poses a most intriguing problem: that of the adaptation of the European to an African environment and climate, although in the case of the highlands of Angola, of one that is modified by the altitude and permits of an easier transplantation.[20] The Portuguese government has been attempting to encourage immigration on a larger scale to Angola. The fact that there has been, over many years, a large migration to Brazil and even to the United States, has made Portugal a population exporting country. Even more recently, in 1954–1956, the Portuguese government has encouraged migrations in the hundreds to Canada, in view of the pressure of population, especially in the Azores and Madeira. Angola offers the attraction of its underpopulation and the considerable areas in the interior whose climatic and other conditions compare favorably with those of Europe. What is more striking is the effort of the government to settle Portuguese families as peasant smallholders, working their own land and tending their own livestock without the help of native labor. This is an un-

---

[18] Article in *Diario de Luanda*, reprinted in *Afrique Nouvelle*, Dakar, French West Africa, December 6, 1955.

[19] Santos, Valdez Thomas dos, *Angola*, *op. cit.*, p. 37.

[20] This problem and how it has worked out in Angola is examined in Ferreira, Vicente, *Regiões de povoamento europeu nos planaltos de Angola Noticias das experiencias de aclimatação da raça europeia na zona inter-tropical*, Roma, 1940. The same author in *Estudos ultramarinos*, Lisbon, 1945, Vol. IV, p. 173 *seq.*

heard-of procedure in Africa and one that will be looked upon as unique in the annals of colonization if continued on an appreciable scale. The experiment was started in 1952 on the plateau at Cela, some 200 miles inland from Luanda and 4000 feet above sea level. If successful the plan will include several thousand families, who will produce coffee, rice, soya beans, and orchard fruits. The land was not used by the Africans, for it was largely swamp land since drained and reclaimed.[21]

A word about the "native policy" because it is the so-called "Angola case" that has brought about the severest strictures in recent years of slavery or near slavery conditions. One recent writer tells us that "on the evidence I collected there are more slaves in Angola than there were fifty years ago."[22] A Native Affairs Department was set up as long ago as 1913 and, under the decree of 1914, forced labor was authorized, so that workers were secured on the basis of recruitment in the villages and among the tribes. In 1922 this was modified so that chiefs received compensation for labor thus made available. The Native Labor Code of 1928 restricted the recruitment system and made such labor usable only for public purposes, that is, as a sort of *corvée*. The Colonial Charter of 1933 forbade government intervention in labor recruiting. Authority is maintained to requisition labor for certain specified purposes. The government of the province, under the law of 1935 requires five days a year of work for public purposes such as roads from each male citizen and such labor can be commuted for a cash payment.[23]

[21] Article in *The Times*, London, September 22, 1955. Résumé in *The Colonial Review*, London, December, 1955, Vol. IX, No. 4, p. 119. "The government of Portugal is essaying an experiment unparalleled in Africa south of the Sahara today."

[22] Davidson, Basil, *The African Awakening*, London, 1955, pp. 195–196. This is a very strong indictment in which the writer finds practically nothing of any good in Portuguese attitudes or administration in Angola.

[23] As long ago as 1906, H. W. Nevinson published *A Modern Slavery* (London), a study of indentured labor and recruitment. This writer sent out by *Harper's Magazine* stated that "I have heard the slaves in Angola estimated at five sixths of the population . . ." (p. 48), and later comments that as of 1905, "slavery exists quite openly throughout Bihé in the three forms of family slavery among the natives, domestic slavery to the Portuguese traders and slavery on the plantations" (p. 100). Another British traveler in Angola, speaks glowingly of "The progressive Portuguese colony of Angola" and especially of its excellent road system and fast-growing agriculture. Barns, *Angolan Sketches*, London, 1928, p. 29. The *New York Times* correspondent, Leonard Ingalls, writing under the title "Portugal Facing Big Job in Angola" (August 5, 1956), states that "The government still retains a policy of forced labor, and in many cases able-bodied

Agriculture in Angola operates on three levels: the first that of the indigenous population raising crops for subsistence living; the second, the Europeans or descendants of Europeans of whom we have spoken who have become farmers in their own right; and, finally, the plantations for the raising of coffee, sugar cane, cotton, sisal, and other tropical products. Agriculture has been considerably facilitated by the existence of the railway system which is one of the more advanced in this part of the world. The line running from Benguela inland connects with the Belgian Congo and allows for overland transportation of goods and passengers to Mozambique on the east coast and to the Union of South Africa. Angola has been steadily increasing its exports, and during and since the last war has augmented its trade with the mother country. Woods and forest products, livestock and rice, mandioca, tobacco, wheat, and the products of the palm tree all enter into the commercial exports of Angola. It is the country producing the largest amount of bees' wax in the world.[24]

The mining of diamonds represents one of the most interesting of Angola's economic activities and the diamonds extracted from its soil are held by those who are well informed on the subject to be quite equal to the ones produced in South Africa. Manufacturing on a small scale has begun and promises to increase in importance in the near future; sugar refining, soap, oils, canned fish, chalk, bricks and tiles, frozen meats, and various fibers are produced in Angola. The fishing industry is one of the most significant, particularly in the regions of Mossmedes, Benguela, and Luanda.

The industrialization of Angola is being carried out along the lines of the six-year plan for general, economic development of the whole empire.[25] One of the features of Angola is the excellent

---

African men, with no choice of employment, are compelled to work for long hours and at low pay on plantations. However, the administration has recently indicated that it intends to discontinue the policy."

[24] The increase of international traffic and the growth of inter-African trade has made the Caminho de Ferro de Benguela of far greater importance and has required large investments to modernize. *Affrica*, Rome, July–August, 1955, No. 7–8, p. 244. This excellent Italian review of things African contains numerous items on the Portuguese area.

[25] Ferreira, Vicente, *Angola e os seus problemas* (in *Estudos Ultramarinos*), Lisbon, 1954, Vol. II, p. 166 *seq.* The author in a penetrating examination of Angola's problems, notes the recurring deficit as one of the gravest drawbacks to expansion. This accords with the emphasis laid by the Salazar regime on a balanced budget.

road system that covers a good portion of the country. This system has made it possible to set up the provincial administration more effectively and has also reduced immeasurably the dependence on native porters for transportation and liberated them from one of the most burdensome of economic servitudes.

In public instruction, the Portuguese have sought to avoid the rigors of segregation and, of course, have nothing remotely comparable to the *apartheid* arrangement in the Union of South Africa. In Angola, as in the other territories, the conception is that education must be adapted to the level of civilization of the native and not to his color. In other words, the native who has assimilated Portuguese speech and thought habits encounters no difficulty in making his way in any line of activity he may choose. "Official instruction in Angola, as in the rest of the Portuguese territories, is not subordinated to racial discrimination. There exist nevertheless two systems of instruction; one for the natives and another for the whites and *assimilados*, but this difference is functional and the result of variation in social and intellectual development."[26]

Elementary education, or "rudimentary" as the Portuguese expression has it, is for the native children and is carried out by the Catholic missions in agreement with the Portuguese government. The number of schools is some 600 and the number of pupils about 20,000. The elementary or general system — without reference to race — takes care of whites and *assimilados*, that is to say, those who already know Portuguese and do not have to devote their time the first years in absorbing the elements of the language.

Secondary education is imparted in public and private high schools or *liceus*, the great majority of which are under Catholic auspices. In addition to what may be called the ordinary classical course as followed in these institutions, the province has facilities for commercial, industrial, and agricultural technical training.

The problem of Angola, from the human point of view, is demographic, that is to say, an insufficient population for the land area involved and in terms of the natural resources available. There is also the fact that at present the overwhelming majority of the inhabitants are natives who have not yet attained the status of

---

[26] *Angola, provincia de Portugal em Africa*, Luanda, 1953, p. 65, also *Provincia de Angola — Estatistico de Educação, Ano Lectivo de 1954*, Luanda, 1955.

assimilados.[27] For the most part these natives belong to the Bantu family and have demonstrated, during the long period of Portuguese penetration, a considerable capacity for resistance.[28] The social problem has been acute for a number of specific reasons. The first is the small number of Portuguese colonists, especially of those who intend to settle permanently in agriculture or industry. Many of the earlier colonists were definitely on the predatory side, and contributed to the antagonism of the natives and Europeans prior to the present century.[29]

The experiment in biracialism which worked so significantly in Brazil, the Cape Verde Islands, and Goa was less feasible on a large scale and with rapidity in territories like Angola. Here, the handful of Portuguese settlers came up against a massive native population, whose tribal organization and attachment to their own community posed great difficulties in assimilation. In Brazil, the Negro was the slave imported from Africa and therefore as much a newcomer as the Portuguese himself; both of them were in a novel environment and obliged to make their way as best they could in circumstances which were strange. The uprootedness of both European and African *vis-à-vis* the Brazilian milieu meant that both of them evolved together, acquiring the same habits and customs as time went on, and giving each other, in a certain sense, mutual support in the struggle for survival. This was not the case in Africa where the Negro was at home and the Portuguese the newcomer. Aside from the ravages of slavery and the complications that the traffic caused in the relations of the two races, the fact that the Negro lived already in normally established communities, meant quite simply that intermingling was infinitely more arduous. Whereas the Portuguese emigrant to Brazil found it relatively easy to share with the Negro from Dahomey, the Senegal, or Guinea coast the adventure of the new world, the same Portuguese, if transported to Angola, found it inordinately difficult to penetrate and, much less, assimilate the pre-existent, compact community social order that was already there.

[27] Statistics in cases of this sort are always a bit arbitrary. The Angola government suggests roughly about 96 per cent against 4 per cent. *Angola*, *op. cit.*, p. 40.

[28] Cadornega, Oliveira, *História das guerras angolanas*, Lisbon, 1942.

[29] Fuentes, Angela, "O comercio de Angola — suporte económico da colonia durante a primeira fase do seu desenvolvimento" in *Boletim do Instituto de Angola*, Luanda, 1954, No. 3, p. 43.

It is well to emphasize that as yet the biracial society is a long way from conclusion in these African territories. But the essential thing is that the Portuguese have not gone there to impose a superior ethnic point of view or to coerce the native in social terms. One writer has said judiciously that the Portuguese in Africa do not have the color bar; what they have is a civilization test, which is something else again.[30] Whatever may be the failings in practical terms, often the consequence of financial limitations, the Portuguese regime has never set up as its goal an all-white "colony" in the heart of Africa, with several million black men condemned everlastingly to the limbo of rigorous segregation.

MOZAMBIQUE

Across Africa on the other side is the immense territory of Mozambique, colonized for the first time in 1505, and since incorporated as a province of Portugal, after various territorial adjustments with Great Britain. It covers an area of 297,654 square miles with a population estimated at 5,732,317 in 1954. According to this same official source, of this total number of inhabitants, the "civilized" were placed at 91,954 and the primitive at 5,640,363.[31]

The statistical tables show that there are about 84,000 Portuguese in the province and if the total number of civilized is taken and this number subtracted, it is evident that the natives who have been completely assimilated are still very few in number, some seven to eight thousand. It should be added as a unique feature of Mozambique that there are around 13,000 Indians established in the country, with an influence comparable to that exerted in Kenya and other territories of East Africa. The process of miscegenation has been advancing at a regular rate with 13,259 individuals in this category in 1935; 15,784 in 1945, and 25,149 in 1950, the year of the last general census.[32]

The influences on Mozambique are equally apparent in the proportions of the various religious groups. Of the total population, 5.1 per cent is listed as Catholic and 10.6 per cent, or more than

[30] Campbell, Alexander, *The Heart of Africa,* London and New York, 1954, p. 378.

[31] *Anuário Estatístico — Provincia de Moçambique,* Lourenço Marques, 1954, p. 21.

[32] *Recenseamento Geral da População em 1950,* province of Mozambique, Lourenço Marques, 1953, "Civilized Population," p. xxxi.

double, as Moslem, largely to be accounted for by the Indian population. The overwhelming mass of 82.6 per cent profess some form of paganism. Protestants, incidentally, for there are evangelical missions in these various Portuguese territories, have 1.7 per cent of the inhabitants.[33] In spite of the low percentage of those able to read and write, there has been appreciable progress over the past ten years, to the extent that the figures on this one point have doubled. At present, of the noncivilized inhabitants of Mozambique, about 165,000 speak Portuguese and of this number roughly 60,000 read and write the language. The means have been lacking for anything like a massive attack on the problem of making Portuguese the second language of the natives.[34] The natives belong generally to the Bantu family, the most important tribes in the north being the Yaos and the Makwa. In the south are Zulu peoples with racial attachments in South Africa.

The relations between the civilized and the more backward peoples of Mozambique are governed by the general idea that the mores and usages of the aborigines shall not be disturbed insofar as they are not contrary to morality or the basic laws of the community. The problem of miscegenation in this area presents certain difficulties which are greater than elsewhere, owing to the very great variety of human elements available.[35] A goodly number of the teachers in the elementary schools are Negroes and it is expected that, with the functioning of the recently established Bureau for Professional Guidance, there will be a marked advance in native education.[36]

---

[33] *Recenseamento Geral da População em 1950*, Lourenço Marques, 1935, "Non-Civilized Population," p. xii.

[34] *Ibid.*, p. xi.

[35] Alberto, V. M. Simões, "Características da mestiçagem Moçambicana," in *Boletim da Sociedade de Estudos de Moçambique*, Lourenço Marques, No. 90, January–February, 1955.

[36] Freitas, Gustavo de, "Mozambique. Native Cultural Policy," in *Civilisations*, Brussels, Vol. VI, 1956, No. 1, p. 122 *seq.* In *African News*, published by Ruth Sloan Associates, Washington, D. C. (Vol. II, No. 7, September, 1955), there is a lead article entitled, "Portuguese Colonial Policy — a Critical View." The point is made that up to 1920 Portugal had no well defined colonial policy but that the amputations and humiliations suffered led to a change and one of the leading figures after this date in the reorientation was General Norton da Matos in Angola. There is reference to the effort to settle white Portuguese on the Angolan plateau and create a new Portugal in Africa. The article stresses the nonracial aspect of Portuguese policy but claims it is only one side of the picture for the chances of a native becoming an *assimilado* are relatively slim.

For a long time Mozambique was organized administratively in such a way that a private enterprise, the Mozambique Company, chartered in Lisbon in 1891, exercised rights over a vast area of 59,315 square miles, called Manica and Sofala, where it had a monopoly of agriculture, commerce, industry, mining, communications, taxation, and customs duties; that is to say, a veritable state within the Portuguese state. Beira on the coast was the port of the Company and anyone who is a philatelist is perfectly aware of the picturesque stamps issued by the Company as part of its activities. At the expiration of the fifty-year period, the arrangement was not renewed and the territory reverted to Portuguese administration, to form today the united province of Mozambique.

The province produces principally sugar, maize, cotton, copra, sisal, and various mineral products. The economy in many ways follows the pattern of Angola and the other areas already mentioned. There is an excess of imports over exports and the budget in general has tended to show a slight deficit. Some effort has been made to overcome the unfavorable balance of trade through the encouragement of local industry capable of producing articles now purchased abroad, such as cotton weave, wheat flour from the United States and Canada, and dairy products, especially powdered milk and similar articles.[37] A notable feature of the economy of the province has been the large importation since 1948 of tractors, automobiles, and, especially, rolling stock for the railways since Mozambique is an important railroad center for all southern Africa and with its connections via Rhodesia and South Africa with the Atlantic coast it plays a role of vital importance in any defense scheme for that part of the continent. A glance at the map will show that the Portuguese control the two sides of the continent and are therefore in a singularly strategic position with reference to interior transportation from coast to coast.

Timber resources are abundant and stock raising offers an increasingly important possibility of expansion. Mining in Mozambique is by no means negligible, with extensive coal fields near Zumbo, and gold deposits are abundant in many parts. Mozambique has

[37] Santos, Manuel Pimentel Pereira dos, "Present Tendencies in the Economy of Moçambique" in *Boletim da Sociedade de Estudos de Moçambique*, Lourenço Marques, March–April, 1953, No. 78, p. 133. A good general survey of economics is Spence, C. F., *The Portuguese Colony of Moçambique, An Economic Survey*, Capetown–Amsterdam, 1951.

often been identified with ancient Ophir as a land where gold abounded. Tin and asbestos are also present in various parts of the province.

The problems of education and relations with the indigenous population are very similar to those of Angola. For the entire province there are reported 155 institutions for elementary instruction, that is, for the "civilized" of which 72 are state and 55 Catholic. Rudimentary education, and it has already been stated that this refers to the noncivilized, was given in 1626 establishments of which the overwhelming majority (1566) were in the hands of Catholic mission communities and 26 in those of non-Catholic Christian groups. Normal education, technical training, commercial and industrial education is provided as well as the usual secondary education at the classical level. A total of some 250,000 students were listed as matriculated in the various institutions of the country.[38] Religiously, Mozambique is of considerable interest especially since the establishment here and in Angola of the regularly organized dioceses and the raising of the Archbishop of Lourenço Marques to the cardinalate dignity.

The size and geographical position of Mozambique promises much for the future. The World War interfered seriously with a number of ambitious projects to develop its economy, but the six-year plan envisages an expansion which will bring a wider prosperity to the entire territory.[39]

Attention will be given in the following chapter to Goa and the minor Portuguese establishments in India, in the light of the conflict that has developed between Portugal and the Indian Union over their cosovereignty. Aside from Goa, Damão, and Diu, with the smaller enclaves inland, the most important Portuguese-controlled area in the East is Macau. Something has been said about this province in the discussion of Portuguese penetration of the Far East. It remains, however, to describe briefly certain features of this last foothold of Portugal on the China coast which still remains as a bastion of its expansion to the Pacific Ocean.

---

[38] *Anuário Estatístico, op. cit.*, pp. 132–133.

[39] "During the last twenty-five years the Portuguese overseas territories have been making steady progress. Indeed 'steady' is hardly an adequate word for, in some respects, the progress, especially in Angola and Mocambique — has been sensational" ("The Portuguese Empire" in *The British Survey*, London, April, 1954, No. 61, p. 18).

MACAO

Macao is situated at the mouth of the Canton River and today, with the two adjacent islands of Taipa and Coloane, forms a single province. The area is only six square miles and the population, according to the census of 1950, is 187,772, of whom less than 5000 are Europeans and the vast majority Chinese.[40] What conceivable reason can the Portuguese have for hanging on to this tiny piece of territory, microscopically insignificant on the edge of the vastness of China and which cannot possibly produce any positive advantage to the economy of the nation? The reason lies deep in history and the national emotions. Macao is the symbol of Portuguese presence in the China seas and of the contact that dates from the beginning of the sixteenth century between the Portuguese West and the Far East. Macao has been defended against invaders and pirates, against every type of marauder and trespasser. The Dutch were held off and, during the Spanish period, Macao remained loyal to the crown in abeyance. Nor did Macao bow even when the British occupied it in the early nineteenth century under pretense of protecting it against French encroachments.[41] There was a time, a little later, when Macao acquired the reputation of the most vice-ridden spot in the Far East, and the movement of tourists toward its gaming rooms and opium dens was supposedly a source of considerable revenue to the state. All that has changed. During World War II, when the tidal wave of Japan swept clear to the Northern Territory of Australia, Macao managed somehow to remain aloof from occupation. Never did the Japanese occupy Macao, although there were innumerable incidents between pro-Japanese and Nationalist Chinese and bands of Chinese armed by Japan were poised more than once on the frontier.

Recent events have affected Macao most directly, for its population has increased substantially, thanks to the thousands of refugees who have poured out of Communist China toward the two islets

---

[40] *Anuário Estatístico de Macau*, Macau, 1953–1955. For current events in Macao, economic and social, the best source is *Macau. Boletim informativo da repartição provincial dos serviços de Economía e estatística geral*, published every fortnight by the Macao Provincial government. Also *Statesman's Year Book*, 1955, p. 1341.

[41] "Macao: une province portugaise en terre chinoise," in *Politique Etrangère*, Paris, February, 1956, p. 85 *seq.*

of hope on the coast: British Hong-Kong and Portuguese Macao. In general, however, the racial propensity of the Portuguese has not operated in Macao. There are certainly some four or five thousand mixed bloods, principally of Portuguese with Malay and Indian rather than with Chinese, for the well-known tenacity of the Chinese to stick by custom and family has made anything like a large-scale intermingling out of the question. Even the Portuguese language has not become the ordinary vehicle of expression, but rather it is Cantonese for the majority of the inhabitants and English for other purposes. A curious Macao dialect has developed which would appear to be a sort of Portuguese superimposed on a Chinese structure. Religiously, the advance of Catholicism has been mediocre, due in large part to the fact that conversion among the Macao Chinese is considered as equivalent to becoming a European.

Educationally, the Chinese schools dominate with nearly 20,000 pupils in these private establishments as against some 2500 in the Portuguese primary and secondary schools, under both official and Catholic auspices. The colleges of São Paulo Grande and São José constitute two important foundations for the diffusion of both Portuguese culture and the Catholic faith in the Orient.[42]

Economically the two industries that have meant the most to Macao are the manufacture of matches and of firecrackers. In 1951, for the lover of statistics, the province produced 3750 tons of firecrackers of all kinds and capacities. Fishing is important and occupies about 20,000 inhabitants, while the making of paper and paper articles holds an important place. The commercial life of the province is very much controlled by the Chinese Merchants Association, which has made it difficult for Portuguese enterprises to establish themselves in the territory. A motion-picture company, Eurasia Films, has opened a studio in the province and to date has

[42] Macao as a basis for Catholic missionary activity both locally and in China has always been of fundamental importance. This city was originally called "City of the Name of God" for "whilst Macao was founded as a place of trade, it speedily became the headquarters of Christian missionary activity in the Far East, and its importance in this respect continued long after its commercial prosperity was a thing of the past" (Boxer, C. R., *Fidalgos in the Far East, op. cit.*, p. 157). The brilliant role of Macao as a Christian center is admirably summed up in "I quattro secoli di Macao cristiana" in *Osservatore Romano*, Vatican City, August 17–18, 1956. Among other things notes the Vatican journal, "Macao had the merit of seeing formed the first seminary for native clergy in 1732."

produced a single film in Portuguese and Chinese under the title, *Novos rumos*. Add to the above economic activities gambling, racing, and other forms of entertainment and the area has managed to carry on quite effectively. The principal problem of Macao has been to adjust itself to the new relations with China. Prior to the coming into power of the communists, Macao served as an important shopping center and assembly point for goods coming out of China. With the cessation of such commerce, Macao has had to find a new orientation. There is obviously a certain amount of clandestine trade and one of the major sources of income for Macao is the flow of gold from elsewhere in Asia to Peking. Food products, particularly, are exported to China and frequently with little reference to the legal niceties involved. The movement of this type of product in 1951 was as follows:

	In Tons	
	Import	*Export*
Rice	24,200	4,300
Dried fish	406	1,750
Fruit	11,000	
Vegetables	24,800	19,600
Flour	2,500	[43]

The excess of imports is generally re-exported toward neighboring China. The trade with Portugal itself is ridiculously small, and there is some commercial movement with Mozambique and with Timor, from which the coffee consumed in Macao comes. Various plans for economic improvement exist and as in Goa and Timor, there is a projected development scheme which involves everything from improved housing to road building and the dredging of harbors.[44] The three-year period from 1951 to 1954 was one during which large sums were devoted to education, medical care, social services, and the missions.[45]

[43] *Anuário Estatístico de Macau*, Macau, 1953.

[44] *O plano de fomento de Macau e as obras levadas a efeito nos últimos tres anos* (1951–1954), Macao, 1955.

[45] *Ibid.*, p. 7:

Education	1,550,000 *patacas*
Medical aid	4,610,000 *patacas*
Public improvements	13,015,000 *patacas*
Social services	5,140,000 *patacas*
Catholic missions	1,760,000 *patacas*

(The *pataca* is the currency of Macao and worth about 15 to 20 cents.) Medical and social services are detailed in Silva, Rodrigues da, *Assistencia em Macau*, Macao, 1954.

The atmosphere of Macao, in spite of the circumstances of the present day, is optimistic. The government is moving ahead with proposals for large-scale investments and improvements as though the menace of Communist China were on another planet.[46] There have been rumblings from Peking regarding Macao, as yet hardly threatening and certainly not ominous. In fact, there have been evidences from time to time of recognition of the Portuguese presence unofficially, as during a recent devastating fire in one of the poorer quarters of Macao which provoked large-scale aid from Canton in food and clothing. The government of Mao and Chou En-lai has not expressed itself in anything like the lively terms of aggression that have been directed at Taiwan and the off-shore islands under Nationalist Chinese control. The very weakness of Macao may be its advantage, although this has not been a determining factor in the Portuguese State of India.

TIMOR

The last of the overseas provinces is that of Timor, the largest of the Lesser Sunda Islands in the Malay archipelago. Take your map of the huge area from south east Asia east to Australia and north to the Philippines and you will discover Timor more or less midway between Java and New Guinea and directly north of the state of Western Australia. The Portuguese occupy, actually, the eastern part of the island, 11,868 square miles, as well as the little enclave of Ocussi-Ambeno on the former Dutch half which is now Indonesian.[47] The Portuguese were there in the sixteenth century, in

[46] The former governor of Macao, Captain Joaquim Marques Esparteiro, in a report entitled *Algunos problemas magnos de Macau. Breve memória descritiva e justificativa*, Macao, 1952, emphasizes how the very considerable material progress of the past few years "has been made possible in Macao with its own resources" (p. 12). The Portuguese administration is perfectly aware of the uneasy relations with China when the governor says that "since there are no diplomatic relations with China, the present Chinese authorities consider their territorial waters inviolable and this leads to numerous incidents especially in shipping, between the Portuguese and Chinese." He then adds that the basic reality of Macao's life is that "From the Chinese point of view everything takes place almost as though a situation of war existed" (p. 27).

[47] Boletim Trimestral de Estatística Provincia de Timor, Dili, 1956 and 1957. Oliveira, Luna de, *Timor na história de Portugal*, Lisbon, 1949–1952, 3 vols. A most readable chapter on Timor under title, "Turbulent Timor" in Boxer, C. R., *Fidalgos in the Far East*, *op. cit.*, p. 173 *seq.* de Castro Afonso, *As possessões portuguesas na Oceania*, Lisbon, 1867. Faria de Moraes, A., *Subsídios para a historia de Timor*, Bastorá (Portuguese India), 1934.

the great drive that took them from Molucca down through the islands as far as Australia. In 1613, the Dutch landed on its shores and waged war against the Portuguese and their Timorese allies. The British were involved and it was not until the nineteenth century that the division of sovereignty between the Dutch and the Portuguese was established. Until 1896, Portuguese Timor was attached administratively to Macao, but at that time it became a separate colony with the capital at Dili. The convention of 1904 fixed the boundary and determined the jurisdiction over the various enclaves.

The present population of Timor is 442,378, of a mixed Malayan-Papuan-Polynesian race. The Portuguese have always attempted to preserve what is possible of native organization and society and this was no different in Timor. The island was found to be organized into what have become known as *regulados*, under two or three of the principal families. These "kingdoms" were divided into *sucos*, or communities of villages, which together formed one of the many minor kingdoms. This social order was respected and it is curious to note that in 1952, when the Minister for Overseas Affairs visited Timor, he was received by aboriginal representatives who continued to bear the titles and exert, at least in theory, the functions of those who were the traditional leaders of Timorese society.[48]

The white population is very small, probably not more than 2000 in all, of whom 500 are Portuguese and the rest Arabs and others who have settled there for trade purposes. Until 1921 there was no substantial progress in such matters as the construction of roads or effective occupation of the interior. Under the governorship of Sousa Gentil, a program that aimed at linking the island with good roads was inaugurated. The economy of the province at present consists principally of forest products such as sandalwood and rosewood, coconuts, coffee, and cacao. There are few industries, principally textiles on a modest scale and the curing of skins.

In February, 1942, the Portuguese part of the island was occupied by the Japanese in connection with their general push into Netherlands East Indies. From that date until the end of hostilities the

---

[48] *Relação da primeira viagem do Ministro do Ultramar ás provincias do Oriente, no ano de MCMLII*, Lisbon, 1935, p. 50 *seq.* "Aspectos da vida de Timor. Organização social indígena" in *Clarim*, Macao, April 12, 1956. See also, Esteves Felgas, Hélio A., *Timor português*, Lisbon, 1956, for a general, up-to-date survey of Timor in every aspect of its life.

island was cut off from Portugal and absorbed within the "co-prosperity sphere" of which the Japanese propagandists talked so much. Portugal protested against this usurpation of its rights in view of its own nonparticipation in the war, and as soon as conditions in the Far East warranted, Portuguese ships and means of assistance were immediately sent to impoverished Timor. For several years after 1945, the budget was in deficit and the main task was the reconstruction after the Japanese devastation. Dili, for one thing, had been almost destroyed, and other parts of the island had suffered in like manner. By 1953, the revenue had reached 63,000,000 escudos with expenditures only slightly larger. Imports and exports were fairly balanced at around 50 million *escudos* each.

This concludes the brief survey of the Portuguese world outside Europe. Just what is its status today and how is it governed? After 1930, there was a fundamental change in the outlook toward the empire. With the Colonial Act, a new era was opened for the overseas territories, based on certain fundamental conceptions: the unity of the entire nation, in Europe and elsewhere; and the necessity for a decentralization of administration to encourage activity on the part of the individual governments in what were later to become the provinces. Salazar stated at the conference of colonial governors in 1934 that "just as Minho and Beira are under the central government, so are Angola, Mozambique and India. We are a juridical and political unity and our aspiration is to move toward a similar economic unity."[49] In Title II of the Colonial Act, the protection and defense of the interests of the native populations is guaranteed and social and economic justice is promised them.[50] The intention is to encourage private initiative and local administrative autonomy in the provinces while at the same time, through the Ministry of Overseas Affairs and the corporative organizations, retain the supreme control. The national government retains the right to modify the statutes regarding the overseas possessions, loans that may be floated for development, agreements with foreign countries, and concessions that may be made. The local decentralization is assured by provision for representation through municipal councils, and local boards of one or another kind, according to the size and

[49] *Portugal. Breviário da pátria para os portugueses ausentes, op. cit.*, p. 211.
[50] Frochot, Michel, *L'empire colonial portugais*, Paris, 1942, p. 20.

resources of each territory. The native is not excluded from such administration, for aboriginal chieftains and "regents" are chosen in villages and similar jurisdictions. Provision is made for the expansion of the Portuguese languages since chiefs are obliged to concern themselves with the learning of the national language. "The creation and suppression of these local organizations is a matter for the governor of the province, with the approval of his Council and the final word of the Minister of Overseas Affairs. Authority at the top — liberty at the bottom."[51]

According to the supplementary modifications, approved November 15, 1933, which became effective in 1934, a charter for the overseas territories was applied. This, together with the *Administrative Reform for Overseas Territories*, constituted the basis of the juridical attachment of these areas to Portugal. The basic idea, without entering upon the details, are three: (1) moral and spiritual assimilation, (2) political centralization for the whole, and (3) administrative and financial autonomy.

The broad tendency has been to strive for an equilibrium between the strong, centralized authority of Portugal itself and a recognition that affairs in Goa, Timor, or São Tomé can scarcely be handled in detail from Lisbon. The fundamental theory behind the whole thing, with the later modifications of 1951, is that the empire is a whole; that it is a family and that the purpose is to assimilate, within the pattern of a common Portuguese nationhood and way of life, these diverse peoples. Portugal combines in a sense the technique of France and Belguim, that is, the intention of improving the social and economic standard and making into populations capable of understanding European ideals the peoples of Africa and Asia over whom it exerts authority. It does not envisage the British idea of ultimate separation or some loose arrangement comparable to the Commonwealth.

The latest developments in the evolution of the empire are significant. The year 1955 was a particularly important year from the juridical point of view because of certain basic modifications introduced into the imperial system. The Organic Overseas Law of 1953 had paved the way for this reorientation and in view of the situation in India, an amendment was introduced in May, 1955, to the Act which provided for greater flexibility in Goa and the

[51] *L'empire colonial portugais*, Documentation française, *op. cit.*, p. 24.

other territories. "The working and functions of government boards and the principles of administration in the State of India may differ from those provided in the present law whenever this is deemed advisable in view of the conditions prevailing in that State."[52] Portugal does not propose, therefore, to control strictly the details of administration in India where the situation is eminently fluid and the need for a high degree of autonomy self-evident.

On December 21, 1955, Portugal brought action against the Indian Union before the International Court of Justice of The Hague, taking advantage of Portuguese entrance into the United Nations and demanding that facilities be granted for access to the enclaves that the Indian Union had taken by force. On April 15, 1956, Portugal confirmed its determination to secure a ruling on its sovereign rights from the international tribunal.[53]

Portugal has taken an increasing part in the various efforts internationally to encourage collaboration among the powers interested in Africa in the solution of problems common to all of them. In addition, within the empire, a growing sense of the need of collaboration has led to a much larger integration of technical and scientific experience than in the past, as illustrated by the more frequent visits of officials of the home government to the overseas territories and such events as the First Congress of Portuguese Economists which met in Luanda, Angola, in September, 1955, and the Fifth Congress of Africanists that gathered in São Tomé in 1955.

---

[52] Moreira, Adriano, "Portuguese Overseas Territories, 1955" in *Civilisations*, Brussels, Vol. VI, No. 2, 1956, p. 287.

[53] *Notícias de Portugal*, Lisbon, May 1, No. 471, p. 2.

Chapter VIII

GOA, PORTUGAL, AND MR. NEHRU

THE question of Portuguese India has become one of the *causes célèbres* of our time. The repercussions of the conflict of interest between Portugal and the Indian Union have affected not only the relations of the West with India but have involved such extraneous influences as the Soviet Union, which has placed itself on record as unequivocally on the side of India in this controversy. Since the problem is of the greatest importance in a world that is beset with problems, it may be useful to examine first of all the nature of Goa and the Portuguese territories in India and, second, the case for and against Portuguese sovereignty and, finally, some of the implications of the question.[1]

The Portuguese State of India, to give the territory its proper name, is composed of three districts, Goa, Damão, and Diu, situated on the west coast of India; the first two adjacent to the state of Bombay in the Union and the latter further north, near the state of Saurashtra. The districts cover an area of 1537 square miles with a population of 637,591. The most important of the regions is, of course, Goa itself, which in turn is divided between Old and New Goa, the former with reference to the conquest and occupation in the first part of the sixteenth century. The old part comprises the principal island of Goa and the smaller islands situated at the mouth of the Mandovi and Zuari rivers, several islands more distant, and the three districts of Bardez, Mormugão, and Salsete. Damão is to the north of Bonbat on the Gulf of Cambay

[1] A good summary of the background and actual situation is the article, "L'Etat portugais de l'Inde et l'Union indienne," in *Chronique de Politique étrangère*, Brussels, Vol. IX, No. 1, January, 1956, pp. 5–39.

and is, in turn, constituted by three smaller subdivisions: Damão itself, Dadrá, and Nagar Avely, while Diu, the smallest of the three, is a tiny island south of the Katiawar peninsula and a still smaller bit of land called Gogola, on the continent itself. The distribution of population by each of the three regions is as follows:[2]

Goa — 547,448
Damão — 69,005
Diu — 21,138

One of the most important elements in the situation is the large emigration from Goa and the other territories of Portuguese India elsewhere, since, for economic reasons, the population finds it necessary to seek betterment abroad. It is estimated that there are some 80,000 Goans in Bombay and 20,000 elsewhere in India; some 20,000 to 30,000 in Karachi in Pakistan and another 30,000 in Kenya in Africa, while there are a scattered 20,000 here and there in the Middle East.

From the religious point of view, the population of Portuguese India may be divided in the following manner:

Hindus — 388,488
Christians (almost all Catholics) — 234,275
Moslems — 14,162

Presently the Catholic population represents approximately 36.7 per cent of the total, having fallen, over the period from 1881–1950, from 50 per cent. This was due almost entirely to emigration, since Goan Christians have been far more inclined to migrate and settle elsewhere than have the Hindus. If one takes into account this displacement of population, Catholics form, actually, something like 50 or more per cent of all Goans everywhere. The Christians are the descendants of the early converts of the so-called "Velhas conquistas," while the more recent territorial acquisitions, the "Novas conquistas," are basically Hindu. Nevertheless it has been remarked that "united for centuries to the Portuguese tradition, the Goa Hindus differ fundamentally from the inhabitants of the adjacent areas, that is, the Indian Union."[3]

[2] *The Statesman's Yearbook, 1955*, London, 1955, p. 1336.

[3] *Chronique de politique étrangère, op. cit.* The estimates of religious affiliation vary slightly, and in some cases it is stated that the majority of Goans

Agriculture is the basis of the economic life of Goa and, as in most underdeveloped countries, the number of farm workers who do not till their own land is high.[4] There is little industry and it has only been in recent years that mining has begun to expand to any appreciable degree. The financial situation, however, is sound, thanks in large degree to the policy of the home government and the reforms of Dr. Salazar in Portugal. One of the sources of revenue has been the Mormugão railway which, up to the time that the Indian Union closed the frontier, was an important outlet for the Indian hinterland. It is not Portugal, however, that holds the privileged place in the export and import balance of Goa, for the mother country and other overseas territories probably do not have more than 10 per cent of such participation and, for imports, about 3 per cent.

There are, in the entire Portuguese State of India, about 4500 civil servants of Goan origin, and not more than thirty or, possibly, forty from metropolitan Portugal.[5] In the address that Dr. Oliveira Salazar delivered on April 12, 1954, over a national hookup, he explained precisely what Goa meant to Portugal in economic terms: ". . . whatever its moral value for us, it may be said that demo-

---

are Christians, taking into account those that have migrated. "Portuguese India with a population of 600,000 is partly Christian and partly Hindu by a half to half proportion — a proportion which tilts in favour of the Christians if the thousands of Goan immigrants who still retain their Portuguese nationality are taken into account" (Boman-Behram, B. K., *Goa and Ourselves*, Bombay, 1955, p. 54). Another writer indicates that "the number of Christians is slightly larger than that of Hindus: 350,000 against 310,000" (de Prelle, Alain, *Gazette de Lausanne*, December 28, 1948). This includes Goans living abroad. The *Anuário da Arquidiocese de Goa e Damão para 1955* (Bastorá, Portuguese India, 1955, p. 1244), edited by F. Francisco Xavier Gomes Catão, gives the following religious figures for Portuguese India: Total Catholic population — 278,799; Goan Catholics abroad — 89,034; Non-Catholic population — 343,165.

[4] "Plano de productividade agrícola em Goa," in *Boletim Geral do Ultramar*, Lisbon, January, 1956, pp. 239–240.

[5] Indian propaganda has insisted on the economic exploitation of Goa for the benefits of Portugal. "The trade policy of Goa is determined in Lisbon for the sole interests of Portugal" (Menon, K. N., *Portuguese Pockets in India*, New Delhi, 1953, p. 61). The same writer adds that "the main cause for the backwardness of Goa's economy is the callous and indifferent policy of the colonial government which has done nothing to foster industry or promote agriculture" (*ibid.*, p. 66). "Goa's trade policy is determined in the sole interests of Portugal" (*Portuguese India Today*, published by The National Congress of Goa, Bombay, 1950, p. 16); also emphasized in Gaitonde, P., and Mani, A. D., *The Goa Problem*, Indian Council of World Affairs, New Delhi, 1956, pp. 17, 18.

graphically, economically, and financially, the Portuguese State of India does not count in the Portuguese world taken as a whole." The entire trade between European Portugal and Portuguese India represents about 0.75 per cent per thousand of metropolitan trade. The budget of Portuguese India has amounted to about two hundred thousand *contos* for receipts and expenditures and these expenditures have all been for local administration with the exception of the very small item of eight hundred *contos* to Portugal toward the operation of one of the agencies devoted to the overseas possessions. "The mother country spends about seven thousand contos a year in the Portuguese State of India and recently, as a result of measures in aid of shipping, many tens of thousands of contos."[6]

If the Portuguese State of India has cost the government money rather than serving as a source of income and of "exploitation" as is asserted by certain sectors of opinion, there is an additional element of some importance, and that is the degree to which Goans have found a place for themselves in the Portuguese world, thanks to their common citizenship. Aside from the fact just noted that almost all officeholders in Goa itself are Goans, there has been a steady flow abroad, especially to the African colonies and, for that matter, to Portugal itself. This is true in the professions, public service, and, very especially, among the clergy, for Goa with its numerous religious vocations has poured out ecclesiastical man power to every part of the Portuguese world. There was a Goan governor of Macau in 1824; a governor of Quelimane, Tete, and Sofala in Mozambique in 1838; a Goan governor of Goa itself in 1843; of Angola in 1917; and of Timor in 1933. As far back as 1839, Dr. Isidore Emilio Batista, a Goan from Loutulim, was professor at the Polytechnical Institute of Lisbon. Dr. Gama Pinto was the founder of the Institute of Ophthalmology and Dr. Alfredo da Costa achieved a name in the Maternity Hospital in Portugal. Goans participated actively in the army and occupied numerous military posts and from as early as 1826 the Indian territory had two members of Parliament in Lisbon.[7] An Indian commentator on the Goa question remarks that "when under the British hegem-

---

[6] Address of Dr. Salazar, "Goa and the Indian Union," in *Portugal. Bulletin of Political, Economic and Cultural Information*, Lisbon, March-April, 1954, p. 3.

[7] Saldanha, *A Short History of Goa*, Nova Goa, 1935, p. 135.

ony we Indians were struggling as clerks, there was a Goan minister in the Portuguese cabinet and a Goan as ambassador of Portugal in Argentina."[8] On the ecclesiastical side Goa has given the Portuguese territories a numerous contingent of priests and bishops. Only recently, for example, Msgr. José Felipe Carmo Colaço, rector of the Major Seminary of Rachol in Goa, was designated Bishop of the Cape Verde Islands. During the second half of the nineteenth century, priests from Goa were among the most active in the spreading of the faith in Cape Verde, Portuguese Guinea, and elsewhere in Africa.[9]

From the administrative point of view, Portuguese India has evolved along similar lines to the mother country. As a result of the proclamation of the Republic, a certain decentralization was introduced and India was granted a limited autonomy; later as a consequence of the revolution of 1926, the overseas territories have been closely attached to European Portugal under the Colonial Act, and the Organic Charter of the Portuguese empire. In 1933 the clauses of the colonial act were incorporated into the new constitution as part of the basic law of the land.[10] In April, 1955, the National Assembly approved a new law granting ample autonomy to Portuguese India in administrative and fiscal matters. The Ministry of Overseas Affairs continues to exert general supervision over the appointment of functionaries and the determination of the budget while the governor, named for a term of four years, is in charge of both civil and military affairs. He is assisted in an advisory capacity by a Government Council, composed of appointed and elective members. The governor general presides over the destinies of Goa with governors responsible to him in Damão and Diu. There is a system of districts composed of a given number of villages and local communities, each with a local council of three members, two of whom are chosen by election. The judiciary is independent, and Goa, together with Macao and Timor, the

[8] Boman-Behram, *op. cit.*, pp. 25–26.

[9] Gomes Catão, F. X., "A diocese de Cabo Verde e o Clero de Goa," in *O Heraldo*, Nova Goa, May 12, 1956. The new diocese of Sá da Bandeira in Angola has been given a Goan bishop in the person of Msgr. António Ribeiro Santana and eight Goan priests have gone out to the African territory with the new prelate ("Goa and Portuguese Africa," in *Revue du Clergé Africain*, Mayidi, Belgian Congo, No. 3, May, 1956, p. 298).

[10] *Principes et réalisations de l'Etat nouveau portugais*, Lisbon, n.d., publications of the National Secretariate of Information, p. 68.

three Far Eastern territories, forms a judicial district with a court sitting in Goa. The civil police force is made up of Goans, as constituted by the decree of April 4, 1946, under a Portuguese commandant. Religiously, there is freedom of worship, and the special arrangement known as the *Padroado,* to which mention has been made previously and regarding which further comment is reserved for the end of this chapter, was formally abolished in 1951.

There is no restriction on education and provision has been made for government schools, mission institutions, and private educational establishments. The 339 elementary schools in 1952 served 12,453 pupils, excluding the 177 mission schools. Four secondary schools, a teaching institute and a medical school complete the general picture of educational activity in the area. The private schools include those in which instruction is given in Marathi, Gujarati, and English, the latter represented by 67 such institutions with nearly 12,000 students.[11] Technical education is cared for by five official and four private institutions and an agricultural school at Sanguem.

Economically, as has been indicated, Portuguese India is relatively well off.[12] Although the soil is fertile, only about a third of the land is actually cultivated and one of the distressing features of the economy is the tendency of the Goans to abandon agriculture thus producing a serious lack of man power. Although rice is cultivated in quantities, the crop is barely sufficient for local consumption. Coconuts, mahogany from the forest lands — 116 square miles — and betel nuts constitute important items of local production. The economic blockade imposed by India in 1954 has forced the local government as well as that of Lisbon to take measures for the increase on a substantial basis of agricultural and food production.

[11] *Statesman's Year Book,* 1955, *op. cit.,* p. 1341.

[12] The budget of Portuguese India for 1954, to take a typical year, was as follows, in *contos:*

	Ordinary	*Extraordinary*	*Total*
Revenue	137,613	56,873	194,486
Expenditures	129,012	65,464	194,476
Balances	+8,601	—8,591	+10

Of this total 52,362 *contos* have been earmarked for the Development Plan (48,000) and Communications (2,632). A grant of 2,340 was made for sanitation. The broadcasting station in Goa got an extraordinary grant of 900 *contos.* As may be seen the budget is perfectly balanced within the limits of its income (*Portugal. Bulletin of Political, Economic and Cultural Information,* Lisbon, January–February, 1954, p. 31).

The area contains a considerable amount of iron and manganese and since 1948 serious efforts have been made to extract these minerals. One of the attractive features of Portuguese India, from the point of view of mining, is the facility of transportation, for the mines which are farthest from the sea are only some thirty to forty miles away. Investment in the mines runs to about ten million dollars, of which capital perhaps three fourths is Indian.[13] This industry employing about 25,000 has had to be adjusted to meet the political challenge, especially after the expulsion of Indian laborers in 1954. Indian corporations such as Chowgule and Company and Bhandekar and Company have continued, in spite of tension, to promote the mining development of the region.

The government of India has applied increasingly severe restriction of an economic sort on Portuguese India in the hope, quite apparently, of strangling the small community or at least of producing a state of stagnation that would jeopardize seriously its capacity to survive. As of August 1954 the following restrictions were put into effect:

1. The communications with Damão and Diu were cut. Postal contact was suspended on May 25, 1955. Indian vessels were no longer authorized to touch at Portuguese Indian ports. The bus service between Belgaum and Mapuça was cut.
2. Imports and exports were cut off.
3. Restrictions were placed on the transfer of money from India to the Portuguese zone.[14]

---

[13] *Mining in Portuguese India: Export*

	Iron Ore		*Manganese Ore*	
Years	*Tons*	*Value in Rupees*	*Tons*	*Value in Rupees*
1949	49,188	1,274,151	11,197	567,371
1950	70,948	1,774,727	20,145	1,271,335
1951	280,610	8,064,629	61,874	7,746,450
1952	464,596	14,913,926	137,463	19,859,141
1953	852,762	28,599,919	207,361	29,253,443
1954	1,228,114	36,620,614	101,796	10,780,673
1955 (half year)	772,424	21,600,000	94,946	7,750,000

Portuguese India News Bulletin (In English), Nova Goa, November 8, 1955, p. 12.

[14] A remarkable achievement is the manner in which the Portuguese reorganized rail communication within their Indian territory. The Indian government refused all collaboration on its end and did everything possible to paralyze the operation of the line in Goa territory. Portugal reacted at once with personnel from Mozambique and Europe. Fuel was sent from Africa. The service of the railway was actually stepped up over what it had been when it was a small

The result has been a very considerable effort to find new markets and reorient business operations elsewhere, especially with and through Pakistan. The Pakistani government has supported Portugal in this respect and Karachi has become one of the major points for communication with Goa and other areas.

The story of the Indian-Portuguese conflict belongs to the contemporary scene of international tension, nationalism, and territorial claims, and in view of the repercussions across the world in terms of the North Atlantic Pact Organization, as well as within the framework of the colonial problem, it may be useful to outline the way in which the controversy has built up to the proportions it has reached today.

During the last part of the nineteenth and the first part of the twentieth centuries, Portuguese India was outside the scope of the political movements corresponding to the National Congress in India. There is little to show that the Goans were concerned particularly about the struggle for separation that was going on in what was then British India. As a result of the Portuguese revolution of 1926 and the reorientation in terms of political expression, a number of Goans, particularly Dr. T. Bragança Cunha, founded the "Goa Congress Committee" in 1928 at Bombay, where there is a large Goan colony, recognized by the Congress, although it was definitely refused affiliation because of its foreign character, in 1934. In 1946 a movement for the liberation of the Portuguese territories was organized by the Indian socialist, Dr. Ram Manohar Lohia, who undertook to provoke within Portuguese India a civil disobedience movement as a protest against what was called the restrictions on liberty. On June 9, this leader, together with several others — Bragança Cunha, Ram Hedge, José Loyola, Parshottam Kakodhar, and Laxmikant Whembre — were arrested and deported to Portugal where they were released under a partial amnesty in 1950. During the course of this campaign, the various nationalist groups of Goan integrationists formed the National Congress (Goa) at Bombay, and it was at this time that the Indian Congress declared that Goa should be returned to India. With the procla-

---

segment of the much longer line running into India. The tonnage transported shot up from 6500, in December, 1955, to 28,800, in January, 1956. Portuguese technical skill was amply demonstrated in this minor equivalent of the Berlin "airlift" (*Noticias de Macau*, Macao, May 1, 1956).

mation of Indian independence and the definitive cessation of British rule, the New Delhi government stated its purpose as that of eliminating the last vestige of foreign domination on the subcontinent.

During 1949 and 1950, the Goan National Congress, which had been relatively inactive since its foundation, lost some of its adherents through the separation of the extremists who formed a number of new parties. In February, 1950, the Indian government demanded that Portuguese India be absorbed and suggested a referendum under United Nations control. The Portuguese government replied firmly that a transfer of sovereignty was out of the question. The issue was therefore clearly drawn and, from this point on, the tug of war between Lisbon and New Delhi took on a marked character of increasing tension and bitterness.

It may be well to note that the first issue, as expressed, involved the demand that Portugal acknowledge the *right* of India to claim Goa and the other territories and that Portugal's *duty* was to accept the principle of annexation. The Lisbon regime refused point blank to compromise on the basic assumption that a shift of sovereignty was to be contemplated. In other words, India proposed no discussion or mutual examination of the problem, but the simple retirement of Portugal and the incorporation of Goa, Damão and Diu.[15] The Portuguese in the course of the crisis have indicated their willingness to work out with India any of the difficulties inherent in the juxtaposition of their territories and the Indian Union but without accepting the premise that the point of departure of all discussion is acceptance of the fact that Portuguese India is to cease to exist. During the course of the visit of the

---

[15] The Portuguese constitution of 1933 specifically forbids any alienation of the national territory, including the overseas possessions (*Political Constitution of the Portuguese Republic. Colonial Act*, Lisbon, 1948, 2 ed., Article I, p. 3, and Article II, p. 4). Prime Minister Nehru has steadily refused to accept any other basis for negotiation than the acceptance by Portugal of the cession of its territories to the Indian Union. This seems to contradict Mr. Nehru's basic conviction about not attending conferences in which the issue is decided beforehand. The Indian leader stated publicly on accepting the invitation to the London conference of August, 1956, regarding Suez: "It has always been quite clear to the Government that they could not participate in any conference which bound its participants beforehand as to the conclusions to be reached" (*The New York Times*, August 9, 1956, under title of "Text of Nehru's Acceptance of Bid to Suez Talks"). How then does the Indian government square this principle with the insistence that Portugal accept a conclusion, namely, cession, before entering upon talks?

Minister of Overseas Territories in 1952, Portugal reiterated this position in the plainest possible terms.[16]

In January, 1953, the Indian government repeated the demand for discussions but without making reference to a possible plebiscite. On the reception of the Portuguese refusal, the Indian legation at Lisbon was closed. Lisbon did not close its own legation in New Delhi in the hope that the deterioration of relations would not be permanent.

In February of 1954, when Dr. Gaitondo, a partisan of Goa's attachment to India, was arrested and deported, the Indian government launched what has become since then one of the most massive campaigns of propaganda against Portugal, with constant accusations regarding the repressive measures Portugal is said to use in its territories to stifle the legitimate voice of the Goan people.[17] During this same spring Prime Minister Nehru made abundantly clear that one of the major arguments of the Indian government against the continuation of Portuguese rule was the fact that Portugal belonged to the North Atlantic Treaty Organization and because of this affiliation, the territories in India might be subject to use by the powers associated in that pact for military or naval purposes which would seriously menace India's neutrality.[18]

In June of 1954, the National Congress (Goa) launched the passive resistance movement which is called "Satyagraha" and prepared for the entry in Portuguese India of numbers of these manifestants on August 15, the anniversary of Indian independence. This policy about which the Indian government has been most

[16] *Relação da primeira viagem do Ministro do Ultramar ás provincias do Oriente,* Lisbon, 1953, 2 vols. The first volume includes the addresses and impressions of Commander Manuel María Sarmento Rodrigues while in Portuguese India.

[17] From this date on, Indian press and official statements are one long lamentation of Portuguese repression and terrorism. "The Government of India sent a note to the Portuguese Legation — protesting against the arrest of 20 Goans by the Portuguese authorities in Goa on June 13 for hoisting the Indian national flag. In their note the Government, it is learnt, have stated that they cannot remain silent spectators to the continuance of the repressive policy followed by the Portuguese authorities" (*The Overseas Hindustan Times,* New Delhi, July 1, 1954).

[18] The government expressed concern that the NATO agreement included Portuguese India. Reference was also made to the Portuguese statement that the treaty of 1642 with England included a British obligation to protect and defend Portugal's possessions overseas (*The Hindu Weekly Review,* New Delhi, April 19, 1954).

equivocal, apparently supporting and then disowning, constitutes one of the most original and, at the same time, dangerous methods for the exertion of pressure to be found in contemporary political practice. The idea consists simply of mobilizing hundreds or thousands, if it is possible, of individuals who are presumedly unarmed and march them across the border into the territory whose sovereignty the nation responsible for the movement is seeking to undermine.[19] On the other side, Goan separatists, in obvious connivance with the Indian authorities, arranged to "liberate" the tiny enclaves of Dadra and Nagar-Avely, which are surrounded by Indian territory and quite inaccessible to the Portuguese authorities once the Indians refused them transit facilities.[20]

Thus far in the controversy, the Indian authorities had employed four procedures for pressure on Portugal: denunciation and the usual propaganda build-up, with glaring accusations of terrorism,

---

[19] "A batch of 500 Indian volunteers will start satyagraha in Goa on August 15th, Indian independence day, according to Goan nationalist sources in Bombay. These sources said the volunteers, who would belong to all parties, including the Congress, the Praja-socialist and the Jan Sangh, and drafted from all parts of Bombay state, would leave for the Goan border by train and bus" (*The Overseas Hindustan Times*, New Delhi, July 8, 1954). The definition of "Satyagraha" is contained in numerous Indian writings. "While Satyagraha in its intense form and in its most comprehensive aspect is a creed, a way of life . . . in its broader aspects it may be said to be a nonviolent weapon for the use of individuals as well as groups and masses in fighting against all evil and injustice, social, economic and political. It is an alternative to all other kinds of weapons and remedies which involve hatred and violence to persons and property." Diwakar, R. R., *Satyagraha. The pathway to peace* (Patna, India, 1950), p. 22.

[20] The full story of this act of aggression has yet to be told. The defenders of the tiny enclaves were Portuguese Indians, to a man, since India had made impossible reinforcements from the rest of Portuguese India. In Dadra, for instance, there was not a single European Portuguese nor a single soldier. The small police force that resisted was made up entirely of Portuguese Indians. Their chief, Aniceto de Rosario, went down fighting for Portugal (*Distortions in in the Case of Goa. Heraldo Replies to The Examiner*, Nova Goa, 1954, p. 5). Mr. Nehru has revealed his own bitterness at the lack of support for "liberation" from the Goans themselves when he stated in a speech on May 21, 1955, that "If Goans themselves did not exercise their right of self-determination, it was possible it might create an adverse reaction throughout the world" (*The Overseas Hindustan Times*, New Delhi, May 26, 1955). India has pretended that "Goan nationalists" liberated the enclaves. The evidence is fairly conclusive that these tiny territories are now ruled by Indians as the Portuguese have always been claiming. One R. G. Kamat in a letter to the *Times of India* remarks that "The Goans can expel the Portuguese from India just as soon as the territories of Dadra and Nagar-Avely are run by Goans and not by Indian citizens" (quoted in *O Heraldo*, Nova Goa, January 12, 1956).

repression, and the massing of troops; second, the toleration if not the actual support of the allegedly peaceful infiltration or "Satyagraha"; third, the economic blockade which was less effective in the case of Goa, Damão, and Diu which have access to the sea than to the two landlocked enclaves; and, finally, the actual invasion of the enclaves and their occupation, which constituted an act of violence, and the exact contrary of the policy Mr. Nehru has always preached of negotiation and discussion rather than direct action for the achievement of the ends of Indian objectives. On July 25, 1954, the Portuguese foreign office announced policy that "The Portuguese territory of Dadrá has been the object of armed aggression originating in the neighboring Indian Union."[21] It was apparent that in numerous villages and border communities not only in the enclaves but elsewhere armed Indians had penetrated Portuguese territory.

Portugal demanded the retirement of the Indian consuls at Goa and Mormugão, and New Delhi retaliated by demanding that the Portuguese consular representative in Bombay leave the country. Moreover, the Indian government refused flatly to allow Portuguese troops to cross to their own enclaves to maintain order. The Portuguese, in view of the fast-deteriorating situation, proposed to India that neutral observers be designated to study the situation. This was, perhaps, a precaution in view of the difficulties expected on August 15, and the desire to demonstrate the degree of complicity of India itself in the encouragement, active or tacit, of the "satyagrahis."[22]

[21] Full text of the protest and details of the incidents in *Noticias de Portugal*, Lisbon, July 31, 1954. This is the weekly bulletin of the National Secretariate of Information. "There were huge demonstrations in Lisbon and elsewhere and the Portuguese press was ardent in its affirmations of solidarity in the face of the aggression. Mr. Nehru has gone much too far in his dangerous game. He has allowed that a cowardly act of force be unleashed against a pacific country." *Diário da Manhã*, Lisbon, July 23, 1954, noted that the action of the New Delhi government in settling honorably this incident would reveal its real intentions. The Indians indicated they had no intention of allowing the re-establishment of Portuguese control over the enclaves: "The Deputy foreign minister Mr. A. K. Chanda, assured the Rajya Sabha on Monday that every step would be taken by the government of India to see that Indian territory was not violated in any manner by Portuguese troops trying to cross to the enclaves" (*The Overseas Hindustan Times*, New Delhi, September 23, 1954).

[22] *The New York Times* (August 11, 1954) notes that Portugal had made

After this flare-up the matter died down perceptibly until early in 1955 when, on January 12, the Indian government handed the Portuguese a note in which it reiterated that any attempt on the part of the Portuguese government to deport Indians, including Goan *satyagrahis*, to serve sentences in penal establishments in Portugal, or other Portuguese territories in Africa, would have serious and far-reaching repercussions in India. The Indian government repudiated the Portuguese government's contention that it had a right to defend itself in Goa against depredations, incursions, and all the multiple forms of penetration the Indians were devising against the territories. "The Government of India categorically refused to accept the view that Indians, including Goans, who have the courage to resist Portuguese colonialism, are criminals." The New Delhi government claimed in this same communication that it had done its best to dissuade citizens from taking part in the *Satyagraha* movement.[23]

The Indian government in taking this position has assumed what, by any standard, is a most extraordinary role. It claims that people living under Portuguese rule have the perfect right to rebel against this government because it is "colonialist" and therefore an abomination in the sight of the Lord. The Portuguese are tyrants and agents of fascism because they are not amused by the idea of mobs of Indians barging over their frontiers bent on destruction and agitation. Do the Indian leaders really think that a principle of this sort, if carried out widely, would bring anything but complete chaos in international relations? It smacks ominously of the manner in which Hitlerite Germany bellowed threats on neighboring countries for their violation of the proper conduct toward their German citizens and urged every kind of pressure to make life wretched for the Poles, Czechs, and the rest. It belies the avowed program in international matters which the Indian government and Mr. Nehru, in particular,

---

this proposal and that India had accepted. "India in her note to Lisbon categorically denied Portugal's allegation of complicity in the merger movement and at the same time maintained that 'Indians in Portuguese possessions are as much entitled to their freedom as those in the Indian Union and are determined to win it but the government and people of India have always been anxious to find a solution by conference and negotiation.'"

[23] *Foreign Affairs Record*, New Delhi, Ministry of External Affairs Publicity Division, February, 1955, Vol. I, p. 3.

have espoused over and over again.[24] One wonders if the principle of mutual respect for the territorial integrity of neighbors applies exclusively to Burma, Bhutan, Tibet, but not to Goa. Nonaggression takes a strange turn when masses of human beings are dispatched across the frontier in the attempt to coerce the Portuguese into submission or, what is worse, produce a situation in which force has to be used to stop them and then, with the martyrdom of these unfortunates, decry Portuguese tyranny and imperialism. Noninterference obviously applies to everyone except the Portuguese territories with which India manages to meddle with extraordinary consistency.

But since the term "colonialism" is employed by New Delhi as an expression of opprobrium and since Portugal is plainly a colonialist state insistent on maintaining a position it has held for four hundred years — long before the existence, let it be mentioned, of anything remotely resembling an Indian nation under one government — none of the ordinary principles of proper international conduct apparently apply.

During the early months of 1955 the tension rose again with border incidents repeating themselves frequently. The Portuguese government expressed, on June 8, 1955, its great disquietude at the progress of anti-Portuguese agitation along the frontier and in the Indian press and the multiplication of episodes that foreshadowed another trial of force on August 15. The press of India was accused of exaggerating grotesquely the situation of unrest within the Portuguese territories; of laying claim to support from Portuguese Indians, which did not in fact exist; and of condemning the legitimate measures taken by the government to maintain peace, without which it would have abdicated all pretension of an established authority. Various Goan newspapers in India, which were hostile to annexation, were assaulted or closed. Various citizens of Bombay of Goan origin who were not favorable to the campaign for integration, such as Pompeia Viegas, Secretary of the Indo-Portuguese

---

[24] The famous five principles about which the Indians talk endlessly are: (1) mutual respect for each other's territorial integrity and sovereignty, (2) nonaggression, (3) noninterference in each other's internal affairs for any reasons of a political, economic, or ideological character, (4) equality and mutual benefit, (5) peaceful coexistence. See *Foreign Affairs Record*, New Delhi, June, 1955, Vol. L, pp. 131–132. These principles are stated in the joint Nehru-Bulganin statement after the Soviet visit.

Institute, Joel Boavida, director of the paper *Ave Maria*, and Vitoriano Rodrigues, were deported. Prominent political figures of India devoted their time to meetings and addresses on behalf of Goan liberation, and this effort culminated in numerous border incidents, some of the most serious of which occurred between April 26 and May 4 on the frontiers of Damão. On May 18, a group of some fifty-five individuals under the socialist leader Goray invaded Portuguese territory and stoned the frontier guards. On May 29, a group of about seventy, under the leadership of S. P. Limae, invaded Goan territory for the same purpose of provoking disorders and were ultimately conducted back into India by the local authorities. That these were not individual, irresponsible, sporadic moves is demonstrated by the fact that the invading group had paraded through the streets of the Indian town of Belgao before moving on to the border. The Indian government did nothing to prevent these manifestations.[25] The list of assaults on the frontier from January, 1955, to June includes at least eighteen specific incidents. The Indian press responded by accusing the Portuguese of widespread arrests in Goa and of firing on the Indian border police.[26]

On February 17, anniversary of the arrest of Dr. Gaitondo, Madame Joshi, president of the National Congress (Goa), crossed the frontier at the head of some fifty *satyagrahis* for the purpose of holding a meeting at Mapuça, and was promptly arrested for her pains. In April the Liberation Committee took over the direction of these operations and on May 11, a Goa Satyagraha Committee was constituted, presided over by Peter Alvares. Between May 18 and August 9, the Committee sent thirteen groups into Goa, running anywhere from 50 to 125 "volunteers," almost all of them of Indian nationality. The Portuguese have claimed that the majority, if not all, of these so-called volunteers have been hired to take part in the demonstrations and this had been virtually admitted by Nath Pai, president of the International Union of Socialist Youth,

---

[25] *Incidentes de fronteira e actividades anti-portuguesas na União Indiana*, Lisbon, 1955, communiqué issued by the Portuguese Ministry of Foreign Affairs, June 8, 1955.

[26] *The Overseas Hindustan Times*, New Delhi, June 23, 1955. There is no denial of the crossing of passive resisters, for the issue of the Indian paper notes that "another group of 33 satyagrahis led by Modak Guruji, . . . crossed into Goa the same day."

who stated that each satyagrahi cost about 20 rupees a day for expenses.[27]

At first the satyagrahis were small groups belonging to a single political party. Later, as the technique became more refined, they were composed of individuals of various political persuasions and from many parts of India. There were women and children among them and it is well known that the groups on their way to penetrate Portuguese territory were feted en route and offered facilities by the local authorities. Poona and Belgaum became well-known centers of their organization and among the leaders are such figures as Atmaram Patel of the Workers and Peasants Party, V. C. Deshpande of the Hindu movement Mahasabha, a member of parliament, and T. K. Chaudhri of the Revolutionary Socialist Party, also a member of parliament.

The preparations for August, 1955, were far more serious than the year before when *The New York Times* announced that the much-heralded march into Goa had fizzled out with a handful of teen-agers making a nuisance of themselves.[28] According to the best figures, on August 15, 1955, 1711 volunteers entered Goa and 1250 entered Damão, among these some 300 Congress members. The manifestation ended up with some 15 dead and 38 wounded. The next day the extreme left in India responded by a series of strikes. In Bombay, the rioting that began over the Goa incidents ended with the Indian police wounding a couple of dozen demonstrators. The political invasion did not work and India settled down to a discussion of what to do next. "The violence of the Portuguese reaction stunned the Indians and halted the peaceful resistance for the time being."[29]

Moreover, the whole theory of peaceful resistance seemed to be

---

[27] *Chronique de politique étrangère*, p. 33. "The trial of Mrs. Sudhabai Joshi, President of the National Congress (Goa) who offered stayagraha in the Portuguese settlement on April 6, would commence towards the end of this month before the Portuguese military tribunal. Mrs. Joshi has been charged with 'treason' and with 'violating' the Portuguese territory by entering it without documents and 'legal formalities' for the purpose of *creating an environment* for the integration of Goa with India" (italics mine since the expression is a classic in euphemism) (*Overseas Hindustan Times*, New Delhi, October 27, 1955).

[28] *The New York Times*, August 15, 1954. Among other incidents then was the attack by a group of volunteers under the leadership of Jan Sangh against the settlement of Diu.

[29] *Ibid.*, August 17, 1955, report by A. M. Rosenthal.

blowing up. "The official philosophy of India is non-violence and most Indians talk of it as an accepted way of life. But the fact is that India, non-violent in philosophy, always teeters on the edge of a frightening, catastrophic sort of violence."[30] The system of putting on pressure through these forced marches and offering of one's body to policemen and frontier guards has certain disadvantages in the specific case of Goa. In the first place, it is all coming from India and one wonders if the Goans are quite so keen to be liberated as is depicted in India. If they were, the small Portuguese force in the country could certainly not cope with a tremendous uprising to support the invaders and neither in 1954 nor in 1955 did anything of the sort mature. Were the Goans as eager to integrate with India as they are said to be, then the territories of Portuguese India would be as difficult to govern as Cyprus is for Great Britain, and the comparison is not entirely out of place because the population is about the same, with the added aggravation that in Goa huge and populous India is just over a land frontier, more than willing to profit from every evidence of unrest in the Portuguese zone. The fact that the Portuguese have shown a decided disposition to crack down hard if the need arises has produced something of a shock.

The events of August 15 produced a fine assortment of the usual terror stories and accounts of sadistic police and army men in Goa mowing down innocent Indians. Homer A. Jack, an American newsman who visited Goa at the time, wrote two articles for the *Hindustan Times* of Bombay (August 19 and 20, 1955) and his account has been produced in the form of a pamphlet by the newspaper, the title of which is sufficient to indicate the tenor of his account: "Callous Mentality of Portuguese." This correspondent, after giving us a bloody account of the savage Portuguese, ends up with the comment that "satyagraha is an honest method and wonderful too."[31] In the publication called *The Story of Goa*, published by the Information Service of India in London, the peaceful policy of India is contrasted with "the massacre of satyagrahis" who were "mowed down by Portuguese troops."[32]

[30] *Ibid.*, August 21, 1955.
[31] *Goa, 15th August, 1955*, Bombay, 1955, p. 15.
[32] *The Story of Goa*, 1955, p. 12. See also *Foreign Affairs Record*, New Delhi, September, 1955, Vol. I, No. 9. Satyagraha casualties were given as follows: killed, 18; convicted, 13; in detention, 26.

In spite of the unpromising results of the experience on August 15, the policy was not abandoned. As of August 18, the communist party of Gujerat announced that it would take over the movement if the Liberation Committee were no longer inclined to do so. The Alvares faction of the Liberation Committee approved a continuation of the method and asked if it was to be carried out on October 2, the anniversary of Gandhi. On August 31 and on September 1, two groups entered Goa. On the sixth of that month, Mr. Nehru declared his opposition to the entry of such volunteers into Portuguese India and closed the overland frontier between the two countries.[33] In connection with this discussion, Mr. Nehru raised a matter which was new in the debate, namely that the emphasis should be placed on the fact that the Portuguese must leave India rather than on the necessity for annexing Portuguese India to the Union. The most remarkable part of this statement which made the rounds of the world press was that the Indian prime minister, in an outburst which was anything but in line with his professed devotion to democracy, added that "we will not tolerate the presence of a colonial power. We will not tolerate the Portuguese even if the Goans want to keep them. Goa will undoubtedly become a part of India."[34] In other words, no matter what the Goans want — and heretofore the Indians have never admitted that Goa wanted anything but instant annexation — the preference will play no part in the ultimate decision, because the Portuguese must go since India wants it.

Mr. Nehru himself has followed a confused policy regarding the satyagrahis. While expressing admiration for them, he hesitated for a long time to condemn this method of international pressure. It has been said that one reason for the decision to actively discourage the volunteers was the threat from Pakistan that the same method would work just as effectively in the case of the critical Kashmir situation. One wonders just what Mr. Nehru would say if five or ten thousand Pakistani satyagrahis marched into Kashmir, which he claims for India, and announced that they were employing

[33] *Le Monde*, Paris, September 8, 1955: "Certain members of parliament in New Delhi qualified Mr. Nehru's policy as vacillating, indecisive and bound to fail. They claimed the decision to disapprove passive resistance against Portuguese territory as sabotage of the efforts by the opposition to place foreign policy on a united plane."

[34] *Ibid.*

a method which the Indians themselves had acclaimed as the acme of proper international relations and which the Pakistanis intended to use in settling border difficulties and annexing territory.[35]

While there has been, perhaps, a lessening of tension, thanks to the hesitations about the utility of the satyagrahis, India has not diminished the massive propaganda campaign against the Portuguese. A Goan nationalist, Telho Mascarenhas, has had charge of the Portuguese language broadcasts over the New Delhi station and a clandestine station operates in Indian territory under the name of *Azad Goa Radio.* The daily newspaper *Heraldo,* in Nova Goa, runs a regular daily column in English on its last page, devoted almost entirely to pointing out the distortions of the *Bharat* (Indian) radio and press. For example, in June, 1956, it was stated from Indian sources that Goan nationalists had wounded the Portuguese governor general near Pangim, in Portuguese India. There was no basis at all to the story and the Goa press replied at once.[36]

The most difficult point of all is to determine the will of the Goan people themselves. There seems little doubt that of the *émigrés*, some of those who have achieved a position of some importance in India (that is, the *élite*), are favorable to annexation. It must be emphasized, however, that of these almost all have lost contact with affairs in Portuguese India and cannot claim to speak for their former compatriots.[37] One of their principal arguments is

[35] *The New York Times,* September 7, 1955: "The Indian parliament gave its backing today to Prime Minister Jawaharlal Nehru's renunciation of peaceful invasion as a weapon to force the Portuguese out of their colony of Goa. . . . Mr. Nehru and his party had walked a thin line before August 15, not openly sponsoring the peaceful invasion but not doing anything to discourage it."

[36] *O Heraldo,* Nova Goa, June 15, 1956. Reply under title, "Down With the Criminals."

[37] A good review of the Portuguese-Indian controversy is contained in *The British Survey* (London, November, 1954, No. 68). Among other things this authoritative — and impartial — examination of the situation notes that "there seems to be a remarkable consensus of opinion among responsible foreign reporters who have been in Goa that the general feeling of the population is against any change" (p. 20). The opinions of such different observers as Roy Trumball of the *New York Times,* André Siegfried writing in *Figaro* of Paris, and others concur in the conviction that the population of Goa is quite unaware of the reality of the Indian contention that it suffers from "oppression." Evelyn Waugh noted after a visit that the Goans tended to compare their relatively high standards with India and were not impressed by what they saw across the frontier.

The panorama of Goan nationalist parties is an amazing one, for the multiplicity and capacity to proliferate:

that as long as Portguese sovereignty continues, Goa will remain a stagnant pool on the coast of Malabar and will not participate in the growing prosperity and future development of India. It would seem that it is this group of Goans, more or less "assimilated" into Indian national life, in whom the Indian government has placed its confidence. Most Goans in India, and especially those in modest circumstances, seem to have remained passive or positively loyal to Portugal up to date. The confusion of parties and movements and the doubtful character of some of the leadership has not been such as to inspire unreserved ardor for liberation. The efforts of the Goan Liberation Council to secure Catholic signatures for a manifesto of solidarity with the aims of liberation

---

National Congress (Goa). Founded in 1946 with marked left-wing tendency. After some dissension, the leftist tendency again prevailed in 1953–1954 under the Peter Alvares, Indian socialist of Goan origin. The Congress has produced various offshoots such as the dissident movement headed by J. C. Carvalho and that under the direction of Mme. Sudhabai Joshi. Telho Mascarenha is one of the active members of the Congress group, and editor of the paper *Ressurge Goa*. Another member, Antonio Furtado, former community treasurer in Portuguese India, edits a review *Free Goa* and was named by the nationalists administrator of the occupied enclaves of Dadra and Nagar-Avely.

Goan People's Party. Divakar Kakodkar and George Vaz, who founded the anti-Fascist Goan Youth League in 1944, broke from the Congress and formed the Goan People's Party. It is, in reality, identified with the Indian communist party. Members of this party were largely active on August 2, 1955, in the occupation of the tiny enclaves.

United Front of Goans. In 1950, Francis Mascarenhas and Waman Desai quit the Congress and founded the United Front of Goans and whose purpose is an autonomous state of Goa within the Indian Union as against the idea of many Indians that Goa should become a part of the Maharashtre State and lose its identity. Waman Desai, who was charged in Goa with embezzlement, is most active.

Azad Gomantak Dal. Early in 1954, V. N. Lawande, expelled from the Congress, founded the *Azad Gomantak Dal* (Free Goan Group) at Belgaum with the support of the Mahasabha, or Hindu extremists, and the Jan Sangh. The tendency here is Hindu communalist and it is active in clandestine activity within Portuguese India.

Goan Action Committee. Founded in 1954 by Tristao Bragança Cunha, a Goan of Marxist convictions, the intention was to co-ordinate the action of the various groups whose aim was Goan "liberation."

Goan Liberation Council. In August, 1954, a number of Catholics in Bombay formed this group under the presidency of A. Soares. The latter was active in the struggle against British rule and since identifying himself with the effort to annex Goa, he has directed his attention principally against what he calls the fascist character of the regime in Portugal. They are aware of the importance of negotiating with the Indian government in the event of annexation, to assure the maximum of religious guarantees to the Goans.

met with only mediocre success. The outlook would seem to favor an intensification of the pressure and the increase of every effort to mobilize Goans resident in India for liberation. Neither of the two governments have shifted the basic position, nor give signs of so doing. As things stand now, the area of possible compromise is most narrow and gives little hope of fruitful conversations between the two states. Whatever may be the political outlook for Portugal in the long run, the roots of culture and of religion that have been struck in Goa remain deep and permanent "nor can a certain immortality be denied to a city which knew St. Francis Xavier, the Apostle of the Indies and Camões. . . ."[38]

I think it may be useful to suggest the main line of argument of the two sides in this conflict and I propose to present them as objectively and dispassionately as possible. Suppose we take the case of India, first of all. It runs something like this:

1. The creation of the independent India in 1947 implies the completion of Indian unity by the incorporation of all territories that form a part of the Indian subcontinent. Therefore there is no room for pockets or enclaves such as those held by France and since given up, and those still held by Portugal.
2. The geographical unity of India demands that these minor areas still in European hands be eliminated and the natural unity of India be rounded out.
3. Historically Goa has been Portuguese for 400 years and several of the other areas for only 200. There is no basic historical argument that Portugal should hang on to territories that were occupied as commercial outposts a few centuries ago but which have remained in essential racial structure, religion (Hindu), language (Kokoni), and way of life quite indistinguishable from the surrounding Indian territories.
4. Portuguese rule represents colonialism of the worse type, and there are several arguments against it:
   a) Colonialism is outmoded and no longer atune with the century.
   b) Portuguese colonialism has been a heavy burden on the Goan community.
   c) Portugal is backward-minded and under a semifascist dictatorship and can no longer pretend to maintain this anachronism.
5. Portugal is a member of NATO and has evoked this treaty in its defense. India belongs to no bloc and does not intend that

[38] Spate, *India and Pakistan*, *op. cit.*, p. 622.

any portion of her soil shall be used as a military or naval base for the NATO.[39]

6. The people of Goa want liberation and favor integration and are kept from expressing themselves by the repressive measures of the Portuguese. It is a matter of self-determination and deserves to be recognized.
7. Portugal would gain infinitely more in Indian friendship and respect if Portuguese India were given up gracefully, following the French pattern.[40]

On the Portuguese side the contention runs more or less as follows:

1. Portuguese India belongs obviously to the Indian land mass, but geography does not and never has determined historical or cultural affiliation.
2. Historically Goa existed long before an Indian nation came into being and to claim Goa today by the present India is as logical as for Greece to claim the conquests of Alexander or for Italy to lay claim to the lands that Rome held under its sway.
3. Goa is distinct from the rest of the Indian area. Its people are separated by a different cultural tradition and an attachment that sets them quite apart from their neighbors.
4. The fact that half of Goa is Christian and that the Christian tradition has been so significant there is an element of the first importance for the West. Moreover, the hostility of the Indian government to missionaries would jeopardize most seriously Goa itself if it were ever incorporated.
5. The demand for Goa is the fruit of Indian nationalism, xenophobia, and general frustration.
6. Goa economically can mean nothing to India and will contribute nothing to her well-being.
7. The Goans themselves are Portuguese on a level of full equality with the mother country and have evidenced no mass desire for

---

[39] Nehru invokes the Monroe Doctrine as a justification for India's attitude. He compares the refusal of the United States to tolerate political interference in this hemisphere as comparable to India's desire. "I submit that in the existing conditions the Portuguese retention of India is a continuing interference with the political system established in India today. . . . we cannot possibly accept such interference or such a foothold, however small it may be" (Nehru in speech to parliament, July 26, 1955, *Foreign Affairs Record*, New Delhi, July, 1955, Vol. I, No. 7, p. 143).

[40] The cession by France of its possessions in India undoubtedly influenced the Indians to exert increasing pressure on Portugal. "Undoubtedly the proximity of a solution with France stimulated the Indian government to seek an identical arrangement with Portugal" (*Le Monde*, Paris, August 10, 1954). The French, ever since 1947, have envisaged the liquidation of their tiny "comptoirs," a policy diametrically opposite to that of Portugal. Also, Coret, Alain, *La Cession de e'clude française*, Paris, 1955.

attachment to India. The present campaign is artificial and part of India's means of stimulating nationalism at the expense of Portuguese interests.

8. Legally, India has no claim to Portuguese India since the present India is the independent continuation of British-ruled India and under British domination no question was ever raised of the Portuguese territories.
9. The Indian position is vague and generally untenable because it proceeds on the assumption that Portugal must give up Goa and then talk, which would amount to conceding the premise and then discussing consequences.
10. India is fighting this matter under the banner of anticolonialism. Portugal is not, and never has been, colonial in the pejorative sense employed by India. To assume an "imperialism" in the case of the Indian territories is to fly in the face of the realities.[41]

There are, of course, all sorts of subsidiary and marginal arguments. These, I think, represent basically the manner of looking at the situation of the two powers involved.

International politics, like all politics, is unquestionably the science of the possible. One has the feeling, on the examination of the material involving Goa, that Mr. Nehru has taken an intransigent position that assumes the solution before it is discussed. One is particularly struck by the constantly repeated theme in all the Indian declarations, that Portugal must give up its sovereignty over Goa before negotiations can be undertaken. But it is precisely the question of Portuguese sovereignty that is the crux of the whole matter and to ask Lisbon to abandon its claims and then enter into discussion — one wonders about what — would seem rather to assure the impossibility of fruitful negotiations.

[41] The Portuguese are exceedingly proud of the degree to which they have achieved racial integration and harmony in India. Colonel Rémy, the famous French Resistance hero, visited Goa recently and has written of his impressions on his return. He tells one incident of an Indian minister of state who crossed the frontier and was received politely, if with surprise, by the Portuguese officials. Among other places, he visited a school and noted Moslems and Christians side by side with a goodly number of Parsis, Brahmins, and untouchables. Every gradation of color was represented and the minister asked: "How do you manage to get them all together?" One of the pupils, a sixteen-year-old lad, rose and said, "The reason is that we are all Portuguese" (Colonel Rémy, article, "Quando um Ministro da União Indiana pediu asilo em territorio portuguễs" in *Diario de Noticias*, Lisbon, July 27, 1955). Colonel Rémy has published a detailed account of his impressions under the title, *Goa, Rome d'Orient*, Paris, 1955. See also an excellent brief statement by the Swiss newspaperman, René Lombard, *Enquête à Goa*, Lausanne, 1956, with a preface by Gonzague de Reynold.

Geographical contiguity is perhaps less important in the determination of national affiliation and even political adherence than other factors, such as culture, a long association, tradition, and a way of life. If the Indian contention that what is geographically a part of the Indian subcontinent must belong to it politically, it is difficult to see just how Burma and Ceylon are going to remain independent, or how Nepal, Bhutan, and Sikkim in the Himalayas can remain outside the orbit of New Delhi control. The existence of Pakistan is the most cogent of all arguments that political unity does not necessarily follow geographical or even economic lines. East Pakistan is certainly a part of Bengal from every point of view except the political and yet the force of circumstances led to the acceptance of the formation of Pakistan and the partition of India, against which Mr. Nehru inveighed for years and about which he said some very unpleasant things.[42] If unity among nations is so sacred a thing that everything else must be sacrificed to it, then just how does India find it possible to accept a divided Korea and a divided Vietnam, both of which came about with considerable Indian approval?

International politics in our age has presented the Goa issue as one of the innumerable facets of the East-West rivalry. When Mr. Dulles spoke of the "province" of India in the joint statement with the Portuguese Foreign Minister Dr. Cunha, the Indian government was incensed, and went in for a hysteria of criticism of the imperial sympathies of the United States in its support of archaic and retrograde Portuguese colonialism. Mr. Nehru spends a good deal of his time issuing joint statements with such ardent defenders of democracy and anti-imperialists as Comrades Kruschev and Bulganin and Chou En-lai. Undoubtedly, from the diplomatic point of view, Mr. Dulles' statement was slightly less than felicitous. But it is equally plain that nothing short of denouncing Portugal and

[42] Nehru, Jawaharlal, *The Discovery of India, op. cit.*, p. 508 *seq.* In these pages Mr. Nehru argues that only on an "all-India basis" can the country survive and that partition means some very disastrous things. Yet partition came and India had to swallow the unpalatable fact and Pakistan continues to exist and gives every promise of remaining a factor in international life indefinitely. If Pakistan exists, regardless of geographical unity, and in spite of the dire calamities foreseen by Mr. Nehru, it is odd that Indian welfare depends to such a high degree on the expulsion of the Portuguese and the annexation of 600,000 of their citizens.

its presence in India will satisfy New Delhi.[43] The United States is in the singularly embarrassing position of not wishing to alienate India any more than is necessary and, at the same time, since Portugal is an ally and a partner in the North Atlantic Pact, it is hardly feasible to go about demanding that the property of one of your friends be handed over to one who displays anything but a warm and understanding friendship.

The Soviet Union is bound by no such scruples and has played Indian sensitivity to the hilt on this issue. The visit of Secretary Kruschev and Bulganin to India gave rise to a formal statement on the matter which apparently made Indian public opinion extremely happy.[44]

The religious problem is something else again. The Portuguese claim fundamentally two things about Portuguese India: that it has been a beacon light of Christianity in the paganism of the East and that its incorporation within India would seriously menace the faith and the freedom of worship of the inhabitants. The Indian critics tend to answer that Portguese India is only partly Christian and still has a majority of Hindus and others, and that, even if incorporated, India has given full guarantees for the respect of the religious sentiments and the freedom of action of the people.[45] We

---

[43] *The New York Times*, December 11, 1955, report of A. M. Rosenthal. "There can be little doubt that Prime Minister Nehru considers the presence of Portugal a much greater danger than China. The Indian government was perfectly willing to accept communist occupation of Tibet as reasonable and entered into an agreement with Peking relative to Indian interests in that remote land. The attitude of Nehru during his visit to China makes it self-evident that a tyranny when exercised by Asiatics is tolerable but a European government of any kind is quite insufferable no matter how just it may be" (*O Heraldo*, Nova Goa, June 26, 1956).

[44] The Soviet statement said: "Our frank statements on Goa and the Kashmir question have aroused great dissatisfaction in the reactionary press and among some foreign statesmen. It is known that Portugal's small colony, Goa, is still preserved on age old Indian territory. Suffice it to look at the map of India and at this 'possession' of the Portuguese usurpers to become convinced that the Indian government justly and lawfully raises the question of reunifying this Indian territory with its motherland, India. The Soviet government supports this just demand of India and holds that the preservation of the colonial regime in our times is a disgrace for the civilized nations" (*The New York Times*, December 30, 1955).

[45] "It is ridiculous of Portugal to appeal to Catholic susceptibilities in an attempt to retain possession of Goa, when religious toleration is the guiding policy of India, and Mr. Nehru has reaffirmed that the cultural, social and lingual distinction of Goa, will be respected in merger with India" (*The Overseas Hindustan Times*, New Delhi, September 2, 1954).

have already noted the figures on the Christian population of Portuguese India. This area has long been rich in religious vocations and has been called by the traditional title, "Rome of the East."[46]

Would Goans run the risk of suffering for their religion in the event of merger with India? The Portuguese say yes; the Indians emphatically deny this possibility. The problem becomes particularly difficult to assess in view of recent Indian action regarding foreign missionaries and restrictions on Catholic activity of various kinds. When India became independent, the optimistic school of thought expected that Catholic missions — and by extension all Christian missions — would enjoy greater favor since it would be evident that they were not the instrument of Western imperialism. Another trend of thought insisted that the secularist nature of the Indian state and the strong current of Hindu nationalism would be an impediment for the work of the missions. In April, 1953, the Indian Minister for Home Affairs declared that evangelizing should be limited to Indian citizens. It was clear from what Dr. Katju, the minister, had to say later that he objected to the presence and propagation of Christianity in India because it involved comparisons between different faiths and this was very harmful.[47] In a later statement, the minister deplored what he called the antinational activity of the missionaries. The danger lay in the fact that "antinational" covered the conversion of an Indian from Hinduism to Christianity. There was a great deal of confusion as to precisely what the government, through the Home Affairs minister, meant. Earlier in the year Dr. Katju had stated that the missionaries were "free to come and work in this country, but that they would not be allowed to act against the country's interests or indulge in objectionable methods for proselytization."[48] In May, 1954, Mr. Nehru assured the Christian Council of India and Pakistan that there was

[46] On religious vocations, "the largest center for vocations in all India is the Portuguese territory of Goa. The profoundly religious population has enjoyed four and a half centuries of Catholic life . . . and many congregations whose principal purpose is the encouragement of vocations have their houses here" (*Osservatore Romano*, Vatican City, March 10, 1955).

[47] See the three excellent articles on the subject by Monsignor S. M. Shaw in *The Tablet*, London, August 7, 14, 1954, under the title, "Indian Nationalism and the Missions."

[48] *The Overseas Hindustan Times*, New Delhi, April 15, 1956, report on a parliamentary speech of the minister under the section, "Home Affairs."

no hostility to Christianity and that indeed the Christian faith was considered as part of the Indian scene, so deep were its roots. On the other hand, if the proposal that Christians limit their efforts to propagation without conversion, the whole reason for being disappears. Father Jerome d'Souza, S.J., has undertaken to clarify this problem as to the degree to which Catholic missions are threatened in India by the present trend of things. The present attitude seems to be that missionaries are to come under the same classification as foreigners in general and their entry into India is to be determined by the same regulations.[49] The whole thing is bound up with Indian nationalism and the desire to "Indianize" as rapidly as possible not only other agencies for education and culture, but the Churches as well. There have been difficulties in certain Indian states and in some cases the central government has undertaken to undo injustices perpetrated locally. The situation has remained tight, as is evidenced by the decisions in 1956 to restrict foreign missionaries by various means: by insisting that they cannot enter until no Indian is available; that they perform some specificed social or medical service; and the like.[50] Government permission will have to be obtained for the opening of new houses or religious centers. Catholic objections to the state policy on nonofficial schools has also been prominent, especially the statement of the hierarchy of India in the spring of 1956, in which "State interference," and actual persecution in one diocese was denounced as well as many restrictions which make the effective work of the Church in this field more and more difficult.[51]

How does all this apply to Goa? It is self-evident that Goa is a stronghold of Catholic faith and practice and that it is the Portuguese contention that, in spite of all the promises given by the Indians, there would be danger that this tiny community would at once be lost in the ocean of India's hundreds of millions.

Valerian Cardinal Gracias of Bombay has undertaken to reply to this objection and at the same time to give assurances that Catholicism would actually enjoy an added advantage if Goa were merged since this would increase India's Catholic population and

[49] "The Missions in India: Uneasiness and Hope," Jerome d'Souza, S.J., in *The Sword*, London, September–October, 1954, p. 22 *seq.*

[50] *Universe*, London, August 26, 1955.

[51] *Ibid.*, April 20, 1956.

make available the large number of clergy that Goa provides.[52] The Cardinal, in this excellent statement, points out that the guarantees of the Indian constitution and the hope that in time the present difficulties which are inevitable in a new nation may be worked out so that the interests of the Christian minority may be amply protected. Cardinal Gracias has also spoken out on the Goa issue in view of the tendency in some quarters to assume that the defense of Portugal in India was a Catholic issue and involved, strictly speaking, a matter of Catholic survival. "When five million Catholics in the Indian Union are being allowed to live their religious life, are restrictions going to be placed on the quarter of a million Catholics in Goa? And when large Catholic communities are flourishing in Mangalore, Kerala, Tamilnad, and Bihar, is it likely that that of Goa is going to be stamped out of existence?"[53]

There has been some question about the discrepancy of views between the Portuguese government and the Sacred Congregation of the Propagation of the Faith on the Goa issue. In late 1954, Dr. Salazar noted in an address certain divergences of viewpoint as regards the Catholic problem in that area. This was interpreted as a conflict between the traditional Portuguese thesis of the *Padroado*, that is, the civil collaboration in the spread of the faith and certain concessions to the State in ecclesiastical matters, and the policy of the Propaganda in matters of missionary activity in the world. The assumption was that the Propaganda preferred to dissociate missionary activity entirely from the State — any State — while Portugal was keen about retaining the privileges that had been granted it historically.[54]

[52] Gracias, Valerian Cardinal, "Catholic and Indian," published in *World Mission* and reproduced in *The Examiner*, Bombay, April 16 and 23, 1956.

[53] "The Future of Goa" in *The Sword, op. cit.*, pp. 25–26. The Archbishop of Bandalore, Msgr. Pothacamury, secretary of the Indian Bishops Conference, analyzes the problem frankly and with restrained optimism in *The Tablet*, London, July 28, 1956. We find also that Goan Catholics are fervent in their desire to remain attached to Portugal. "More than 8,000 Catholics marched in a dawn pilgrimage on Tuesday from the city of Goa to the Church of Bom Gesu in Old Goa to pray before the body of St. Francis Xavier for the preservation of Goa's independence from India" (*Universe*, London, August 17, 1956).

[54] The problem raised here is scarcely one that can be treated honestly in a few lines. The so-called question of the *Padroado* and the conflict with the Propaganda has a long history and led at one time to what was considered the "Goa schism." Much of the conflict stemmed from Portugal's privileged position over all India ecclesiastically and to the effort of Gregory XVI to bring about certain changes in the Indian missions. The relations between Portugal and the

There are Catholic arguments on both sides. Msgr. T. D. Roberts, S.J., former Archbishop of Bombay, stated not long ago that the incorporation of Goa into India would be an advantage to the Church in the latter country. The majority of bishops in Indian sees outside South India are Goans and there are 250,000 Goans, more or less, in India itself. If Goa were merged, these Goans would have a far more effective voice in Indian affairs than now, and their status as members of a diaspora would disappear. "Incorporation would improve relations with Indian government and assuage the current antagonism toward foreign missionaries by intense Hindu nationalism." The definite discrepancy seems to be that, in the minds of many Catholics in India, Portugal conceives of Christianity as Portuguese and definitely attached to the Lusitanian way of life and outlook whereas the Propaganda prefers what Archbishop Roberts called the Jesuit conception originated by Father Robert di Nobili who became a Brahmin in order to make Indians Christians.[55]

The Holy See itself has been most careful to avoid making of this issue a religious one. To say that the defense of Portuguese sovereignty in India is essentially a defense of the faith and of its maintenance there is part of the whole problem. There is also the political one and very especially the moral question of giving up at the arbitrary demand of India what Portugal has governed for centuries. And there is always the prestige element which plays so decisive a role in the conduct of international affairs. "Therefore," it has been stated in Vatican circles, "contrary to some assertions, the question of Goa is not, in itself, a religious question. What stands, acute and tense, is the political question."[56]

Holy See and Portuguese claims over large areas in the East all conspired to make this a classical example of the tension caused by the system of patronage and the desire of the Holy See to organize mission activity along nonnational lines. See da Silva Rego, António, *O Padroado português do Oriente*, *op. cit.*, p. 248 *seq.* Also de Sá, Artur Basílio, *Documentação para a historia das missões do padroado português do Oriente*, Lisbon, 1956. Also de Figueiredo, P. Niceno, *Pelo clero de Goa*, Bastorá, Portuguese India, 1939.

[55] *Catholic Herald*, London, December 17, 1954.

[56] *Osservatore Romano*, "La questione di Goa," Vatican City, July 29, 1955. The Portuguese government has not posed the question as a "religious" issue. Dr. Paulo Cunha, Minister of Foreign Affairs, in a press conference, August 15, 1955, "The presence of the Portuguese in Goa is certainly not a religious matter. Nor has the Portuguese government ever pretended that it was, in spite of what Mr. Nehru has erroneously concluded. But it may very well be a problem

The conflict over Goa is, of course, a conflict of attitudes. The expression that the Portuguese use of a "Christian beacon" in India is in itself offensive to Indian ears for it implies, as does Portuguese political rule, a remnant of the past with which the country is eager to break. The French were able to give up their Indian possession with less difficulty than would be the case in Goa, for the latter has always been independent ecclesiastically, whereas French India was directly under the Propaganda.

Is there any prospect of a decent settlement of this question? One writer has suggested that it might perhaps be well to let Portugal continue its rule as a monument to a fascinating past and a very great century of achievement for surely 2000 troops in Goa can constitute no threat to the Indian Union.[57] And still another suggestion, which may have some worth, is that Goa, in Portuguese hands, might well play a very real role in the movement of Indian population toward Africa. It is well known that hundreds of thousands of Indians have settled in Africa and that this migration will probably continue until it is cut off either at the source or on the receiving end. Lourenço Marques is the natural port of entry for these Indians in South Africa and there might be a future for many of them in the racially unconscious Mozambique. "Instead of bullying the Portuguese over Goa, Mr. Nehru might do very much better to try to make Goa a bridgehead to Africa, the natural link with Lourenço Marques." Goa would then become a means of strengthening the connection with a continent where Indians are a very important element.[58]

As things stand the dialogue has been broken and there is only the slightest chance that anything else than the adamant positions that have been taken will be forthcoming. The Portuguese have, however, maneuvered Mr. Nehru and the Indian government into a peculiarly tight and uncomfortable spot. Obviously, India could take Goa in a few hours by police or military action. The Portuguese know this and are quite aware that they are incapable, from Europe, of defending Goa adequately unless NATO were to come to their

with religious overtones" (*Noticias de Portugal*, Lisbon, No. 433, August 20, 1955, p. 8).

[57] Msgr. S. M. Shaw, *The Tablet*, *op. cit.*, August 21, 1954.

[58] Rodeur, Paul, "The Price for Goa," *The Tablet*, London, August 6, 1955.

support, and this has been ruled out.[59] Mr. Nehru has reiterated over and over again that violence is out and that only "peaceful means can be used to secure India's position." Portugal can therefore take the position that since she has no intention of backing down and will not abandon Goa except by force, India will have to take the territory by arms. The minute this happens, the whole elaborate structure of Indian pacificism, nonviolence, and nonaggression collapses. By what logic will India be able to pretend afterward, if she does use force, that the philosophy behind every act of Indian diplomacy is peace and nonviolence? Nehru and his government would have to betray what they have erected into a state policy to secure Goa. Would it be worth it?

The present stage is one of recrimination. The examination of the statements from both sides indicates fairly clearly that the shrillest denunciations emanate from the Indian spokesmen. Mr. Nehru is much addicted to addressing huge gatherings in which temperance of expression is not the unvarying rule. Speaking at Bombay in June, 1956, he found nothing better to hurl at the Portuguese than the accusation that Salazar belonged mentally to the fifteenth century.[60] The Indian prime minister has made a world-shaking issue out of the case and with a petulance somewhat unbecoming a leader of a great nation. In his Independence Day address at the Red Fort in Delhi in 1954, he called Goa, "a test not only for India and Portugal but for all the nations of the world."[61] Goa was proclaimed a symbol of hated colonialism which must be extirpated. Mr. Nehru has demanded peremptorily that

---

[59] The Indian press reported that Lord Home, Britain's Secretary of State for Commonwealth Relations, had indicated that Portugal could not invoke NATO obligations in the case of Goa. When asked whether Britain had any obligations either under the NATO arrangement or the ancient Anglo-Portuguese treaty, Lord Home stated: "I think it will be stretching NATO too far." Moreover Portugal had not, said the Secretary, asked Britain to act under the treaty of alliance between the two (*The Overseas Hindustan Times*, New Delhi, August 18, 1955). The United States ambassador to India, Mr. Sherman Cooper, was reported to have said in Madras that his country "would stop its arms aid to any country that utilized the arms to assist the Portuguese in Goa" (*ibid.*, October 20, 1955).

[60] Reported in detail in *O Heraldo*, Nova Goa, June 6, 1956, under the title, "Words, Words, Words. Nehru Sacrifices an Excellent Opportunity to Remain Silent."

[61] *The Overseas Hindustan Times*, New Delhi, August 19, 1954.

the Western powers stand up and be counted on the Goa issue. On June 4, 1956, the prime minister urged the Western powers, "some of whom have been accusing India of adopting a neutralistic attitude, to inequivocally state whether they approved of Salazar's assertion of being the standard bearer of western civilization in the Orient. He asked the western powers why they were neutral on the Goa issue which was fundamentally a colonial issue."[62] The Indian government apparently finds that the absence of enthusiastic support from the West against Portugal is a crime against humanity, whereas the kind of *camaraderie* in which the Indian leadership engages with every communist regime across the world is a wholly laudable effort to maintain the peace.[63]

Salazar has never assumed this blatant tone in replying to the attacks from India. The Portuguese leader's attitude can be summed up in his speech of November 30, 1954, to the National Assembly:

> India does not want to cease its needling nor does it want an open war with its armies in action. Can the Indian Union continue indefinitely this way? It can. The thousand and one administrative annoyances, the impertinent diplomatic notes, the unfounded demands, the press and radio campaigns regarding facts that either do not exist or have been distorted, the specious interpretation of treaties and laws can all go on, but it is a woeful lack of dignity and greatness for a nation like the Indian Union.[64]

World opinion has not reacted with anything like unanimous approval of Indian pressure politics. The leading Italian paper, *Il Giornale d'Italia,* commented that "The pacifist and neutralist government of Nehru does not lose time nor does it allow itself to be deterred by excessive scruples when concerned with the conquest of foreign territories. Nehru's offensive is not, however, aimed exclusively at Portugal. In point of fact it is a complete anti-European

---

[62] *Ibid.*, June 7, 1956. Nehru also asked the Catholic Church to remain aloof from the controversy. "Mr. Nehru told a cheering crowd of 30,000 that he wanted a clear answer from the United States, Great Britain, France and other western nations to India's demands for Goa" (*The New York Times*, June 5, 1956).

[63] The absolutely ludicrous is reached when the Bulgarian chargé d'affaires in India, Ivan Montafchiev, announced to the local Rotary Club that Bulgaria supported the "just aspirations of the Indian people for the liberation of Goa." And this because "Bulgarians hated enslavers" (*The Overseas Hindustan Times*, New Delhi, June 21, 1956).

[64] *Noticias de Portugal*, Lisbon, No. 396, December 4, 1954.

offensive."[65] *The Times* expressed concern that the communist agitators and irregular elements would only lead to greater and greater violence that would get completely out of hand.[66] The *Neue Zürcher Zeitung* expresses skepticism regarding these "liberation" movements that come from outside. "An attack on Goa would completely destroy the thesis of peaceful co-existence which India constantly flaunts."[67] The *Washington Post* spoke out very strongly on the matter by saying that "what is happening in India is strangely similar to the communist technique. . . . If it had not been for the firm stand taken by Prime Minister Salazar, Portuguese India would have been indianized today—and indianized against the law by dishonest processes."[68]

[65] *Il Giornale d'Italia*, Rome, July 31, 1954.
[66] *The Times*, London, August 3, 1954.
[67] *Neue Zürcher Zeitung*, Zurich, August 7, 1954.
[68] *The Washington Post*, Washington, D. C., August 12, 1954.

Chapter IX

PORTUGAL AND ITS PLACE IN THE WORLD

THIS chapter is not intended as an exhaustive examination of the foreign relations of Portugal in modern times but it would be impossible, however, to conclude these pages on Portugal and its role in the world without reference to certain events which have made the country an important and vital factor on the international scene. The geopolitics of the situation makes Portugal *malgré lui*, a decisive element with reference to the western Mediterranean, the entrance to the Straits of Gibraltar, and the whole South Atlantic, including the coast of Africa. The position of the Azores, Madeira, and the Cape Verde Islands gives Portugal a high degree of control over the routes toward the African continent and between Europe and South America. The relative independence of the Portuguese coast itself, by virtue of its remoteness from the center of Europe, provides an important approach route to the continent and, by the same logic, an exit in difficult times when the continental land mass is under occupation, as was amply demonstrated in the period of Napoleonic control and repeated during the years when the Nazis surged over all Europe, only to stop at the Pyrenees. Portugal's African interests *plus* the strong historical link with Great Britain afford an extraordinarily promising possibility for the partnership between Europe and Africa, of which Premier Salazar has spoken, and to which as acute an observer as B. H. Liddell Hart refers.[1]

---

[1] Hart, B. H. Liddell, *Defence of the West*, London, 1950, p. 252: "Economically Africa is far more important to us than the Middle East. . . . it would profit us to concentrate more effort there . . . a further advantage is that the other states which have large possessions in Africa — France, Belgium, and Portugal — are the three foreign states who are most closely linked to us in Europe."

From all that has been suggested heretofore, it is evident that at the present time Portuguese foreign policy must de dominated by five major premises or constants:

1. The relations with Spain;
2. The alliance with Great Britain;
3. The defense of the integrity of the empire in Africa and Asia and the problems that necessarily follow from this world-wide position;
4. Relations with Brazil, as the other Portuguese-speaking power in the world;
5. Membership in the NATO system.

We might add, as a result of the admission of Portugal to the United Nations, that the Lisbon government has now assumed a further obligation of foreign policy since Portugal will be required to accept, as a member of the international organization, numerous responsibilities with which she was not burdened before.

The first and fundamental aspect in the analysis of Portugal in the world is the question of relations with Spain. There is no need at this point to reiterate the purely historical considerations that have cropped up again and again in these pages; that Portugal was invaded by the Spanish time after time and the Portuguese in their turn invaded Spanish territories, all part of the inevitable dream of Iberian unity that unquestionably existed in many sectors of Spanish opinion far into modern times.[2]

The ideal of Iberian unity is no longer realistic and much less feasible. One of the concrete results of the experience of the Spanish Civil War and the aftermath was to bring about the *rapprochement* diplomatically of the two peoples in an atmosphere of cordiality which had long been lacking in the relations between the two. It would seem that all idea of an ultimate merging of the two states has been abandoned as unrealistic and out of keeping with the realities of Portuguese and Spanish life.

The opening scene in this short account of Spanish-Portuguese relations is 1931. This was a crucial moment for both nationalities, for the Portuguese were definitely launched by then on the *Estado*

---

[2] An indication of this is the comment of Conde De Limpias in his *De Política exterior de España a principios del siglo* XX, Madrid, 1914, p. 153, in which he states that the separation of the two nations "was suicidal for Portugal and harmful to Spain" and opines that a high degree of statesmanship might well lead to a similar consummation in the Iberian peninsula in terms of unity as occurred in Italy under Cavour or Germany under Bismarck (p. 168).

Novo and the broad directives for social and political action that Salazar had outlined were clear. The new constitution was to come into effect two years later to give consistency and form to the emerging regime. On the other side of the frontier, the monarchy had fallen, as inexorably as it had in Lisbon in 1910, to give way to a republic. On the surface it might have seemed that the institution of republicanism in Spain would bring the nation closer to its sister republic in the same peninsula. It was rather the contrary. Portugal was in full reaction against the excesses of Jacobin republicanism while Spain was embarking on the dangerous and antinational policy that had brought so much havoc to its Iberian neighbor. The demagoguery and socialism of Manuel Azaña, Largo Caballero, and the rest of the Spanish political and syndicalist leaders was not likely to arouse much enthusiasm in the breast of Oliveira Salazar, nor were the ideas of the Portuguese prime minister capable of provoking the sympathy of those who were shouting clichés and political slogans in Spain.

What was infinitely more dangerous was the revival under the Azaña government of intrigue against Portugal, in part at least fomented by Portuguese refugees after the unsuccessful rebellion of 1931 and members of Freemasonry who undertook to secure funds and assistance in Spain for their work in Portugal. Since Freemasonry was forbidden in the Portugal of Salazar, this was definitely a cause of tension. It has been amply demonstrated that Azaña provided financial aid for a conspiracy against Portugal in one of those fantastic and improbable plots that seem to prosper so luxuriantly in the fertile Iberian soil. Arms were to be acquired for the refugees, and the intermediaries, especially one Echevarrieta, were to be compensated with concessions in Angola once the Salazar government had been overthrown. Several Spanish republican ministers were involved in the transfer of arms and munitions to the Portuguese border in this absurd effort to bring about a change of regime in the neighboring country. The Portuguese government was perfectly aware of these maneuvers and the Portuguese press commented on the implications of it — especially the role of certain important political personalities who, from Paris, were endeavoring to undermine the new regime. It has since appeared that the Spanish republican leader and minister, Martínez Barríos, was responsible for selling thousands of bombs for the purpose of assisting in the overthrow of General Carmona of Portugal.[3]

This type of thing, during the five-year period of the Spanish republic, was not likely to endear the increasingly extremist governments in Madrid to corporative Portugal. This is a necessary background comment on the problem of the Portuguese attitude during the Spanish Civil War. Aside, however, from basic political sympathies, once the civil war had broken out in Spain, certain very plain facts of geography became involved. After the initial maneuvering of the two forces: the Nationalist from Morocco and the Republican in the peninsula, it became clear that the basic purpose of the Spanish armies under General Franco was to open the way from south to north, to the end that the Nationalist zone in Navarre and the center might be attached to that of the south, especially after Seville, Granada, and most of Andalusia had been liberated. It was logical that this process of unification should take place up the peninsula through Estremadura along the Portuguese frontier. Just as the rebellion had suffered setbacks in Madrid and Barcelona, so was it successful in Zaragoza from which it extended its control to Jaca, Huesca, Calatayud, and Teruel, where General Saliquet brought these territories rapidly into the Nationalist camp. Zamora, Burgos, and Pamplona represented no problem, for the strength of Nationalist sentiment in this area was very great. In Segovia, Ávila, and elsewhere north of Madrid, the Nationalists prevailed as they did in all Galicia with no fighting at all. Córdoba, Jérez de la Frontera, and Cádiz joined the Nationalist cause as soon as the movement, initiated on the eighteenth of July, indicated that it was something more than a sporadic military uprising with only the scantiest prospects of success.

On August 3, 1936, the forces under Commander Castejón left Seville with troops that had been transported from Africa by air, and on the seventh of that month, General Franco himself transferred his headquarters to Seville to take charge of the supreme operations. By August 10, the armies were at Mérida in a lightning

---

[3] These details are to be found in Comín Colomer, Eduardo, *Historia secreta de la Segunda República*, Madrid, 1954, Vol. I, p. 205 *seq.* Also Pedro Aurioles, article on Martínez Barrios and his machinations in the newspaper *Pueblo*, Madrid, February 3, 1953.

dash aimed at sweeping the Republicans from Estremadura and opening up a corridor from south to north. The Battle of Badajoz has gone down in history as one of the bloodiest engagements of this eminently bloody war. The armies of Castile and Andalusia were able to combine after this operation and, in spite of the torturous character of the route, managed to keep in touch with each other. On August 26, General Franco was at Cáceres and the way was open for advance up the Tagus valley toward such strongly defended spots as Talavera, looked upon by the Republicans as one of the outer defenses of Madrid itself. This is not the place to recount the story of the Spanish Civil War, but simply to indicate that within six weeks of the outbreak, the Portuguese frontier was sealed off from Republican Spain, and the Nationalists, from then until the end of the war in the spring of 1939, were in direct contact with Portugal. The Lisbon government, aside from its sentiments, could not but take this fact into account.

No nation was as close to the hostilities and none more alarmingly affected by what was happening in Spain. Premier Salazar recognized fully the implications of the civil war and was not in the least led astray by the propaganda clichés about democracy versus totalitarianism. In an official statement, dated September 10, 1936, the Portuguese leader expressed deep concern at what was transpiring and called attention especially to the campaign of vilification going on in the world press, particularly in Britain and France, against Portugal and its position. "We are tired of calling Europe's attention to the fact that the Spanish civil war, independently of the will of the parties in conflict, is, on the basis of all evidence, an international battle."[4]

Portugal's stake in the conflict was fundamental and far greater than that of any other single power, including the only other power with a common land frontier with Spain — France. The first effect was to cut rail communications with the rest of Europe which, of necessity, traverse Spain.[5] But, since most of the Portuguese trade was carried on by sea in any event, this forced insularity was not particularly grievous. The political repercussions were far more menacing for the stability of the Portuguese regime. It was perfectly

[4] Salazar, *Discursos, op. cit.*, Vol. II, 2 ed., p. 185.

[5] See Toynbee, Arnold J., *Survey of International Affairs. The International Repercussions of the War in Spain, 1936–7*, the publication of the Royal Institute of International Affairs, London, 1938, p. 201 seq.

evident that the triumph of the Popular Front in Spain, especially after a bloody civil war, would mean a tremendous swing to the Left, and possibly the institution of the brand of sovietism preached by Largo Caballero and the extremists. If the rest of the peninsula went Left, socialist or, worse, communist, Portugal would be in a most precarious position. There was the danger, too, that a victorious Left would be in a far more favorable position to do what Azaña had tried to do under peace conditions: encourage and aid Portuguese exiles desirous of finishing off the Salazar regime. The insulation of Portugal from the Republicans in Spain did not prevent certain manifestations at home of unrest, especially the outbreak of a mutiny on September 8, 1936, on two warships in Lisbon harbor.[6]

Once more in its history, peninsular affairs took precedence over all else in the mind of the Portuguese government. One of the matters of principal interest is to note how the Lisbon regime was forced to oscillate between its immediate anxiety about what was happening beyond the frontier and the traditional bonds with Great Britain. Up to 1936, Portugal had followed a position essentially the same as Britain's in the international field. She participated in World War I and suffered considerably in her African territories from German depredations. The Portuguese government had supported Britain in the attempts in 1934 and 1935 to stem the tide of Italian aggression in Ethiopia and had deplored the wanton act of aggression against the land of the Negus.

On the other hand, as the evidence poured in that the Spanish republicans were strongly supported by the Soviet Union and were receiving aid from that country as well as from international communism through the International Brigades, Portuguese resistance stiffened. Portugal's position then and now was crystal clear: "Our position as regards communism is definitely fixed. On the contrary to what they do, we do not intend to go abroad to fight them, but we will not consent that communism enslave us at home. A policy of generosity and tolerance has its limits as imposed by the need of security."[7]

From general sympathy, the problem of collaboration with the Spanish Nationalists quickly became a practical one. Portugal became an important basis for the entrance of war materials into

[6] Salazar's speech, to which I have referred, was made after this mutiny.
[7] Salazar, *op. cit.*, Vol. II, p. 189.

National Spain which was soon to become a complicating feature of the so-called nonintervention policy of the powers.[8] It has been indicated that a Spanish Nationalist Junta functioned in Lisbon with financial support from the noted Spanish financier, Juan March, for the recruitment of volunteers and the transportation of supplies to the Nationalists.[9] The sympathy that the Portuguese felt for the Nationalist cause produced a violent reaction in Republican propaganda circles and among those aiding the republic abroad. "Fascist" Portugal became almost as popular a scapegoat as Franco himself. We find every accusation launched against Salazar's government: that it permitted a loan of 80,000 pounds sterling for the Nationalists; that planes over Badajoz came from Portuguese airfields; that Portuguese warships escorted National vessels; and, all in all, a "sinister" campaign of Salazar on behalf of the rebels.[10] The Portuguese public sentiment in favor of the Nationalists was both comprehensible and no different from the encouragement coming from France to the Republicans. The Portuguese press was favorable and "Radio-Club" of Portugal was a potent factor in maintaining the morale of the Nationalists, especially of the valiant defenders of the Alcázar who received their messages, and informed the beleaguered men and women of the true story of the Nationalist advance up from Andalusia.[11]

---

[8] Julio Alvarez del Vayo complains that as of late August the republican situation deteriorated and this was due in large part to foreign assistance to the "rebels." "Badajoz was captured, thanks partly to the cooperation of the Portuguese frontier authorities who, not content with allowing munitions lorries to be unloaded in Portuguese ports . . . handed over to the insurgents all republican combatants who attempted to fall back into Portugal" (*Freedom's Battle*, London-Toronto, 1940, p. 35). See also *Documents on German Foreign Policy, 1918–1945*, Department of State, Washington, D. C., 1950, on the efforts made in Portugal by Nationalist representatives to secure war materials through Portuguese ports (pp. 8, 15, 26). The German chargé d'affaires, Count Du Moulin, informed the Foreign Ministry in Berlin under date of August 22, 1936: "The Portuguese government determined on the clear policy of complete support for the rebels as far as it was possible to do so and maintain the semblance of formal neutrality" (p. 54). Emphasis is laid from this German source on the opposition of Great Britain to the Portuguese position which risked bringing about a wider conflict.

[9] Esch, P. A. M. van der, *Prelude to War. The International Repercussions of the Spanish Civil War, 1936–1939*, The Hague, 1951, p. 40.

[10] *Foreign Intervention in Spain. A Collection of Documents*, London, 1938, edited by "Hispanicus," p. 320 seq., under title "Portuguese Intervention."

[11] McNeill-Moss, Major G., *The Epic of the Alcázar. A History of the Siege of the Toledo Alcázar, 1936*, London, 1937, p. 279.

The most complicated feature of this complicated era was the effort to put into effect a policy of nonintervention and seal off the Spanish Civil War as much as possible from the rest of the world. The French were alarmed at the prospects of rival interventions in the conflict, in spite of their own willingness to allow arms to move southward toward Spain and early in August approached the British and Italian governments to suggest that an arrangement for nonintervention be worked out. The British government agreed on August 4 and a similar note was sent to the other interested powers: Germany, the Soviet Union, the Netherlands, Czechoslovakia, and Poland. After a certain amount of preliminary sparring, the first meeting of the nonintervention committee took place on September 9, 1936, with the representatives of twenty-six nations present. On top of the endless discussions of the subcommittee charged with working out a feasible system of control, the Spanish Republican government appealed to the League of Nations. The nonintervention committee functioned for over two years and devoted a great deal of time and effort to prove that Italy and Portugal were intervening in the civil war. It was during the second phase of the committee that provisions were drawn up to prevent war material reaching Spain by land or sea. There was the further problem of volunteers or foreign troops on both sides, about which the committee was also deeply concerned.

The Soviet representation on the committee demanded, among other things, that naval forces be deployed along the Portuguese coast to prevent supplies from entering what was already beginning to be called "Franco Spain." In August the Portuguese government indicated its acceptance of the principles of nonintervention but with specific reservations which were the result of its peculiar position *vis-à-vis* the conflict. France and Great Britain took action even before the agreement was drawn up and on August 27, 1936, Portugal approved it. The latter country became the crux of the whole international control system because if Lisbon refused to implement the agreement or failed to carry out its provisions, the way was open for a heavy traffic in arms with Spain and neither Italy nor Germany had committed itself not to send arms to Portugal which, in turn, could be transmitted into Spain. Portugal was the only invited nation not present at the opening meeting of the committee on September 9, having expressed a desire to have more precise information as to the nature of the committee's work before sending a delegate.

The Spanish Republican government published a series of documents purporting to show how Portugal was serving the rebel cause, and the Soviet Union chose Portugal as the principal objective of its diatribes both in the League of Nations and in the nonintervention committee, proposing that a commission be sent to inspect the Hispano-Portuguese frontier. By the end of October, all the member states save, of course, the Soviet Union had accepted the fact that there was no way to prove violations of the agreement on the part of Portugal, among others.[12]

The civil war gave promise of lasting for a long time and the nonintervention committee was thus able to settle back and take things more leisurely. As regards Portugal, the Lisbon government refused to accept international supervision of its land frontier and Great Britain assumed the sole obligation, in the name of nonintervention, of this task. By March, 1937, the entry of volunteers was made illegal. At this time a British corps of observers were on the Hispano-Portuguese frontier, an arrangement to which Portugal consented in view of its relations with Great Britain, a system that lasted for only a few months.[13] It was in October of 1936 that Portugal broke off relations with the Republican government, although this was not followed up until December of 1937 when an agent was appointed to represent Portuguese interests in Nationalist Spain.[14]

The successful conclusion of the civil war removed, of course, this active center of anxiety. "Portugal's harmony of sentiment remained intact with Spain throughout the civil war — it was indeed strengthened by the understanding of which the substance was embodied in the Pact of Friendship and Non-Aggression concluded on March 17, 1939."[15] A new chapter opened in Hispano-Portuguese

---

[12] Peers, E. Allison, *Spain in Eclipse, 1937–1943*, London, 1945, 2 ed., p. 30. Also Padelford, Norman J., *International Law and Diplomacy in the Spanish Civil Strife*, New York, 1939, p. 71.

[13] Toynbee, *op. cit.*, p. 253.

[14] The Portuguese case is available in documented form in Salazar, *Discursos*, *op. cit.*, Vol. II, with the official declarations on the rupture with Spain, nonintervention, the withdrawal of volunteers, etc. Also de Osório Andrade, Gilberto, *Os fundamentos da neutralidade portuguesa*, *op. cit.*, p. 292.

[15] Hodgson, Sir Robert, *Spain Resurgent*, London, 1953, p. 89. The conditions of the treaty are: the two parties undertake to respect fully each other's

relations with the institution of the new regime in Spain whose essential features resembled so markedly those of Portugal itself.

This second period embraces the time during which the Spanish government was setting its house in order and laying the foundations of the new order. It also involves the trying six years of the World War which threatened the integrity of Portugal, if not its peace and well-being at home. The first document in the establishment of what was to become known as the Iberian bloc, was the nonaggression pact of March, 1939, just before the formal ending of the civil war itself. The way had been prepared for this agreement in the numerous declarations of solidarity that had emanated from both Portuguese and Spanish sources. In an interview in May, 1938, with the Portuguese journalist, Armando Boaventura of *O Século* of Lisbon, General Franco noted that Portugal was the first country "to actually recognize Nationalist Spain." The unfortunately bad relations of the past are over, the Spanish leader declared, and the hatreds and misunderstandings of the liberal period gone forever. "The Spanish army saved Spain in the same way that the Portuguese saved Portugal on May 28, 1926." And he added, "I hope that Spain may have a regime of order, unity and discipline comparable to that of Portugal."[16] In June of that same year, in receiving the credentials of the Portuguese ambassador in Burgos, General Franco assured Portugal that in the future the bonds of close fraternity would bind the two people together.[17]

The nonaggression pact of 1939, which is the cornerstone of the new Iberian situation, specifically recognizes the existence of prior treaties in the case of Portugal which bind her to Great Britain. The creation of this unity did not overlook the fact that one of the contracting parties was already bound to a third, and in this case a world power which, if involved in war, might easily enmesh Portugal in the conflict. This odd situation of the Portuguese

---

frontiers and territory and to commit no act of agression or invasion the one against the other. Each party promises to give assistance to any aggressor against the other and to allow no attack against the other to be directed from its own territory. Each undertakes to enter into no pact or alliance against the other and which aims at aggression against the other. Each undertakes to safeguard the principles of the treaty in future treaties with a third power (Peers, *Spain in Eclipse*, *op. cit.*, p. 145).

[16] *Palabras del Caudillo, 19 abril, 1937 — 7 diciembre, 1942*, Madrid, 1943, pp. 494–495.

[17] *Ibid.*, p. 72.

alliance with Great Britain and with Spain simultaneously posed certain difficulties during the war years when Portugal's policy was one of official neutrality, and today it poses difficulties because Portugal belongs to the North Atlantic Defense Community whereas Spain, as yet, does not.[18] Moreover, in creating this arrangement between the two states, Spain and Portugal have contributed to the regional organization of peace which has been long recognized, both under the League of Nations and the United Nations, as essential segments of the larger international structure.

The outbreak of the World War led Premier Salazar to make a formal declaration of Portuguese neutrality and noted that the alliance with Great Britain did not oblige the nation to deviate from this course in connection with the war that was just beginning. "It is hoped that Providence will preserve the Portuguese people in peace and that neither the national dignity, interests nor obligations will be compromised."[19] The Portugal of the war years is the story of a delicate equilibrium maintained between the two belligerents. The danger was greatest when France went under, and still more grave when Vichy France disappeared and German troops were poised on the Pyrenees. Portugal held its doors remarkably open, however, for the flow of refugees and others who sought to get out of Europe to America through this last exit on the entire continent.[20]

In February of 1942, Premier Oliveira Salazar made the journey to Seville to meet with General Franco and the Minister for Foreign Affairs of Spain, Ramón Serrano Suñer. The entrance of the United States and several of the Hispanic-American republics into the war had changed the whole panorama of the conflict, and in the specific case of Spain had tended to produce a certain tension between Madrid and the Hispanic-American world, a factor which undoubtedly drew her closer to Portugal. Moreover it was felt that a re-examination of the 1939 treaty and the Protocol of July, 1940, that had followed it, was in order. The 1942 interview was another link in

[18] See Trelles, Camilo Barcia, "La política internacional peninsular," in *Cuadernos de Política Internacional*, Madrid, April–June, 1950, p. 9 *seq.* Also in the same review (January–March) is the study of the significance of this agreement by José Sebastián de Erice y O'Shea.

[19] Salazar, *Discursos*, *op. cit.*, Vol. III, p. 174.

[20] Serrano Súñer, Ramón, *Entre Hendaya y Gibraltar*, Madrid, 1947, pp. 150–151.

the large number that were being forged between the two countries and in which the able Portuguese ambassador to Madrid, Pedro Teotonio Pereira, was one of the main instruments. A Spanish diplomat who was present has reported on how it was General Franco himself who was responsible for the discussions and worked out the bases of many of the points of agreement.[21] It became clear toward the end of that year that the visit must be returned and a meeting was so arranged in December of 1942 when General Gómez Jordana, the new Minister of Foreign Affairs, visited Lisbon, and in the midst of speeches and banquets, the solidarity of Iberia was reaffirmed. The significance of the phrase "Iberian bloc" was considerable, as employed by General Jordana. The purpose was not merely to crown the structure of Iberian understanding, but to "approach Spain to the British sphere."[22] Spain was seeking, in this critical winter of 1942 when the fortunes of war had swung so definitely against the Axis, to approach Great Britain and the best way, in fact the only way, was through Portugal. The new achievement was hailed as indicative not only of peninsular solidarity, but of a new force in world politics whose weight might be of some importance for the cause of peace and international understanding.[23] In the allied countries, the act was interpreted as an indication of neutral intentions and a refusal to be drawn into the hostilities.[24]

---

[21] Doussinague, José María, *España tenía razón*, Madrid, 1950, p. 116. Serrano Súñer refers to this visit in *Entre Hendaya y Gibraltar*, *op. cit.*, p. 269. If the allies were certain that Portugal as well as Spain would resist invasion from the Axis, the Germans and Italians were equally sure that Portugal would resist the allies. "If Portugal were attacked by the Anglo-Saxons, Spain would not hesitate to enter the conflict. Agreements on this point exist between Franco and Salazar" (Ciano, Galeazzo, *Diario, 1941–1943*, Milan, 1946, Vol. II, p. 174).

[22] Doussinague, *op. cit.*, p. 118: "This visit was a public avowal of Spain's move toward the area of British policy."

[23] Del Rio Cisneros, Agustín, *Política internacional de España*, Madrid, 1946, p. 171 *seq.*, which reproduces an article on the Iberian bloc by this newsman, published in *El Español* of December 26, 1942.

[24] *The New York Times*, December 25, 1942. "The move — the Iberian bloc — can be interpreted therefore as an attempt to strengthen the neutrality of both counties"(*The Philadelphia Evening Bulletin*, December 22, 1942). "A development which tends to strengthen the belief that the Spanish Generalissimo really means to stay neutral and would offer more than token resistance to a Nazi invasion is the formation of the so-called Iberian bloc. Spain's Iberian bloc policy is, under the circumstances, reaffirmation of its determination to resist Nazi pressure." Peter Lyne, writing from London in *The Christian Science Monitor*, notes that "interpretation of the Spanish-Portuguese pact to keep

It would be somewhat of a digression to list the various efforts on the part of the Portuguese and Spanish governments to bring about, not peace, because that was out of the question in the midst of the war, but at least some preliminary discussions or exchanges of views as to the possibility of peace and the kind of peaceful settlement that might come after the war. It was quite evident that after the visits of 1942 both General Franco and Premier Salazar were interested in sounding out other neutral governments as to any basis for peace gestures that might be found. We find, for example, in a personal communication from the Spanish foreign minister to Nicolás Franco, Spanish ambassador in Lisbon, dated May 11, 1942, the statement: "Please explain to Oliveira Salazar that General Franco and his government are not convinced the time has come to negotiate peace but that it is time to talk about it. Peace, like war, must be prepared and it is indispensable to create the necessary atmosphere for it. Spain does not have any illusions about pointing out the way to peace for that has been done clearly by His Holiness Pope Pius XII. No one can deny the right of the Spanish and Portuguese governments to follow his lead."[25]

Portugal's position was, during the last war, appreciably different from that of Spain. One reason was the exposed position of the island provinces in the Atlantic and their high strategic value for both the Allies and the Axis, if either one or the other should succeed in occupying them. The other factor was that Portugal was the only Iberian state with vital interests in the Far East which was directly affected by the Japanese expansion. In a curious way, the interests of Portugal and the United States coincided perfectly in the mutual desire to liberate the occupied islands of

---

the two countries out of war is that it can most probably be taken at its face value as an intention of the Iberian peninsula to keep out of war." As far back as 1940 when the original treaty had been signed, the Japanese immediately took it to be a sign of British domination. The Tokyo *Asahi* (quoted in Spanish Legation dispatch No. 299 of August 29, 1940, from Tokyo to Madrid, in Ministry of Foreign Affairs archives). "Moreover the conclusion of a mutual aid pact between Spain and Portugal can be considered as a victory for British diplomacy."

[25] Personal letter to Ambassador Nicolás Franco, May 11, 1943 (in archives of the Ministry of Foreign Affairs, Madrid). This was the same sentiment expressed by Cardinal Plá y Daniel in his pastoral in May, 1945, when he spoke of "the clear mission of Spain and Portugal, to remain an island of neutrality and peace in western Europe."

the Pacific from Japanese control. The third factor, on which I have dwelt from time to time, was the ancient alliance with Britain which gave Portugal a rather special category among the neutral nations.

Sir Winston Churchill emphasizes what he calls "another burning question for us," that is, how to obtain the use of the Portuguese Atlantic islands.[27] The United States and Great Britain bent every effort during the critical years of 1941–1943 to keeping Portugal neutral — not a difficult task, since this was Premier Salazar's most ardent wish also. In 1942 the American government began a program aimed at securing certain strategic materials from Portugal, such as cork, and preventing the Germans from importing wolfram. Former Secretary of State Cordell Hull claims that Dr. Salazar was a harder bargainer than the Spanish, even, for "he realized and valorized his strong bargaining power" and his control over the air facilities in the Azores and at Lisbon, which was one of the few tiny spots still classified as free Europe.[28] In November of 1942 an agreement was concluded for the sale to Portugal of certain materials and in return the Portuguese committed themselves to selling a larger share of their exportable strategic material to the Allies than to the Axis. The negotiations over wolfram, the details of which need not be entered into here, are as laborious and wearisome as in the case of Spain and, after all sorts of vicissitudes, the United States and Great Britain secured an agreement that was basically quite favorable. Every sort of pressure was brought to bear on Portugal to get her to cut off wolfram to Germany or at least reduce it appreciably. The Americans wanted a total embargo of wolfram; the Portuguese were not ready to take any such drastic measures. The United States was willing to deprive itself of Portuguese wolfram if none of this product went to Germany. When the Germans stopped the Portuguese ship *Serpa Pinto* and forced the passengers to abandon it, the reaction in Portugal was strongly against the Axis. In June, 1944, the complete embargo on wolfram was finally secured.

---

[27] Churchill, Winston, *The Second World War: The Hinge of Fate*, London, 1951, Vol. IV, p. 705. There was actually a projected assault on the Portuguese islands in the event of necessity, under the code name of *Lifebelt* (*ibid.*, p. 748).

[28] Hull, Cordell, *The Memoirs of Cordell Hull*, London, 1948, Vol. II, p. 1335.

There was certainly no thought in the minds of the allied statesmen that the hesitations or reservations displayed by the Portuguese government could possibly be sympathy for the Axis cause as such and much less a moral intelligence with Nazism. As severe a critic of dictatorship — and especially of the Iberian variety — as the British ambassador in Madrid, Sir Samuel Hoare, writes feelingly that "it is sufficient to say that Salazar never left a doubt in my mind as to his desire for a Nazi defeat, or his unshakable belief in the fundamental principles of European civilization."[29]

The problem of leasing the Portuguese islands was another matter of paramount importance to the Allies. Early in 1943 the American government was convinced that the main body of the Portuguese army was in the Azores and that the very real danger existed of a German invasion of the mainland. Conversations had taken place with Brazil, as they had regarding the wolfram affair, to the end that should Germany invade Portugal, Brazil should garrison the Azores and other islands to prevent their falling into Nazi hands.[30] The negotiations for the cession of facilities in the islands have been published *in extenso* by the Portuguese government, from the communication of the British ambassador in Lisbon, Sir Ronald H. Campbell, on June 16, 1943, to Premier Salazar, until the conclusion of the agreements.[31] Every aspect of the current problem was examined, in the light of the North African invasion and the greater capacity of the Allies to give Portugal effective assistance in the event of invasion. "His Majesty's Government have reviewed the situation in the light of the facts. . . . They have come to the conclusion that the use of facilities in the Portuguese Atlantic Islands, particularly in the Azores . . . would be a decisive factor in the early defeat of the German submarine campaign . . . and consequently a vital contribution to an early victory of the United Na-

---

[29] Hoare, Rt. Hon. Sir Samuel Viscount Templewood, *Complacent Dictator*, New York, 1947, p. 112. The two pages in this work devoted to the interview with Salazar are full of praise and admiration for the Portuguese leader with his urbanity, graciousness, humanity, and "encyclopedic knowledge of Europe." It was precisely this encyclopedic knowledge that prevented Salazar, during the war years, from oversimplifying complex issues.

[30] Hull, Cordell, *op. cit.*, Vol. II, p. 1339.

[31] *Documentos relativos aos accordos entre Portugal Inglaterra e Estados Unidos da America para a concessão de facilidades nos Açores durante a guerra de 1939–1945*, Lisbon, 1946, published by the Ministry of Foreign Affairs of Portugal.

tions."[32] Salazar accepted in principle and insisted that other governments, especially the United States, join in the guarantee to the Portuguese possessions in the Far East. This, of course, was because of the Japanese aggression in Timor. On August 17, 1943, the agreement was entered into by Portugal with Great Britain but not with the United Nations as a whole. It was clear that Salazar found it far more reasonable to grant facilities to an ally rather than to a grand alliance or to the United States, with which Portugal had no diplomatic ties of any special character. The Americans were especially keen about securing bases for the construction of the type of air facilities needed for the prosecution of the war. On November 28, 1944, United States Ambassador R. Henry Norweb communicated to the Foreign Office the willingness of the United States to accept the participation of Portugal in the liberation of Timor "recognizing that this Portuguese territory lies within the large area of operations undertaken in the Pacific."[33] This was linked to the concession on the island of Santa Maria in the Azores for the facilitation of the movement of armed forces to the various war theaters. Finally, in November, 1944, this arrangement was completed to terminate six months after the conclusion of hostilities. Cordell Hull has stressed the fact that allied pressure on Portugal was exerted at a distance, whereas the Germans were on the Pyrenees and that, in spite of this, the flow of strategic materials from Portugal to the Allies was far larger than that which went to the Axis.[34]

The end of the war relieved Portugal, as it did all neutrals, of the terrifying possibility that war would overwhelm them. The Portuguese had accept the Allied landing in North Africa with serenity and had watched the ebbing fortunes of the Axis with what must have been indescribable relief. The years since 1945 may be summarized very rapidly. Portugal, like Spain, Ireland, Italy, and a number of others, was left in outer darkness when the United

---

[32] *Ibid.*, p. 3. Portugal's attitude during the war may be compared to that of Spain, one of "benevolent neutrality" toward the Allies. Salazar stated in a speech to the National Assembly on May 8, 1945, that "The active guard of the key positions of the Atlantic, the concession of bases in the Azores, with many other related and reciprocal services, the greater and best part of our economy in the service of the Allies, financial assistance, transatlantic shipping made this neutrality a collaborationist neutrality" (Salazar, *Portugal and the Peace*, Lisbon, 1945, p. 15).

[33] *Documentos . . . 1939–1945, op. cit.*, p. 41.

[34] Hull, *op. cit.*, Vol. II, pp. 1343–1344.

Nations was formed and, although never submitted to the same virulent attack as was the Madrid government, nevertheless the stigma of "fascism" was attached to the Salazar government. In the years immediately following the war, Portugal suffered a number of economic reverses: the poor sardine catch, a disastrous wheat crop, and her balance-of-payments problem became acute. The European Recovery Program was one way of relieving this distress and Portugal was among the sixteen nations invited in July, 1947, to the Paris meeting for European Economic Cooperation. In the autumn of 1948, the Portuguese government submitted a program covering a four-year period and asked for a sum necessary to cover the anticipated balance of payments deficit to 1950.[35]

In addition to this economic collaboration, Portugal's ties with the West have been strengthened by various bilateral and multilateral defense agreements. Various aviation agreements were signed in 1948, and in 1949 negotiations were undertaken to associate Portugal with the North Atlantic Pact, culminating in the formal adherence of Portugal to this combination on April 4, 1949.[36] Five years later, when the anniversary of the Pact was celebrated in Lisbon, Foreign Minister Dr. Paulo Cunha hailed it as a cornerstone of Portuguese foreign policy and an indispensable contribution to the welfare of the free world.[37] In September, 1951, Portugal signed with the United States a new agreement for certain rights in the Azores and it is expected that this will provide for their use by the North Atlantic Treaty powers in the event of hostilities. War matériel from the United States, under the Mutual Defense Assistance program, has included aircraft, aeronautic instruments, and other forms of aid

[35] *Foreign Policy Reports*, "Spain and Portugal — a Dilemma for the West," by Olive Holmes, New York, Vol. XXV, No. 4, May 1, 1949, pp. 49–50.

[36] Address of Premier Salazar to the National Assembly, July 25, 1949, on the Atlantic Pact. Published in French in pamphlet entitled, *La Pensée de Salazar. Le Portugal et le Pacte de l'Atlantique*, Lisbon, 1949. In this speech Salazar analyzes the pact from the point of view of Portugal's traditional policy and notes candidly in passing that "Although we are obligated by the terms of the Pact and its general end, but not by the ideological affirmations that have been expressed to the end of making the political regimes of the member states uniform." In other words, Portugal is willing to commit itself internationally but has no intention of submitting to political influences from outside to the vain effort to shape and modify her regime to meet the demands of other members who consider it a dictatorship.

[37] *Portugal. Bulletin of Political, Economic and Cultural Information*, Lisbon, March–April, 1954, p. 22.

of a technical character. A three-year military expenditure program substantially larger than in the past was announced in 1951 as well as an increase in the army to place Portugal in a more advantageous position from the point of view of its commitments under the pact.

The admission of both Spain and Portugal to the United Nations and the agreements between the United States and the Madrid governments have, to be sure, completely changed the situation as regards the West. The result has been an intensification of Hispano-Portuguese ties, as evidenced by the state visit to Spain, in 1953, of President Craveiro Lopes.[38]

The latest step on the part of co-operation by Portugal has been the placing at the disposal of the United States and the other Western powers of two strategically situated air bases on metropolitan territory. Col. Fernando Santo Costa, Minister of Defense, announced on June 29, 1956, that the two bases of Montijo and Espinho would be expanded and made available to the NATO nations. In view of the danger to the Keflavik base in Iceland and the uncertainty of the situation in North Africa, Portugal becomes a key position in the whole scheme of Atlantic defense. The United States, at the same time, was negotiating for the renewal of the ten-year agreement, expiring in September, 1956, which entitles the Americans to build and maintain bases in the Azores.[39]

Portuguese interests, as indicated at the beginning of this chapter, reach out in all directions, embracing four of the continents. The political independence of Brazil has not diminished the strong bonds of solidarity that the Portuguese have always maintained with the former colony, and this cordiality has been heartily reciprocated. There have been astonishingly few incidents of discord between the two countries and aside from the minor frictions, which take such undramatic forms as a common orthography for the Portuguese language or customs duties on Portuguese translations of foreign books into Brazil, the contacts between the two have evolved harmoniously. The visit of former President Café Filho to Portugal and the more recent one of President Juscelino Kubitschek de Oliveira attest to the feeling that Portugal is still the cultural and

---

[38] *Portugal. Bulletin of Political, Economic and Cultural Information*, Lisbon, May–June, 1953.

[39] *The New York Times*, June 30, 1956.

spiritual center of the Portuguese-speaking world. A steady stream of Brazilian visitors find their way to Portugal and keep alive this sense of continuity.

Portugal, with its less than nine million people in Europe, is the center of the Portuguese world which culturally, linguistically, and spiritually includes not only the empire whose general character we have described, but Brazil with its territory covering half of South America and representing 50 million Portuguese-speaking people.

Chapter X

CHURCH, STATE, AND RELIGION

"There are some who surmise that in these mundane conflicts, there are other than human forces engaged, and to one who examines the matter curiously, what happened in Russia in 1917 may yet be counterbalanced by something that happened in Portugal the same year, an event that is still having powerful repercussions."

Alan Gordon Smith, The Western Dilemma, *London, 1954, pp. 183–184.*

No account of the evolution of Portugal to what it is today would be complete, or anywhere near complete, unless some attention were devoted to the revival of religion, the reintegration of the Portuguese people into their traditional Catholic background, the harmonization of relations with the Holy See, and, above all, the impact on the nation of the extraordinary event at Fatima in 1917.

In the atmosphere of the persecution that followed the separation in 1910 and the prevalence of a type of Jacobinism that recalled the France of the worst anticlerical moments of the nineteenth century, the Church began gradually to adjust to the new circumstances. The disestablishment and seizure of properties posed novel problems for the hierarchy and it is not easy for a religious institution of long tradition in the country to reorient its economic life along strictly private lines overnight. Even before the National Revolution with its encouraging reaction to anticlerical extremism, and much before the Concordat of 1940 which brought peace to the Portuguese Church, there were many signs of stirrings in the liturgical movement, popular devotions, and propaganda on behalf of the faith. The liturgical congresses of Vila Real in 1926 and Braga in 1928 contributed to an intensification of the appreciation of the liturgy and, above all, focused attention on the reform and re-establishment of the very ancient and special rite belonging to Braga.[1]

Even in the nineteenth century, when the winds of liberalism and the effects of the Pombaline reform were still felt, Portuguese Catholics had given lively evidence of their faith and especially of their attachment to Rome and the teachings of the Holy See. Much later, Premier Salazar could say that in all its Christian history, Portugal had never given birth to a major heresy nor had it fallen into collective schism of any kind. When Pius IX submitted the question of the proclamation of the dogma of the Immaculate Conception to the bishops of the world, the Portuguese were unanimous in supporting the initiative. In 1873 the cornerstone was laid for a national monument in commemoration of the proclamation of the dogma of papal infallibility. Popular associations sprang up over the country as relations between the State and the Church worsened. The Apostolate of Prayer, inaugurated in Lisbon by Father António Marcocci, was a powerful influence in villages and towns all over the land in the restoration of popular piety.

The hope for the restoration of the spiritual health of Portugal seemed remote in those years when a raucous, shrill, taunting republicanism brought pressure to bear on every form of Christian life in the effort to impose a social order in conformity with the thought of Auguste Comte. It was a far throw from the age when Portugal had raised up saints and produced missioners by the hundreds for the hazardous task of spreading the faith beyond the seas.

Suppose we turn for a moment from the Church in chains to the men and women of Portugal who have been raised to the honor of the altars. Everyone is familiar with St. Anthony of Padua, who might far more properly be called St. Anthony of Lisbon

[1] Coelho, António, O.S.B. (1892–1938), directed the liturgical review *Opus Dei* and published a five-volume work, *Curso de liturgia romana* (Braga, 1926–1930), which won international praise.

for it was in the Portuguese capital that he was born, supposedly in 1190 or 1195.[2] His teaching and work as a Franciscan scarcely need repetition. He is considered the patron saint of Portugal, although a good part of his life was spent at Padua and in the Italian universities of the time.

The Blessed Teresa, Sancha, and Mafalda form a fascinating trinity in the narrow world of the specially chosen of God. The devotion to them is deep in the spiritual practice of the Portuguese people and dates from the thirteenth century when these three daughters of Sancho I all died in the odor of sanctity. Teresa was the wife of Alfonso XI of León, by whom she had three children. In later life she entered the convent at Lorvao and took the Cistercian habit, dying in 1250. Her sister, Sancha, entered the convent of Cela which she herself had founded, and died in 1229 — while the last of the three, Mafalda, wedded to Henry I of Castile, returned to Portugal to become a religious. It was Pope Clement XI in 1705 who confirmed the validity of the devotion to Teresa and Sancha and later, in the same century, the Sacred Congregation of Rites confirmed the same privileges for Mafalda.

The most striking of Portugal's saints was unquestionably the great St. Elizabeth, daughter of Pedro III of Aragon, who was married in 1281 to Diniz, King of Portugal. A widow in 1325, she took up residence near the Santa Clara convent in Coimbra without becoming a professed religious. Her exemplary life as wife and mother and her infinite compassion for the wretched and miserable had won her a reputation for saintliness. She was beatified in 1516 and canonized by Urban VIII in 1625.[3]

St. John Brito was born in Lisbon in 1647 and in 1673 embarked for India where he spent years in the work of conversion. Sent to the Malabar coast in 1674, it was in the Maduré mission that St. John realized his most notable work. He was reputed to have made 12,000 conversions in a period of ten days and a prince of Maravá, who had become interested in Christianity, implored the great missionary to cure him of an ailment that had defied all treatment. John Brito performed the cure and the prince was converted but

---

[2] Lopes, Fernando Félix, *Santo António de Lisboa, Doutor Evangélico*, Braga, 1946.

[3] Vasconcelos, António de, *Evolução do culto de Dona Isabel de Aragão*, Coimbra, 1894, 2 vols.

intrigue eventually led to John's imprisonment and martyrdom in 1693. He was beatified by Pope Pius IX in 1852 and on June 22, 1947, he was canonized by His Holiness Pope Pius XII.[4]

But to return from this digression to the thread of our narrative regarding the situation of the Church prior to the restoration of political and social normality. Many of the great traditions of Portuguese piety such as the Corpus Christi processions were suspended during this period of darkness and it was in the midst of the greatest tribulation, of local persecution and the World War, that the Blessed Virgin appeared to the three children at the Cova de Iria. Of this stupendous event we shall say something a little later.

The official secularism of the Republican regime tended quite naturally to deprive the Church of many of the charity functions which had been its traditional task. Many of the social services in its hands were now laicized, although the religious institutions and especially the communities continued, to the best of their ability, to carry on this mission. The work of the secular clergy was distinguished by two outstanding enterprises: the *Oficina de São José* in Porto and the *Colegio da Regeneração* in Braga. The first of these two foundations was directed for years by Sebastião Leite de Vasconcelos, later Bishop of Beja, and destined for instruction in the trades and crafts as well as the religious formation of abandoned children. Dating from 1884, this foundation was imitated by similar ones in several other Portuguese cities. The *Colegia da Regeneração* was founded in 1869 and had as its purpose the rehabilitation of prostitutes.

During the days of the monarchy, the Catholic interests of Portugal had never been properly organized except at the parish and, at the most, the diocesan level. A few vague attempts in the direction of creating a national organism had been made, notably in the *Centro Nacional* in 1894, the purpose of which was the diffusion of the social teachings of Leo XIII. The Catholic Congress of 1903

---

[4] On April 27, 1947, over the National Broadcasting service, His Eminence Cardinal Cerejeira exalted the work of St. John Brito on the occasion of his canonization. "Saint John Brito is the synthesis of the missionary work of Portugal itself. The destiny of both the Saint and of Portugal are the same. The canonization of Saint John Brito assumes, therefore, the character of a national event of the first importance" (*Avante*. Organ of Catholic Action of Goa, Nova Goa, September, 1947, Vol. I, No. 12, pp. 381–382).

in Porto undertook to revive this movement or something similar in view of the hostility of the State, even at that time, to the religious orders. The atmosphere was definitely not propitious, during the stormy decade that preceded the fall of the monarchy, for the institution of a Catholic political party or even of a movement with influence on political life.

One of the earlier manifestations of the sentiment of need for organization outside politics was the *Associação Católica*, formed in Porto in 1872 under the direction of Conde de Samodães and Visconde de Azevedo. This organization was in response to the rapid spread of secularist ideas in the country after the usurpation by the united Italy of the temporal sovereignty of the Church. The Association was expanded elsewhere in Portugal and was responsible for a number of congresses, including the Marian in 1904. The seventh centenary of St. Anthony led to an international congress in Lisbon in 1895, and out of it grew the society "Os amigos de Santo António" which founded, in Porto, the *Círculo Católico de Operários*. In protest against the restrictions on the religious congregations, the Catholic students of Coimbra founded, in 1903, the *Centro Académico de Democracia Cristã*. Since 1922 the group has published the review *Estudos*. In 1902 the *Associação promotora da Educação e Instrução Popular* was founded in Lisbon, to become, a few years later, the *Liga de Acção social Cristã*. Out of this grew the women's organization and various others which have since constituted Portuguese Catholic Action. After 1910 the necessity was imperative for the defense of the most vital interests of the Church and the bishops insisted in their pastorals on the need for united action and constant vigilance in the face of the hostility of the State. In 1913 the *União Católica* was established, and two years later the *Centro Católico português*, with the result that in the elections of 1915 Catholics were represented as such in parliament, with António Augusto de Castro Meireles a deputy and António José da Silva Gonçalves in the Senate. The Center enjoyed the support of the Portuguese bishops and from time to time was attacked violently by certain of the monarchist factions. The situation in these years between 1915 and 1920 in Portugal was quite similar in many ways to that in Spain after the advent of the Second Republic in 1931; that is, the Catholics were faced by the problem of what attitude to take toward the State as an institution. Was its republicanism of such a nature that no remedy could be reasonably sought except the return to the monarchy, or was there a chance that under the republican order, Catholics could introduce the type of modification they desired without affecting the basic structure of the State? In every election in which the Center took part, it elected at least one deputy. The reappearance of the daily newspaper *Novidades* in 1923, as an organ of Catholic opinion, was one of the most significant achievements in making Catholic expression effective.

The nineteenth century is filled with complaints from the highest ecclesiastical sources regarding the decline of religious institutions and the meager influence of the episcopacy and clergy on the affairs of the country. The bishops lamented in 1862 that the situation was distinguished by "decadence and depression," and Pope Pius IX, in a message to Portugal, expressed his deep sorrow over the "deplorable state of the Church in that land."[5] The improvement toward the end of the century was largely the result of the apostolic zeal of such eminent prelates as Cardinal Américo Ferreira dos Santos Silva (1830–1890) and Cardinal José Sebastião Neto (1841–1920). In the present century the number of pastorals from members of the hierarchy has increased and its influence in general become more evident, thanks to the synods of Braga and Coimbra in 1918 and 1923, respectively, and the Plenary Council for all Portugal in 1926.

The Revolution brought a truce and, as we have already noted, a change of atmosphere regarding the Church. The new leaders were not sectarian fanatics nor philosophical secularists. They understood perfectly that there was no sense in suppressing the Church in a country where it had held sway for centuries. The culminating note of the whole period and the greatest achievement of the present regime *in re* the Church is the Concordat of 1940, a fundamental document which arranged the definitive peace between the two authorities.

The Constitution of 1933 specifies, in Article 45, that "Public or private worship of all religions is free, with liberty of organization in accordance with the norms of law and order, and for the formation of organizations which the State recognizes legally." Article 46 states that the regime of separation of Church and State is

[5] Oliveira, Manuel de, *História eclesiástica de Portugal*, *op. cit.*, p. 391.

maintained with reference to the Catholic Church and any other religion or religious group in Portuguese territory. Diplomatic relations with the Holy See are established. Moreover no church, temple, or other ecclesiastical edifice can be destined by the State for a nonreligious purpose. Cemeteries are secularized and burial services of any religion may take place in them.[6]

The law of separation — which is retained in the new constitution — had deprived the Church integrally of almost all its properties, in a manner as drastic as that of France. From 1910 on, the Church had been obliged to reorganize its corporate life from the bottom up. The new constitution, while retaining this important item of the old, was inspired by a very different spirit "completely opposed to the hostility that had marked the separation in the document of 1911."

The Concordat of May 7, 1940, canceled out the discriminatory features of the former legislation and paved the way for a normal, healthy growth of the Church.[7] Salazar explained clearly the purpose of the new agreement with his customary clarity: "We had no intention of simply righting the wrong that had been done for over the last thirty years but to go much further and in the return to the best tradition, reintegrate in this respect Portugal on the classical course of its historical destiny. We return, with all the force of a nation reborn, to the great source of our national life . . . and without any sacrifice of the material progress of our time, we aim to place ourselves on the same spiritual level as eight centuries ago."[8]

The Concordat recognizes the legal personality of the Church and guarantees it full liberty of worship, organization, and administration. Provision is made for religious care in public institutions and in the armed forces. The organization and maintenance of private schools is recognized as legitimate, and in the state institutions Catholic doctrine and moral principles are taught. Catholic

---

[6] *Constituição política da República portuguesa*, Lisbon, 1948, Title X, Articles 45–48.

[7] Pérez Mier, Laureano, *Sistemas de dotación de la Iglesia Católica*, Salamanca, 1949, p. 242.

[8] Text of the Concordat in *Concordata e accôrdo missionário de 7 de maio de 1940* (Secretariate of National Propaganda, Lisbon, 1943). Comment in Amedeo Giannini, "Il concordato portoghese," *Rivista di Studi Politici Internazionali*, Florence, Vol. X, 1943.

marriages are recognized by the civil authority. The properties that had been taken from the Church are restored. Exemption from taxation is provided for seminaries, churches, and ecclesiastics in the performance of their duty. Provision is also made for the Portuguese nationality of a certain number of the ecclesiastical functionaries. The Holy See, before making an episcopal appointment, communicates the name of the proposed candidate to the government and a period of thirty days is allowed for the presentation of any objections.

As to the economic arrangement, Article V of the Concordat provides that "The Church is free to carry out among the faithful collections of any kind or impose any contribution it may wish for the carrying out of its purposes, in the interior or exterior of the churches or in any building that belongs to it." It is therefore clear that the Portuguese State does not underwrite or subvent in any way the Church in Portugal or its ministers, nor has the Church been compensated for the properties seized during the confiscations of the nineteenth century or after 1910. The State accepts no obligation to aid the Church or even to urge the citizenry to support it financially. Cardinal Cerejeira expressly emphasized that from the economic point of view the Church got nothing. The Church in Portugal continues to live exclusively on the generosity of the faithful. A Protestant writer has noted in this respect that "There is no State Church, union of Church and State or public subsidy to the Church as such in the home country (Portugal)."[9]

The Concordat further provides for the ecclesiastical organization of the country in three archbishoprics with their suffragan dioceses, a total of eighteen dioceses.[10] The Concordat was the crowning feature in the Catholic renaissance. As we have noted, during the entire decade of the 1930's, there had been a steady improvement not only in the effective apostolate of the Church, but especially in the number and variety of Catholic organizations that were being founded. Portuguese Catholic Action as such was established by the hierarchy in 1933, divided as it is in the European countries into the four branches and in 1947 had some eighty to

[9] Bates, M. Searle, *Religious Liberty: an Inquiry*, New York and London, 1945, p. 97.

[10] The best single source for information regarding Catholic life in Portugal is the *Anuario Católico de Portugal*, Lisbon, 1947, and the more recent edition, 1953.

ninety thousand members, affiliated with over 3500 local sections.

Of considerable interest is the status of the Church in the Portuguese overseas world. The "Missionary Agreement" that accompanies the Concordat fixes the situation outside the continent with considerable precision. On September 4, 1940, the bull *Sollemnibus Conventionibus* established the ecclesiastical divisions overseas. Certain readjustments were made in Africa such as the separation of Portuguese Guinea from dependence on the Cape Verde Islands and in the Far East, the Archdiocese of Damão was made the center to which Cochim, S. Tomé de Meliapor, Macau, and Timor were suffragan. The traditional Padroado was retained in part, even outside the Portuguese possessions themselves in certain limited cases.

The major problem posed in Africa and Asia, however, is not one of organization; it is rather the identification of "national mission" and "spiritual mission" which has annoyed a number of non-Catholic commentators. The *Colonial Act* in Article 23 states that "The State guarantees liberty of conscience in its overseas territories and freedom of worship, the only limitation being the rights and interest of Portuguese sovereignty, the maintenance of public order and conformity with international conventions." In the following article (24) it is provided very clearly that "The Portuguese Catholic missions overseas, as agencies of civilization and national influence and the establishments for the formation of personnel for their service and that of the Portuguese *Padroado*, shall enjoy all legal rights and shall be protected and aided by the State as teaching institutions."[11]

Cardinal Cerejeira called this agreement "a splendid tribute of confidence on the part of the Holy See in the missionary effort of Portugal."[12] It was preceded by other legal dispositions such as the *Estatuto Orgánico das Missões Católicas Portuguesas* of 1926 in which the principle of State support for the missionary is recognized. In many ways the experience of Portugal follows the same line as that of France, in which anticlerical governments at home were not particularly disinclined to maintain the tradition of support

---

[11] *Constituição política*, *op. cit.*, p. 69. See also "Survey of Portuguese Catholicism" in *Informations Catholiques Internationales*, Paris, February 15, 1957, p. 18.

[12] Quoted in Oliveira, *op. cit.*, p. 402.

of Catholic missions in the colonial areas, construing them undoubtedly as important and vital agents for the maintenance of European prestige and national influence.

Here again we are up against the problem of fundamental cultural assimilation as opposed to "adaptation" on the part of the missionary to the milieu in which he finds himself. The Portuguese unquestionably have conceived of their mission task as that of lifting the aborigine up from his present state through the spread of the Catholic faith and with it Portuguese culture which will provide a window on the world and an opportunity for spiritual and intellectual expansion.

The Accord provides further that if the number of Portuguese missionaries is insufficient, the ordinaries may, by agreement with the Holy See and Lisbon, call in foreigners. Recognized missionary agencies are to be subsidized by both the metropolitan and provincial governments overseas. Provision is also made for the granting of lands and other facilities to the missions. The training of missionaries, their travel, and other details of their activity will be provided for at State expense. The Holy See has especially recommended the *União Missionária do Clero* and the *Sociedade Portuguesa das Missões Católicas Ultramarinas* in the encyclical *Saeculo exeunte octavo* that every effort be made to imitate the glories of those ages when Portuguese missionaries bore the brunt of propagating the Christian faith.[13]

An interesting problem and one that has been raised from time to time is that of the non-Catholic missions in the Portuguese territories outside Europe. They operate in the African territories primarily and according to Protestant sources, have suffered from "deliberate hindrance, discrimination and persecution through a long period of years."[14] They have made use of the possibilities of protection of the various treaties and agreements into which the major powers have entered and which protect the interests of foreign missionaries laboring in the field. The Berlin Act of 1885, the Brussels Act of 1890, and the Anglo-Portuguese Treaty of 1891 provide that religious activity shall be free and untrammeled and in the case of the last-mentioned document, that the missionaries of each shall be granted the right to full protection. The postwar

[13] *Novidades*, Lisbon, July 2, 1940.
[14] Bates, M. Searle, *op. cit.*, p. 99.

settlement of 1919, while modifying some of the previous agreements, retained the guarantees in principle. The listing of grievances, particularly in the two large territories of Angola and Mozambique, includes such items as the following:

1. Exemption from duties and other burdens of the Catholic, but not the Protestant missions;
2. Difficulties in securing permits to open new stations;
3. Refusal of authorities to recognize, in some cases, Protestant marriages;
4. Action on the part of authorities to prevent attendance at Protestant schools;
5. Protestant missions must provide at own expense teachers of Portuguese;
6. Discrimination against Protestant Africans in government service, higher schools, etc.

Aside from the specific charges, the principal consideration is the fundamental problem of the theory behind the Portuguese action. It is not, perhaps, easy to convince the non-Catholic that any area where preference is shown for Catholic mission activity is not necessarily obscurantist and hopelessly backward. Progress spiritually is not necessarily equated with multiplicity of sectarian missions. The national unity that springs from the retention of the common Catholic faith is something very precious to the Portuguese as a people and they are loath to introduce in the more backward parts of the empire the variety of religious experiences which can very easily militate against the solidarity which is their aim. Portugal may be wrong in thinking that it has a mission in the world and that in the overseas territories it is responsible for the elevation of the moral and intellectual tone of the native population. But if the nation does not abdicate, there is a certain logic in giving preference to what is, for all purposes, although not formally proclaimed so, the religion of the overwhelming majority of the Portuguese people. In sound democracy, this majority is sufficiently impressive to justify the application of a policy which undoubtedly meets with the approval of all but a tiny minority of the nation.

That this is understandable and even reasonable may be adduced from a comparable experience on the Protestant side. I cite the case of Greenland which, from the geographical and human point of view, may seem far removed from the regions about which I have been writing. But the analogy is very close. Denmark rules Greenland as a colony and recently, by the legislation of 1950, has provided for representation of the Greenlanders and a general liberalization of what has been heretofore a fairly closed corporation. Nevertheless, the education in Greenland for the native population is Lutheran, and the country has been literally handed over, in matters of spiritual guidance, to the Lutheran Church under the direction of the Bishop of Copenhagen. Does one suppose that Denmark would view with enthusiasm the proposal that Catholic missionaries be admitted to Greenland and carry on their activities in precisely the same manner as the Danish Lutherans? This is the case of a non-European community governed by a European state, where religion, education, and political administration are so intertwined that it is difficult to separate one from the other. There can be little question that the Danish regime in Greenland has profited from the Danish Lutheran monopoly in terms of strengthening the attachment of the island's population to Denmark itself.[15]

The identification of missionaries with their country of origin is by no means a Catholic monopoly. All over the mission world, Protestant missions from the United States and Great Britain cling with an astonishing tenacity to their national character and I can speak from some personal experience of the dozens of "American schools" in South America which are centers of evangelical activity and adhere at the same time very definitely to their American character. The Portuguese can scarcely be blamed if, in their view, the wisest policy is to so act as to make of the territories overseas harmonious units of the empire and in furthering this end to prefer that the same religious influence which shaped their own history be diffused in their possessions.

This is neither the place nor the occasion to recount the now

[15] In *Skolevaesenet kirken og andre kulturelle forhold*, Copenhagen, February, 1950, a publication of the Greenland Commission, we have an account of the connection of the Church in the colony and education. Also *Greenland*, Copenhagen, published by the Royal Danish Ministry for Foreign Affairs; article, by Eske Brun, "The Greenland Administration." "The 1950 legislation also includes an act relating to the Greenland Church and one on education. Pending the implementation of these, Greenland education is administered by the Church" (p. 40). In the official report on Greenland for 1954, *Report on Greenland*, published by the Greenland Department of the Danish Government, it is noted that the schools have been detached from the exclusive supervision of the Church but that the board managing them includes the Dean of Greenland, an ecclesiastic, and that religion (Lutheran) is a part of the curriculum.

well-known apparitions at Fatima in 1917 and their import for all mankind. In the preface of his deeply moving account of Fatima, the late William Thomas Walsh asks: "Why should she (the Blessed Virgin) have appeared in Portugal in 1917, and in such a deserted and inaccessible place as the Serra da Aire? . . . The Portuguese have an idea that they were favored partly, at least, because their country has always been called *a terra de Santa Maria* and in the Serra about Fatima, regardless of revolutions and apostasies in other places, the poor have clung for centuries with unwavering devotion to the recitation of her Rosary."[16]

Father C. C. Martindale has recalled how the history of Portugal is interwoven with devotion to our Blessed Lady: "A real substantial fact that went to the creation of Portugal and also was productive of legends, was devotion to our Lady."[17] It is perhaps bad history but popular legend that Afonso Henriques, who carved out medieval Portugal, was born a cripple and miraculously cured by our Lady. In the long story of Portugal's glory and her misery that we have recounted in the preceding pages, how often the hand of God seems to have been specially lifted on behalf of this small, tenacious, and, in spite of buffetings and deviations, essentially pious people. It was on the eve of the feast of the Assumption that the armies fought at Aljubarrota and before this event Nun' Álvares, since beatified, prayed to our Lady for Portugal and her cause.[18] Boniface IX declared all the cathedrals of Portugal dedicated to our Lady and the Immaculate Conception was the special devotion of the Braganças.[19]

Pope Benedict XV in a reply to the Portuguese hierarchy in 1918 wrote that he could not believe that the spiritual depression of the Church in Portugal would continue but that on the contrary he was filled with hope for the future. "This hope is confirmed by our knowledge of the burning love for the Immaculate Virgin for which this portion of the Lord's flock is so greatly renowned."[20]

---

[16] Walsh, William Thomas, *Our Lady of Fatima,* New York, 1949, p. vii.

[17] Martindale, C. C., S.J., *The Meaning of Fatima,* New York, 1950, pp. 11–12.

[18] *Acta Apostolica Sedis,* Vol. V, 1918, p. 102.

[19] John IV proclaims his confidence in the Immaculate Conception and proposes the formal recognition of Our Lady Immaculate as Patroness of Portugal. Ryan, Archbishop Finbar, *Our Lady of Fatima,* Dublin, 1948, p. 25.

[20] Barthas, C., and Fonseca, G. da, *Our Lady of Light,* Milwaukee, 1947, p. 2.

Coming a year after the great event at Fatima, there was more than ordinary prophecy in these words of the Supreme Pontiff. It was Pope Benedict XV who, torn by sorrow at the conflagration devouring the world in 1917, urged a crusade of prayer and the invocation, "Queen of Peace, pray for us." This was dated May 5, 1917, and eight days later three little shepherds in Portugal saw in amazement Our Lady of the Rosary appear to them.[21] Pope Pius XI confirmed once more the patronage of our Lady over Portugal in 1936 and ten years later her statue at Fatima was solemnly crowned in commemoration of the third centenary of the consecration of Portugal to her.

Fatima, as everyone knows who has been there, is a parched, dry, barren piece of land which, in its desolation, reminds one of that other land across the Mediterranean which was so specially the chosen of God. The Blessed Virgin seems to have frequently evidenced a predilection for deserts or, at least, spots on the earth's surface which were far from lush or delectable to the eye. There was the land of Palestine itself; there was that stony hillock called Tepeyac in Mexico, and there is Fatima, all arid and uninviting.

The message of Fatima has embraced the whole world and in the revelations transmitted to the three children, the future of mankind is, in effect, outlined. Portugal itself could not but feel the consequences of this transcendental event that took place on its soil and that at first shook the torpor of believers and stunned those who would not believe. The hidden miracle of Fatima has changed the face of the Portuguese nation, not by spectacular cures or sudden recoveries as in the case of some of the maimed and the diseased, but the subtle infiltration of a new spirit in the hearts of both the humble classes and the leadership of the nation. "For years Our Lady of Fatima has been touching the hearts of the Portuguese people from the humblest to the most cultivated, and it would seem, most particularly the cultivated."[22] There is something deeply moving in the accounts of how Jacinta, one of the three, became singularly devoted in her prayers to the intentions

---

[21] Ryan, *op. cit.*, pp. 25–26.

[22] Figueiredo, Antero de, *Fátima. Graça, segredos, mistérios*, Lisbon, 1936, pp. 320–321.

of the Holy Father and insisted on the need for constant supplications on his behalf and on behalf of Portugal.[23]

And would it not be proper to see in this an extraordinary coincidence that a place called Fatima, whose name the Blessed Virgin has taken, is of Moslem origin, and was the name of a daughter of the Prophet. How much one may hope that in the mysterious designs of God, this link in nomenclature may yet serve as the bridge by which the Christian world may establish dialogue with Islam.[24]

But whatever may be the ultimate repercussions of what three children saw at the Cova de Iria that May day in 1917, Portugal itself will never again be the same. "A whole nation has been shaken out of its torpor and touched by a supernatural wave."[25] There can be little doubt that this grandiose manifestation of the supernatural was in a very real sense the response of Heaven to what was transpiring in Portugal during those tragic years after 1910.[26] But whatever may be the case, Fatima has transformed Portugal and it was on a barren Portuguese hillside that the Blessed Virgin revealed the secret of the future.

---

[23] Oliveira, José Galamba da, *Jacinta. Episódios inéditos das aparições de Nossa Senhora*, Fatima, 1942, p. 157.

[24] Marchi, João De, *Era uma Senhora mais brilhante que o sol*, Cova de Iria, n.d., p. 21.

[25] Moresco, Luigi, *Gli occhi che videro la Madonna*, Rome, 1942, p. 18.

[26] Fischer, L., *Fátima, a Lourdes portuguesa*, Lisbon, 1930, p. 44.

BIBLIOGRAPHY

THE following bibliography is far from what could be called "exhaustive." It includes a number of works on some of the major topics treated with reference to Portugal and the Portuguese world. Some of the books, articles, and other sources cited in the footnotes are not repeated here to avoid making the bibliographical index overly long.

GENERAL

The formation of Portugal. The Middle Ages and early modern period. General histories and accounts of the country and people.

Almeida, Fortunato de, *História de Portugal*, Coimbra, 1922–1929, 6 vols.

Almeida, João de, *O fundo atlante da raça portuguesa e a sua evolução histórica*, Lisbon, 1950.

Ameal, João, *Bref résumé de l'histoire du Portugal* (translation by Jean Bayle), Lisbon, n.d.

——— *História de Portugal*, Porto, 1940.

Azevedo, J. Lucio de, *Epocas de Portugal Económico*, Lisbon, 1929.

Azevedo, Luiz Gonzaga de, *História de Portugal*, Lisbon, 1935–1942, 5 vols.

Barbera, Martín Domingues, *Caminos de Portugal*, Madrid, 1944.

Bataillon, Marcel, *Etudes sur le Portugal au temps de l'humanisme*, Coimbra, 1952.

Bell, A. T. G., *In Portugal*, London, 1912.

——— *Portugal of the Portuguese*, London, 1915.

——— *Portuguese portraits*, Oxford, 1917.

Birot, Pierre, *Le Portugal*, Paris, 1950.

Bridge, Ann, and Lowndes, Susan, *The Selective Traveller in Portugal*, London, 1949.

Carnarvon, Herbert, Earl of, *Portugal and Gallicia*, London, 1837, 2 vols.

Carqueja, B., *La population de Portugal. Le Portugal et son activité économique*, Lisbon, 1932.

——— *O povo português*, Porto, 1916.

Carvalho, Joaquim de, *Estudos sobre a cultura portuguesa de século XV*, Coimbra, 1949.

——— *Estudos sobre a cultura portuguesa do século XVI*, Coimbra, 1947–1948, 2 vols.

Casanovas, Francis de, *Le peuple portugais et ses caractéristiques sociales*, Lisbon, 1937.

Castro, José Ferreira Borges de, *Collecção dos tratados, convenções contratas e actos públicos desde 1640 até o presente*, Lisbon, 1856–1879, 30 vols.

Castro e Almeida, Virginia de, *Itinéraire historique du Portugal*, Lisbon, 1940.
Caters, Christian de, *Portrait de Portugal*, Paris, 1940.
Correia, Araújo, *Portugal económico e financeiro*, Lisbon, 1938, 2 vols.
Costa, A., *Dicionario corográfico de Portugal continental e insular*, Porto, 1929–1949.
Coutinho, B. X., *Acção do Papado no fundação e independência de Portugal*, Porto, 1939.
Crawford, Oswald, *Portugal, old and new*, London, 1882.
Diercks, Gustav, *Das moderne Portugal*, Berlin, 1913.
——— *Portugiesische Geschichte*, Berlin and Leipzig, 1927.
Ferrarin, A. R., *Storia del Portogallo*, Milan, 1940.
Figueiredo, Fidelino de, *Pyrene*, Lisbon, 1935.
Fullerton, Alice, *To Portugal for pleasure*, London, 1945.
Gama Barros, H., *História da administração pública em Portugal nos séculos XII a XIV*, Lisbon, 1895–1914, 3 vols.
Giménez Caballero, E., *Amor a Portugal*, Madrid, 1949.
Girão, Aristides de Amorim, *Atlas de Portugal*, Coimbra, 1941.
——— *Geografia de Portugal*, Coimbra, 1942.
Goldring, Douglas, *To Portugal*, London, 1934.
Gonçalves Cerejeira, M., *Clenardo e a sociedade portuguesa do seu tempo*, Coimbra, 1949, 3 ed.
Gonçalves, Ernesto, *O destino da pátria portugalense*, Funchal, 1941.
Greenwall, H. J., *Our oldest ally*, London, 1943.
Herculano, Alexandre, *História de Portugal desde o começo da monarchia até o fim do reinado de Affonso III*, Lisbon, n.d., 8 vols., 8 ed.
——— *História da origem e establecimento da Inquisição em Portugal*, Lisbon, 3 vols.
Konetzke, Richard, *Geschichte des Spanischen und Portugiesischen Volkes*, Leipzig, 1939, Vol. VIII of the *Grosse Weltgeschichte* of the Bibliographisches Institut of Leipzig.
Latino Coelho, J. M., *História de Portugal desde os fins do século XVIII até 1814*, Lisbon, 1874–1891.
Lautensach, H., *Portugal das Land als Ganzes*, Gotha, 1932.
Legrand, Théodoric, *Histoire du Portugal du XI siècle à nos jours*, Paris, 1928.
Leite de Vasconcelos, José, *Religiões de Lusitania*, Porto, 1924.
Livermore, H. V., *A History of Portugal*, Cambridge, 1947.
Macauley, Rose, *They went to Portugal*, London, 1946.
McMurdo, Edward, *History of Portugal*, London, 1888–1889, 3 vols.
Marden, Philip S., *A wayfarer in Portugal*, Boston and New York, 1927.
Marvaud, Angel, *Le Portugal et ses colonies*, Paris, 1912.
Matoso, A. G., *História de Portugal*, Lisbon, 1939.
Mendes Corrêa, A., *Os povos primitivos da Lusitania*, Porto, 1924.
——— *Raça e nacionalidade*, Porto, 1939.
——— *Raizes de Portugal*, Porto, 1944, 2 ed.
Meneses, Luis de, *História de Portugal restaurado*, Lisbon, 1679–1698, 2 vols., and 1731, 4 vols.
Morse Stephens, H., *Portugal*, London, 1891.
Múrias, Manuel, *Portugal império*, Lisbon, 1939.
Murphy, James, *Travels in Portugal*, London, 1795.
Nowell, Charles E., *A History of Portugal*, New York, 1952.
Oliveira Martins, Joaquim Pedro de, *A vida de Nun'Alvares*, Lisbon, 1944, 6 ed.
——— *Historia da civilisação ibérica*, Lisbon, 1883.

——— *História de Portugal*, Porto, 1886, 4 ed.
Osorio de Oliveira, *Psicologia de Portugal e outros ensaios*, Lisbon, 1934.
Papy, Louis, and Gadala, Th., *Le Portugal*, Grenoble, 1935.
Peres, Damião, *Como nasceu Portugal*, Barcelos, 1938.
——— *História de Portugal. Edição monumental do 80 centenário da fundaçao da nacionalidade*, Barcelos, 1928–1935, 7 vols.
——— *História de Portugal. Palestras na emissora nacional. Origens e formação da nacionalidade*, Porto, 1951, Vol. I.
Pimenta, Alfredo, *Elementos de história de Portugal*, Lisbon, 1935, 2 ed.
——— *Subsidios para a história de Portugal*, Lisbon, 1937.
Poinsard, L., *Le Portugal inconnu*, Paris, 1910.
Pommeranz-Liedtke, G., and Rickert, G., *Portugal-Aufstrebender Staat am Atlantik*, Berlin, 1939.
Portugal. Breviário da Pátria para os portugueses ausentes, Lisbon, 1946.
Reynold, Gonzague de, *Portugal*, Paris, n.d.
Ribeiro, Orlando, *Portugal, o Mediterrâneo e o Atlântico. Estudo geográfico*, Coimbra, 1945.
Rollão Preto, *A monarquia e a restauração da intelligencia*, Lisbon, 1920.
Saraiva, António José, *História da cultura em Portugal*, Lisbon, 1950–1955, 2 vols.
Schäfer, Henrich, *Geschichte von Portugal*, Gotha, 1836–1837, 5 vols.
Schneider, Reinhold, *Portugal. Ein Reisetagebuch*, Munich, 1931.
Schulten, Adolf, *Viriato* (translated by Alfredo Ataide), Porto, 1940, 2 ed.
Sergio de Sousa, Antonio, *História de Portugal*, Barcelona, 1929.
Sousa Silva Costa Lobo, A. de, *História da sociedade em Portugal no século XV*, Lisbon, 1903.
Southey, Robert, *Letters written during a journey in Spain and a short residence in Portugal*, London, 1808, 2 vols.
T'Serstevens, A., *L'itinéraire portugais*, Paris, 1940.
Van Balen, W. J., *Portugal de tuin van Europa*, 'S-Gravenhage, 1930.
Van der Elst, J., *Le Portugal*, Paris, 1951.
Vasconcelos, A. G. Ribero de, *D. Isabel de Aragão: a Rainha-Santa*, Coimbra, 1894.
Watts, Henry E., *The Christian recovery of Spain*, New York, 1894.
Young, George, *Portugal old and young. An historical study*, Oxford, 1917.

THE CHRONICLES

The following is a listing of some of the principal chronicles of Portuguese history. In most cases the editions have been numerous and many can be found in easily available form. In general a modern edition is indicated.

Albuquerque, Afonso de, *Cartas*, Lisbon, 1884–1935, 7 vols.
Alvarez, Fr. João, *Chrónica do Infante Santo D. Fernando*, Coimbra, 1911.
Barros, João de, and Couto, Diogo do, *Décadas da Asia*, Lisbon, 1777–1788.
Castanheda, Fernão Lopes de, *História do descobrimento e conquista da India pelos portugueses*, Coimbra, 1924–1937, 3 ed., 4 vols.
Chrónica do Condestabre de Portugal, Dom Nuno Alvares Pereira, Coimbra, 1911.
Comentários do grande Afonso de Albuquerque, edited by A. Baião, Coimbra, 1923.
Corrêa, Gaspar, *Lendas da India*, Lisbon, 1858–1866, 4 vols.

Diário de viagem de Vasco da Gama, Porto, 1945.
Freyre de Andrade, Jacinto, *Vida de D. João de Castro*, Lisbon, 1561.
Gois, Damião de, *Crónica do felicíssimo Rei D. Emanuel*, Coimbra, 1926, 2 vols.
——— *Crónica do Serenissimo Príncipe Dom João*, Coimbra, 1905.
Lopes, Fernão, *Crónica de D. Pedro I*, Barcelos, 1932.
——— *Crónica de D. Fernando*, Barcelos, 1933.
——— *Crónica de D. João I*, Lisbon, 1944.
Mendonça, Jerónimo de, *Jornada d'Africa*, Lisbon, 1904, 2 vols.
Pina, Ruy de, *Chrónica de D. Sancho I, D. Afonso II, D. Sancho II, D. Afonso III, D. Diniz, D. Afonso IV*, Lisbon, 1726–1728.
——— *Chrónica de El-Rei D. Duarte*, Lisbon, 1790.
——— *Crónica de El-Rei D. João II*, Lisbon, 1792.
Zurara, Gomes Eanes de, *Crónica da tomada de Ceuta*, Coimbra, 1915.
——— *Crónica do descobrimento e conquista da Guine*, Paris, 1841. In English translation by C. R. Beazley and E. Prestage, London, 1899, 2 vols.

THE AGE OF THE DISCOVERIES AND COLONIAL EXPANSION

Beazley, C. R., *The life of Prince Henry the Navigator*, London, 1914.
Bensaude, Joaquim, *Histoire de la science nautique portugaise*, Lisbon, 1914–1919, 7 vols.
Blake, J. W., *European beginnings in West Africa, 1454–1578*, London, 1937.
Boxer, Charles Ralph, *Fidalgos in the Far East, 1550–1770*, The Hague, 1948.
Campos, J. J. A., *History of the Portuguese in Bengal*, Calcutta, 1919.
Cayolla, Julio, *A restauração e o império colonial*, Lisbon, 1944.
Cogan, Henry, *The voyages and adventures of Ferdinand Mendes Pinto of Portugal, during his travels for a space of one and twenty years in the Kingdoms of Ethiopia, China, Tartaria, Cauchin-China, Calaminham, Siam, Pegu, Japan and a great part of the East Indies*, done into English by H. C. Gent, London, 1653.
Collis, Maurice, *A viagem maravilhosa. Fernão Mendes Pinto*, Porto, 1951.
——— *The land of the great image*, London, 1942.
Correia, Germano, *História da colonização portuguesa na India*, Lisbon, 1952, 4 vols.
Cortesão, Armando, *Cartografia e cartógrafos portugueses dos séculos XV e XVI*, Lisbon, 1935, 2 vols.
Cortesão, Jaime, *Teoria geral dos descobrimentos portugueses*, Lisbon, 1940.
Coutinho, B. X., *L'idée de croisade au Portugal au XV siècle*, Louvain, 1946.
Danvers, F. C., *The Portuguese in India*, London, 1894, 2 vols.
História da expansão portuguesa no mundo, edited by António Baião, Hernani Cidade, Manuel Múrias, Lisbon, 1937–1940, 3 vols.
Jayne, K. G., *Vasco da Gama and his successors*, London, 1910.
Le Gentil, G., *Fernão Mendes Pinto. Un précurseur de l'exotisme au XVI siècle*, Paris, 1947.
Ley, Charles David, ed., *Portuguese voyages 1498–1663*, London, 1947.
Major, Richard H., *The life of Prince Henry of Portugal, surnamed the Navigator*, London, 1868.
Malheiro Diaz, Carlos, *História da colonização portuguesa do Brasil*, Porto, 1921–1924.
Múrias, Manuel, *História breve da colonização portuguesa*, Lisbon, 1940.
Oliveira Martins, J. P., *The golden age of Prince Henry the Navigator*, London,

1914 (translated with additions and annotations by J. J. Abraham and William Edward Reynolds).
Osório, João de Castro, *A formação orgánica da expansão portuguesa*, Lisbon, 1938.
Peres, Damião, *História dos descobrimentos portugueses*, Porto, 1943.
Pires de Lima, Durval, *O Oriente e a Africa desde a restauração a Pombal*, Lisbon, 1946.
Prestage, Edgar, *The Portuguese pioneers*, London, 1933.
Reparaz, G. de, *La época de los grandes descubrimientos españoles y portugueses*, Barcelona, 1931.
Rey, Charles F., *The romance of the Portuguese in Abyssinia*, London, 1929.
Ricard, Robert, *Les portugais et l'Afrique du Nord de 1521 à 1557*, Coimbra, 1941.
Sanceau, Elaine, *Henry the Navigator*, London, n.d.
——— *Indies adventure. The career of Afonso de Albuquerque*, London, 1936.
——— *Portugal in quest of Prester John*, London, 1944.
Welch, Sidney Read, *Portuguese rule and Spanish crown in South Africa, 1581–1640*, Capetown, 1940.
Whiteway, R. S., *The rise of the Portuguese power in India, 1497–1550*, London, 1899.

BRAZIL

I suggest a few titles regarding the beginnings of Brazil as part of the Portuguese epic. This is necessarily a somewhat arbitrary choice from a massive number of books and other publications on the subject.

Almeida Prado, J. F. de, *A Bahia e as capitanías do centro do Brazil*, São Paulo, 1945.
——— *Os primeiros povoadores do Brasil 1500–1530*, São Paulo, 1939.
——— *Pernambuco e as capitanias do Norte do Brasil*, São Paulo, 1939.
Azevedo, J. Lucio de, *História do Padre António Vieira*, Lisbon, 1931.
——— *Os jesuitas no Grão Pará*, Coimbra, 1930, 2 ed.
Boxer, Charles R., *Salvador de Sá and the struggle for Brasil and Angola, 1602–1686*, London, 1952.
Buarque de Hollanda, Sergio, *Raizes do Brazil*, Rio de Janeiro, 1936.
Caio Prado Junior, *Formação do Brasil contemporâneo*, São Paulo, 1942.
Capistrano de Abreu, J., *Caminhos antigos e povoamento do Brasil*, Rio de Janeiro, 1930.
——— *O descobrimento do Brasil.*
Cortesão, Jaime, *A carta de Pero Vaz de Caminha*, Rio de Janeiro, 1943.
——— *Cabral e as origens do Brasil*, Rio de Janeiro, 1944.
Coutinho, Gago, *Descobrimento do Brasil*, Rio de Janeiro, 1943.
Duarte Leite, *Descobridores do Brasil*, Porto, 1931.
Ferreira Reis, Artur Cesar, *A política de Portugal no vale amazónico*, Belem do Pará, 1940.
Freyre, Gilberto, *Casa grande e senzala*, Rio de Janeiro, 1938, 3 ed.
——— *Interpretación del Brasil*, Mexico, 1945.
——— *Sobrados e mucambos*, São Paulo, 1936.
Gay, João Pedro, *História da república jesuítica do Paraguai*, Rio de Janeiro, 1942, 2 ed.
Greenlee, W. B., *The voyage of Pedro Alvares Cabral to Brazil and India*, London, 1938.

Macedo Soares, José Carlos de, *As fronteiras do Brasil no regime colonial*, Rio de Janeiro, 1939.
Marcondes de Souza, T., *O descobrimento do Brasil*, São Paulo, 1946.
Pandía Calogeras, J., *Formação histórica do Brasil*, São Paulo, 1946.
Peres, Damião, *O descobrimento do Brasil*, Porto, 1949.
Sanmartin, Olinto, *Bandeiras no sul do Brasil*, Porto Alegre, 1949.
Simonsen, Roberto C., *História económica do Brasil, 1500–1820*, São Paulo, 1937, 2 vols.

THE MODERN PERIOD

Abreu, Jorge de, *A revolução portuguesa, o 31 de janeiro*, Lisbon, 1912.
Agostinho, José, *História da república*, Porto, 1915, Vol. I.
Almeida, António José de, *Quarenta anos de vida política e literaria*, Lisbon, 1933–1934, 4 vols.
Ameal, João, *Panorama do nacionalismo português*, Lisbon, 1932.
Andrade, Anselmo de, *Portugal económico*, Coimbra, 1918.
Azevedo, J. Lucio de, *A evolução do sebastianismo*, Lisbon, 1947, 2 ed.
——— *História dos cristãos novos portugueses*, Lisbon, 1922.
——— *O Marquês de Pombal e a sua epoca*, Lisbon, 1922.
Beirão, Caetano, *El-Rei Dom Miguel I e a sua descendencia*, Lisbon, 1943.
Beneyto, Juan, *Antonio Sardinha y la cuestión peninsular*, Valencia, 1927.
Bollaert, William, *The Wars of Succession in Spain and Portugal*, London, 1843, 2 vols.
Botelho Moniz, Jorge, *O 18 de abril (elementos para a história duma revolução vencida)*, Lisbon, 1925.
Braga, Teófilo, *Discursos sobre a constituição da república portuguesa*, Lisbon, 1911.
——— *História das ideias republicanas em Portugal*, Lisbon, 1880.
Brandão, Raúl, *Vale de Josafat*, Lisbon, 1933.
Brazão, Eduardo, *Relações externas de Portugal: reinado de D. João V*, Porto, 1938, 2 vols.
——— *Relance da história diplomática de Portugal*, Porto, 1940.
Cabral, Antonio, *As minhas memórias políticas*, Lisbon, 1929–1931, 3 vols.
Cabral de Moncada, L., *Mística e racionalismo em Portugal no século XVIII. Uma pagina de historia religiosa e politica*, Coimbra, 1952.
Campos, Enrico de, *Quem são os assassinos do Dr. Sidónio Paes?* Coimbra, 1919.
Campos, Ezequiel de, and Quirinode, J., *A crise portuguesa*, Lisbon, 1923.
Campos, Fernando, *A genealogia do pensamento nacionalista*, Lisbon, 1931.
——— *O pensamento contra-revolucionario em Portugal (Século XIX)*, Lisbon, 1931.
Carneiro de Moura, *Portugal e o tratado de paz*, Lisbon, 1918.
Carqueja, Bento, *O futuro de Portugal. Portugal após a guerra*, Porto, 1920.
Casimiro, Augusto, *Portugal e o mundo*, Coimbra, 1921.
Castro, Américo, *España en su historia: cristianos, moros y judíos*, Buenos Aires, 1948.
Chagas, João, *Portugal perante a guerra*, Porto, 1915.
Cheke, Marcus, *Dictator of Portugal. Marquis of Pombal*, London, 1938.
——— *Carloa Joaquina. Queen of Portugal*, London, 1947.
Correia dos Santos, J. A., *A revolução de 14 de maio*, Lisbon, 1915.
Costa Cabral, F. A., *João II e a renascença portuguesa*, Lisbon, 1914.
Costa Lobo, S. S., *Origens do sebastianismo — história e prefiguração dramática*, Lisbon, 1909.

Couto, A. M. do, *Carta sobre a origem e efeitos do sebastianismo*, Lisbon, 1810.
Duhr, Bernhard, *Pombal, sein carakter und seine Politik*, Freiburg, 1891.
Duynstee, F. X., *De Kerkvergolging in Portugal*, Leiden, 1914.
Gomes, Francisco Luis, *Le Marquis de Pombal. Esquisse de sa vie publique*, Lisbon, 1869.
Gomes da Costa, *Portugal na guerra. A guerra nas colonias, 1914–18*, Lisbon, 1925.
Lavradio, Marques de, *D. João e a independencia do Brasil. Ultimos anos do seu reinado*, Lisbon, 1937.
Leitão, Joaquim, *A comedia politica (uma epoca)*, Lisbon, 1910.
——— *Diário dos vencidos (uma epoca)*, Lisbon, 1911.
——— *Os cem dias funestos (uma epoca)*, Porto, 1912.
Llanos y Torriglia, Félix de, *Cómo se hizo la revolución en Portugal*, Madrid, 1914.
——— *Mirando a Portugal*, Madrid, 1917.
Luz Soriano, S. J. de, *História do reinado de El-Rei D. José e da administração do Marques de Pombal*, Lisbon, 1867, 2 vols.
Macedo, J. A. de, *Os sebastianistas*, Lisbon, 1810.
Machado, Bernardino, *Da monarquia para a república*, Coimbra, 1912.
Machado Santos, *A ordem pública e o 14 de maio*, Lisbon, 1916.
——— *A revolução portuguesa. Relatório*, Lisbon, 1911.
Magalhães, Luis de, *A crise monárchica*, Porto, 1934.
——— *Portugal e a guerra*, Lisbon, 1916.
——— *Tradicionalismo e constitucionalismo*, Porto, 1927.
Magno, David, *A situação portuguesa*, Porto, 1926.
Malheiro Dias, Carlos, *O estado actual da causa monárchica*, Lisbon, 1912.
Marnoco e Souza, J. F., *Constituição política da república portuguesa. Comentário*, Coimbra, 1913.
Martinho Nobre de Melo, *O problema da moeda e as finanças portuguesas*, Lisbon, 1924.
Menezes, Carlos J. de, *Os jesuitas e o Marques de Pombal*, Porto, 1893, 2 vols.
Montalvor, Luis de, *História do regime republicano em Portugal*, Lisbon, 1930–1932, 2 vols.
Morote, Luis, *De la dictadura a la república. La vida política en Portugal*, Madrid, 1911.
Murphy, James, *A general view of the state of Portugal*, London, 1798.
Neves, Hermano, *Como triunfou a república*, Lisbon, 1910.
Oliveira Lima, Manuel de, *D. Miguel no trono, 1828–1833*, Coimbra, 1933.
Oliveira Martins, *Portugal contemporáneo*, Lisbon, 1881, 2 vols.
Paxeco, Oscar, *Os que arrancaram em 28 de maio*, Lisbon, 1937.
Pequito Rebelo, José, *Espanha e Portugal*, Lisbon, 1939.
——— *Terra portuguesa*, Lisbon, 1929.
Pereira, António Manuel, *Organização política e administrativa de Portugal desde 1820. Bases gerais*, Porto, 1949.
Pereira de Magalhães, Felix, *Apontamentos para a história diplomática de Portugal desde 1826 até 1834*, Lisbon, 1871.
Peres, Damião, *A diplomacia portuguesa e a successão de Espanha, 1700–14*, Barcelos, 1931.
Pimenta, Alfredo, *A questão monarquica*, Lisbon, 1920.
——— *As bases da monárquia futura*, Lisbon, 1923.
——— *A situação política*, Lisbon, 1918.
——— *Cartas monárquicas*, Porto, 1923.

——— *D. João III*, Porto, 1936.
——— *Política monárquica*, Lisbon, 1917.
——— *Política portuguesa*, Coimbra, 1913.
Pimenta de Castro, *O dictador e a afrontosa dictadura*, Weimar, 1916.
Pimentel Cordeiro, *O povo e a república*, Lisbon, 1910.
Pinheiro Chagas, Alvaro, *O movimento monárquico, O 28 de janeiro e o 5 de outubro*, Porto, 1913.
Prestage, E., *Diplomatic relations of Portugal, 1640–1668*, Watford (England), 1925.
Queiroz Velloso, J. M. de, *D. Sebastião, 1554–1578*, Lisbon, 1935.
Ramos Ascensão, Leão, *O integralismo lusitano*, Lisbon, 1943.
Raposo, Hipólito, *Dois nacionalismos*, Lisbon, 1929.
Rebello da Silva, L. A., *História de Portugal nos séculos XVII e XVIII*, Lisbon, 1860–1871, 5 vols.
Rebello de Bettencourt, *Teófilo Braga. Mestre nacionalista (Teófilo Braga e Antonio Sardinha)*, Lisbon, 1942.
Ribeiro, Armando, *A revolução portuguesa*, Lisbon, 1914.
Ribeiro, Raphael, *O exército e a politica*, Lisbon, 1924.
——— *O iberismo dos monárquicos*, Lisbon, 1943.
Ribeiro Lopes, Arthur, *Histoire de la république portugaise*, Paris, 1939.
Rocha Martins, *D. Carlos. História do seu reinado*, Lisbon, 1926.
——— *D. Manuel II. História do seu reinado e da implantação da república*, Lisbon, 1931.
——— *Memórias sobre Sidónio Paes*, Lisbon, 1921.
Roque da Costa, Constancio, *Questões económicas, financeiras, sociais e coloniais*, Lisbon, 1916.
Sardinha, António, *A aliança peninsular*, Porto, 1930, 2 ed.
——— *Durante a fogueira (El-Rei D. Carlos)*, Lisbon, 1927.
——— *O valor da raça (Introducção a uma campanha nacional)*, Lisbon, 1915.
——— *Processo dum Rei (A legalidade da república)*, Porto, 1937.
Smith, John, *The life of the Marquis of Pombal*, London, 1943, 2 vols.
Sousa Viterbo, F. M. de, *O prior de Crato e a invasão hespanhola de 1580*, Lisbon, 1897.
Steffanina, Celestino, *Subsidios para a historia da revolução de 5 de outubro de 1910*, Lisbon, 1913.
Suárez Inclán, Julián, *Guerra de anexión en Portugal durante el reinado de Don Felipe II*, Madrid, 1897–1898, 2 vols.
Teixeira de Sousa, *A força pública na revolução*, Coimbra, 1913.
——— *Para a historia da revolução*, Coimbra, 1912, 2 vols.
——— *Responsabilidades históricas*, Coimbra, 1917, 2 vols.
Telles, Bazilio, *Do ultimatum ao 31 de janeiro*, Porto, 1905.
Van Steen, M., S.J., *De Gevangenschap en Uitzetting der Portugeesche Jezuiten in October 1910*, Nijmegen, 1912.
Vasconcelos, Joaquim C. de, *O movimento nacional de 18 de abril*, Porto, 1925.
Vide, Fernão de, *O pensamento integralista*, Lisbon, 1932.
Vieira de Castro, Luiz, *A Europa e a república portuguesa*, Coimbra, 1922.
——— *D. Carlos I*, Lisbon, 1943, 3 ed.
——— *Dom Carlos I. Elementos de história diplomatica*, Lisbon, 1936.
Vilhena, Julio de, *D. Pedro V e o seu reinado*, Coimbra, 1921, 3 vols.

PORTUGUESE CULTURE

The following are a very limited number of references to Portuguese letters and certain aspects of Portuguese cultural life with no pretention of completeness.

Ameal, João, *Littérature portugaise*, Paris, 1949.

Bell, A. F. G., *Portuguese literature*, Oxford, 1922.

——— *Studies in Portuguese literature*, Oxford, 1914.

Braga, Teófilo, *Historia da literatura portuguesa*, Porto, 1908–1918, 4 vols.

Burton, Richard F., *Camoens, his life and his "Lusiads,"* London, 1881, 2 vols.

Castro e Almeida, Virginia, *Vie de Camoens*, Paris, 1934.

Cidade, Hernani, *Lições sobre a cultura e a literatura portuguesas*, Coimbra, 1933.

——— *Lições de cultura e literatura portuguesa*, Coimbra, 1948.

——— *A literatura portuguesa e a expansão ultramarina. As ideas, os sentimentos, as formas de arte*, Lisbon, 1943.

——— *A literatura autonomista sob os Felipes*, Lisbon, 1948.

——— *Luis de Camões: O épico*, Lisbon, 1950.

——— *Luis de Camões. A vida e a obra lírica*, Lisbon, 1943.

Costa, J., *Alma portuguesa (ensaio de crítica literaria)*, Porto, 1907.

Dalgado, Mons. Sebastião Rodolfo, *Influencias do vocabulario português em linguas asiáticas*, Coimbra, 1913.

Figueiredo, Fidelino de, *A poesia épica no século XVI*, São Paulo, 1950.

——— *Historia da literatura classica*, Lisbon, 1922, 3 vols.

——— *Historia literaria de Portugal (séculos XII–XX)*, Coimbra, 1944.

Fortes, A., and Forjaz de Sampaio, A., *História da literatura portuguesa*, Lisbon, 1936.

Higgins, M. H., and Winton, C. F. S. de, *Survey of Education in Portugal*, London, 1942.

Houwens Post, H., *Het heroieke leven van Luis Vaz de Camoens. Portugees Renaissancedichter en avonturier, 1524–1580*, Amsterdam, n.d.

Le Gentil, George, *La littérature portugaise*, Paris, 1935; 2 ed., 1951.

Lopes, David, *A expansão da lingua portuguesa no Oriente nos séculos XVI, XVII e XVIII*, Barcelos, 1936.

——— *Os arabes nas obras de Alexandre Herculano. Notas marginais de lingua e de historia portuguesa*, Lisbon, 1911.

Lopes, O., and Martins, J., *Breve história da literatura portuguesa*, Lisbon, 1945.

Mendes dos Remedios, *História da literatura portuguesa desde as origens até a actualidade*, Coimbra, 1930, 6 ed.

Pereira da Silva, L., *A astronomia dos Lusiadas*, Coimbra, 1915.

Pimpão, Alvaro da Costa, *História da literatura portuguesa*, Coimbra, 1947, Vol. 1.

Regio, J., *Pequena história da moderna poesia portuguesa*, Lisbon, 1941.

Ribeiro da Cunha, A., *A lingua e a literatura portuguesa. História e crítica*, Braga, 1948, 3 ed.

Rodrigues Lapa, M., *Lições de literatura portuguesa. Epoca medieval*, Lisbon, 1934.

Rossi, G. C., *La prosa romantica portoghese*, Rome, 1949–1950.

——— *Storia della letteratura portoghese*, Florence, 1953.

Veiga Simões, *A nova geração (Estudo sobre as tendencias actuais da literatura portuguesá)*, Coimbra, 1911.

THE OVERSEAS EMPIRE

Almeida, Fortunato de, *Portugal e as colonias portuguesas*, Coimbra, 1920, 2 ed.

Almeida, João de, *O espíritu da raça portuguesa na sua expansão além mar*, Lisbon, 1933.

Andrade, João Corvo de, *Estudos sobre as provincias ultramarinas*, Lisbon, 1883–1887, 4 vols.

Andrews, C. F. W., *Portuguese East Africa: economic and commercial conditions*, London, 1948.

Alves Roçadas, *O sul de Angola*, Lisbon, 1908.

Brásio, P. António, *Monumenta missionária africana*, Lisbon, 1952. 5 volumes to date.

Brito Camacho, *Moçambique, problemas coloniais*, Lisbon, 1926.

Cadbury, W. A., *Labour in Portuguese West Africa*, London, 1910.

Cadornega, A. de O., *História geral das guerras angolanas*, Lisbon, 1940–1942.

Caetano, Marcelo, *Portugal e o direito colonial internacional*, Lisbon, 1946.

——— *Tradições, principios e métodos da colonização portuguesa*, Lisbon, 1951.

——— *Os nativos na economia africana*, Coimbra, 1954.

Capelo, H., and Ivens, R., *De Angola a contra costa*, Lisbon, 1881.

——— *From Benguela to the territory of Yaca*, London, 1882, 2 vols.

Carvalho, Henrique Augusto Dias de, *Guiné. Apontamentos inéditos*, Lisbon, 1944.

Castro, Albero Osório de, *A ilha verde e vermelha de Timor*, Lisbon, 1943.

Castro, Gonçalo Pimenta de, *Timor. Subsídios para a sua história*, Lisbon, 1944.

Cerqueira, Ivo de, *Vida social indígena na colonia de Angola: usos e costumes*, Lisbon, 1947.

Cordeiro, Luciano, *A questão de Zaire*, Lisbon, 1883.

Childs, Gladwyn Murray, *Umbundu kinship and character*, London-New York, 1949.

Corrêa, Armindo Pinto, *Timor de Lés-Lés*, Lisbon, 1940.

Correia, E. A. da Silva, *História de Angola*, Lisbon, 1940, 2 vols.

Costa, Augusto da, *Portugal, vasto império*, Lisbon, 1934.

Cunha, Amadeu, *Serpa Pinto e o apelo de Africa*, Lisbon, 1946.

Cunha, J. M. da Silva, *Política indígena*, Lisbon, 1950–1951.

——— *O sistema português de política indígena*, Coimbra, 1953.

Delgado, Ralph, *O reino de Benguela*, Lisbon, 1945.

——— *Ao sul de Quanza*, Lisbon, 1944, 2 vols.

Denuit, Désiré, *Voyage dans l'Angola*, Antwerp, 1938.

Diniz, J. de O. Ferreira, *Populações indígenas de Angola*, Coimbra, 1918.

Duarte, Teófilo, *Estudos coloniais*, Lisbon, 1942.

Egerton, F. C. C., *Angola without prejudice*, Lisbon, 1955.

——— *Angola in perspective*, London, 1957.

Esparteiro, Joaquim Marques, *Alguns problemas magnos de Macau*, Macao, 1952.

Felgas, Hélio A. Esteves, *Timor português*, Lisbon, 1956.

Felner, A., *Angola, colonização dos planaltos e litoral do sul de Angola*, Lisbon, 1940, 3 vols.

Fernandes, Abílio José, *Missões em Timor (1561–1931)*, Macao, 1931.

Fernandes, J. A., *Timor, impressões e aspectos*, Porto, 1923.

Freyre, Gilberto, *O mundo que o português criou: uma cultura ameaçada; a luso-brasileira*, Lisbon, n.d.
——— *Um brasileiro em terras portuguesas*, Lisbon, n.d.
——— *Aventura e rotina*, Lisbon, n.d.
Galvão, Henrique, *História do nosso tempo*, Lisbon, 1934, 2nd edition.
Galvão, Henrique, and Selvagem, Carlos, *Império ultramarino português*, Lisbon, 1950–1953, 4 vols.
Gonçalves, Júlio, *Os portugueses e o mar das Indias* (*Da India antiga e sua historia*), Lisbon, 1947.
Jakob, Ernst Gerhard, *Das portugiesische Kolonialreich*, Leipzig, 1940.
Lavradio, Marques de, *Portugal em Africa depois de 1851*, Lisbon, 1935.
Leitão, Humberto, *Os portugueses em Sólor e Timor de 1515 a 1702*, Lisbon, 1942.
Lemos, Alberto de, *História de Angola*, Lisbon, 1932.
Lopes de Lima, *Ensaios sobre a estrutura orográfico-histórica das colonias portuguesas*, Lisbon, 1844.
McCulloch, Merran, *The Ovimbundo of Angola*, London, 1952.
Magnino, Leo, *L'Africa portoghese*, Florence, 1942.
Martins, Rocha, *História das colonias portuguesas*, Lisbon, 1933.
Mello, Lope Vaz de Sampayo e, *Política indígena. Questões coloniais*, Porto, 1910.
Mendes Corrêa, A. A., *Raças do império*, Porto, 1943.
Morais, A. Faria de, *Sólor e Timor*, Lisbon, 1944.
Moreira, Adriano, *Administração da justiça aos indígenas*, Lisbon, 1955.
——— *Política ultramarina*, Lisbon, 1956.
Mousinho de Albuquerque, *Moçambique, 1896–1898*, Lisbon, 1899.
Negreiros Almada, *História etnográfica da Ilha de São Tomé*, Lisbon, 1895.
Norton de Matos, *Memórias e trabalhos da minha vida*, Lisbon, 1944, 4 vols.
——— *A situação financeira e económica da provincia de Angola*, Lisbon, 1914.
Oliveira, Boléo, *Moçambique*, Lisbon, 1951.
——— *Apuntamentos para uma geografia física de Goa*, Lisbon, 1955.
Oliveira, Humberto Luna de, *Timor na história de Portugal*, Lisbon, 1953, 3 vols.
Oliveira, Mauricio de, *Africa de sonho*, Lisbon, 1932.
Ornelas, Ayres de, *O ultramar português*, Lisbon, 1918.
Paiva Couceiro, *Angola*, Lisbon, 1910.
Penha Garcia, Conde de, *A partilha da Africa*, Lisbon, 1901.
Pereira, André Gonçalves, *Sobre os nacionalismos africanos*, Lisbon, 1956.
Ribeiro Lopes, Artur, *A convenção secreta entre a Alemanha e a Inglaterra sobre a partilha das colonias portuguesas*, Lisbon, 1933.
Rémy, Goa, *Rome de l'Orient*, Paris, 1955.
Serpa Pinto, Carlota de, *A vida breve e ardente de Serpa Pinto*, Lisbon, 1937.
Serpa Pinto, *Como eu atravessei a Africa do Atlántico ao Mar Indico*, London, 1881.
Silva, Fernando Emygdio da, *L'Essor colonial portugais*, Lisbon, 1941.
Silva Correia, Elías Alexandre de, *História de Angola*, Lisbon, 1937, 2 vols.
Sommaruga, Rodolfo, *Le potenze europee in Africa dal Congresso di Berlino a Versailles* (*1878–1919*), Milan, 1938.
Spence, C. F., *The Portuguese colony of Moçambique*, Capetown, 1951.
Teixeira da Mota, A., *Guiné portuguesa*, Lisbon, 1954, 2 vols.
Vasconcelos, Ernesto J. de C. e, *As colonias portuguesas*, Lisbon, 1921, 3rd edition.
Villas, Gaspar do Couto Ribeiro, *História colonial*, Lisbon, 1938.

ANGLO-PORTUGUESE RELATIONS

Jerónimo da Camara, Manuel, *Portugal e a Inglaterra*, Lisbon, 1909.
Marques Guedes, *Aliança inglesa (1373–1943)*, Lisbon, 1943.
Osório de Andrade, Gilberto, *Os fundamentos da neutralidade portuguesa*, Recife (Brazil), 1943, and Lisbon, n.d.
Sousa, Carlos Hermenegildo, *A aliança anglo-portuguesa*, Porto, 1939.

THE CHURCH AND RELIGION

I have included in this listing of references a few items on Our Lady of Fatima.

Almada, José de, *Investigação sobre o estado actual do Padroado do Oriente*, Lisbon, 1917.
Almeida, Fortunato de, *Historia da Igreja em Portugal*, Coimbra, 1910–1922, 4 vols.
Alves da Cunha, *Portugal. A sua acção missionária*, Lisbon, 1929.
Ameal, João de, *João de Brito, heroi da Fe e do Imperio*, Lisbon, 1941.
André, P. J., *L'Islam noir*, Paris, 1924.
Anuário Católico de Portugal. 1947, Lisbon, 1947, and 1953 (new edition).
Barthas, C., and Fonseca, G. da, *Fatima merveille inouïe*. Arras-Toulouse, 1942. English with title, *Our Lady of Light*, Milwaukee, 1947.
Barros Gomes, Henrique de, *O Padroado da Coroa de Portugal nas Indias Orientais e a Concordata de 23 de junho de 1886*, Lisbon, 1887.
Bussière, Th. de, *Histoire du schisme portugais dans les Indes*, Paris, 1854.
Cardaire, Captain, *Contribution à l'étude de l'Islam noir. Etudes Camerounaises*, Douala, Cameroun, 1949.
Correia, J. Alver, *Missões franciscanas portuguesas de Moçambique e Guiné*, Braga, 1934.
Costa Lima, Joaquim da, *A acção missionária dos jesuitas portugueses*, Lisbon, 1929.
Couto, Mons. Gustavo, *A obra dos capitães e missionários portugueses nas terras de ultramar*, Lisbon, 1926.
Cunha e Costa, *A Igreja Catolica e Sidónio Paes*, Coimbra, 1921.
Dias, António Joaquim, O.F.M., *As missões católicas na evolução politico-social da Guiné portuguesa*, Coimbra, 1943.
——— *A dilação da Fé no imperio português*, Lisbon, 1936.
D'sá, *History of the Catholic Church in India*, Bombay, 1910 and 1924, 2 vols.
Farinha, António Lourenço, *A expansão da Fe*, Lisbon, 1942–1946, 3 vols.: *Na Africa e no Brasil; No Oriente;* and *No Extremo Oriente.*
Felix, José Maria, *Fátima e a redenção de Portugal*, Vila Nova de Famalicão, 1939.
——— *Pio XII e Portugal*, Famalicão, 1952.
Ferreira da Silva, Francisco, *A obra missionária na provincia de Moçambique*, Porto, 1911.
Figueiredo, Antero de, *Fatima: Graças, segredos, mistérios*, Lisbon, 1949.
Figueiredo, Niceno de, *Pelo clero de Goa. Duas lendas: o cisma de Goa e a ignorancia do clero goês*, Bastorá (Portuguese India), 1939.
Fischer, Luiz, *Fatima á luz da auctoridade eclesiástica*, Lisbon, 1932.
Groves, C. P., *The planting of Christianity in Africa*, London, 1948–1955. Three volumes published to date.

Jann, Adelhelm, *Die Katolischen Missionen in Indien, China und Japan. Ihre Organisation und das Portugiesische Patronat vom 15 bis ins 18 Jahrhundert*, Paderborn, 1915.
Lopes Akpoim, C., *O Padroado em face da política do Vaticano e da política da República*, Nova Goa, 1928.
Lopétegui, S. J. León, *El despertar cristiano de Africa*, Bilbao, 1945.
Lourenço, Joaquim Maria, *Situação jurídica da Igreja em Portugal. Análise histórico-jurídica e crítica das relações da Igreja Católica com o estado português*, Coimbra, 1943, 2 ed.
McNabb, Vincent, *St. Elizabeth of Portugal*, London, 1937.
Martindale, C. C., *Portuguese pilgrimage, July 1–September 4, 1947*, London, 1948.
Melo, S. J. Carlos Mercês de, *The recruitment and formation of the native clergy in India* (16th–19th century), Lisbon, 1955.
Melo e Alvim, *Fátima, Terra de Fe*, Lisbon, 1943.
Missões franciscanas portuguesas no seu cinquentenário, 1898–1948. Commemorative edition of *Missões franciscanas*, Lisbon, June–September, 1948.
Moresco, L., *Gli occhi che videro la Madonna*, Rome, 1942.
Oliveira, Augusto, *Lei de separação. Subsídio para o estudo das relações, do Estado com as igrejas sob o regime republicano*, Lisbon, 1914.
Oliveira, Miguel de, *História eclesiástica de Portugal*, Lisbon, 1948. 2 ed.
Paiva Manso, Visconde de, *História eclesiástica ultramarina*, Lisbon, 1872.
Pequito Rebelo, José, *Meditações de Fátima*, Lisbon, 1942.
Pimenta, Alfredo, *A República Portuguesa em face da Igreja Católica e a política do Centro Católico*, Lisbon, 1925.
Rego, A. da Silva, *Curso de missionologia*, Lisbon, 1956.
Ryan, Most Reverend Finbar, *Our Lady of Fatima*, Dublin, 1948, 4 ed.
Seabra, Eurico de, *A Igreja, as congregações e a República*, Lisbon, 1914.
Silva, Abundio da, *Igreja e a política*, Porto, 1911.
Silva Rego, António da, *O Padroado português do Oriente. Esboço histórico*, Lisbon, 1940.
Tucker, John T., *Angola, the land of the blacksmith prince*, London, 1933.
Walsh, William Thomas, *Our Lady of Fatima*, New York, 1947.

CONTEMPORARY PORTUGAL AND THE ESTADO NOVO

Almeida, João de, *O Estado novo*, Lisbon, 1932.
——— *Nacionalismo e Estado Novo*, Lisbon, 1932.
Ameal, João, *A revolução da Ordem* (*Estudio político*), Lisbon, 1932.
——— *No limiar da Idade nova. Ensaios contemporaneos*, Coimbra, 1934.
——— *Construcção do Novo Estado*, Lisbon, 1938.
Anselmo, Manuel, *As ideas sociais e filosóficas do Estado Novo*, Porto, 1934.
A Obra de Salazar na pasta das finanças, 27 de abril de 1928 a 28 de agosto de 1940, Lisbon, 1941.
Araujo, Correia, *Directrizes económicas do Estado Novo*, Lisbon, 1935.
——— *Realidades e aspirações de Portugal contemporaneo*, Rio de Janeiro, 1938.
Azpiazu, Joaquîn, *El estado corporativo*, Madrid, 1934. English translation by Rev. William Bresnahan, O.S.B., *The corporate state*, St. Louis and London, 1951.

Bagger, Eugene, *Portugal, anti-totalitarian outpost*, Lisbon, 1947. Originally published in *The Catholic World* (New York), December, 1946.
Bainville, Jacques, *Les dictateurs*, Paris, 1939.
Baldi-Papini, V., *Portogallo Nuovo*, Florence, 1936.
Belgrano, Mario Carlos, *El Nuevo Estado del Portugal. Ensayo jurídico-político* Buenos Aires, 1943.
Bernardo, Héctor, *El régimen corporativo y el mundo actual*, Buenos Aires, 1943.
Bizarri, Aldo, *Origine e caratteri dello Stato Nuovo portoghese*, Milan, 1941.
Bragança-Cunha, V. de, *Revolutionary Portugal, 1910–1936*, London, 1937.
Brongersma, E., *De Opbouw van een corporatieven Staat*, Utrecht, 1940.
Cabral de Moncada, Luis, *Do valor e sentido da democracia*, Coimbra, 1939.
Cabrita, Henrique, *Esta é a verdade sobre Salazar*, Lisbon, 1934.
——— *Ordem corporativa*, Lisbon, 1934.
Caetano, Marcello, *Lições de Direito corporativo*, Lisbon, 1935.
——— *O sistema corporativo*, Lisbon, 1938.
——— *Posição actual do corporativismo português*, Lisbon, 1950.
——— *Problemas da revolução corporativa*, Lisbon, 1941.
Campos, E. de, *Problemas fundamentais portugueses*, Lisbon, 1946.
Campos, Fernando, *O principio da organização corporativa através da história*, Lisbon, 1938, 2 ed.
——— *Paginas corporativas*, Lisbon, 1941.
Carmo Couto, João Xavier do, *O homem que rehabilitou Portugal*, Lisbon, 1940.
Carneiro Pacheco, *Portugal renovado*, Lisbon, 1940.
Castro, A., *Introducção ao estudo da economia portuguesa*, Lisbon, 1947.
Chesnelong, Charles, *Salazar*, Paris, 1939.
Constituição política da República portuguesa. Acto colonial, Lisbon, 1948. English text, *Political constitution of the Portuguese Republic*, Lisbon, 1948.
Corte-Real, João Afonso, *O Chefe do Estado, General António Oscar de Fragoso Carmona (Subsidios biográficos)*, Lisbon, 1941.
Costa, Augusto da, *A nação corporativa*, Lisbon, 1934.
Cotta, Freppel, *Economic planning in corporative Portugal*, London.
Cunha, Leal, *A obra intangivel do Dr. Oliveira Salazar*, Lisbon, 1930.
——— *Ditadura, democracia ou comunismo? O problema português*, La Coruña, 1931.
Cunha Gonçalves, Luis da, *Causas e efeitos do corporativismo português*, Lisbon, 1936.
——— *Principios de direito corporativo*, Lisbon, 1935.
D'Aguiar, Armando, *O homem e o ditador*, Rio de Janeiro, 1934.
D'Almeida, Vitor, *Salazar*, Rio de Janeiro, 1938.
Derrick, Michael, *The Portugal of Salazar*, London, 1938.
Descamps, Paul, *Le Portugal. La vie sociale actuelle*, Paris, 1935.
Doctrine and Action. Internal and foreign policy of the New Portugal 1928–1939. Antonio de Oliveira Salazar (translated by Robert Edgar Broughton), London, 1939.
Editions of the SNI Lisbon (National Information Service):
Salazar says: for the understanding of our policy, 1950.
At the opening of the political year, 1951.
The problem of the presidential succession, 1951.
Portugal and the Far East, 1949.
Our national interests, 1946.

Reforming the constitution, 1949.
My deposition, 1949.
Egerton, F. C. C., *Salazar, Rebuilder of Portugal*, London, 1943.
Ferreira, Emilia A., *Corporativismo português (Doutrina e aplicação)*, Lisbon, 1951.
Ferro, António, *Salazar. O homem e a sua obra*, Lisbon, 1935, 3 ed. translated in English as *Salazar. Portugal and her leader*, London, 1939.
——— *Viagem á volta das ditaduras*, Lisbon, 1927.
Garnier, Christine, *Vacances avec Salazar*, Paris, 1952.
Giannini, Amedeo, *La costituzione portoghese del 1933*, Rome, 1935.
Gilles, P., *Le redressement financier au Portugal*, Paris, 1938.
Gonçalves Caetano, *O estado corporativo e a politica do imperio no direito constitucional português*, Lisbon, 1935.
Gonçalves de Andrade, José, *Doutor Oliveira Salazar. O seu tempo e a sua obra*, Porto, 1937.
Graux, Lucien, *Le Portugal économique*, Paris, 1937.
Guimarães, Antonio, *Salazar, o homem do momento*, Rio de Janeiro, 1936.
Guyomard, George, *La dictature militaire au Portugal. Impressions d'un français retour de Lisbonne*, Paris, 1927.
Jorge Norberto, *A revolução de 28 de maio e a obra de Oliveira Salazar*, São Paulo, 1938.
Krop, F. J., *Portugal onder Salazar of het herstel van een klein en dapper volk*, Rotterdam, 1939.
Leach, Leonard, *Report on the economic conditions in Portugal*, London, 1928.
Leffe, André de, *La renovation du Portugal par le Président Salazar*, Poitiers, 1942.
Luambo, Manuel, *O humanismo financeiro de Salazar*, Lisbon, 1944.
Manoilesco, Mihail, *Portugalia Lui Salazar*, Bucharest, 1936.
Marques, H., *Essencia do corporativismo em Portugal*, Lisbon, 1949.
Marques Guedes, Armando, *Uma experiencia económica e financeira*, Lisbon, 1936.
Mascarenhas, Telo de, *Sob o signo da Revolução nacional*, Lisbon, 1938.
Mattos, J. Rodrigues de, *Corporativismo em Portugal*, Lisbon, 1937.
Mayer, Anton, *Portugal und sein Weg zum Autoritären Staat*, Berlin, 1939.
Neves da Costa, *Para alem das ditaduras, soluções corporativas*, Lisbon.
Nunes, Leopoldo, *Carmona (Estudo biográfico)*, Lisbon, 1942.
——— *O ditador das finanças*, Lisbon, 1930.
Oliveira, Aguedo de, *Filosofia e moral política do Estado Novo. A nova constitucionalidade*, Lisbon, 1937.
Oliveira Salazar, Antonio de, *A questão cerealifera: o trigo*, Coimbra, 1916.
——— *Laicismo e liberdade*, Funchal, 1925.
——— *O agio do ouro, sua natureza e suas causas (1891–1915)*, Coimbra, 1916.
——— *Discursos*, Coimbra, 1937–1943, 3 vols. from 1928 to 1943.
Ovalle Castillo, Darío, *Oliveira Salazar, Restaurador de Portugal*, Santiago de Chile, 1941.
Overseas Economic Surveys. Portugal. Economic and commercial conditions in Portugal with annexes on Madeira and the Azores, London, 1941.
Pabón, Jesús, *La Revolución portuguesa*: Volume I. *De Don Carlos a Sidonio Paes*, Madrid, 1941; Volume II. *De Sidonio Paes a Salazar*, Madrid, 1945.
Pereira, Pedro Teutonio, *A batalha do futuro*, Lisbon, 1937, 2 ed.

Pereira dos Santos, Francisco, *Un Etat corporatif: la constitution sociale et politique portugaise*, Paris, 1940, 2 ed.
Pimenta, Alfredo, *Nas vesperas do Estado Novo*, Porto, 1937.
Pinto da Costa Leite, João, *A doutrina corporativa em Portugal*, Lisbon, 1936.
Poncins, Léon de, *Le Portugal renaît*, Paris, 1936.
Posada, Antonio, *De Viriato a Salazar*, São Paulo, 1939.
Rendeiro, José Licinio, *Tres homens da historia contemporanea* (Salazar, Mustafá Kemal, Pilsudski), Porto, 1938.
Ribeiro, A. M., *Organização politica e administrativa de Portugal*, Porto, 1949.
Ribeiro, José T., *Legislação corporativa*, Coimbra, 1946.
Romano, Raul, *Salazar*, São Paulo, 1949, 2 ed.
Sanson, Odette, *Le corporatisme au Portugal*, Paris, 1937.
Schreiber, Emile, *Le Portugal de Salazar*, Paris, 1938.
Sieburg, Friedrich, *Neues Portugal: Bildnis eines alten Landes*, Frankfurt-am-M., 1937.
Silva, Fernando Emygdio da, *Trois images du Portugal* (*le redressement financier, l'essor colonial, la paix monétaire*), Coimbra, 1938.
——— *La politique monétaire du Portugal*, Paris, 1937.
Teixeira, Luiz, *Perfil de Salazar. Elemento para a história da sua vida e da sua época*, Lisbon, 1938.
Thomas, Joaquim E., *La realización portuguesa del Estado corporativo*, Lisbon, n.d.
Van Leisen, Herbert, *Genève-Lisbonne. Le rideau de fer levé sur le monde ibérique*, Geneva, 1947.
Vieira, Arthur, *Proyecto de la nueva constitución portuguesa. Traducción y estudio*, Santiago de Chile, 1932.
Wallich, H., *The financial system of Portugal*, Lisbon, 1951.
Wanderley, Arnobio Tenorio, *Salazar e o problema da liberdade*, Pernambuco, 1938.
West, S. G., *The new corporative state of Portugal*, London, 1939.
Wylie Fernandez, Tomaz, *Professor Oliveira Salazar's record. Portugal's financial reconstruction*, Lisbon, 1939.
Zapp, Manfred, *Portugal als autoritäter Staat*, Berlin, 1937.

INDEX